MW00654564

To Marianne Mastropolo,

Atila Sinke Guimarães

March 9, 2012

COLLECTION

Eli, Eli, lamma sabacthani?

Volume II

ANIMUS INJURIANDI – I

(Desire to Offend)

Atila Sinke Guimarães

"What is most important in this Council is not the letter of the decrees it promulgated. They still need to be translated into life and action by all of us. Its spirit, its more advanced tendencies, this is what is the most important." [1]

[1] Statement by Karl Rahner in Anton Holzer, *Vatikanum II - Reformkonzil oder Konstituante einer neuen Kirche* (Basel: Saka, 1967), p. 324

ISBN-13: 978-0-9819793-2-8

Library of the Congress Number: 2010928090

First edition 2010 by Tradition in Action, Inc.

Printed and bound in the United States of America

The picture on the front cover is a reproduction of *The Mocking of Christ* by Giotto, Scrovegni Chapel, Padua, Italy / The Bridgeman Art Library International

Cover by the TIA art desk

Tradition in Action, Inc.
P.O. Box 23135
Los Angeles, CA 90023
www.TraditionInAction.org

TABLE OF CONTENTS

INTRODUCTION

§ 1   Volume I of this Collection, *In the Murky Waters of Vatican II*, dealt with the Council's ambiguity with regard to the **letter of the conciliar documents**. This second volume will study the **spirit of the Council** in order to learn how those texts should be understood, as well as to gain a broader perspective of the conciliar movement.[1]

§ 2   How does one study the spirit of documents such as those of Vatican II? Or of movements such as Progressivism that inspired it and was celebrated at it?

§ 3   Theoretically and generically, the spirit of a law, rule, code or constitution is the set of principles that inspire it and govern its application. When these principles are not clearly spelled out by the law or set of laws in question, they can usually be determined by considering the known thinking of the actual legislator or the authors who influenced those laws. For example, the work of Montesquieu, *De l'esprit des lois*, which influenced the foundation of the Modern State, sets out the fundamental principles of its laws and institutions.

§ 4   When there is no statement of principles of the legislators or those who inspired them, the spirit of the law normally can be determined by studying how it has been applied by the courts and obeyed by the people.

Thus, the spirit of the law is a certain unity of thinking that is not necessarily expressed; it is a more or less explicit body of doctrine. This body can be – according to its nature – a body of legal doctrine, moral doctrine, philosophical doctrine or perhaps even theological doctrine. By analogy, the spirit of a movement can be determined by distinguishing the thinking that inspires it.

To explain the body of doctrine that influences a given set of laws or that characterizes a given movement is to determine its spirit.

§ 5   If we were to apply this theoretical and general meaning of *spirit* to the expression *spirit of the Council* and proceed to delimit the body of doctrine that influenced Vatican II, the entire Collection *Eli, Eli, Lamma Sabacthani?,* from this Volume on, would be an attempt to define the spirit of the Vatican II documents and the spirit of the progressivist movement. This is not, however, the course of action that will be followed here.

---

[1] The first part of this Introduction – with some minor differences – was published previously in Volume IV, which came to light before this Volume II.

§ 6

The analysis of *spirit of the Council* in Volumes II to V will consider the expression in a practical, specific and analogical sense, that is, **it will give less consideration to the body of doctrine that inspired the Council and much more to the state of spirit unleashed by it or the mentality that has since become increasingly manifest inside the Church.**

§ 7

Although, in theory, to use *spirit* to mean *state of spirit* can be a simplification, it seems that in the specific case of the Council, the first and most important thing to do is to determine its state of spirit or mentality. Far more than being a mere codification of rules or laws, the conciliar documents have brought about the greatest change in Holy Mother Church and in the religious mentality of Catholics throughout the world that History has ever seen. Therefore, to determine the broader meaning of these documents, they must be considered together with the changes to which they gave rise. It is indispensable, therefore, to become familiar with the conciliar mentality.

How can this mentality or state of spirit be defined?

§ 8

***First*, this state of spirit can be defined as the assumption by conciliar and post-conciliar Church leaders of an attitude of tolerance toward error and evil, as well as toward their agents.**

In the Council's opening speech, John XXIII described this new position as one that "shows mercy" for those in error, and that "spreads everywhere" the Church's love for the "brotherly unity of all," referring in this way to the world and the false religions. [2]

Tolerance for error and evil inevitably generated hostility toward the previous Catholic militancy. That is, it created hostility toward the main characteristic of the Holy Catholic Church,[3] which forms the perfect likeness of Our Lord who said: "I came not to bring peace, but the sword" (Mt 10:34; Lk 12:51).

§ 9

***Second*, the state of spirit born at the Council can be defined as the adoption of a generally hostile attitude toward the militancy of the Catholic Church - both past and present.**

Once tolerance toward error and evil has been admitted, it is simple to see why the meaning of *aggiornamento*, the adaptation of the Church to the world, would no longer imply combating the funda-

---

[2] Cf. *Opening Speech* of the Council, October 11, 1962, in Walter M. Abbott, S.J., *The Documents of Vatican II* (Piscataway, NJ: New Century Publishers), 1966, pp. 716-717.

[3] See Chap. II §§ 1, 22, Note 42 ; Volume XI, *Ecclesia*, Chap. VII, 1.

mental errors of the world. On the contrary, it implies a conflict against the sacral and hierarchical characteristics of the Holy Church, which are diametrically opposed to the vulgarity and egalitarianism of the modern world.

§ 10

Third, the state of spirit born at the Council can be defined as the adoption of a general hostility toward the sacral and hierarchical characteristics of the Holy Catholic Church.

This characterization of the state of spirit of the Council - tolerance for evil and hostility toward the militant, sacral and hierarchical characteristics of the Church - is, in our view, the best possible definition of the *spirit of the Council*.

§ 11

This will be confirmed by the following general arguments that will be analyzed over the course of the Collection:

1. It is consistent with the general orientation of the pontificate of John XXIII, which was faithfully followed by Paul VI, John Paul II and Benedict XVI;

2. It explains the dogmatic relativism and moral laxity that have pervaded the interpretation of Catholic doctrine since the Council;

3. It explains the general climate of the conciliar reforms in regard to both the de-sacralization of the Church and the dissolution of her hierarchical structure;

4. It explains ecumenism and secularization – adapting the Church to other religions and to the world – both notable characteristics of the conciliar era;

5. It sheds light on innumerable ambiguities in the official documents of Vatican II.

§ 12

For these reasons, **the Author has adopted this definition of the _spirit of the Council_: tolerance for evil and hostility toward the Church's militancy, sacrality and hierarchical character.**[4]

---

[4] A demanding Reader could request a more detailed explanation of the expression *spirit of the Council*. In response, we acknowledge that the expression *spirit of the Council* can be used in other ways. For example, it can be understood from two different standpoints:

With regard to its normal applications, the expression *spirit of the Council* may be interpreted as:

a. Its doctrinal sense, as in the ambiguous dogmatic, moral or social excerpts used in the conciliar documents. As a rule, this interpretation reflects a body of doctrine that does not appear *per se* in the excerpts, but can be found elsewhere. In this sense, the *(spirit of the Council)* would refer to a clear and coherent doctrine – Progressivism – expressed in places outside the conciliar texts.

b. The spirit of the authors who inspired the conciliar documents. In this sense, the *spirit of the Council* would be that of the progressivist current to which the majority of these authors belong.

c. The spirit of the pastoral norms contained in the conciliar documents. In this sense, the spirit of the Council would be closely linked to the texts themselves.

d. The general line of the institutional reforms initiated by John XXIII and carried on by Paul VI, John Paul II and Benedict XVI, which usually are founded on the progressivist interpretation of ambiguous Vatican II texts. In this sense, the *spirit of the Council* would be a determined intention of these Popes that became apparent in its application and that can be found in the common denominator of their reforms.

e. A blurry mirage of hopes for the future that generally coincide with progressivist aims. In this sense, the *spirit of the Council* would have little to do with the texts of the conciliar documents.

f. A state of spirit of adaptation to the modern world and other religions. In this sense, the *spirit of the Council* would be the reflection of the progressivist mentality.

So, the expression can have many meanings. It was necessary, then, to define the meaning that we will be using, as we did in the text (§§ 6, 12).

With regard to precision of terms, the expression *spirit of the Council* is inappropriate on two counts:

g. Based on its application to the different topics we set out in letters a-f of this Note, the expression *spirit of the Council* could mean a number of different things: the *spirit of the doctrinal excerpts* used in the Council documents; the *spirit of the authors* who wrote the conciliar documents; the *spirit of the pastoral guidelines* of the Council; the *spirit of the reforms* of the Council; the *spirit of the ardent supporters* of the Council or the *state of spirit of adaptation* to the modern world and other religions.

As we saw in the text (§§ 3, 4), *spirit* is a kind of common denominator of the various parts of a group of laws or the guidelines for a general framework of principles. This common denominator or the general framework permits the ambiguous passages to be better understood. Seeking to define this kind of spirit, however, is better suited to fields of an inductive nature, such as Law. It is much less appropriate for matters of a deductive nature, such as Theology.

Thus, some of the above applications of *spirit of the Council* do not seem appropriate. Rather than the *spirit of the authors,* it seems more fitting to say the *thinking of the authors*; rather than *spirit of its supporters*, it is better to say the *doctrinal dreams of its supporters*. To interpret *state of spirit* or *mentality* as meaning *spirit* also seems an inappropri-

§ 13

In addition to the general intent expressed by John XXIII in the opening speech of Vatican II, two actions of Paul VI mark the institutionalization of tolerance in the Conciliar Church: the abolition of the *Index Librorum Prohibitorum* [Index of Forbidden Books] and the establishment of the International Theological Commission (ITC).

§ 14

On the day before the Council closed, December 7, 1965, Paul VI reformed the Sacred Congregation of the Holy Office and abolished the *Index* by means of the *Motu proprio Integrae servandae*. This action was intended to signify establishing freedom of thought and expression inside the Church. Henceforth, anyone could think, say or write whatever he wanted without fear of anathema. That is to say, everything unorthodox, immoral and dishonorable that has been said and written regarding Holy Mother Church from that time until today was, in effect, permitted by the pontifical authority of Paul VI. The body of post-conciliar work is, therefore, the authorized expression of the spirit of the Council insomuch as it reflects tolerance.

§ 15

The same could be said about Paul VI's establishment of the International Theological Commission in 1969 as an organ in some ways parallel to the Congregation for the Doctrine of the Faith. Prior to its establishment, the Holy Office – the Congregation responsible for guarding and maintaining the unity of Faith and the purity of Morals – traditionally consulted its own group of advisers. Founding a new commission with privileges and special rights autonomous to the

---

ate simplification. Instead of in its proper sense, the expression is used in its analogical meaning - as we explained in the text (§ 7).

The expression would be appropriate only in two of its applications that deal with matters of an inductive nature: It seems correct to use the *spirit of the pastoral guidelines* of the Council and the *spirit of the re-forms* of the Council.

h. The instability and fluidity of the expression *spirit of the Council* also makes it unsatisfactory. If, as we have just shown, the word *spirit* cannot be appropriately used in several of its applications, it would be even more inappropriate to package all the meanings together under the general expression *spirit of the Council*. This would make it prey to a fundamental inaccuracy, rendering the term unfit for interpreting documents as important as those of Vatican II.

i. For these reasons, the use of the expression *spirit of the Council* would seem to demand some kind of typographical mark to indicate our reservations. However, with the explanation given in the text and in this Note on the exact meaning in which this Collection adopts the expression, we will dispense with the need to italicize or underscore the term.

authority of the Congregation for the Doctrine of the Faith signified the end of doctrinal unity in the Catholic Church and the establishment of freedom of opinion in religious matters. [5]

---

[5] a. The ITC was set up by Paul VI *ad experimentum* on April 11, 1969 ("Comissionis Theologica statuta ad experimentum," AAS, August 8, 1969, pp. 540-541). It was established definitively by John Paul II on August 6, 1982 with the *Motu proprio Tradecim anni iam* (*Insegnamenti di Giovanni Paolo II*, Libreria Editrice Vaticana, vol. 3, pp. 183-187). The ITC purpose was to legitimize theological pluralism.

b. Addressing the subject of research standards for theologians, the 1967 Synod of Bishops affirmed: **"For theologians to carry out their mission in a normal way, they must be assured the freedom both to open new trails and to update older bodies of learning**" (*La Documentation Catholique* 64, 1967, 1986, in Joseph Comblin, "La théologie catholique depuis la fin du pontificat de Pie XII" In V.A., *Bilan de la théologie au XXe siècle*, Tournai/Paris: Casterman, 1970, vol. 1, p. 480).

c. At the same Synod, Cardinal Leo Jozef Suenens proposed the establishment of the ITC (*ibid.*, p. 481; Leo Josef Suenens, *Souvenirs et espérances*, Paris: Fayard, 1991, pp. 64, 152-153, 190).

d. Toward the end of 1968, a few months before Paul VI actually set up the ITC, a petition signed by theologians associated with the magazine *Concilium* made this request: **"The undersigned theologians find themselves constrained to openly and gravely call attention to the fact that the liberty of theologians and of theology** in the service of the Church, which was restored by the Vatican Council, **should not be imperiled.** ... Well aware that we, as theologians, can be led astray in our theology, we are convinced, nonetheless, that **erroneous theological ideas cannot be corrected by coercive measures. Today they can be corrected effectively only through objective scientific discussion free of any coercion**, where the truth can conquer by its own merits. ... **Any type of inquisition, however subtle it may be, harms the development of a sound theology**, as well as seriously damages the credibility of the whole Church in today's world. ...

"Today, as we face the growing possibility of a new threat to unimpeded theological studies, **we find ourselves compelled to present a series of constructive proposals. It seems to us imperative they be carried out** so that the Pope and the Bishops will properly and honorably be able to fulfill their mission regarding their function as theologians in the Church.

"[Proposal] 1. Since the internationalization [of the Curia] inaugurated by Pope Paul VI, **various organs of the Roman Curia, and especially the Congregation for the Doctrine of the Faith, must stop giving the impression of favoring a certain theological school of**

thought, insomuch as the composition of its members does not reflect the legitimate plurality of contemporary schools and modern theological thinking. ...

"[Proposal] 4. **The International Theological Commission** proposed by the Bishops' Synod **should be established immediately in a way that proportionately integrates the various theological tendencies and schools of thought.** The Congregation of the Faith should collaborate closely with this commission. Further, with regard to questions of the Faith, **the juridical powers of the Congregation,** like that of the Bishops' commissions ... **should be officially delimited in explicit terms**" (V.A. "Declaration" published in a supplement of *Concilium*, Portuguese ed., January 1969).

Among those who signed this "Declaration" were Fathers Karl Rahner, Yves Congar, Marie-Dominique Chenu, Edward Schillebeeckx, Hans Küng, Joseph Ratzinger, Walter Kasper, Johann Baptist Metz, Piet Schoonenberg and Pierre Benoit.

Everything leads one to believe that Paul VI established the International Theological Commission to satisfy the demands of the '67 Synod and the requests of these theologians.

e. Cardinal Suenens, who originated the idea of founding the Commission, addressed the question of the ITC's independence from the unity of teaching of the Magisterium, represented by the Congregation for the Doctrine of the Faith. He said: "On my first trip [to Canada in 1967], I **advised that an international theological commission be established in Rome with the aim of eventually freeing ourselves from the monopoly of advisers chosen too exclusively by the Holy See. With this, we would broaden our information base and increase the credibility of Rome's doctrinal interventions**. The text of this speech appeared in the *Minutes of the Congress*, as well as in the final chapter of my book *La corresponsabilité dans l'Église d'aujourd'hui* [Co-responsibility in Today's Church]. The proposal was acted upon, and today it is a reality. The international body was formed, and we already owe some important and invaluable studies to it" (*Souvenirs et espérances*, p. 190).

Even more explicitly, he stated: "**At a post-conciliar Synod, I proposed the creation of an international theological commission with the precise aim of breaking this monopoly (of the Holy Office) that hindered free dialogue at the highest level**" (*ibid.*, p. 64; pp. 152-153).

f. During an interview, Fr. Chenu made this comment: "You know that the idea of creating a theological commission was based on the desire of the Council and came into being after much consideration. After all, the Pope already has his own theological commission, the Congregation for the Doctrine of the Faith, formerly known as the Holy Office. These experts are at his full service. **Creating another theological commission, therefore, was to allow for autonomous research.** ...

These were, then, the two milestones that established tolerance inside the Church. It was these two acts that released the brakes
that had restrained doctrinal abuse and upheld the unity of Faith and
Morals (2 Thes 2:6).

§ *16*   Thus, Paul VI cut the silver cord closing the "Aeolian bag"
that kept the riotous winds of error and heterodoxy from escaping
into the Church.[6] Who should bear responsibility for the tempests that
were unleashed when it opened? The winds themselves? Or the Pope
who unleashed them?

Four months after founding the ITC, Paul VI expressed his
intent to establish greater tolerance, along the same lines of the program already being followed. He said:

"*Question* - **Isn't this commission somewhat out of line with the
Magisterium?**

"Answer - **It tends to be**" (*Jacques Duquesne interroge le Père Chenu
– Une théologie en liberté*, Paris: Centurion, 1975, p. 5).

g. Msgr. Philippe Delhaye, secretary-general of the ITC from 1973 to
1988, spoke to the Author of this Work about the increasing pluralism of
the organization. He said that when the Commission was founded, there
were 30 members and "we all thought more or less the same way about
problems. There were several more forward-looking thinkers, but the
majority thought along the same lines. Today, however, **for 30 persons
there are 30 opinions**" (Louvain-la-Neuve, March 1,1983).

h. There are, nevertheless, some who think that the ITC adopts the
exemplary behavior of submission to the Congregation for the Doctrine
of the Faith (Gino Concetti, "La Teologia al servizio del Magistero,"
L'Osservatore Romano, December 23, 1988, p. 3). Even if this opinion
were objective, it seems clear that the potential of autonomy exists.
Further, nothing stands in the way for the ITC to realize *in tempore
opportuno* the objectives for which it was created.

[6] During his adventures after leaving Troy, Ulysses received from Aeolus,
the son of a god, a bag that contained all the winds that could disturb
Ulysses' return trip to his island home of Ithaca. The bag was closed
with a shining silver cord bound so tightly that not so much as a tiny
breeze could escape. With Ithaca in sight, the hero allowed himself a
brief repose. During his slumber, his crew, moved by curiosity and envy,
opened the sack. The winds that were released carried the ship away
from the shore and out to the high sea. Ulysses would undergo nine
years of trials before he would finally find his way home. (Homer, *Odyssey*, trans. by E.V. Rieu, New York: Penguin Books, 1982, cant. X, 1-
100).

"We will have a period in the life of the Church and, consequently, in that of each one of her children, **of greater liberty, that is, of fewer legal obligations and internal inhibitions. The former discipline will be reduced, arbitrary intolerance and despotism abolished, the prevailing laws simplified, and the exercise of authority tempered.** That sense of Christian liberty which so marked the first generation of Christians when they understood they were released from observing the Mosaic Law and the complicated ritual precepts will be fostered (Gal 5:1)."[7]

In fact, John XXIII had already symbolically paved the way for Paul VI to adopt this position. In his Council journal, Henri Fesquet noted: "Some time ago, when receiving a visitor who asked him what he hoped from the Council, John XXIII pointed to the window and said: 'A current of fresh air in the Church.'"[8]

Everything leads one to believe, therefore, that the responsibility for releasing the new winds that are ravaging the Catholic Church should be attributed to John XXIII and Paul VI.

§ 17 Although he did not agree with this analysis of the post-conciliar situation, then Cardinal Ratzinger – today Benedict XVI – nonetheless provided evidence confirming it when he spoke about the devastation being wrought in the Church by "latent forces" opposed to the traditional way of being. Would this process have been possible without the tolerance of John XXIII, Paul VI and other authorities of the conciliar Church? Although he did not answer that question, the Cardinal added:

"It is my impression that **the devastation which the Church has suffered** these last 20 years **is due** not so much to the Council itself, but **to the chain reaction set off inside it of latent forces that are aggressive, polemic, centrifugal and perhaps irresponsible."**[9]

*

§ 18 The Volumes that study the spirit of the Council will provide examples from every corner of the Church where the conciliar winds are blowing. There will be quotes from persons directly or indirectly

---

[7] Paul VI, Speech to the National Federation of Schools for Obstetricians on July 6, 1969, in *Insegnamenti di Paolo VI*, Tipografia Poliglotta Vaticana, vol. 7, p. 1004.

[8] Henri Fesquet, *Le Journal du Concile* (Forcalquier: Robert Morel, 1966), p. 44.

[9] Joseph Ratzinger, "Ecco perché la fede é in crisi," interview by Vittorio Messori, in *Jesus* (Milan), November 1984, p. 70.

linked with Vatican II. Even the latter are expressive of the spirit of the Council since they reflect the tolerance shown by the highest authorities for demonstrations of hostility toward the militancy, sacrality and hierarchical character of the Church.

§ 19   Undoubtedly, there have been occasional instances where the Holy See has "condemned" certain theological abuses, such as the cases of Hans Küng, Edward Schillebeeckx, Leonardo Boff, Pedro Casaldáliga, Raymond Hunthausen, Charles Curran, John McNeill and, more recently, some Catholic theologians from the East. These "condemnations," however, stopped short of declaring the strange theories of these authors heterodox or of applying the corresponding sanctions of excommunication and suspension of orders.[10] In general, they were admonishments about just some aspects of the doctrines disseminated by these authors, and the sanctions applied were light. Volume IV will examine in more detail the mildness and inefficiency of the Vatican "condemnations."[11]

---

[10] We have in our hands the text of the "Speech to the Bishops in Colombia: Reflections on the case of Archbishop Marcel Lefebvre" ("Alocución a los Obispos en Colombia – Reflexiones sobre el caso de Monseñor Marcel Lefebvre"), a speech delivered by Cardinal Joseph Ratzinger during a theological course for the Colombian Bishops (*Curso de Profundizacion Teologica para los Señores Obispos,* July 11-22, 1988). The text is duly authenticated by the seal of the Colombian Bishops' Conference. Referring to the Vatican's supposed "condemnation" of the progressivists, the Cardinal stated: "**The myth that the Vatican takes a hard hand against the theses of progressivists is false.** Right up to the very date [of Msgr. Lefebvre's break on June 30, 1988], basically **only admonitions were issued, never canonical penalties in the proper sense**" (*El Catolicismo*, Bogotá, August 28, 1988, p. 12).

Journalist Vittorio Messori, who was well acquainted with Cardinal Ratzinger since he interviewed him for his book *The Ratzinger Report*, said this about the Cardinal's mode of action: "As a matter of fact, **Ratzinger never took measures against anyone**. Leonardo Boff 'had coffee with him' – as Boff himself described his meeting with the Cardinal – and this made him an international star. Today it is no longer possible to apply disciplinary measures because they boomerang against the Church. When a Third World priest falls under the scrutiny of the Congregation [for the Doctrine of the Faith], he is acclaimed by the press and becomes a gigantic Prometheus" (Stefano Paci, "O Prefeito e o quarto poder," *30 Dias*, April 1992, pp 52-53).

[11] Among the various "condemnations" made by the Congregation for the Doctrine of the Faith is the paradigmatic case involving Fr. Hans Küng, which will be analyzed in Volume IV, *Animus Delendi I*, Chap. III.1.E,F. This analysis seems to provide a sufficient example of the Holy See's supposed "rigor" with regard to post-Council abuses. The cases of Arch-

§ 20

      Vatican sanctions no longer sound like doctrinal condemnations. They seem more like prudential censures made by "moderates" of the official Vatican line against the "radicals" of Progressivism's extreme left. Both would appear to be striving to reach the same goal, and their only disagreement is methodology. In much the same manner, the moderate *Gironde* and the radical *Montaigne* parties fought each other during the French Revolution. Yet after the river of blood under Robespierre and the blasts of gunpowder under Napoleon had passed, it was the moderate *"Girondist* spirit" that installed the revolutionary *Jacobin* victories in the new institutions and, consequently, in the minds of the people.[12]

---

bishop Hunthausen and Fr. McNeill will be studied in Vol. III, *Animus Injuriandi II*, Chap. III.3; the instance of Bishop Casaldáliga in Vol. V, *Animus Delendi II*, Part I, Chap. V, Note 24, and that of Fr. Leonardo Boff in the Introduction of Vol. V Note 9 o-p. The Holy See's unequivocal desire to be mild and tolerant and to avoid taking punishments to their final consequences is quite obvious in all of these "condemnations."

[12] a. By *Girondist spirit* we refer to the mentality of the "moderates" who took positions analogous to those advocated by the *Gironde* before the Terror. We do not, however, mean to affiliate post-revolutionary "moderates" with the *Girondist* party, as described, for instance, by Alphonse de Lamartine in his well-known *Histoire des Girondins*.

b. In this sense, the "spirit of the *Girondists*," or "moderates," survived even into the Restoration and played a part in the victory of the revolutionary principles. This is described by the celebrated writer Victor Hugo: "During the Restoration, the nation became accustomed to calm debates, which were not present during the Republic, and to a peaceful grandeur, which was absent during the Empire. A strong and free France was an encouraging sight for the other peoples of Europe. The Revolution spoke under Robespierre; the cannon spoke under Bonaparte; under Louis XVIII and Charles X intelligence had its turn. In that period the winds stopped blowing and the torch was relit. We saw, sparkling from its serene heights, the pure light of the mind. A magnificent, timely and enchanting spectacle! For 15 years, in perfect peace and in broad daylight, we witnessed the action of these great principles, so old for the thinker, so new for the statesman: equality before the law, liberty of conscience, speech and the press, and open access for all to any office. So it was until 1830" (*Les Misérables*, Paris: Garnier-Flammarion, 1967, vol. 2, p. 353).

c. François-René de Chateaubriand affirmed essentially the same thing: "The Restoration gave a stimulus to the intelligence; it liberated the thinking repressed by Bonaparte. The mind, like a caryatid freed from the building weighing over it, raised its head once more. The Empire had struck France dumb; in the Restoration, freedom touched her and returned her power of speech. Gifted orators appeared who took up where

§ 21

Therefore, despite episodic clashes in some phases, the radical and moderate currents complemented each other through the course of the revolutionary process.[13] The "condemnations" by the Vatican "moderates" of the post-conciliar *arditi,* or radical progressivists, seem to follow this same pattern.

In any case, when citing statements of *arditi* theologians, this Collection will pay special attention to the points that were not "condemned."

Presenting statements by theologians who hold different positions in the conciliar theological spectrum will reflect the tolerance of Vatican II and, thus, help us to define its spirit.

*

---

the Mirabeaus and Cazalès had left off, and the Revolution continued on its course" (*Memoires d'outre tombe*, Librairie Générale Française, 1973, vol. 2, p. 447).

[13] In *Revolution and Counter-Revolution*, Prof. Plinio Corrêa de Oliveira refers to the upheavals of 1789 to exemplify the metamorphoses of the revolutionary process: "The revolutionary process is the development by stages of certain disorderly tendencies of Western Christian man and of the errors to which they have given rise. In each stage, these tendencies and errors have a particular characteristic. The Revolution, therefore, makes metamorphoses in the course of History. The metamorphoses observed in the grand general lines of the Revolution recur on a smaller scale within each of its great episodes. Hence, the spirit of the French Revolution, in its first phase, used an aristocratic and even ecclesiastical mask and language. It frequented the court and sat at the table of the royal council. Later, it became bourgeois and worked for a bloodless abolition of the monarchy and nobility and for a veiled and pacific suppression of the Catholic Church. As soon as it could, it became Jacobin and became inebriated with blood in the Terror. But the excesses committed by the Jacobin faction stirred up reactions. The Revolution turned back, going through the same stages in reverse. From Jacobin it became bourgeois with the Directory. With Napoleon, it extended its hand to the Church and opened its doors to the exiled nobility. Finally, it cheered the returning Bourbons.

"Although the French Revolution ended, the revolutionary process did not end. It erupted again with the fall of Charles X and the rise of Louis Philippe, and thus, through successive metamorphoses – taking advantage of its successes and even its failures – it reached its present state of paroxysm. The Revolution, then, uses its metamorphoses not only to advance, but also to carry out its tactical retreats that have so frequently been necessary" (York: American Society for the Defense of Tradition, Family and Property, 1993, pp. 24-5).

§ 22   To what extent, one may ask, does this exposition of the spirit of the Council reflect the spirit of the progressivist current? To the degree that the spirit of the Council is tolerant of the progressivist current, the statements of the latter will reflect and express the former.

The position of Vatican II toward Progressivism, however, is not just one of tolerance, but also of sympathy. The Pontiffs from John XXIII until today have made no secret of their ardent support for progressivist thinking.[14]

---

[14] a. Trying to find the middle road between the "right" and "left" positions of John XXIII, journalist Silvio Tramontin made this commentary that reflected a general opinion: "At times, he [John XXIII] has been defined by the progressivists as a standard-bearer, a demiurge to which they attribute not only the summoning of the Council, but all the progress made by today's Church" ("Giovanni XXIII: di 'destra' o di 'sinistra'?" *Avvenire*, June 1, 1993).

Further on, Tramontin provided these facts from the life of Angelo Roncalli: "The progressivists and those who see the person and work of Pope John as 'progressivist' can find many signs of such behavior since his youth: his union activity (which is quite significant, given that it took place at a time when Pius X was not favorable toward Christian labor unions); his solidarity with the Ranica strikers; his correspondence with Adelaide Coari, one of the most controversial exponents of Catholic feminism; the reprimand he received from Cardinal de Lai for materials he was reading (especially [Louis] Duchesne's *Storia della Chiesa Antica*), and a suspicion of Modernism because of his friendship with Buonaiuti" (*ibid.*).

Tramontin also dealt with his term as Pope: "As Pope, he granted an audience to Kruschev's son-in-law and his wife, an incident that probably gained votes for the Italian Communist Party in the 1963 elections. Above all, he called the Council, which restored a voice to the Bishops" (*ibid.*).

Archbishop Emeritus of Trent Alessandro Maria Gottardi, a long–standing disciple of John XXIII, reported some of the vanguard actions of the then Patriarch of Venice: "What drove Cardinal Roncalli, as he was at that time, was his desire for the people to be an active part of the Church. This explains his efforts, for example, to facilitate the participation of the faithful in religious functions at St. Mark's Basilica. I also remember when a conference of the Italian Socialist Party, dominated by the figure of Pietro Nenni, was held at the Venice Lido in 1956. Roncalli invited all the faithful to give a warm welcome to the socialists. One must remember that political divisions were very strong at that time" (Personal Memoires, in Massimo Iondini, "L'Angelo della semplicità," *Avvenire*, June 1,1993).

b. It is difficult to deny that John XXIII opened the doors of the Church to the modernist-progressivist movement. Condemned by St. Pius X at the

beginning of the century and later by Pius XII during the '40s, this movement had continued to spread surreptitiously during the period preced-
ing the Council. Alluding to this "opening," Cardinal Congar stated: "Pius
X was the Pope who confronted the modernist movement, understood
as 'the theoretical and practical subordination of Catholicism to the
modern spirit.' The crisis was contained, but problems remained. The
studies of the movement continued to follow their irrepressible course,
both from outside and within, at times meeting with resistance, problems, controls and restraints. Later, the situation changed drastically.
There was John XXIII (1958-1963), the Council (1962-1965), the
aggiornamento..." (Yves Congar, *Église Catholique et France moderne*,
Paris: Hachette, 1978, pp. 37-38).

c. In this "changed situation," John XXIII rehabilitated various theologians formerly considered suspect by the Holy See or even condemned
for heterodoxy. Some were exponents of the *Nouvelle Théologie* (New
Theology). Philippe Levillain wrote: "Among the advisers [of the theological commission that prepared the Council], one noted the presence
of Frs. Congar, de Lubac, Hans Küng and others. The whole group of
theologians implicitly condemned by the Encyclical *Humani generis* in
1950 had been called to Rome at the behest of John XXIII" (*La mécanique
politique du Vatican II*, Paris: Beauchesne, 1975, p. 77).

The list of the most important exponents of the *Nouvelle Théologie* that
gained prominence under John XXIII includes Karl Rahner, Yves Congar,
Henri de Lubac, Marie-Dominique Chenu, Edward Schillebeeckx, Hans
Küng and Joseph Ratzinger.

Cardinal Congar confirmed the words of Levillain: "Fr. de Lubac later told
me that it was John XXIII himself who had insisted that we both become
members of this commission [that prepared the Council]" (*Jean Puyo
interroge le Père Congar – Une vie pour la verité,* Paris: Centurion, 1975,
p. 124; see also Karl Heinz Neufeld, "Au service du Concile, évêques et
théologiens," V.A., *Vatican II: Bilan et perspectives, vingt-cinq ans après
– 1962-1987*, ed. R. Latourelle, Montreal/Paris: Bellarmin/Cerf, 1988,
vol. 1, pp. 110-111).

d. The opening speech of Vatican II and the papal intervention that caused
the schema *De fontibus Revelationis* to be withdrawn from the debates
of the Council Assembly contributed powerfully to the predominance of
the progressivist current (Vol. I, *In the Murky Waters of Vatican II,* Chap.
IV.§ 2, Note 2; Chap. VI, §§ 50, 83, Note 47).

e. The plan to reformulate Vatican II, as well as the Council's most
progressivist Constitution, *Gaudium et spes*, likewise counted on John
XXIII's personal support, as attested by Msgr. Philippe Delhaye: "At the
end of November 1962, John XXIII asked Cardinals Montini and Suenens
to propose a new program involving the study of relations between the
Church and the modern world. After reviewing the plan, the Holy Father
approved it and asked Cardinal Suenens to propose these suggestions

to the assembly. This was done on Monday, December 3. The Prelate gave no indication that the initiative came from above, but the authority and precision of the suggestions were such that many suspected what was later confirmed about the papal origin of the plan for the Council and the schema to study the Church and the modern world ("Histoire des textes de la Constitution pastorale" in V.A., *L'Église dans le monde de ce temps – Constitution pastorale 'Gaudium et spes,'* Paris: Cerf, 1967, vol. 1, p. 217).

f. According to Cardinal Franz König, the *Pastoral Constitution on the Church in the Modern World (Gaudium et spes)* marked a complete turnabout in the Church with regard to the *Syllabus* of Pius IX and the Encyclical *Pascendi* of Saint Pius X, which condemned Modernism. König states: "Much importance is attached to the fringe group [that is, the *arditi,* hotheads] who tried to push forward, even in the face of opposition to the authentic progress that the Vatican was making for the first time in the Church by recognizing the positive character of History, the sciences and the arts – in short, human categories that the *Syllabus* had condemned less than 100 years ago and that *Pascendi* again censured less than 48 years ago ... This document [*Gaudium et spes*] represents an about-face in the Church's conception of History and closes the era of the *Syllabus* and *Pascendi*" (*Chiesa dove vai? – Gianni Licheri interroga il Cardinale Franz Koenig,* Rome: Borla, 1985, pp. 104, 108).

g. It also befell John XXIII to inaugurate a new, more egalitarian way of being in the Church when he proposed ridding her of "her imperial mantle." "Did John XXIII not explicitly propose ridding the Church of 'her imperial mantle?'" asked Msgr. Ignace Ziade, the Maronite Archbishop of Beirut ("Un nouveau style de papauté" in V.A., *La nouvelle image de l'Église – Bilan du Concile Vatican II,* Paris: Mame, 1967, p. 131).

There was also the emergence of the expression "Church of the poor," a term used by John XXIII himself in his message of September 11, 1962 (Yves Congar, *Le Concile au jour le jour – Deuxième session,* Paris: Cerf, 1964, p. 51). On the egalitarian and de-sacralizing character of the "Church of the poor," see Volume XI, *Ecclesia,* Chap. III *passim;* Volume IV, *Animus Delendi I,* Chap. VI.2, *passim;* in this Volume see Chap. III, Appendix I, Part I, 1, 2.

h. Thus it comes as no surprise to hear Lucio Lombardi of the Italian Communist Party praising the Pontiff: "We finally arrived at the brief but resplendent pontificate of John XXIII. We saw the explosion of a thirst for justice, a craving for freedom, a rejection of the 'consecration' of the capitalist regime and the 'excommunication' of Socialism, an ardent desire for fraternal dialogue with the 'infidels'" (Eulogies of John XXIII, *V.A., Il dialogo alla prova,* Firenze: Vallecchi, 1964, p. 91, in Philippe de la Trinite, *Dialogue avec le marxisme? – Ecclesiam suam et Vatican II,* Paris: Cèdre, 1966, p. 50).

i. As for Paul VI, "the Pope of the Council and the post-Council," according to *L'Osservatore Romano* (November 21, 1985, p. 6), it is well known that he belonged to the group of Cardinals who led the progressivist wing, with whom he frequently met. Cardinal König attested to this in an interview with G. Licheri: "I, along with my whole group – Suenens, Döpfner, Liénart, Frings – frequently met with the Archbishop of Milan [Cardinal Montini] to discuss and exchange ideas. He was completely on our side" (*Chiesa dove vai?*, pp. 24-5).

Another quote of the former Archbishop of Vienna reveals the same idea: "The Council truly renewed the face of the Church, opened its doors to the modern world and overcame many prejudices. I returned to Vienna very satisfied because something that seemed impossible had been accomplished, and this was due as much to the merit of Pope John as to Paul VI, who, even before being elected, had joined the Cardinals in emphatically upholding the need to continue on the path established by John" (*ibid.*, p. 43).

j. Like his predecessor, Paul VI vigorously supported the harbingers of the *Nouvelle Théologie*. Even before he became Pope, Msgr. Montini had a great admiration for some of these liberal theologians, such as Fr. de Lubac. In fact, *Méditations sur l'Église* by the French Jesuit "was so dear to Msgr. Montini that he read the book until it was worn out" (Giacomo Martina, "Le contexte historique dans lequel a surgi l'idée d'un nouveau Concile Oecuménique," V.A., *Vatican II: Bilan et perspectives*, vol.1, p. 71).

After he was elected Pope, Paul VI chose to honor de Lubac by inviting the theologian to concelebrate High Mass in the Basilica of St. Peter with him, 12 heads of religious orders and 10 other *periti*. ("Paolo VI annunzia l'inizio dei processi di beatificazione di Pio XII e Giovanni XXIII," November 18, 1965, *Insegnamenti di Paolo VI*, Tipografia Poliglotta Vaticana, vol. 3, pp. 625-626; J. Ratzinger, *Problemi e risultati del Concilio Vaticano II*, Brescia: Queriniana, 1967, pp. 151-152; H. Fesquet, *Le journal du Concile*, p. 1063; K. H. Neufeld, *Au service du Concile*, pp. 109, 115). On February 2, 1965, Paul VI publicly cited de Lubac in order to "pay special honor and homage" to him ("Au service du Concile,""Au service du Concile," p. 117; H. Fesquet, *Le journal du Concile,* p. 993). He also invited him to dinner following the closing ceremony of the Council (K. H. Neufeld, *ibid.*, p. 122).

k. Paul VI also received Fr. Karl Rahner on a number of occasions, praised his work and encouraged him to proceed with it. For example, on November 7, 1963, the Pontiff told Rahner to "continue to enrich Catholic theology with your sincerity and your science" (biographical cover note of K. Rahner, *Escritos de teología*, Madrid: Taurus, 1964, vol. 4). He also thanked the theologian for his contribution to the conciliar work (Battista Mondin, *Os grandes teólogos do século vinte*, São Paulo: Paulinas, 1979, vol. 1, p. 98; Antoine Wenger, *L'Église de son temps – Vatican II – Chronique,* Paris: Centurion, 1964, vol. 2, p. 254).

l. On two occasions Paul VI granted private audiences to Fr. Yves Congar, which increased his prestige and standing (*Jean Puyo interroge le Père Congar*, p. 118; H. Fesquet, *Le journal du Concile*, pp. 280, 297). On one of these occasions, he referred to Fr. Congar as "one of the theologians who most contributed to prepare Vatican II and whose thinking is held in the highest esteem by the Council Fathers" (H. Fesquet, *Le journal du Concile*, p. 280).

In his journal on the Council, Fesquet commented on Paul VI's support for Congar: "During a private audience, the Supreme Pontiff clearly supported Fr. Congar, thus silencing all the unfavorable comments of those who .... were trying to discredit the thinking of one of the greatest Catholic theologians of our times" (*ibid.*, p. 297). Congar himself testified to the Pontiff's esteem: "One day Paul VI solemnly told me, 'I thank you for what you have done for the Church. I say this not in my name, that is, the Pope's, but in the name of Jesus Christ'" (Y. Congar, "O Papa também obedece," interview by Stefeno Paci, *30 Dias*, March 1993, p. 26).

m. Paul VI gave prestige to an *avant-garde* progressivist work by Fr. Marie-Dominique Chenu, *Pour une théologie du travail* – formerly viewed with reservations on the part of Rome – by summarizing it in a chapter of the Encyclical *Populorum progressio* (*Jacques Duquesne interroge le Père Chenu*, p. 114).

Paul VI appointed Rahner, Congar, de Lubac, Joseph Ratzinger and von Balthasar to the International Theological Commission. The same Pontiff also sanctioned and honored the theological work of Fr. Jean Daniélou by making him a Cardinal.

n. In contrast, during the Council Paul VI did not give the conservative wing any prestige whatsoever and consistently turned a deaf ear to their requests. Moreover, he censured them through his Secretary of State, Cardinal Cicognani, for trying to "make other 'alliances' to the detriment of the conciliar assembly" (Ralph Wiltgen, *The Rhine Flows into the Tiber*, Devon/England: Augustine, 1978, p. 248). For more information on the openly hostile action of Paul VI against the program of the conservatives, see Volume I, *In the Murky Waters of Vatican II*, Chap. VI. §§ 85-102.

o. John Paul II also harbored a blatant admiration for the *Nouvelle Théologie* and its vanguard thinkers. Fr. Malinski, a close friend of Cardinal Wojtyla, noted that in a study circle that met at the Polish College during the Council, Wojtyla stated: "Eminent theologians such as Henri de Lubac, J. Daniélou, Y. Congar, Hans Küng, R. Lombardi, K. Rahner and others played an extraordinary role in these preparatory works [of the Council]" (Mieczyslaw Malinski, *Mon ami Karol* Wojtyla, Paris: Centurion, 1980, p. 189).

p. Italian journalist G. Marchesi points to two instances where John Paul II personally favored de Lubac: "In reference to personal encounters between John Paul II and Fr. de Lubac before the latter was el-

§ 23

It was their mentors, condemned or suspected of heterodoxy before the Council [15] who laid the foundation of the conciliar doctrine

---

evated to the Cardinalate, one can recall two episodes: The first was the preface that de Lubac wrote at Karol Wojtyla's request for the French translation of his work *Amour et responsabilité* (Paris, 1965, pp. 7-8). The second was in May 1980. While speaking during a papal visit to the *Institut Catholique de Paris*, John Paul II became aware that Fr. de Lubac was present in the room. He paused in his speech and said, 'Allow me to pay my respects to Father de Lubac'" (Giovanni Marchesi, "L'influsso di de Lubac su von Balthasar," *La Civiltà Cattolica*, May 17, 1997, p. 368, note 2).

q. Rocco Buttiglione, a professor at Rome's Lateran University and the University of Urbino, considered an expert on the life and thinking of John Paul II, affirmed that Cardinal Wojtyla aligned himself with the progressivist wing of the Council by taking a stand in favor of the *Nouvelle Théologie* against the "right-wing Roman theology" (Rocco Buttiglione, *Il pensiero di Karol Wojtyla*, Milan: Jaca Books, 1982, pp. 226-227).

r. John Paul II raised Frs. de Lubac, von Balthasar and Congar to the Cardinalate, thereby honoring the progressivist current of thinking that they represented. To Cardinal Ratzinger – also formerly under suspicion – he entrusted the direction of the Congregation for the Doctrine of the Faith (Alain Woodrow, "A Rome: Trente théologiens du monde entier pour accomplir le Concile," *Information Catholique Internationales*, May 15, 1969, p. 9).

s. John Paul II should be credited with the letter written in his name by Cardinal Agostino Casaroli to Msgr. Paul Poupard, Rector of the *Institut Catholique de Paris*. This letter praised the work of the Jesuit priest Pierre Teilhard de Chardin, one of the most controversial representatives of the *Nouvelle Théologie* ("Lettera del Card. Casaroli al Rettore dell'Istituto Cattolico di Parigi," *L'Osservatore Romano*, June 10, 1981, p. 1).

t. On the occasion of Fr. Rahner's birthday in 1984, John Paul II sent the Jesuit theologian "a warm message of congratulations to express his personal esteem" (Message of congratulations on the 80th birthday of Karl Rahner, in "Il teologo gesuita Karl Rahner morto in una clinica di Innsbruck,"*L'Osservatore Romano*, May 1, 1984, p. 4).

[15] The Encyclical *Humani generis* of Pius XII (1950) took a general stand against the *Nouvelle Théologie*. The encyclical crystallized the widespread reaction in the '40s against Progressivism. Some exponents of the *Nouvelle Théologie* were punished both before and after the document was released.

a. Fr. Chenu's book, *Une école de théologie: Le Saulchoir*, was published in 1937 and placed on the *Index in 1942* (*Jacques Duquesne interroge le Père Chenu*, p. 120). He also lost the rectorship of the Dominican College of Le Saulchoir.

and applied those same condemned principles with the open support of the highest echelons of the Conciliar Church.[16]

Thus, the spirit of the progressivist current reflects the spirit of the Council to a considerably large degree.

§ 24   Based on what this Introduction has expounded, the spirit of the Council differs from the spirit of the progressivist current only in those points that the Vatican explicitly and consistently condemned in the post-conciliar period. In all other points, one must assume the Vatican's sympathy or, at the very least, its tolerance.

In addition to examining conciliar tolerance, the Volumes of this Collection that study the *spirit of the Council* will analyze the hostility of that spirit toward various characteristics of the Catholic Church, notably her militancy and her sacral and hierarchical nature.

§ 25   The exposition of this hostility will be divided into two major parts: *First,* a presentation of the *animus injuriandi* (desire to offend), and *second,* a presentation of the *animus delendi* (desire to destroy).

The presentation of the *animus injuriandi* will describe the principal offenses against the Holy Church made during the post-conciliar period (this Volume II) and the offenses perpetrated against the Catholic Faith in the same period (Volume III). This division is not rigorous, since many offenses in one sphere overlap those in the other. For example, the denial of the virginity of Our Lady, which could be treated as an offense against the Faith, has been placed with offenses against the sacrality of the Church and her devotions in Chapter III of this Volume II.

---

b. In the '50s, Fr. Congar was prohibited from re-editing and translating his book *Vraie et fausse réforme dans l'Église*. Further, he was moved to Jerusalem, thence to Cambridge, and finally to Strasbourg (*Jean Puyo interroge le Père Congar*, pp. 106, 108-109, 111-112).

c. Cardinal de Lubac's *Catholicisme* (1938) was, in the Cardinal's own words, "the object of the strongest suspicions." Moreover, the theologian lost his chair at the University of Lyon-Fourvière (Angelo Scola, "Viaggio nel Concilio e dintorni," *30 Giorni*, July 1985, p. 11).

d. Rahner and Ratzinger were also under suspicion of heterodoxy by the Holy Office (A. Woodrow, "A Rome: Trente théologiens du monde entier pour accomplir le Concile," p. 9).

[16] In addition to citing quotations, this volume will try to show how the attitude of the ecclesiastical structure favored each of these authors. This will allow the Reader to better evaluate the veracity of this statement.

§ 26

What is meant by the word offense? In this Collection, offense refers to any affront to the honor of the Church and the honor of her doctrine.

An affront to the honor of the Church is an offense to the love which the Church has for herself: that is, the love that the parts of the Mystical Body of Christ – the Hierarchy and the faithful – mutually give to one another, as well as the love for its sacred institution which they comprise. An affront to the honor of the Church may range from a simple injury to the gravest blasphemy. The Introduction to Volume III will explain that praising heretics is included in this type of offense.

An affront to the honor of Catholic doctrine is anything that tries to debase or denigrate the high degree of love and veneration that the Catholic Church has for revealed truths and for the body of doctrines distilled from those truths with the continuous assistance of the Holy Ghost. An affront to the honor of Catholic doctrine habitually reveals itself as an outburst of hatred, quite often devoid of clear, calm reasoning. At times, however, it dons the deceitful guise of sophistry. In such cases, a brief overview of Catholic doctrine on the subject will be presented to provide the Reader with criteria to gauge the *animus injuriandi* that inspired it.

§ 27

It is not the intention of the Author to consider every error that tarnishes a doctrine as an offense against the honor of the doctrine. If this were the case, practically the whole Collection would have to be devoted to this consideration only. For this reason, the Author emphasizes **offenses against the honor of doctrine,** not merely **offenses against doctrine**. Offenses against the honor of doctrine are insults directed against the love that Catholics nurture for doctrine, more than the denials of its content.[17] As such, offenses against the love of doctrine express the *animus injuriandi* of those who perpetrate them.

§ 28

The presentation of the *animus delendi* will examine the plan of auto-demolition or self-destruction of the Holy Church, as conceived and executed by conciliar progressivists. Volume IV will deal with the plan of auto-demolition as a whole. Volume V will focus on the two main initiatives of the Council – secularization and ecumenism – that aim to destroy the position the Church has held for about two millennia with regard to the world and false religions. The Author's intent in exposing this planned self-destruction of the Church and the reforms relating to secularization and ecumenism is to reveal the *ani-*

---

[17] Attacks against the Faith will be studied in Volumes VI to XI of this Collection.

mus delendi of the authors cited. As such, it seems expressive of the spirit of the Council.

*

§ 29   It is not the custom of Catholics to judge intentions: *De internis nec Ecclesia* (the Church does not judge interior intentions). How then, does this Work intend to judge the outrageous and destructive intentions of the authors cited?

Once intentions are openly expressed, they leave the realm of hidden thoughts and unexpressed aims and enter the public domain. Thus the aphorism no longer applies to them.

The Volumes dealing with the *spirit of the Council* will consider the *animus* of the conciliar current insomuch as it has been revealed, and not on the basis of what secretly underlies the thinking of each author mentioned. With this, the objection is answered.

*

§ 30   Basic common sense tells us that, in matters of affronts and insults, nuances and subtleties are of little account. For example, if a person publicly affronts another and says, "Perhaps you are a thief," the use of the word "perhaps" makes little difference. What remains in the minds of those who hear his words is the accusation: The victim's honor has been questioned. The label of "thief" has stained his good name and moral integrity.

If this is a serious affront in the case of an individual, it becomes even more serious when the person attacked represents a people. Thus, if someone were to say publicly about a queen, "Perhaps she is a promiscuous woman," what stays in the mind of the hearers is the accusation of "promiscuous woman," an insult to the queen and, by extension, to the whole kingdom. Someone who would argue that the use of the word "perhaps" diminishes the gravity of the insult would only show his total lack of common sense, as well as his sense of honor and propriety.

If this applies to private individuals and public figures, it also clearly applies to the Holy Catholic Church. Therefore, in the analysis of the *animus injuriandi* of the conciliar progressivists in this Volume, the nuances and subtleties that color the insults of the offenders are of little account.

*

§ *31*

Volume I systematically analyzed the impossibility of studying *the letter* of the Council documents because of an inherent and intentional ambiguity in them. The nature of *the spirit* of the Council is analyzed in this Volume II, *Animus Injuriandi I*, and in Volume III, *Animus Injuriandi II*, which show the sacrilegious and hostile attitude of representatives of Progressivism toward the Holy Church and the Catholic Faith.

This Volume II will present a list of affronts against the Holy Catholic Church. Doing so, the Author believes he offers the Reader an opportunity to evaluate how far the spirit of tolerance allows the leaders of the conciliar theology to go.

The criterion used to select the affronts is the *sensus fidelium*,[18] or Catholic sense, especially in regard to the honor of Holy Church.

The plan of exposition progresses from the gravest offenses to the lesser ones.

*   *   *

---

[18] Volume I, *In the Murky Waters of Vatican II*, Introduction, note 1.

Chapter I

APOLOGIA FOR BETRAYAL

§ 1   To begin the analysis of the affronts against the Church made by progressivist thinkers, we will expose their very strange eulogy of betrayal as one of the most significant examples of just how far Vatican II's spirit of tolerance can go.

    Holy Mother Church has always been model of and inspiration for honor in its noblest aspects, i.e., in the homage she pays to virtue and fidelity. In this she imitates Our Lord Jesus Christ, who was divine Virtue and Fidelity Incarnate. The highest source of honor, virtue and fidelity is the internal life of the Most Holy Trinity.

§ 2   The apologia of betrayal offends the three actual foundations of honor – that of the Church, Our Lord and the Holy Trinity – as we will see below. By praising betrayal, these authors principally affront Catholic honor, although countless other errors might also be attributed to them. From this perspective, we will set out the eulogy of betrayal as the progressivists understand it.

    Among the authors cited in this Chapter, theologian Hans Urs von Balthasar stands out as the one who most extensively deals with the topic. Even though he was not present at the Council, he strongly represents its spirit.

1. Credentials of Urs von Balthasar as a Representative of the Spirit of the Council

§ 3   Hans Urs von Balthasar is indisputably one of the most important representatives of contemporary theology. In 1984, John Paul II granted him the Paul VI International Prize,[1] which pretends to be a kind of "Nobel Prize" [2] of the Church. During an audience at the

---

[1] John Paul II granted von Balthasar the Paul VI International Prize at a solemn audience in Clementine Hall in the presence of 16 Cardinals and numerous other Prelates and civil dignitaries. He was the first theologian to receive the prize, awarded every two years by the Paul VI Institute in Brescia ("Hans Urs von Balthasar ha meso la sua conoscenza al servizio del vero che promana da Cristo," *L'Osservatore Romano*, June 24, 1984, pp. 1, 4; H.U. von Balthasar, "La mia opera è abbozata più che terminata," *L'Osservatore Romano*, June 25-26,1984, p. 4).

[2] H.U. von Balthasar, interview with Erwin Koller, "Cento domande a von Balthasar," *30 Giorni*, June 1984, pp. 8-9; *30 Dias*, November 1989, p. 26.

Vatican, the Pontiff addressed von Balthasar with words of praise, telling him that he hoped that the award "recompenses you for your arduous efforts and encourages you to continue your study, which has already produced such significant results."[3] Later, repeating the words of Paul VI, he implied that von Balthasar was a prophet. [4]

The unquestionable glorification of Fr. von Balthasar's theses took place in 1988, when John Paul II gave him the Cardinal's hat. Since von Balthasar was not a Bishop, the theologian did not have the normal positions that would lead to the Cardinalate. The obvious objective of the papal choice was to endorse the theological opinions of von Balthasar.

Something similar had already taken place in 1983, when the same Pontiff made Fr. Henri de Lubac a Cardinal. Thus, these two leaders of the New Theology – de Lubac and his disciple von Balthasar – became Cardinals of the conciliar Church. In fact, von Balthasar never actually received the red hat because he died a few days before the ceremony. Notwithstanding, John Paul II's intent in conferring the honor was to glorify von Balthasar's theses.[5] Hearing of his death,

---

[3] John Paul II, "Hans Urs von Balthasar ha meso la sua conoscenza," *L'Osservatore Romano*, June 24, 1984, p. 1.

[4] Addressing the complementarity between theology and the Magisterium, John Paul II exalted the theologian, saying that **"Paul VI ... recalled these grave, prophetic words of Urs von Balthasar**: 'In the Church the faults of Christians, even of those with the mission to preach, is never reason to diminish the absolute character of the Word'" (Apostolic Exhortation *Quinque iam anni, Insegnamenti di Paolo VI*, VIII, 1970, p. 1422 in "Hans Urs von Balthasar ha meso la sua conoscenza," pp. 1, 4).

In its turn, the Science Commission of the Paul VI Institute, which unanimously chose von Balthasar for the Paul VI International Prize, justified its choice saying: "His broad and profound learning, his multifaceted and encompassing work, and his original and bold concepts have objectively earned the Swiss theologian Hans Urs von Balthasar a prominent position among the leading theologians of this century. ... In fact, he is the only eminent contemporary Catholic theologian who by himself dared to carry out the formidable assignment of [writing] a theological *summa,* which by the unity of its conception and grandeur of its foundation can justly compete with the great syntheses that marked Western theology" ("La motivazione del Premio," *L'Osservatore Romano*, June 24, 1984, p. 4).

[5] Several months after his death, John Paul II referred to him as a Cardinal, according to "L'incontro di Giovanni Paolo II con la Commissione Teologica Internazionale," *L'Osservatore Romano*, October 6,1988, p. 6.

John Paul II and his Secretary of State Agostino Casaroli expressed great consternation.[6]

Another sign of John Paul II's great admiration for the theologian was his encouragement of the foundation of the "Casa Balthasar." This institution, established at the initiative of Cardinal Joseph Ratzinger, aims to form priests following the thinking of von Balthasar and Lubac.[7]

---

[6] When he heard about von Balthasar's death, John Paul II sent this telegram to Bishop Joseph Gandolfi, president of the Swiss Episcopal Conference: "Perplexed by the news of the sudden death of the Reverend Lord Doctor Hans Urs von Balthasar, **a praiseworthy figure so important to the life of the Church because of his theological knowledge, whom I recently raised to the College of Cardinals**, I express my deep condolences to you and the whole Church in Switzerland.

"Remembering in my prayers the **most esteemed deceased,** who passed away in the peace of the Lord, I wholeheartedly give my apostolic blessing to you and those who mourn him in the Christian hope of resurrection" ("Il cordoglio del Santo Padre per la morte di von Balthasar," *L'Osservatore Romano*, June 28,1988, p. 1).

Cardinal Agostino Casaroli, then Secretary of State, sent Dietrich von Balthasar, the brother of the theologian, this message: "Given the sudden death of your brother, the Reverend Lord Doctor Hans Urs von Balthasar, recently raised to the College of Cardinals, the Holy Father expresses his sincere condolences to you and the other relatives and collaborators of the most esteemed deceased. In the Christian hope of resurrection, he grants his apostolic blessing to those who mourn him. I personally share your sorrow and assure you of my prayers for the dearly beloved deceased" ("Telegrama inviato al Dott. Dietrich von Balthasar," *L'Osservatore Romano*, June 28, 1988, p. 1).

In his speech at the Consistory receiving the new Cardinals, John Paul II referred to von Balthasar with these words: "**Sadly,** as you already know, **the Lord God** – by a mysterious design of His providence – **called to Himself Hans Urs von Balthasar, a renowned man and most esteemed theologian, whom today we would like to see among the [new] Cardinals receiving all our congratulations and marks of esteem.**

"Taken from us by sudden death, we commend him to the goodness of the merciful Redeemer so that, as a reward for his earthly merits and his long life of study and teaching and in recompense for the Cardinal's dignity that he lost, he may be granted the best, richest and most secure rewards of Heaven" ("Nella prospettiva ecclesiologica del Concilio," *L'Osservatore Romano*, June 29.1988, pp. 1, 4).

[7] Robert Moynihan, "Casa Balthasar," *30 Dias*, August-September 1990, pp. 56-57.

Perhaps even more expressive than this news report is the letter that the then Prefect of the Congregation for the Doctrine of the Faith sent to

§ 4

Many known theologians have also expressed their great consideration for von Balthasar.

Cardinal Henri de Lubac, his master, called him "perhaps the most cultured man of his time."[8] He judged his work to be "of such great proportion and depth that the Church has seen nothing like it in our epoch. The Church will draw benefits from his work for a long time."[9]

De Lubac considers von Balthasar's thinking crucial to understand Vatican II: "In the future, when someone explores this new treasure, he will realize that perhaps no tool is more useful than the work of Hans Urs von Balthasar."[10]

Fr. Joseph Fessio, SJ, director of Ignatius Press. Fr. Fessio himself describes Cardinal Ratzinger's letter in an appeal to his supporters for financial help:

"On July 19 of this year [1990], Cardinal Joseph Ratzinger wrote me a letter requesting help for an important project that should interest every practicing Catholic, and especially you who read the books of Ignatius Press.

"What is this project? How does it concern Ignatius Press? As you know, the main goal for establishing IP in 1978 was to make translations of the works of Henri de Lubac, Hans Urs von Balthasar and Adrienne von Speyr available. I was convinced then – as was Cardinal Ratzinger, and I had the joy to learn that Pope John Paul II shared our opinion when I had the opportunity to dine with him privately – that these authors were the best guides for the authentic renewal of the Church desired by Vatican Council II.

"Cardinal Ratzinger wanted to found a Lubac-Balthasar-Speyr Association with a twofold goal: 1. To spread the works of these three authors and promote studies and a spirituality based on them; 2. To open a house [Casa Balthasar] in Rome where youth considering the priesthood and religious life could retreat for a period of discernment while receiving a spiritual and intellectual formation according to the spirit of the Association. ...

"Any help you can give to this worthy project, eagerly desired by the Holy Father himself ... would be greatly appreciated" ("Cardinal Ratzinger asks for help," Ignatius Press Catalog 1990, New Fall Books, San Francisco).

[8] Henri de Lubac, *Paradoxe et mystère de l' Église* (Paris: Aubier-Montaigne, 1967), p. 184.

[9] *Ibid.*, p. 180.

[10] *Ibid.*, p. 181.

Noting that the great topics of the Council had already been analyzed by von Balthasar in his works, De Lubac states:

"First it must be said that there is not one single topic dealt with by Vatican Council II that this work [the ensemble of von Balthasar's theological studies] does not address in depth, following the same lines the Council would later draw. Church, Revelation, ecumenism, the priesthood, the liturgy of the word and the liturgy of the Eucharist have an important place in his work. In it one also finds fruitful perspectives about dialogue, the signs of the times and even the role of social communication. ...

"Before the Conciliar Fathers called for the dominant role of Jesus Christ to be affirmed in the documents on the Church and Revelation, Balthasar had already done this magnificently. He was also ahead of those at St. Peter's Basilica who asked that the Holy Spirit not be forgotten. The role of the Virgin Mary in the mystery of the Church as its symbol and fulfillment is one of the preferred themes of his meditations.

"Politely, but with all the force of love, he denounced 'power' and 'triumph' as perpetual temptations for churchmen and reminded them to bear witness through 'service.' His spiritual diagnosis of our present civilization was very profound. Although he did not end by fully drawing up the famous Schema XIII [*Gaudium et spes*], he was at least a precursor of its spirit, stating that 'just as the Spirit calls the world to adhere to the Church, it calls the Church to deliver herself to the world.' He warned, however, that one could not expect any good from those who too easily made syntheses between the Church and the world.

"Balthasar also presents remedies for false interpretations of the call to *aggiornamento*, which often and inevitably occur. Anyone seeking the Council's doctrinal framework on encounters with non-Christian religions or Atheism in its multiple contemporary forms can refer to Balthasar without risk of deception."[11]

La Civiltà Cattolica, the official organ of the Society of Jesus, warmly praises von Balthasar and attributes to him the role of a "prophet" who paved the way for Vatican II:

"In many of his intuitions von Balthasar was a precursor of Vatican II. With a prophetic eye, one might say, he expressed views about the Church, Christology, ecumenical dialogue and anthropology that the Council would later adopt. It suffices to examine his works

---

[11] *Ibid.*, pp. 181-182.

before the Council was convoked. In them, with an accurate ecclesiological sensibility, von Balthasar's thinking was already centered on Christ as the definitive revelation of God to man, the polarizing center of the encounter between man and God, a universal and concrete reality – unique and unrepeatable – the manifestation of God's love for man and the definitive fulfillment of the history of salvation."[12]

These examples reflect the high regard von Balthasar's thinking enjoys in the official circles of the Church.

The theses of von Balthasar, therefore, seem a good representation of the thinking of the Council and its spirit.

2. The Word Incarnate Seen as Betraying the Eternal Father

In view of such high praise for the theologian, it is very perplexing to analyze some excerpts of his works that reveal very strange theses. As a matter of fact, they give the impression of a lack of respect for the highest values of the Church and the Catholic Faith.

§ 5

In his book, *Le Coeur du Monde* (*The Heart of the World*), he imagines Our Lord Jesus Christ in Hell addressing the Eternal Father in a prayer. Christ declares He has betrayed His Father's justice. Note also that the request made on behalf of the reprobates of Hell is a parody of the words the Savior said to the Apostles. Speaking as if he were Christ, Von Balthasar writes:

"Father, the hour has arrived. Glorify your Son so that your Son may glorify you! ... **Do not refuse me the right to reveal you even in the horrors of Hell and in the form of sin itself,** so that you also may be glorified through me in these members and branches that are mine [that is, the enemies of God], for **henceforth we – they and I – form one indissoluble unity.** Before, Father, you and I were one, and they stood outside of us as enemies. ... Today I stand in the midst of our enemies. **I have become a traitor to your justice, and if You want to strike out at them, strike first at me.** ...

"All that is mine is yours! For this reason even **your enemies – my friends – belong to you.** ... And because **they are now indeed a part of myself,** I once again say: Confirm them in the truth! As you have sent me into the world, so also have I sent them into the world. Sanctify them also in their mission so that, like rays of light they

[12] Giovanni Marchesi, "La teologia di Hans Urs von Balthasar," *La Civiltà Cattolica*, January 1, 1977, p. 9.

may disappear into the darkness, and, as they disappear, they may illuminate the darkness."[13]

Some of these passages shock the *sensus fidelium* and Catholic doctrine. What does Fr. von Balthasar mean when he says that Christ wanted to "reveal God even in the horrors of Hell and in the form of sin itself"? God's Justice reflects Hell.

§ 6   It appears unlikely that he is referring to the traditional version of Our Lord's descent into Hell as Conqueror to enchain the Devil who had theretofore comfortably held dominion over men.[14] Then

---

[13] Hans Urs von Balthasar, *Le Coeur du Monde* (Paris: Desclée de Brouwer, 1956), pp. 87-89.

[14] Even though the descent of the Soul of Our Lord to the Hell where the reprobates dwell is not a matter closed to discussion, we adopt here the judgment of the great Doctor of the Church, St. Robert Bellarmine. He asserts that it is probable that Christ went to "all the infernal places," and, consequently, to the Hell of the condemned souls: *"Probabile est profecto Christi animam ad omnia loca inferni descendisse."* In support of this thesis, the saintly Doctor cites St. Ambrose, St. Gregory of Nyssa, Eusebius Emissenus, and St. Cyril of Jerusalem (*De Christo capite totius Ecclesiae*, lib. 4, c. 16, in *Opera Omnia*, Palermo/Naples/Paris: Pedone, 1872, vol. 1, p. 286).

His arguments are reinforced by this consideration of Francisco Suarez: "'Christ took some action in all the places of Hell; but the most perfect and co-natural way of taking action is by one's actual presence. Furthermore, at His death Christ was proclaimed Lord of the living and the dead so that all – even the devils and the condemned – belong to His kingdom and are subject to His power. Therefore, it was well for him to take possession of His kingdom by His presence and to triumph over all'" (*De mysterio vitae Christi*, disp. 43, sect. 4, n. 1, Paris, 1866, vol. 19, pp. 740-741, *apud* Hector-Raphaël Quilliet, entry *Descente de Jésus aux enfers*, in DTC, Paris: Letouzey et Ané, 1920, vol. 4, col. 612).

In this same sense, St. Thomas argues: "The third reason is that He [Our Lord Jesus Christ] triumphs over the Devil in a perfect manner. Indeed, someone triumphs perfectly over someone else when he not only defeats him in the battlefield, but also invades his actual house and destroys both it and the seat of his kingdom. Now, Christ triumphed over the Devil and vanquished him on the Cross; hence Jn 12:31: 'Now is the judgment of the world; now shall the prince of this world (that is, the Devil) be cast out.' And, in order to triumph perfectly, He wanted to destroy the seat of the [Devil's] kingdom and chain him in his house, which is Hell. So, He descended there, smashed everything that belonged to the Devil, put him in chains, and rescued his prey [that is, the just who were in Limbo as a consequence of original sin]. ...

"Just as Christ received possession of and power over Heaven and Earth, He also wanted to receive possession of Hell so that, in the words of the

Our Lord in triumph went to free the just souls awaiting the Redemption in Limbo. Nor does it seem likely that revealing God "under the form of sin itself" could refer to Christ uniting Himself to human nature in the hypostatic union, as the Church teaches. She instructs that, as God, He took on our nature without having any stain of sin; as God and Man, being pure and innocent, He died for the impure and guilty, thus repairing the infinite offense that our first parents committed against God.

  At first sight the meaning of the supposed request of the Jesus imagined by von Balthasar is that He wanted to be in Hell and from there, in union with the reprobates, to glorify God. And He supposedly took on sin – or at least would desire to do so – also to glorify God.

§ 7 How could one conceive of Our Lord wishing to unite Himself to the condemned souls to glorify God? The hypothesis appears absurd, since the reprobates and the devils suffer the penalty of eternal damnation,[15] and no glory can come from them of their own will. What is the meaning, then, of this incoherent and absurd request that von Balthasar places on the sacred lips of Jesus Christ? Such a hypothesis is irreverent, if not blasphemous.

  To suppose that Our Lord would be or ask to be in the state of sin is also incomprehensible, since it clashes with Catholic sense and the teaching of the Magisterium. Again, it gives the impression of irreverence or blasphemy.

  This impression comes closer to being a certainty as the analysis continues, and we find this disconcerting assertion attributed to the Savior: "I have become a traitor to your justice."

Apostle to the Philippians (2:10), 'In the name of Jesus every knee should bow, of those that are in Heaven, on Earth and in Hell'" (Thomas Aquinas, *In Symbolum Apostolorum Expositio,* a.5, Rome: Marietti, 1954, vol. 2, pp. 204-205). Elsewhere, however, St. Thomas gives a different opinion (cf. *Summa Theologiae,* Rome: Marietti, 1948, III, q. 52, a.2; *III Sententiarum,*d. 22; Paris: L. Lethielleux, 1933).

[15] On the penalty of damnation or eternal loss suffered by the Devil and the reprobates, see St. Thomas Aquinas, *In Aritotelis Librum De Anima* (Rome: Marietti, 1948, a. 21; *Super Epistolam Pauli ad Hebraeos, lectura IV; III Sententiarum* d.15, q.2, 1.3, q.3, ad 5; *IV Sententiarum,* lib. 1, d. 48, a. 3, q.,1; *Summa Contra Gentiles* (Rome: Marietti, 1934), lib. 3, c. 144.

Even pagans like Pilate and his wife acknowledged that Jesus was a just man.[16] Now this Catholic theologian – "the most cultured of our time"– accuses Our Lord of being a traitor! The first question that leaps to the mind of a Catholic is, "What does he mean by this? Is it a joke in poor taste or a disrespectful literary hyperbole?" Unfortunately, nothing in von Balthasar's context leads one to believe it is a joke or a literary metaphor. It seems, by its context, that the author is speaking seriously and really considers Christ a traitor, betraying the justice of God the Father. Several of the texts studied further on confirm the same absurd idea and give the same impression of irreverence.

§ 8   Von Balthasar adds yet another outrageous remark: "For this reason even your enemies – my friends – belong to you!" Could it be that the reprobates have converted and thus become friends of Christ? Or is the author implying there was a struggle between God the Father on the one side and God the Son together with the enemies of God on the other? Or did Christ – in the author's mind – enter into a syncretist coalition with the enemies of God?

Such hypotheses are opposed to Catholic doctrine and clash with the *sensus fidelium* because of their irreverence for the Redeemer's unsurpassed purity and perfect obedience.

The Christ imagined by von Balthasar takes this revolutionary idea even further when he asks to be with the enemies of God, whom he considers his friends, and then states, "Henceforth we – they and I – form one indissoluble unity," and, "they are now indeed a part of myself."

§ 9   St. Thomas Aquinas conceives the existence of a mystical body of the Devil,[17] composed of the enemies of God as a whole, that

---

[16] • "And as he was sitting in the place of judgment, his wife sent to him, saying: Have you nothing to do with that just man" (Mt 27:19).

• "And Pilate said to the chief priests and to the multitudes: I find no cause in this man" (Lk 23:4).

• "And Pilate seeing that he prevailed nothing, but that rather a tumult was made: taking water washed his hands before the people, saying: I am innocent of the blood of this just man; look you to it. And the whole people answering, said: His blood be upon us and upon our children" (Mt 27:24-25).

[17] In *De venerabili Sacramento altaris* (Rome: Marietti, 1939, p. 114), St. Thomas Aquinas teaches: "There are two mystical bodies in this world: the Mystical Body of Christ and the mystical body of the Devil or of the Antichrist. All men belong to one or the other. The Mystical Body of Christ is the Holy Church, His pure and faithful Spouse ... The mystical

is, the devils, the damned who are in Hell and the men still on this earth who fight against the good and the Church.[18] Von Balthasar's excerpt leads one to ask: Was Christ, then, part of this mystical body of the Devil? Would there not have to be a symbiosis between the Mystical Body of Christ and the mystical body of the Devil for Christ to say that the two "form one indissoluble unity" and that the enemies of God are "part of Himself"?

Regardless of the explanation, we can say that the text of von Balthasar is profoundly irreverent, both in a first reading and a second more profound analysis.

So as not to lengthen this Work, we will pass over his enigmatic description of the condemned souls as "rays of light," that "disappear into the darkness, and, as they disappear, they may illuminate the darkness." Let us only say that the key to the enigma again appears to be a symbiosis taking place between the good and the evil.

If an analysis of the parts of this imaginary prayer of Christ is shocking, a study of its ensemble is no less startling.

§ 10

In fact, it is a parody of the sublime prayer that Our Lord addressed to the Eternal Father before the Passion, pleading for himself, the Apostles and the Church. The text follows:

"Father, the hour is come; glorify thy Son, that thy Son may glorify thee. ... I have manifested thy name to the men whom thou hast given me out of the world. Thine they were, and to me thou gavest them; and they have kept thy word. Now they have known that all things which thou hast given me are from thee; because the words which thou gavest me, I have given to them; and they have received them, and have known in very deed, that I came out from thee, and they have believed that thou didst send me.

"I pray for them: I pray not for the world, but for those whom thou hast given me; because they are thine; and all my things are thine, and thine are mine; and I am glorified in them. Now I am no longer in

---

body of the Devil is the totality of the wicked, which plays to him the role of an adulterous nurse. Of this body, he himself is the head and the wicked persons are the members... 'The body of the Devil,' said St. Gregory, 'is composed of all the wicked ones.'"

See also *Summa Theologicae*, III, q.8, a.7; *Super Epistolam Pauli, II ad Corinthios*, 6, 15, lect. III.

[18] "The society of the evil ones is fourfold. That is, it is composed of the devils, public sinners, hypocrites and the reprobates" (Thomas Aquinas, *Super Epistolam Pauli, I ad Corinthios*, chap. X, lect. V, n. 560).

the world, but these are in the world, and I come to thee. Holy Father, keep those whom thou hast given me in thy name; that they may be one, as we are one. While I was with them, I kept them in thy name. Those whom thou gavest me I have kept; and none of them is lost, but the son of perdition, that the scripture may be fulfilled. ...

"I have given them thy word, and the world hath hated them, because they are not of the world; as I also am not of the world. I pray not that thou shouldst take them out of the world, but that thou shouldst keep them from evil. ... Sanctify them in truth. ... As thou hast sent me into the world, I also have sent them into the world. And for them do I sanctify myself, that they also may be sanctified in truth (Jn 17:1-19)."

A simple comparison of the two texts clearly shows that von Balthasar wanted to make a parody of the sublime prayer of Our Lord.

While Our Lord intercedes for the Church and the Apostles who received and knew Him, von Balthasar's Christ intercedes for Hell and sin, which rejected Him. Whereas Our Lord declares Himself a faithful witness of the Father, von Balthasar's Christ proclaims himself a traitor to Him. Whereby Our Lord offers His friends to God, the Christ of von Balthasar offers God's enemies. Christ affirms that the Apostles are one with Him, but von Balthasar's Christ says God's enemies are one with Him. Finally, whereas Our Lord institutes sanctification as the fundamental mission of the Apostles in the world, von Balthasar's Christ establishes in its place a mysterious "disappearance into the darkness."

These are the general lines of the eulogy of von Balthasar for the imagined betrayal of the Word Incarnate.

What should one conclude from this analysis? That the text by von Balthasar simply reveals a strange thinking? Or should one call it blasphemous? [19]

---

[19] The Author of this Volume is well aware of the superiority of the priestly dignity over that of a simple layman, as well as the high degree of study and culture of the cited authors quoted in this Work, superior to that of the average layman.

In acknowledgement of this, he has adopted a constant attitude of respect, endeavoring to let the facts speak for themselves and avoiding direct criticisms whenever possible by asking pertinent questions instead. Nevertheless, the Author will not fail to point out the cases when the honor of the Church is insulted and her doctrine is offended and threatened with destruction. In so doing, he draws inspiration from the example of innumerable Saints. See some of these examples of resis-

Even being as prudent as possible, one must brand such ideas as unusual and extravagant and the state of mind that inspired the text as, at the least, highly irreverent.

3. God the Father Charged with Betraying Our Lord and Assigning Judas to Be His Proxy

The strange defense of treason is not restricted to just one text in the works of von Balthasar. One can find such apologias in various books of his massive theological production.

In the text below, Von Balthasar attempts to generalize his notion of treason by applying it to God the Father, and then indiscriminately to the Apostles and Judas, as well as to the pagans and the Jews.

§ 11   By excessively broadening the notion of treason, von Balthasar confuses the concepts in the mind of the reader and reaps the immediate fruit of this ruse. That is to say, he excuses Judas for the infamous crime of treason and tries to absolve the Jews for the crime of Deicide. He also makes a grave offense against God the Father.

As is known, treason comes from the Latin *tradere*, to deliver. From that root, the word has come to mean betrayal, breach of trust, treachery. To excuse Judas and the Jews, von Balthasar confuses the common meaning of the word treason with its etymological meaning.

"The fundamental concept of *tradere*," writes von Balthasar, citing Popkes,[20*] "becomes present with the appearance of Judas and the [Roman] troops at the end of the scene on the Mount of Olives. 'It is enough. The hour is come: Behold, the Son of man is delivered up into the hands of sinners. Rise up, let us go. Behold, he that will betray me is at hand' (Mk 14:41) ... In predictions of the passion this 'delivery' was already spoken of various times ... always in the passive verb form, linked to the subject 'the Son of man.'...

"Here you have a continuation of a sacred tradition of the Old Testament where God is the one who acts and 'delivers' Israel to its enemies, to imprisonment, and so on. ... This action taken by God is always an act of judgment and, correspondingly, an act of divine wrath.[21*] 'One who is delivered in this way is abandoned by God in the truest sense of the word.' ...

tance in Vol. I, *In the Murky Waters of Vatican II*, General Introduction §§ 7, 18 Notes 3, 166.

[20*] Wiard Popkes, *Christus traditus: eine Untersuchung zum Begriff der Dahingabe im Neuen Testament* (Zurich: Zwingli Verlag, 1967), pp. 25, 41.

[21*] *Ibid.*, pp. 23-24.

"God is the agent of the passive form of delivery that takes place with the inexorability and inevitability of a judicial act, even though 'ire' is no longer present in the one who delivers, but rather His 'set purpose and foreknowledge' (Acts 2:23) and, finally, His love, for 'He spared not even His own Son, but delivered Him up for us all' (Rom 8:32). Despite this, however, a 'condemnation' takes place (Rom 8:3)."[22]

Although von Balthasar still does not call God a traitor in the current meaning of the term, he already has laid the presuppositions for his linguistic ruse: Since God the Father delivered (*tradidit*) His Son, in fact, He betrayed Him. By confusing the current meaning of betrayal, which has deservedly infamous connotations, with the original meaning of *tradere* – which merely means to bequeath, hand over, deliver, transmit – von Balthasar makes a sophism, a deliberately invalid argument that aims to deceive the reader. It is also a grave offense against God in one of the fundaments of our Faith, the sacred relations between the Father and the Son.

§ 12 Below, the Reader will see how the theologian continues to use the same artifice, confusing the current usage of betrayal with the first definition of the verb *tradere*. In this way von Balthasar gives the "delivery" of the Father and the "self-delivery" of the Son equal footing with the treason of Judas and the Deicide of the Jews. By this linguistic sleight-of-hand, an unsuspecting reader, accompanying the text, will find himself pressed to agree with von Balthasar that either all are traitors – God, Christ, Judas and the Jews – or that none is a traitor. By taking advantage of a person's instinctive repulsion to imagine God and Christ as traitors, von Balthasar tries to absolve Judas and the Jews, presenting them as representatives of God who executed the sentence of the Father.

Along these lines, he continues: "Together with the *Verbum-Caro* [Word made Flesh] of the New Testament and the co-humanity present in Him, there is, however, another fact: **Alongside the Father who delivers (the Son) and the Son who delivers himself, there appears a third person, the traitor who delivers (Christ).** Judas, 'one of the twelve,' is the 'one who delivers' (*traditor*). In passing, his action makes him the representative of the unbelieving and unfaithful Israel that rejects its Messiah, who is thus abandoned ...

"The paradoxical game between God who delivers and sinners who deliver and betray unfolds on a razor's edge, even though in

---

[22] Hans Urs von Balthasar, *Mysterium paschale,* in Johannes Feiner and Magnus Löhrer, *Mysterium salutis* (Petrópolis: Vozes,1974), vol. III/6, pp. 71-72.

the Old Covenant God had His juridical agents who were not excused for their action but were judged because of it. **This game can be interpreted as a mystery of God's Providence** (Act 2:23) **and as a relative ignorance on the part of the Jews** (Act 3:17; **see also the attenuating 'repentance' of Judas,** according to Mt 27: 3). **But it can also be abused polemically (and even politically) to define a personal or ethnic black sheep? [infamously guilty]** ...

"On the one hand, **Judas comes to play the 'role' of Israel, the rejected one** ... On the other hand, **he is**, in light of the universalist affirmations of the New Testament, **the visible representative of all sinners – Christians, Jews and pagans.**"[23]

According to Von Balthasar, then, Judas was chosen by God to play the role of His representative, as well as of Israel. He also suggests that the Christians – and not the Jews – bear the major guilt for the "delivery" and crucifixion of Christ.

§ 13   Further on, he tries to acquit Annas and Caiphas, along with all the Sanhedrin, of the crime of Deicide, since they supposedly judged Our Lord merely from a political standpoint:

"The theme of the 'delivery' now unfolds within the dimensions of the theological structure of mankind, constituted by the mass of the non-chosen (pagans), the (Jewish) people chosen from the pagans, and the (Christian) disciples chosen from the Jews. The true 'deliverer' is Judas, one of the Twelve (Mt 10:4, etc.). He 'delivers' Jesus to the Jews, who 'deliver' Him to Pilate (Mk 15:1), who 'hands Him over' first to Herod (who, in his turn, 'sends Him back' Lk 23:7-11) and, finally, 'delivers' Him to the Jews (Mk 15:15; 27:26; Jn 19:16): 'He delivered up Jesus to their will' (Lk 23:25).

"The chain of deliveries is complete: Judas, at depth, shares the common messianic ideal of the Jewish leaders. He denies his New Testament faith. The Jewish leaders, however, always understood the theological aim of the 'Messiah' and 'Son of God' (Mk. 14:61) as something political. Hence the political goal of their accusations against Jesus before Pilate (Lk 23:2) – He stirred up the people, refused to pay taxes, was ambitious for power – is not, as the Jews pretended, a diplomatic disguise for their political purposes, but reveals their pagan way of thinking: 'We have no king but Caesar' (Jn. 19:15).

"It becomes irrelevant, therefore, to ascertain whether Jesus was judged by a Jewish or Roman tribunal, whether He was condemned on account of His pretensions to the title of

---

[23] *Ibid.*, p. 73.

Messiah or as 'king of the Jews' and even, finally, **whether the question of His mission as the Messiah was expressly raised at the Sanhedrin, or whether Jesus' pretensions to personally be the Savior of the latter times implicitly contains His mission.**"[24]

§ 14   The theological-hermeneutic sophism of von Balthasar comes to its end: It would be irrelevant whether Our Lord was the Messiah and whether the Jews knew it. The real reason for the latter to condemn Jesus Christ would be their diplomatic desire to please the Romans. Their fault was only to be influenced by their pagan way of thinking, just as the fault of Judas was to be influenced by the Jewish leaders.

It is not our purpose here to prove that this reasoning is relativist, wrong and anti-Catholic. We transcribed these excerpts to show how a theologian such as von Balthasar is free to propose a thesis highly offensive to the honor of God the Father, making Him an associate of Judas in the infamous act of betraying His Only-Begotten Son.

4. A Sentimental Eulogy of Judas

§ 15   In another work, von Balthasar endorses verses of the socialist French poet Charles Péguy,[25] where he imagines that Christ's love for Judas, as He hung on the Cross, was based not on divine wisdom but, rather, on a worldly and sentimental affection. Péguy fancies a Christ who supposedly became so indignant that the traitor should be damned that He lost control of Himself and "cried out like a mad man." Further, Christ's death was supposedly caused by the frustration of this passionate love:

"Gervaise[26] transcends her own thinking now, describing God's abandonment of Jesus on the Cross: the suffering of Jesus over the infernal desperation of Judas and the impossibility of commuting his eternal condemnation by His temporal suffering. This suffering is so inconceivable it becomes infinite:

---

[24] *Ibid.*, pp.75-76.

[25] Although in this excerpt, von Balthasar does not compromise himself deeply with Péguy's view, he clearly does so in other parts of the same book, *La Gloire et la Croix - Les aspects esthétiques de la Révélation - II Styles: de Jean de la Croix à Péguy* (Paris: Aubier-Montaigne, 1972), pp. 373-375, 377-379).

[26] Gervaise, a fictitious 25-year-old Franciscan nun, teaches the young Joan of Arc her catechism under the portal of the Cathedral. Her words constitute Péguy's poem titled *Mystery of the Charity of Joan of Arc* (*Mystère de la Charité de Jeanne d'Arc,* 1909).

"Being Son of God, Jesus knew everything,
And the Savior knew that this Judas, whom He loves,
Would not be saved even by His full offering.
It was then that He knew infinite suffering;
It was then that He experienced infinite agony.
And He cried out like a madman with terrible anguish ...
And the Father took pity and He had His human death." [27]

Further on, in his comments on Pegúy's *Mystère*, von Balthasar repeats, but greatly intensifies, the idea that Our Lord "cried out like a madman" as a reaction of a passionate and desperate state of mind. He says that "**Jesus cried out in a way more terrible than a reprobate.**" [28]

In addition to the blasphemy of likening the Son of God to a madman and a reprobate, note also von Balthasar's insistence on presenting Judas in a way that elicits pity, if not sympathy.

We will not analyze here von Balthasar's error in Catholic doctrine when he imagines Our Lord in rebellion against the existence of Hell.

§ 16   Von Balthasar continues his sentimental defense of Judas in his book, *The Heart of the World*. First, he poetically presents the traitor as one who was misunderstood and abandoned in order to elicit romantic compassion in his readers. In addition, the author again appears to slide into blasphemy by imagining that Jesus Christ and Judas kissed each other on the mouth "a thousand times." To the ears of today's Western man – whom von Balthasar normally addresses – this phrase insinuates a suspicious relationship of a homosexual nature between the Lamb of God and the traitor.

Von Balthasar imagines Judas speaking: "Into what hole can I crawl so that you will no longer see me, so that I will no longer be a burden to You, so that the stench of my [moral] putrefaction may no longer importune you? I have sinned right to your face and **the mouth which touched Your lips – Your divine lips – a thousand times** has also kissed the lips of the world and said: 'I do not know Him' ...

"It is a beautiful thing when love bends to what is vile, but it is unbearable when love becomes vile with the vile. There is a kind of betrayal that cannot be redressed. A residue remains for all eternity, and my eyes will never again be able to meet Your eyes. I will fling the thirty silver pieces into the temple – but, I beg You, do not confuse this

---

[27] H. U. von Balthasar, *La Gloire et la Croix – Péguy*, pp. 311-312.
[28] *Ibid.*, p. 329.

act with repentance. That pretentious word does not fit here. My soul is sealing its lips tightly to prevent any such word from escaping."[29]

We see, therefore, von Balthasar made a twofold outrage to the Lamb of God: *first*, by considering Christ as a mad man and a reprobate without interior peace; *second*, by creating a sentimental climate with the aim of lessening the just horror we should have for the betrayal of Judas Iscariot.

5. Our Lord Thought to Have Died Like a Reprobate, Cursed by God the Father

§ 17

According to von Balthasar, God the Father's abandonment of Our Lord Jesus Christ would have consisted of a "curse," which would concur with the notion of the Father's supposed betrayal of the Son. He writes:

"The Theology of abandonment can only be realized from a trinitarian perspective. That God 'delivers' His Son is one of 'the most unheard of statements of the New Testament.'

"We should understand 'delivery' in its full meaning, rather than minimize it to a 'mission' or 'gift.' Here one realizes what Abraham did not need to do with regard to his son Isaac: Christ was abandoned by the Father with full deliberation to the fate of death. God released Him to the forces of perdition, be it called man or death ... **Christ is the one cursed by God**. Here we have the *theologia crucis* in its most radical meaning.'[30*][31]

§ 18

We will quote several more excerpts that offend Our Lord, which confirm von Balthasar's view that Christ died without interior peace and suffered like a reprobate:

"God takes upon himself, as Christ the Man, all the guilt of Adam (Rom 5:15-21), to be 'delivered up' (Rom 4:25) as a 'living' personification of sin and enmity (2 Cor 5:21; Eph 2:14) to 'condemnation by God' (Rom 8:3) ... This is not to be taken in a mythical sense, but rather it is the central message of the Bible. **Nor should the meaning be diminished** as far as the cross of Christ is concerned, **as if the Crucified was reciting psalms in an intimate and unperturbed communication with God and died in divine peace.**"[32]

---

[29] H. U. von Balthasar, *Le Coeur du Monde*, pp. 156-157.

[30*] W. Popkes, *Christus traditus*, pp. 286-287.

[31] H. U. von Balthasar, *Mysterium Paschale,* in J. Feiner and M. Löhrer, *Mysterium Salutis,* p. 74.

[32] *Ibid.*, p. 82.

In the work commenting on Péguy's Joan of Arc, von Balthasar repeats his affront by considering, with the utmost impropriety, that Our Lord's suffering was analogous to that of a reprobate:

"Afterwards the question arose of the **meaning of the cry of Christ on the cross: It can only be ... in the fruitful suffering,** not the vain suffering of the reprobates, **even if Jesus cried out more terribly than a reprobate,** and His shout resounded through the Church and the world of all times and eternities: **'O culminating, eternal and effective clamor! - which sounds as if God himself had despaired'** (J. 97. 98). God the Father gauges the abyss of this suffering: **'Even the reprobate, even the thief who has just been damned, were nothing to Him but human reprobates,' but here is His Son who cried out** from the midst of time, His cry encompassing, moreover, the two edges of eternity (J. 116)."[33]

In *The Heart of the World,* von Balthasar presents the Word Incarnate as the abyss into which all the world's bitterness and despair flow:

"He **[the Word] wanted to sink so low that in the future every fall would be a fall into himself. And every streamlet of bitterness and despair would henceforth run down into His lowermost abyss.**" [34]

Von Balthasar thus repeats here the affront that he made before: Our Lord would have died without interior peace, despairing like a reprobate.

6. The Heart of Christ Betrayed God and the World

§ 19

Fancying his thinking sublime, von Balthasar speaks disrespectfully in the texts below about the Heart of Jesus, which he calls the "heart of the world." Further on, in another text, we will see his views about the traditional devotion to the Sacred Heart. According to him, the Heart of Christ, which knows all the human passions – not excluding the evil ones – is the maddest and most superficial of all creatures. It would be the betrayer of the betrayal of the world, the nudity and madness of God. It is the betrayer of those who confide in

---

[33] H. U. von Balthasar, *La Gloire et la Croix - Péguy*, pp. 329-330.

[34] H. U. von Balthasar, *Le Coeur du Monde*, p. 39.
For an analysis of the most profound meaning of this text by von Balthasar, which would imply the notion of a Christ who is co-natural with evil, the reprobates and even Hell, see Vol. III, *Animus Injuriandi II*, Chap. III and Vol. VIII, *Fumus Satanae*, Chap. VI.

it; it falls in love with its enemies; it is the symbol of the breaking of all barriers.

§ 20   To imagine the adventures and follies of the Heart of Christ, one should resort to the world of prostitution. In the Heart of Christ, which is the heart of the world, on the one hand we find grace and, on the other, the dark scum of sin and all that is called betrayal and cowardice, defiance and pride, anguish and infamy. It would be the synthesis between Heaven and Hell. Not even God's betrayal was able to crush this heart. It is the symbol of the disfigured relations of the Trinity in which the Father became the judge, and the Son, the sinner. The Heart of Christ would be the nuptial bed shared by Heaven and Earth. In it two inimical wills unite: that of God and that of the world.

Such is the list of improprieties and offenses contained in excerpts of von Balthasar we will now cite. The theologian expounds his opinion in a context that reeks of an unbalanced Wagnerian sentimentality. The more shocking or bizarre expressions are in bold print:

"Then God created a Heart for Himself and placed it at the center of the world.[35] It was **a human heart**, knowing the impulses and yearnings of human hearts, **experienced in all** its windings and

---

[35] A Reader who is unaccustomed to progressivist authors, and particularly von Balthasar, will understandably have some difficulty following the texts in this Item 6 about the Heart of Christ. Indeed, the author indiscriminately applies diverse meanings to the expression, which can disorient the reader.

To prevent such an effect in our Reader – and primarily to clarify the offenses made by von Balthasar – we present the principal meanings used by the author for the expression Heart of Christ:

a. Heart of Christ = heart of the world. According to several progressivist theologians, the universe as a whole is an 'incarnation' of the Word. Hence the existence of a Cosmic Christ, who in one way or another encompasses the spiritual and material aspects of the universe. The heart of this Comic Christ, then, is a center from which energies emanate in a latent state and into which already spiritualized energies converge after being liberated from the life cycle. Some, like Teilhard de Chardin, imagine this center as the concentration of an energized atmosphere or as a *pneuma* that hovers above creation (Cf. *Le milieu divin,* Paris: Seuil, 1957, pp. 196, 182, 187, 94, 135-138, 144-145, 149, 153-154; *Le coeur de la matière,* Paris: Seuil, 1976, pp. 50, 69).

Others, such as Karl Rahner, imagine that this energized center is found inside the Earth and the souls of the deceased go there (Cf. *Pour une théologie de la mort, in Écrits théologiques*, Bruges: Desclée de Brower,

wanderings, its **changes of humor and sudden impulses** – in a word, **experienced in all the bitter blessings and blessed bitterness that a human heart can savor.** The human heart is the **most foolish,** obstinate, and **fickle of all creatures. It is the seat** of all fidelity and **of all treachery,** an instrument richer than a full orchestra and poorer than a cricket's empty chirping; its incomprehensibility is a mirror image of God's own incomprehensibility.

"This is what God drew from the world's rib as it slept, and He fashioned it into an organ of His divine love. With this weapon He already stood ... deep in enemy territory, and He shared fully in the world's bustle. He knew everything from within. As in a dream, He could listen in this shell to the sea of blood of mankind. The world's betrayal was already known to Him, and, like Hagen, He recognized the vulnerable spot on the back of Siegfried's head." ...

"But God living in the fragile shelter of a heart now becomes easy to touch! How swiftly He could be hurt! ... **What nudity God**

1963, vol. 3, pp. 155-156, 160, 153-154, 115-119, 127). . Von Balthasar appears to favor this latter view, as he insinuates that Hell is the natural habitat of the Heart of Christ.

b. Heart of Christ = divine heart. This would be the love of the Divine Persons, therefore, the Holy Spirit. Such love is paradoxically reflected in the betrayal of one of the Persons by another. Heart of Christ would also be the love of the Word Incarnate for mankind upon the realization of the Redemption. As such, it would be a point that surpasses both good and evil, truth and error, friends and foes, and Heaven and Hell, since for von Balthasar such distinctions were overcome by the love of Christ, symbolized by His Heart.

c. Heart of Christ = human heart. Two applications stem from this: A. Applied directly to Our Lord, it would be His Sacred Heart which, pierced by the lance, gave birth to the Church, as the rib taken from Adam's chest gave birth to Eve. B. Applied directly to man and indirectly to Our Lord, the expression Heart of Christ would take on the unruly passions of human love. Thus, it would be inconstant like the human affections of fallen nature. Such a Heart would be irrational, given over to the excesses of the senses, abandoned to the passions and, finally, moved by carnal attraction.

In every meaning he adopts – one not necessarily connected to another – von Balthasar adds literary hyperboles and poetic-theological effusions. This undoubtedly makes his exposition somewhat obscure and convoluted.

Nevertheless, we hope these explanations will help the Reader comprehend the grave improprieties and offenses to Our Lord.

has assumed! What madness He has committed! He himself betrayed the weak spot of His love. As soon as the news spread that He was dwelling among us in a human heart, each and every one began to whet his arrows at him and test his bow. A shower of arrows will soon fall upon Him. Millions of shots will fly toward the small red spot.

"Nor will His [Christ's] unprotected heart protect Him. A heart certainly lacks the use of reason. **It knows not why it pumps. It will not resist; it will betray Him (because every heart is unfaithful).** For, indeed, it never stands still; it always goes on, it runs. And because love is always effusive, so **also His heart will be effusive toward… the enemy.** This is His joy, to dwell among the children of men; it is His curiosity to know the taste of other, alien hearts. He wanted to savor this taste, and for that He suffered the trial and paid tribute to the taste of the others. He will never forget this taste, even in the most distant eternities. **Only a heart could be commissioned with such adventures; follies best left concealed from reason,** which should be silent. **Follies that only the intercourse with flesh and blood can inspire; follies of a poor heart,** which by enchantment transforms its hidden poverty and arid earthly ground into treasures that surprise the angels of heaven." [36]

Further on, von Balthasar writes: "Who can separate what may no longer be separated? … Let him [the foolhardy one who desires this] first turn his gaze to the grand heart at the center and **celebrate the annihilation of all barriers.** Let him marvel to see the Most High contemplate with such love the lowliness of His creation and choose flesh and blood to be the home and abode of a transcendent grace.

"Celebrate, o my heart, the immensities of the heart of the world! Although the triune ocean of eternal life cascades from above into that little shell, so too billowing up **from below and clashing against him is the opposing ocean of all countries and centuries, the gloomy tide of the world, the black foam of sin, treachery and cowardice, defiance and pride, anguish and infamy. Everything surges up, assaults, plunges and crowds into the heart of the world.** The two oceans clash against each other into that shell, like fire and water, and **the eternal struggle between heaven and hell is decided within that narrow battlefield. … In one stroke it swallows the whole goblet of heaven and hell; and along with the deepest misery it savors the most sublime bliss. …**

---

[36] H. U. von Balthasar, *Le Coeur du Monde*, pp. 40-45.

"This little heart will not burst as it resists the double onslaught, the double storm of love and hate, the double lightning bolt of judgment and of grace. **It will not burst even when the Father, veiled, joins his betrayers and forsakes Him,** leaving Him alone in the midst of the world, tossed about by the most frigid darkness of hell, ablaze with its flames, laughed at by every grimace of sin, filled with unimaginable anguish, buried alive, indescribably perplexed. ...

"Only God can expand that finite bowl to infinity without shattering it. And if a heart can be extended to the proportions of God, here is an even greater miracle: that God was able to reduce Himself to the proportions of man ... **That the Trinity could disfigure itself into the relationship between judge and sinner. That eternal love could assume the traits of divine wrath.** That the Abyss of Being could be drained into the abyss of nothingness.

"But even this mystery is contained within the space of a Heart. In its center Being and Non-being encounter each other. It alone knows the secret of both the knotting and the untying of the riddle. In its axis the beams cross. The whole abyss is encompassed by the arch of his love. Every contradiction grows silent before His sacrifice. ...

"**Sober is the intoxication of this love [reciprocal between God and man], virginal is the bridal bed of heaven and earth.** ...

"**In his own deeds, He [the Word of God] joined together two hostile wills, and by the very act of linking them, He undid the inextricable knot.** He dared to demand everything from His Heart; indeed, by His excessive demands, He launched His Heart into an impossible task. Through such overburdening, the Heart recognized its divine Lord, recognized fortune and love (which always demand the excessive), and opened itself up to obedience.

"He opened himself to the world. He took the world up into himself, and He became the heart of the world." [37]

*

§ 21   For von Balthasar, Our Lord should always be characterized as one who is condemned, destroyed and miserable. The image of Jesus Christ as He really was and is – divine and most holy, the sum of all perfections – he considers "necessarily false." For von Balthasar, who spoke so much on the Heart of Christ, the modern images of the Sacred Heart "are repugnant." He writes:

---

[37] *Ibid.,* pp. 48-52.

"Péguy avoids a Christology that would make Jesus Christ an abstract, insensible and, therefore, inhuman amassing of high points, of supreme values. ... For a theological aesthetics, this has decisive importance. A **Jesus** (like that of so many theologians) **that is nothing but an abstract (and therefore necessarily false) accumulation of 'perfections'** ... **can never become the pattern for** 'classical' **beauty. His image can only degenerate from the emptiness of the Gothic 'beau Christs' to the repugnant modern images of the Sacred Heart."** [38]

Now if the famous Cardinal Hans Urs von Balthasar – praised by John Paul II and considered by many as a "moderate" and even a "conservative" – says this, what will other theologians of lesser renown and a more avant-garde tendency feel free to say?

The spirit of tolerance born at the Council is undoubtedly quite broad...

7. Judas Hanging from the Tree, His Entrails Strewn About: A Symbol of the Church

§ 22

To give the Reader a general view of the offenses and blasphemies hurled at the Holy Church, conciseness is indispensable. This is, however, not an easy matter to achieve. The Author chose some **700 excerpts of progressivist insults** to the Church and the Faith that could have been included in these Volumes, [39] and so far, due to the method of exposition, only 15 have been used. For this reason, an attempt will be made to present the texts in as brief a manner as possible, although always *ipsis litteris*.

One cannot say that objectivity will be compromised by omitting the context since, in order to gauge the gravity of an offense, it is not necessary to have the full context. An offense is judged *per se*. It always reflects the state of mind of the one who made it. This is elementary common sense.

---

[38] H. U. von Balthasar, *La Gloire et la Croix - Péguy*, pp. 375-376.

Fr. Teilhard de Chardin also expresses his aversion to the Sacred Heart of Jesus and the devotion to it: "Historically, as everyone knows, **the devotion to the 'Sacred Heart'** (or Love of Christ) latent in the Church from the beginning, **was expressed in France** during the *grand siècle* in **an amazingly lively fashion. At the same time, it was strangely inadequate with regard to both its object ('reparation') and its symbol (the Savior's Heart shown in very bizarre anatomical contours!)"** (Teilhard de Chardin, *Le coeur de la matière*, Paris: Seuil, 1976, pp. 53-54).

[39] This Volume and Volume III, *Animus Injuriandi II*.

Since the goal of this Volume is just to present the spirit of Vatican II as being tolerant toward theologians who offend the honor of the Church rather than to expose their thinking, this method of exposition achieves its goal.

Should someone want to verify that the contexts confirm the offenses contained in the excerpts quoted, he can go to the sources that are provided.

The Author's comments will be brief, only what is indispensable either to establish necessary premises or to assist the Reader in some nebulous points that may appear.

*

§ 23

Referring to the Church's "guilt" for the Protestant revolt, Fr. von Balthasar has the highly maladroit and offensive idea of comparing the Holy Church to Judas hanging from the tree, his innards strewn about. He says:

"This change of awareness in the theological realm would have been difficult to achieve without the secession of **the Reformation** and its consequences ... What **for us is unforgivable guilt** can be used by God to further His mysterious purposes in the distribution of redemptive grace.

"**When finally the horrible words** *crepuit medius* **could be uttered over a guilty Christendom ... then it was necessary to add also the words that follow:** *'et diffusa sunt omnia viscera eius'* [referring to Judas who 'burst asunder in the midst: and all his bowels gushed out' (Acts 1:18)]." [40]

"**Something of the innermost bowels of the Church had been torn away by the reformers; some fibers of her heart continued to beat outside her body**. ... But that is not all: **profound secrets known only to her saints were taken from her by the**

---

[40] Von Balthasar refers here to the description of Judas' suicide in the *Acts of the Apostles*: "In those days Peter, rising up in the midst of the brethren, said: (now the number of persons together was about one hundred and twenty) Men, brethren, the scripture must needs be fulfilled, which the Holy Ghost spoke before by the mouth of David concerning Judas, who was the leader of them that apprehended Jesus: Who was numbered with us, and had obtained part of this ministry. And he indeed hath possessed a field with the reward of iniquity and, being hanged, burst asunder in the middle: and all his bowels gushed out" (Acts I: 15-18).

**Augustinian monk of Wittenberg and borne off from her trea-
sure in the silence of the night. Now her patrimony lies on the
open road** ...

"So, **the love for the Church** ... **seeks those parts living
outside her walls. ...**

"What a strange new meaning the words of the *Canticle of
the Canticles* ... now take on: *curremos in odorem unguentorum
tuorum* [We shall run after you in the odors of your ointments] – now
that the invisible odors of the beloved are scattered in the most profane parts of the world and suddenly accost the unperceiving Bride,
who hastens after the invisible on difficult roads." [41]

It should be noted that, according to the author, these "odors"
the Church is now running after appear to be the "odors" of the bowels of Judas strewn about on the ground, that is today, the rotten parts
of Christendom that were taken by the Protestants.

8. The Church Accused of Betraying Her Mission

After showing the offenses made by the "moderate" von
Balthasar, who deems God the Father and Jesus Christ traitors and
likens the Church to Judas hanging with his bowels strewn on the
ground, we will present the testimony of other authors who also offend the Holy Church by affirming that she betrayed her mission.

§ 24

Fr. Hans Küng indirectly contends that the Church has "betrayed her very essence" and "denied her origins":

"**What good is it for a Church to be the oldest one** or to
appeal to the 'Fathers'... **if along her history she betrayed her
very essence**, if she no longer represents more than an august monu-
ment to a highly venerable tradition? **Of what purpose is this romantic, restorationist and archaeological ecclesial tradition, if,
during her centuries-old evolution, she denied her origins?** ...
However international, vast, multiform and even ancient she may be,
the Church can alienate herself. She **is no longer the same; she
has turned away from her original nature, strayed from her most
natural path**." [42]

Küng affirms that if the Church refuses to unite with the other
religions, she is "betraying the Gospel":

[41] H. U. von Balthasar, *Abbattere i bastioni* (Turin: Borla, 1966), pp. 69-
70.
[42] Hans Küng, *A Igreja* (Lisbon: Morales,1970), Vol. II, pp. 66-67.

"Is this process of opposition and mutual hostility – which ends by causing division between the Churches – always, necessarily and only a matter of dull intelligences, petty hearts and a legalistic mania? This is often the case, but not always! It can also occur by virtue of an honest conviction that each and every **other attitude would amount to a betrayal of the Gospel of Jesus Christ.**" [43]

§ 25

Bishop Boaventura Kloppenburg, then a member of the International Theological Commission, regarded by some as a moderate and by others even as a conservative, points to several cases where the Church would betray herself. He attacks and insults the customary ways the Holy Church always presented herself until Vatican II:

"**The catholicity of the Church can be betrayed in several ways.** ... The *first* consists of giving in to the temptation of power, either by adopting ways befitting a political power or by being conformed and submitting to the powers of this world, thus turning her back on the poor ... The *second* would be by trying to justify the formation of sects or parties in the bosom of the Church. The *third* results from taking **pride in the catholicity of one's own confession and despising the others.** The *fourth* ... lies in **abusing the term 'Catholic.'**" [44]

*

These are the appalling sketches that result from attributing treason to the holiest of subjects. They offend Catholic honor in the broadest and most fundamental ways: from the honor due to the three Persons of the Blessed Trinity all the way to the honor due to the Redemption of mankind; from the honor of the Savior's earthly mission to the honor of the Church's mission.

This is only a sample of what the Council's spirit of tolerance permits to be said, disseminated and taught.

*   *   *

---

[43] *Ibid.*, pp. 28-29.

[44] Boaventura Kloppenburg, *A eclesiologia do Vaticano II* (Petrópolis: Vozes, 1971), p. 124.

Chapter II

THE MILITANCY OF THE CHURCH
CALLED SHAMEFUL AND INFAMOUS,
FAVORING A CRUEL AND SADISTIC RITE

§ 1 Of the essential attributes of the Church, her militant character is certainly the one that elicits the most hatred from progressivists. Even more than her monarchic and fundamentally non-egalitarian character and her sacral nature, her militant character is the keel of the Bark of Peter that presupposes and synthesizes all her other attributes. For this reason, in this "valley of tears" the Church has always been called the Church Militant in accordance with the words of the 'Lion of Judah' (Gen 49:9; Apoc 5:5) Who taught: "I came not to bring peace but the sword" (Mt 10:34; Lk 12:51).

In principle such spiritual militancy is employed against errors that attack the Holy Catholic Faith and the Mystical Body of Christ either internally or externally.[1] This spiritual militancy, however, is not complete unless it is also reflected in the temporal sphere. Catholic States and, by antonomasia, Christendom, have the right and duty to defend the institutions, laws and customs that distinguish the culture and civilization born from the sacred inspiration of the Church. On her part, the Church should orient and influence the State toward that end. This implies an indirect action over the temporal sphere, represented by the silver key on the coat of arms of the Vicar of Christ.[2]

The coherence of these principles shocks the progressivist current because it summarizes – especially with regard to the militancy of the Church – what they want to destroy.

1. At and after the Council, Popes and Prelates Oppose the Militancy of the Church

§ 2 With the aim of pleasing the progressivist current, Cardinal Stefan Wyszynski, Primate of Poland, addressed these words to the 48th General Congregation at the Council, asking that the Church should no longer be called the Church Militant:

---

[1] Evidence of the militancy of the Catholic Church based on papal documents is presented in Vol XI, *Ecclesia*, chap VII.1.

[2] Cfr. Appendix I §§ 12-14; Vol. XI, *Ecclesia*, Chap. I Note 55.

"Instead of presenting the Church in juridical terms as a perfect society, it is better – at least in countries where she is combated – to present her as a mystery, as a mystical body whose spiritual bonds with the Trinity remain even in those places that lack priests. We do not ignore the existence of the Church's public law, but it is necessary to be realistic. Even when a parish or diocese no longer exists, the Church continues, and it is this intimate presence that saves her. **The expression Church militant is not opportune because it runs the risk of being misunderstood. It is better to speak of the life-giving and sanctifying Church.**

"The Church is for everyone, and not just for those who are Catholics. She exists also for those who attack her. The Church is the source of progress and social peace." [3]

Combating the polemical character of the Church, Melkite Patriarch Maximus IV, spoke in the same tenor as Wyszynski. By describing the previous position of the Holy Church as one of "sterile polemics," he offended the Church. On the occasion of presenting the schema on ecumenism at the second session of the Council, Maximus IV stated:

"This schema pleases me enormously. It is the sign that **we are finally leaving the period of sterile polemics, so harmful to our theology and our spirituality.**" [4]

The same Patriarch criticized as negative the condemnations of the Church included in the schema on the sources of Revelation. These were his words:

"Parts of this schema repeat the traditional teaching of the Church, but **this teaching is presented in the negative form of condemnations and polemics**. This approach does not correspond either to the desire of the Pope or to the experience of the faithful people, which expects from us a serene, positive and rich exposition of the history of salvation to feed their Christian life."[5]

---

[3] Stefan Wyszynski, Intervention in the Conciliar Hall of October 15, 1963, in H. Fesquet, *Le Journal du Concile*, pp. 239-240. Cfr. Giovanni Caprile, *Il Concilio Vaticano II,* (Rome: *La Civiltà Cattolica*, 1964), vol. 3, pp. 95-96; A. Wenger, *Vatican II – Chronique de la Deuxieme session*, p. 49.

[4] Maximus IV, Intervention in the Conciliar Hall of November 19, 1963, in H. Fesquet, *Le Journal du Concile*, p. 341.

[5] Maximus IV, Intervention in the Conciliar Hall of November 14, 1962, in V.A. *A Igreja Greco-Melquita no Concílio* (São Paulo: Loyola, 1992), p. 38.

§ 3   Maximus IV spoke also in the presentation of the schema on the Church. He straightforwardly opposed the militancy of the Church and qualified it as "triumphalism:"

"The comparison of the Church to 'an army in battle order' is not at all opportune. This triumphalism – as it was already stressed in this venerable assembly – **does not find any base in the Gospel. It risks giving a false idea of the Church**, which, as the mystical body of the risen Savior, is called to complete with her Head the redemption of mankind and all creation by believing and suffering,."[6]

§ 4   In his turn, Cardinal Franz König, Archbishop of Vienna, advised the Church to put down her arms against Atheism. At the fourth session on the topic of Communism, the great contemporary enemy of the Church, he stated:

"Priests and Christians must share the life of atheists. These are the true Christian arms. We should not make a new condemnation of Atheism because this will do absolutely no good at all."[7]

König, while president of the Secretariat for Non-Believers, also pronounced the following general decision:

"The Secretariat for Non-Believers does not intend to promote or prepare any battle against Atheism." [8]

§ 5   At the third session, Cardinal Bernard Alfrink, Archbishop of Utrecht, spoke against those who wanted the Council to make a condemnation of Communism:

"What would be the purpose of a new condemnation of Communism? Experience has shown us that even in Catholic regions, a pure and simple condemnation of Communism has not defeated that imminent danger. Further, Atheism and Materialism are spreading everywhere – they exist not just in theory, but in a practical form, and the latter is more contagious for the faithful. Finally, **according to the judgment of competent persons, these condemnations are inefficient. They only entrench atheists in their Atheism and create**

---

[6] Maximus IV, Intervention in the Conciliar Hall of December 5, 1962, *in ibid*, pp.65-66.

[7] F. König, Intervention in the Conciliar Hall of September 28, 1965, in H. Fesquet, *Le Journal du Concile*, p. 885-886.

[8] F. König, Statement, November 20, 1965, *in ibid,* p. 1074.

obstacles to the dialogue that we should try to establish with them. We should avoid any aggressive statements."[9]

Also at the third session Cardinal Suenens insinuated a critique of the image of God presented by the Church, which he called a "caricature."

"It is not a matter of condemning Atheism. This was already done. What is needed is to inquire into its cause, which is a false image of God that men reject, a caricature that should be denounced. [10]

On another occasion, in a discussion about Communism's response to how the Church has presented God, Suenens spoke these offensive words:

§ 6   "Men and **Christians … have made an idol of God, a caricature of God. Before condemning Atheism, it behooves us to know which God it wanted to destroy.** Let us pause a moment to examine some current images of God, which were very common not long ago …

"The God who finds himself in the beginning as an architect and engineer in repose, as one who explains and covers for the ignorance and incapacity of man at his level, is also the one who now guarantees the established order, the *status quo,* who wraps authority with the mantle of divine right and protects the powerful against revolution, who tells the poor to be patient and impedes social reforms: **This God is the opium of the people**.

"**We can analyze various caricatures of God. To cite only one, we think of the caricature of God as Providence who 'providentially' allows us to avoid some disaster, but permits the same disaster to happen to another. It is a type of garbage providence. …**

"**It is quite understandable that this God should die** so that the world can live, and also, so that God can live."[11]

---

[9] Bernard Jan Alfrink, Intervention in the Conciliar Hall of November 5, 1964, in René Laurentin, *L'enjeu du Concile – Bilan de la troisième session* (Paris: Seuil, 1965), p. 181.

[10] Leo Josef Suenens, Intervention in the Conciliar Hall of October 1965, *in ibid.,* p. 183.

[11] L.J.Suenens, *Cristianismo sem Deus*, in V.A., *Cristianismo sem Cristo* (Caxias do Sul: Paulinas, 1970), pp. 63-66.

The statements of these important Prelates concur with the words John XXIII pronounced in the first days of Vatican II, referring to the pre-conciliar position of the Catholic Church:

§ 7

"It is necessary to leave our ghetto. **We have more to do than to throw stones at Communism**."[12]

On another occasion, speaking again about the Communists, he said: "**They say they are the enemies of the Church, but the Church does not have enemies.**"[13]

Regarding the heretics who abandoned the Faith and the schismatics who separated themselves from the Church throughout History, John XXIII delivered this sentence: "**We will not start a historical lawsuit and attempt to know who was right or wrong. Responsibilities lie on both sides. We will only say: Let us meet and put an end to our dissensions.**" [14]

§ 8

Along these lines, Paul VI revealed his opposition to the apologetic character of the Catholic Faith: "**We do not want to make our faith a reason for a polemic.**"[15]

In the next excerpt from this Pontiff, he indicated that the conciliar spirit is opposed to the militancy and honorability of the Church:

"**Towards those who,** as a consequence of blind anti-religious prejudices or unjustifiable positions taken against the Church, **still inflict so many sufferings on her, this Council, instead of pronouncing condemnations against them – whoever they might be – will have only sentiments of goodness and peace**, and will pray for them." [16]

Some days before the closing of Vatican II, at an ecumenical ceremony that took place in the Basilica of St. Paul Outside-the-Walls, Paul VI repeated his anti-militant purposes. In our view, these words

---

[12] John XXIII, Words to a visitor, November 19, 1962, in H. Fesquet, *Le Journal du Concile*, p. 44.

[13] John XXIII, Statement, *in ibid.*, p. 1124.

[14] John XXIII, Speech to the Vicars of Rome of January 9, 1959, *apud* Maximus IV, Letter to Msgr. Pericle Felici of May 19, 1961, in V. A., *A Igreja Greco-Melquita no Concilio*, p. 335.

[15] Paul VI, Speech at the opening of the second Conciliar session of September 29, 1963, in H. Fesquet, *Le Journal du Concile,* p. 177.

[16] Paul VI, Opening speech at the fourth Conciliar session of September 14, 1965, *in ibid*, p. 815; see also R. Laurentin, *Bilan du Concile – Chronique de la quatrième session*, p. 164.

– even though they are clothed in prudent generalizations – are grave offenses because they attribute "non-Christian roots" to the previous Catholic apologetics, describing it as "unworthy of the school of Christ," "offensive," and seeking vain prestige.

Directing himself to the non-Catholic observers, he stated: "Through your persons, we enter into contact with Christian communities that live, pray and act in the name of Christ, with systems of doctrines and religious mentalities – and let us say it without fear – with Christian treasures of high value.

"We acknowledge certain faults and common sentiments on our part that were not good. For these, we ask pardon from God and from you. Now we realize their non-Christian roots and propose to transform them into sentiments worthy of the school of Christ. We renounce a polemics based on offensive prejudices and set aside the pursuit of vain prestige. Above all, we seek to keep in mind the repeated exhortations of the Apostle, over whose grave we gather here this evening: 'Let there be no contentions, envyings, animosities, dissensions, and detractions among you' (2 Cor XII:20)."[17]

At the closing speech of the Council, the Pontiff once again denied the militancy of the Church: "Here [at the Council] the religion of God who became man met the religion (for it is a religion) of the man who became god. **What has taken place here? A clash, a fight, an anathema? It could have been so, but it was not. The old story of the Samaritan was the model of the spirituality of the Council. An unlimited sympathy completely pervaded it."**[18]

§ 9   Considering these testimonies, one can understand why the expression Church Militant was not used in any of the 16 final documents of Vatican II. [19]

---

[17] Paul VI, Speech at the ecumenical ceremony in St. Paul Outside-the-Walls of December 4, 1965, in R. Laurentin, *Bilan du Concile – Chronique de la quatrième session*, p. 179.

[18] Paul VI, Speech at the closing of Vatican II of December 7, 1965, *in ibid*, p. 184.

[19] a. Although we have carefully searched the texts, we cannot find the expression Church Militant in the conciliar texts.

The expression 'militia of Christ' is used once in a quite irrelevant context: "These religious families give their members the support of a firmer stability in their way of life and a proven doctrine of acquiring perfection. They further offer their members the support of fraternal association in the **militia of Christ** and of liberty strengthened by obedience. Thus these

Directing himself to the writers of *La Civiltà Cattolica*, the famous Italian biweekly magazine printed by the Jesuits, John Paul II approvingly points out its change of tone in expressing the militancy of the Holy Church:

§ 10

"Initially the comportment and style of the magazine were combative and frequently sharply polemical in accordance with the climate of tension, if not outright confrontation, that was general. Today the situation has changed very much. With Vatican Council II, the Church wants 'to establish a dialogue inspired only by love for truth' with all men, even with those who do not partake in the Christian faith, but 'have worship of high human

---

religious are able to tranquilly fulfill and faithfully observe their religious profession" (LG 43a).

The word militia also appears in reference to the Church triumphant: "Christ is sitting at the right hand of God, a minister of the holies and of the true tabernacle; we sing a hymn to the Lord's glory with all the **warriors of the heavenly militia**; venerating the memory of the saints, we hope for some part and fellowship with them" (SC 9).

In its proper meaning, the expression Church Militant is never used.

b. Texts abound, however, in which the militant character of the Catholic Church is denied.

This is the case, for example, in setting out norms for the teaching of theology:

"Sacred theology and other branches of knowledge ... must be taught with due regard for the ecumenical point of view, so that they may correspond more exactly with the facts.

"It is most important that future shepherds and priests should have mastered a theology that has been carefully worked out in this way and not polemically, especially with regard to those aspects which concern the relations of separated brethren with the Catholic Church" (UR 10a,b; cfr. UR 18; AG 41e).

The same tone is taken for the norms for the profession of the Faith:

"The way and method in which the Catholic faith is expressed should never become an obstacle to dialogue with our [separated] brethren" (UR 11a; cfr. UR 11b, c, 24; DH 14d).

Regarding the abolition of militancy toward heretics, schismatics or pagans, see UR 7a-c, 9; AG 15d; CD 13b, 16f; OT 16f; AA 31a; NA 2c, 4e. Against philosophical or ideological disputes, see GS 4d, 82c, 85c. Against Catholic militancy in the temporal sphere, see DH 6c, d; GS 84c; AG 13b. Against the war, even a just war, see GS 77b, 81b-d, 82a,d,e. Pacificism is also warmly applauded and defended (cfr. GS 78e, 79c).

values,' and even with 'those who oppress the Church and harass her in manifold ways' (GS 92)"[20]

It is based on this ample foundation of papal statements and pontifical documents that many other Prelates and theologians offend the militancy of the Holy Church.

2. Affronts to the Holy Office and the Inquisition [21]

§ 11   One of the interventions in the Conciliar Hall that most notably marked Vatican II was that of Cardinal Joseph Frings, Archbishop of Cologne. He directed offensive critiques against the Supreme Sacred Congregation of the Holy Office, the former Supreme and Universal Congregation of the Holy Inquisition against the Perfidy of Heretics, or, simplified, the Congregation of the Roman and Universal Inquisition. During the second session of November 8, 1963, Cardinal Frings declared:

"**The way of acting of the Holy Office** in many cases does not correspond to the mentality of our time. It **is harmful for the Church and a cause of scandal for non-Catholics**."[22]

The first point to note is that Cardinal Frings read the intervention prepared by his secretary, then Fr. Joseph Ratzinger, who habitually drew up the interventions of the Cardinal in the Hall.

§ 12   That Fr. Ratzinger was the author of that intervention is a well-known fact. Commenting on that action, Cardinal de Lubac approvingly noted:

"It was a radical critique ... of the methods of the Holy Office ... It is not exaggerated to say that the old Holy Office, as it had always represented itself, was destroyed on that day by Ratzinger in

---

[20] John Paul II, Speech of January 19, 1990, to the writers of *La Civiltà Cattolica* on the occasion of the 140th anniversary of the magazine, *L'Osservatore Romano,* January 20, 1990.

[21] For the Reader to have a broader idea about the Inquisition, we suggest that he consult Vol. III, *Animus Injuriandi II*, Chap. I.3.C.a.ab and Vol. XI, *Ecclesia*, Chap VII §§ 27-46. For the condemnation of Galileo Galilei, see Volume IX, *Creatio*, Chap. I.3.A; see also the booklet by the Author *The End of the Myth of Galileo* (Los Angeles: TIA, 2005). In this Chapter, the treatment of these matters will be brief.

[22] Joseph Frings, Intervention in the Conciliar Hall of November 8, 1963, in B. Kloppenburg, *Concilio Vaticano II*, vol. 3, p. 253; see also H. Fesquet, *Le Journal du Concile*, pp. 303, 317; R. Laurentin, *Bilan de la deuxième session*, p. 121; G. Caprile, *Il Concilio Vaticano II,* vol. 3, p. 212.

union with his Archbishop. Cardinal Seper [head of that Congregation 1968-1981], a very good man, initiated its renovation. Ratzinger [head of that Congregation 1981-2005], who has not changed, continues it." [23]

§ 13   A second point of interest is that the Frings-Ratzinger intervention was probably also a counter-attack against measures of the Holy See, warning the Superiors of Religious Orders to be careful of the 12 *periti* of the *Nouvelle Théologie*. Named in that list were Ratzinger, Rahner, Congar and Küng.[24] Shortly before that intervention, an open letter had been sent, under the influence of the Holy Office, by Cardinal Ilbebrando Antoniutti, Prefect of the Congregation for the Religious, to all the Superior Generals in Rome, which had already caused a book by Fr. Hans Küng to be removed from the Catholic bookstores of the city.[25]

Another offense against the Holy Office was made by retired Archbishop of Bombay (India) Thomas Roberts in a press interview in Rome at the time of the Council. He said:

§ 14   **"The members of the Holy Office use such methods that they would immediately be brought before the English tribunals if they were in Great Britain**. It would be good if today's Inquisition were not to give the same impression as that of the Middle Ages. On my part, I do not clearly see that it is any different. **Certainly it is more difficult to kill and incarcerate in the 20th century, but it continues to ruin reputations and destroy careers.**"[26]

---

[23] Henri de Lubac, *Entrétien autour de Vatican II* (Paris: Cerf, 1985), p. 123.

[24] That intervention was possibly also related to a circular against the theologians of the *Nouvelle Théologie* that was being distributed some days before. On October 29, 1963, the following observations appeared in a Council chronicle: "The rumor is flying that Cardinal Antoniutti, Prefect of the Sacred Congregation of Religious, sent the General Superiors of Religious Orders who have houses in Rome a circular warning them about the 12 *periti*, whose names include Frs. Congar, Küng and Ratzinger" (H. Fesquet, *Le Journal du Concile,* pp. 279-280).

[25] The well-informed Fr. Antoine Wenger, director of *La Croix* and a chronicler of the Council, comments: "We can think that the removal of the book of Hans Küng, *Le Concile, épreuve de l'Église,* and some other works from the Catholic bookstores in Rome at the beginning of the second session had something to do with the intervention of Cardinal Frings" (A, Wenger, *Chronique de la deuxième session*, p. 147, note 1).

[26] Thomas Roberts, Press statement of October 25, 1963, in H. Fesquet, *Le Journal du Concile,* pp. 273-274.

During the Council, the Holy Synod of the Catholic Church of the Melchite Rite made an official statement asking for the reform of the Roman Curia, particularly of the Holy Office. Some of its affirmations were clearly offensive:

"**The reform of the Holy Office is mandatory**. In our opinion, the following are its most urgent reforms:

§ 15

"**First, it is necessary to change the spirit that dominates the Holy Office. It does not seem to us to be the spirit of Christ and His Holy Gospel. The Holy Office inherited from its origins an absolutism in thought and behavior** that existed in the customs of the epoch, but which **rightly cannot be tolerated by our contemporaries. ... Those who belong to the Holy Office ... do not act according to the spirit of Christ; they spread a false idea of Christianity to the faithful and others**.

"**What is particularly shocking to our contemporaries is the self-assurance the Holy Office shows in every domain,** be it dogmatic, moral, politic, artistic and so on, ... in such a way that everything appears evident, clear and sure to it. **The Holy Office acts as if it were infallible. The Holy Office should not be above the law**. It must follow a public legislation well known by others. ... **It is necessary to exterminate from the Church the system of denunciations that is tolerated or perhaps encouraged by the Holy Office. Those who denounce should be severely punished**. Except for very rare and grave cases, **denunciations, even when they report the truth, harm the Church by creating an atmosphere of suspicion, fear and terror**.

"**The terror of the secret of the Holy Office** (*secretum Sancti Officii*) that either forbids one to speak under most grave penalties or gives orders that are repugnant to the conscience **must end**, such as, for example, when under this secret it determines that a Bishop should punish one of his priests, letting it appear that that action comes from the Bishop and not from the Holy Office. These procedures are repugnant to natural conscience and create a climate of suspicion in the Church. **This is immoral**.

"In brief, **the Holy Office can no longer live in the Middle Ages. The Inquisition of Torquemada ended; so also must the Holy Office, heir of its spirit.** Its present day form and procedures must be replaced by a normal Congregation that should take care of the Faith and Morals."[27]

---

[27] Holy Synod of the Greek-Melkite Catholic Church, "Observations on the Schemata of the Council," in V.A., *A Igreja Greco-Melquita no Concílio,* pp. 192-193.

§ 16

Evaluating the tendencies at play in the Council at the beginning of the discussion on the reform of the Roman Curia (the second session), conciliar *perito* and chronicler Fr. René Laurentin summarizes how the progressivist current – to which he belongs as a "moderate" – explains the militancy of the Church, represented by the Holy Office. His synthesis includes offenses, such as the attribution of "moral tortures" inflicted on imaginary "victims" (in fact, dangerous spiritual assailants against Catholic doctrine) during the investigation procedures. Laurentin offers this summary:

"The Fathers are concerned about the judiciary procedures and everything associated with them.

"First, there is a certain spirit, a negative way of dealing with the faith. The concern for detecting error and averting dangers – while necessary – seems to polarize the action of the Holy Office. It does not leave enough room for the more essential matter of making the faith grow and stimulating the spirit of investigation, the evangelical and prophetic spirit and, finally, that liberty, that *parrhesia* [freedom of expression] that are important marks of the faith, according to St. Paul.

"In a parallel way, there is also that high abstraction which orients the conduct of the Holy Office: It judges and condemns the work itself, independent of the author. In our epoch, which is concerned with the rights of the person – proclaimed by the last Popes – this distinction is not well received. If a work is condemned or even discretely retired from the shelves, it soon becomes known, the reputation of the author is harmed, his career and his life itself are broken, sometimes irremediably. **Anyone who has witnessed** (either in close proximity or from afar) **the moral tortures that resulted for a person thus indirectly hit** – and the first half of the 20th century provides many examples of this type, from Fr. Lagrange and Fr. Touzard to Fr. Lubac and Fr. Congar and so many others – **is convinced that this is a problem.**" [28]

Commenting on the Motu Proprio *Integrae servandae* of December 5, 1965, issued by Paul VI to reform the Holy Office, chronicler Henri Fesquet offends the Church in a similar way. He says:

"Without the reform of the Holy Office, no other substantial reform could be brought to term in the Church. **It is not the men who are at fault, but an institution radically addicted to secrecy, a unilateral procedure and a hidden omnipotence.** Even though I know it is wrong to step on a wounded person the moment he is

---

[28] R. Laurentin, *Bilan de la deuxième session*, pp. 124-125.

injured, let me recall … **how many men of the Church suffered because of the Holy Office. Their reputations were soiled, their lives destroyed, their consciences crushed. And how many Christians lost the faith because of that dicastery? It was truly a work of religious sanitization that Paul VI undertook, a work indisputably and urgently needed.** Who could take the schema on religious liberty seriously if the Church had not begun by first applying it to herself?

     "Today that tumor has been cut out, which is an extra cause for joy for the Fathers of the Council on this day of the closing of Vatican II.[29] **The day of December 5 will go down in the history of the Roman Church as a great day for ecclesiastical liberty."** [30]

     Further on, he again offends the militant character of the Church:

     "By not admitting the totalitarian spirit of the Holy Office and the Inquisition, she [the Church] removed her constant temptation to dominate intelligences and consciences."[31]

§ 17   During the Council, there were yet other offenses made against the methods of the Holy Inquisition, even when used by an ecumenical Council. Thus, Cardinal Joseph Beran pretended that the main condemnation decreed by the Council of Constance against the heresiarch John Hus was a "fault" and a "sin." When Cardinal Beran, the Archbishop of Prague, issued this statement, his country was oppressed by Communism. He stated:

     "In my country, Bohemia, the Church today seems to be making expiation for the faults and sins that were committed in times past in her name against liberty, such as the case of the burning of Fr. John Hus in the 15th century." [32]

---

[29] The Motu proprio *Integrae servandae* was published in the *L'Osservatore Romano* of December 6-7, 1965 under the title *La S. Congregazione del Sant' Uffizio diventa "Congregatio pro doctrina Fidei,"* p. 1. The last general assembly of the Council was on the same day of December 7, 1965; the closing, December 8, 1965.

[30] H. Fesquet, *Le Journal du Concile*, p. 1101.

[31] *Ibid.*, p. 1124.

[32] Joseph Beran, Intervention in the Conciliar Hall of September 20, 1965, in R. Laurentin, *Bilan du Concile, Cronique de la quatrième session*, pp. 63-64; cfr. B. Kloppenburg, *Concilio Vaticano II*, vol. 5, p. 45.

§ 18

Later, these words of Beran were praised by John Paul II who took advantage of them to commend the heresiarch John Hus. On a visit to Czechoslovakia, the Pontiff stated:

"I recall **when the Czech Archbishop Cardinal Joseph Beran intervened energetically at Vatican Council II to defend the principles of religious liberty and tolerance, referring regretfully to the life of the Bohemian priest John Hus and deploring the excesses to which he was submitted – then and afterwards.** [33*]

"I still remember those words of the Cardinal Archbishop of Prague about that priest, who had such great importance in the religious and cultural history of the Bohemian people. It will be the mission of experts – the Czech theologians, first of all – to define more precisely the position that John Hus occupies among the reformers of the Church, together with other notable reformer figures of the Bohemian Middle Ages, such as Thomas of Stitne and John Milic of Kromeriz. Despite the theological convictions Hus defended, **one cannot deny the integrity of his personal life and his efforts in the moral instruction of the Nation.**

"**Are these elements not ones that should above all unite – rather than divide – believers in Christ?**"[34]

In the post-conciliar period we find the same spirit as the one that inspired the documents above. Strong offenses made against the Inquisition came from the pen of Fr. Hans Küng in his book *The Church*, which counted on the support of Fr. Joseph Ratzinger. Küng wrote:

§ 19

"The State Church, formed at the time of Constantine, introduced violent procedures against heretics. ... **Obviously, those who fought the heretics very early began to set aside the principle commandment of love** in matters of the faith, and to insult and humiliate those who thought or believed in a different way. **But whoever sows hatred** sooner or later **must harvest blood.** ... For centuries, **what constituted one of the most terrible institutions in the history of the Church that must be seen as one of the most incomprehensible stains in the Body of Christ was being prepared: the Inquisition.**"[35]

[33*] Cfr. *Acta Sinodalia* IV, pp. 313-314.

[34] John Paul II, Speech to the representatives of the cultural world in Prague of April 21, 1990, published under the title "Gli eventi de cui siamo testimoni dimostrano che l'Europa unita non è un'utopia del Medio Evo ma un traguardo raggiungibile," in *L'Os. Rom.*, April 23-24, 1990, p. 4.

[35] H. Küng, *A Igreja*, vol. 1, pp. 359-360.

After the intervention written by Fr. Ratzinger for Cardinal Frings in the Conciliar Hall, it should come as no surprise that Ratzinger made no major objection to the hate-charged tone toward the Tribunal of the Holy Inquisition in his revision of Küng's book, *The Church*. Küng declared:

> "**One cannot deny that theology has failed gravely in resolving the Church-heretics problem,** when she should have been the one to play a critical and constructive role. **It is shameful to contemplate the type of biblical arguments made by great medieval theologians to justify the spiritual harassment, torture and massacre of persons who had different ways of thinking.**"[36]

In the next excerpt, the same theologian defends the heretics, going so far as to compare them to heroes and saints and to lament that their writings were "brutally destroyed."[37] Küng wrote:

> "**If authentic heretics**, the great heretics, **could stand before us, they would certainly tell us that** ... **they had been well-intentioned toward the Church, that they had acted in good faith. But** ... **the majority of heretics from the past can no longer speak and their writings were brutally destroyed.** This makes it easy to deny their good intentions. **But is this legitimate behavior for a Christian? Should he not, on the contrary, presuppose that good faith? A** *benign interpretation* **should also be given to heretics.** ...
>
> "The great heretics did not have easy lives. They dedicated themselves entirely to their task; they did not fear the consequences and subjected everything to their beliefs. They sacrificed everything for the faith, developing an unusual capacity to withstand shock. In this **the great heretics are similar to the great Saints!**"[38]

§ 20   In the 1940s a strong reaction arose against the *Nouvelle Théologie* – a reaction whose symbolic expression was the publication of the Encyclical *Humani generis* of Pius XII (1950). At that

---

[36] *Ibid.*, p. 363.

[37] In Vol. III, *Animus Injuriandi II*, Chap. I, we will analyze in detail what is mentioned only briefly here – the praise of heretics by progressivists.

[38] H. Küng, *A Igreja*, vol. 1, pp. 357-358.

time many of the precursors of Vatican II were either punished – de Lubac, Chenu, Congar and Teilhard de Chardin[39] – or had their writings placed under suspicion of heresy by the Holy Office – Rahner, Ratzinger, von Balthasar, Congar, de Lubac.[40]

§ 21   Referring to these measures of censure, Fr. Congar calls the actions of Rome "stupid" and "imbecile:"

"I kept writing to Fr. Duccatillon, **saying that those measures were stupid** (I used that word or something similar) and that I could not understand them **(perhaps I even used the expression 'imbecile').** I am not a man who takes a tragic view of things. **But it is distressing to be the victim of stupidity.**" [41]

It would be difficult for the spirit of the Council to show itself more opposed to something than the general position it took toward the Supreme Congregation of the Holy Office and the Inquisition.

---

[39] Fr. Chenu's book *Une école de Théologie: le Saulchoir* (1937) was placed on the *Index* in 1942. He also was removed as rector from Le Saulchoir, the Dominican Center of Studies in Paris (cfr. *Jacques Duquesne interroge le Père Chenu,* pp. 119-121).

Cardinal Henri de Lubac's book, *Catholicisme*, was, as the Cardinal put it, "the object of the worse suspicions." Further, the theologian had to relinquish his chair at the University of Lyon-Fourvière (cfr. Interview granted to Angelo Scola, "Viaggio nel Concilio e l'intorni," *30 Giorni,* July 1985, p. 11). He was sent into "exile" in Paris and had his writing subjected to censure from 1950 to 1954 (cfr. Interview granted to Marco Politi, "Irrequieto ma ubbidiente," *Il Messagero*, February 2, 1983, p. 3.

Likewise, Fr. Congar's book *Vraie et fausse réforme dans l'Eglise* was forbidden to be published and translated. He was sent to Jerusalem, Cambridge and later Strasbourg (cfr. *Jean Puyo interroge le Père Congar,* pp. 106, 109, 111-112). This was the period of his "captivity," as he called it (cfr. *Un people messianique,* Paris: Cerf, 1975, p. 8).

As for Fr. Teilhard de Chardin, when he returned to France in 1946, he was again prohibited to spread his philosophical and religious doctrines or to publish the writings that contained them (B. Mondin, *Os grandes teólogos do século vinte,* vol. 1, p. 47). Later, the restless Jesuit moved to the United States, where he died in 1955. For a list of the censures against Teilhard, see H. Küng, *Veracidade, o futuro de Igreja,* (São Paulo: Herder, 1969), p. 104.

[40] The weekly *Informations Catholiques Internationales* reports that Frs. Rahner, Ratzinger, Congar, de Lubac and von Balthasar were under the list of suspects of the Holy Office (A. Woodrow, "A Rome: Trente théologiens du monde entire pour accomplir le Concile," June 15, 1969, p. 9).

[41] *Jean Puyo interroge le Père Congar,* pp. 112-113.

3. Offenses against the Catholic Wars and the Crusades

The texts below spare no adjectives offensive to the militancy of the Church. They present militancy as disconnected from her proper end, which is the defense of the Faith under attacks, and give the impression that the heroes who took up arms under the standard of the Cross through the centuries did so in bouts of personal ire, despising their neighbors. They pretend that evangelical meekness excludes its harmonious counterpart, an avenging but tempered combativeness!

§ 22

The great St. Bernard is called the "Mellifluous Doctor" because of the sweetness of the *Memorare* he dedicated to the Mother of God. At the same time, he was the one who preached the Second Crusade and inspired the foundation of the Order of the Knights of the Temple, undoubtedly the highest archetype of the spiritual-temporal militancy of the Middle Ages.[42] Thus he provides an admirable

---

[42] At the request of the Superior of the Knights Templar, Hugh de Payens, St. Bernard wrote a letter of orientation that established the foundation for the life of the new militia. It reads, in part:

"If I am not mistaken, my dear Hugh, you have asked me not once or twice, but three times to write a few words of exhortation for you and your knights. Since I am not permitted to wield the lance against the insults of our enemies, you ask that I at least might direct my words and my talent against them, and you assure me that I would be doing you no small favor by encouraging with my pen those that I cannot stimulate by taking up arms …

"Go forth confidently then, valorous knights, and repel the enemies of the Cross of Our Lord with a stalwart heart. Know that neither death nor life can separate you from the affection of God which is in Jesus Christ.
…

"To inflict death or to die for love of Jesus Christ is no crime but, rather, worthy of much glory. In the first case, one conquers for Jesus Christ; in the second, it is Jesus Christ whom you conquer; for the Lord accepts with joy the death of the enemy who has offended Him as reparation, and He gives himself with yet even greater joy for the consolation of His fallen knight.

"Thus, the soldier of Jesus Christ kills His enemy with confidence and dies yet more confidently. For when he kills he serves Jesus Christ, and when he dies, he serves himself. He does not take up the sword in vain – for he is a minister of God – to wreak vengeance against the evil ones and defend the virtue of the good. If he kills an evildoer, he is not a man killer, so to speak, but an evil killer, since he becomes the avenger of Jesus Christ against evildoers and a legitimate defender of Christians. And should he lose his life, it is an advantage rather than a loss. Therefore, when he inflicts death on the enemy, it is a conquest for Jesus Christ,

example of the equilibrium that can be reached between these two qualities of meekness and militancy, achieving a balance only possible in a Catholic spirit.

§ 23

The first text is from a speech of John Paul II in Vienna's historic *Heldenplatz* (Hero's Square) during commemorations of the third centennial of the glorious Battle of Vienna (1683). The Pontiff called the efforts of the Catholic hosts to halt the aggression of the Muslim Crescent in that epic fight "disheartening" and "shameful." His words can only leave one perplexed, wondering if perhaps John Paul II would have preferred for Vienna to fall prey to Mohammed's followers in order to avoid the war-related "cruelties that cry out to heaven." Indeed, John Paul II said:

"No one can deny the fact ... that the whole history of the nations of Europe presents not just luminous features, but also dark and terrible ones. ... Repeated times, countries and parties waged war against each other filled with hatred and cruelty. ... Millions of men were killed on account of their race, nation, beliefs or simply because they stood in the way of others. **It is disheartening to see that the Christian faithful were among those who oppressed and persecuted their neighbor. ... We must confess and ask forgiveness for the great faults with which we Christians have stained ourselves** by thoughts, words and deeds and by passive indifference in the face of injustice. ...

"Everyone knows that 300 years ago, just as in 1529, the troops of the Ottoman Empire lay siege to this city. ... **We know that cruelties which cry out to heaven were committed** not only by the Ottoman army but also **by the army of the Emperor and his allies**. However content we may be with the successful defense of the Christian West, **we must become conscious, with shame, of the fact that Christian solidarity then was neither spontaneous** nor European.

"Above all, **we are convinced that the language of arms is not the language of Jesus Christ, nor of his Mother.**"[43]

---

and when he suffers death, he receives eternal happiness. The Christian is glorified in the death of the pagan because Jesus Christ is glorified in it" (St. Bernard, *Obras Completas,* Madrid: BAC, 1955, vol. 2, pp. 853, 855, 857).

[43] John Paul II, "Un'Europa unita dalla fede in Cristo," September 10, 1983, in *Insegnamenti di Giovanni Paolo II*, vol. VI/2, Lib. Ed. Vaticana, 1983, pp. 438-440.

It is perplexing to consider that John Paul II would attribute "cruelties that cry out to heaven" to the Catholic armies that freed the capital of the Holy Roman Empire from an implacable siege by the followers of Mohammed. The Pontiff did not specify what exactly those so-called "cruelties" were. It is certain that nearly 10,000 of the 200,000 Muslim troops of the Sultan of Bagdad died in the battle. Nevertheless, responsibility for these deaths lies with those who obliged the Catholics to take a defensive military action – namely, the generals of the Muslim Crescent.

§ 24   To deem the legitimate defense of the Faith, their countries and their own lives – as was the case for the Catholic combatants who broke the siege of Vienna – as a "cruelty that cries out to heaven" would seem at variance with the traditional teaching of the Church [44] and, as such, an erroneous claim.[45]

It should also be remembered that cruelties like those mentioned by the Pontiff were in fact actually found on the part of Muslim attackers, who, before the battle, beheaded all the combat-worthy Catholic prisoners they held, sparing only children. [46]

Comparing these statements of the Pontiff with the words of St. Bernard leaves a Catholic perplexed, not knowing whom to follow – the great medieval Doctor or John Paul II.

---

[44] On the right to wage a just war and the legitimacy for the public authority to resort to arms in face of an unjust aggression, Yves de la Brière, professor of the *Institut Catholique de Paris*, indicates the following authors: St. Augustine, *De libero arbitrio*, chap. 5; *Contra Faustum Manichaeum*, book 22, 74-78; *Civitas Dei*, book 19, chaps. 7, 12-13, 15; St. Isidore of Seville, *Etymologiarum libri*, book 18, chaps. 1-3; Gracianus, *Concordantia discordantium Canonum*, II, 23; St. Thomas Aquinas, *Summa Theologiae*, II.II, q. 40; Francisco de Vitoria, *De jure belli*; Francisco Suarez, *Disputatio XIII, De bello*; Luigi Taparelli D'Azeglio, *Essai théorique de droit naturel basé sur les faits*, book 6.

He also cites more recent authors: Roberto Regout, *La doctrine de la guerre juste de Saint Augustin à nos jours, d'après les théologiens et les canonistes catholiques*, Paris: Pedone, 1935; Alfred Vanderpol, *La doctrine scholastique du droit de guerre*, Paris: Pedone, 1919 (Cf. Y. de la Briére, *Le droit de juste guerre*, Paris: Pedone, 1938, pp. 18-19, 27-28, 30, 38-40, 43, 46).

[45] Luther claimed that *"proeliari adversus Turcas est repugnare Deo visitanti iniquitates nostras per illos"* [To fight against the Turks is to reject God's punishment of our sins through them] (Statement about the fight against the Turks, DS, 1484).

[46] Cf. Ludwig von Pastor, *Historia de los Papas* (Barcelona: Gustavo Gili, 1912, vol. XXXII, p. 143.

§ 25   Analogous thoughts arise on considering the words John Paul II pronounced in the city of Vilnius to representatives of the academic world of Lithuania. In passing, he stated that the wars of religion constituted a "true night of the faith." It is difficult to conceive of an expression more offensive to Catholic militancy. These were his words:

"The desired 'new alliance' between the Church and culture must dispel the shadows and open the doors to the light. Toward this end, **the promising ecumenical effort among Christians and inter-religious dialogue should also be considered an important 'sign of the times.'** Men of different beliefs are being called to cooperate for the good of humanity. **Under the sad memory of the wars of religion – a true night of the faith – the dawn of a long awaited religious peace is rising,** promoting harmonic cooperation in civil society as well."[47]

§ 26   The same offense against Catholic militancy is found in the letter the Pontiff presented to the Cardinals in the program for the Consistory of June 1994. In it, one reads:

"How can one be silent about the many forms of violence also perpetrated in the name of faith? Wars of religion, tribunals of the Inquisition, and other forms of violating the rights of persons. ... It is significant that coercive methods, harmful to human rights, were also later applied by the totalitarian ideologies of the 20th century, as well as by Islamic fundamentalists."[48]

§ 27   Fr. Congar shares the same horror of battles in defense of the Faith and takes a position against the Crusades as a whole. Showing his revolt against the great surge of grace that poured over the faithful with the appeal of Blessed Urban II to liberate the profaned Holy Land, Congar refers to the "atrocities" committed by the Crusaders in Constantinople during the Fourth Crusade, calling it an "infamy."

What the French Dominican conveniently omits is the fact that Constantinople had fallen into Schism a century and a half earlier and, since then, had constantly manifested its arrogance and rebellious spirit toward the Catholic Church and the Sovereign Pontiff. He only grudgingly admits that the Emperors of Byzantium betrayed the

---

[47] John Paul II, Speech to the representatives of the academic world of the University of Vilnius of September 5, 1993, published under the title "Tra la Chiesa e la cultura è necessaria e urgente una 'nuova alleanza,'" *L'Osservatore Romano,* September 6-7, 1993, p. 9.

[48] John Paul II, Reflection on the grand jubilee of 2000, in "La nave di Pietro fa rotta verso il duemila – Il documento riservato inviato ai Cardinali per il Concistoro de giugno," *Adista* - DOC, May 28, 1994, p. 6.

Crusaders several times, thus causing the destruction of important parts of the Catholic armies. Such treasons justified the siege and conquest of Constantinople from the standpoint either of defending the Faith or of simple military strategy, that is, to prevent having a powerful enemy at one's rearguard.

Taking the relics from the Schismatics – an action deplored by Congar – was in fact nothing more than the Church re-taking what they had lost the right to possess. The burning of convents or the death of Schismatic monks was a sad consequence of the violence found in any war – even a just one – and especially a religious war.

The French Dominican laments "**the Crusades,** above all, the Fourth one which carried out the siege of Constantinople in 1204, burned and pillaged the city, seized relics and destroyed monasteries, causing monks to perish. **The memory of this infamy still lives to this day.**" [49]

To appear impartial, Fr. Congar inserts a small counterweight, but he goes on to repeat his stand against the Crusaders:

"To tell the truth, the facts are not that simple. There were not innocent Greeks on one side and guilty Latins on the other. The Greeks had attacked the Latins various times, ambushed them, waged war against them, destroyed their rearguard ... but this does not justify the taking of Constantinople." [50]

Fr. Von Galli has only negative and offensive words for the militant past of the Church:

§ 28   "We Catholics used to see only distortions in all the non-Christian religions, only the action of the Devil, which was expressed very clearly in our baptismal ceremonies. Fortunately, today things have changed. From now on, our first aim should be to see in the non-Christian religions the absolute and positive values they contain. ...

"As well as recognizing everything that is great and good, **the Christian religion should also admit its own deformations, such as the burning of witches, the persecutions of heretics, the cruelty of the Crusades, etc. We acknowledge that there were many things that were not very honorable.**" [51]

---

[49] *Jean Puyo interroge le Père Congar*, pp. 147-148

[50] *Ibid.*

[51] Mario von Galli, "La relación con las religions mundiales," in V.A. *La reforma que llega de Roma* (Barcelona: Plaza & Jares, 1970), pp. 200-201.

§ 29

What inspired John Paul II and these theologians seems to be reflected in the following excerpts by Fr. Luis Maldonado, a known Spanish theologian from the University of Salamanca. Referring to war in general – regardless of whether it be just or unjust – Fr. Maldonado terms it "bestial" and a "sadistically cruel ritual:"

"The difference between the ethological [concerning animal behavior][52] and the human kingdoms should be obvious. But war confirms that **man can be a truly ferocious beast or the most bestial animal.** From this hecatomb-sacrifice **any act of generosity** disappears. Better, it **ends by becoming a veritable ritual of sadistic cruelty.** Every possible 'paschal' meaning that the old myths of primitive religions attributed to sacrifice vanishes. ... Today war has become total and leads more literally than ever to total annihilation."[53]

§ 30

Shortly before condemning all war, as he just did, Maldonado censured the movement of the Crusades and the preaching of the Church through the centuries that stimulated the combativeness of her children. The Spanish liturgist goes so far as to say that devotion to St. Michael the Archangel is something mythological, a new edition of the cult to Wotan, the god of war among the barbarians. He further affirms that the Crusades would signify the negation of the Gospel. These are Maldonado's words:

"**Christianity**, as a popular religion with a powerful incarnatory dynamism, **was assimilating aspects of new cultures and allowing itself to be impregnated with them indiscriminately, uncritically.** Thus, in the 10th century when the Normans landed on the northern coasts of Europe and later established themselves in Italy and Sicily, this caused a powerful transfusion of Germanic blood from the north of Christendom. Those Normans were still very much like their barbarian forefathers. They quickly adopted Christianity, but **Wotan, the god of war, was still stirring in their blood** and in their spirits.

"**From these new pagan currents, the new threat arose of a** not only ambivalent but **predominantly distorted epiphany of**

---

[52] The *Dictionnaire de la Langue Philosophique* defines **Ethology** as "a little used term to designate the science of *èthè* (plural of *ethos*): the science of character (Stuart Mill); the science of habits and customs described by ethnography (Wundt); or, **today, the science that studies animal behavior in their natural environment**" (Paris: Presses Universitaires de France, 1962). Maldonado employs the adjective ethological in the latter meaning, that is, pertaining to animal behavior.

[53] Luis Maldonado, *La violencia de lo sagrado* (Salamanca: Sígueme, 1974), p. 135.

the sacred. Therefore, **a new attempt to sacralize war was to be expected. In fact, this took place with the Crusades**, which were the first official, solemn version of holy war in Christianity. It began in 1095 at the Council of Clermont, when the Pope launched a dramatic appeal to the Western Church, asking her to unite in a holy war against the new civilization of Islam.

"This call marks the beginning of the movement of **the Crusades, a traumatic experience for Western civilization** that had a profound and lasting influence on its religious consciousness, particularly in regard to its attitude toward war. ...

"On the mythological plane, **many of Wotan's attributes were transferred to the Archangel St. Michael, chief of the heavenly armies** in the Christian tradition. Churches were dedicated to St. Michael in places theretofore consecrated to Wotan, and a 'Mass of St. Michael' was instituted to obtain victory in times of war. ...

"In short, **Christendom sent to the land of Jesus an army charged with a mission that was the very negation of the Gospel's teaching: to install the Kingdom of God by means of the sword. The Pope promptly promised plenary indulgences to those who died in the Crusade. And the liturgical books provided the proper prayers, e.g., the blessing of the sword that dates from the 11th century** ...

"The apex of this evolution was the founding of a new religious order, the Knights of the Temple or the Templars, who installed themselves near the Temple of Solomon and promised in solemn vows to combat the enemies of God."[54]

It is often said that the only condemnation made by Vatican II was against war and violence (cf. GS 77). Here we can understand how the Catholic just war incites the hatred of important representatives of the progressivist current. Also we see how the desire to offend manifested in these selections is expressive of the spirit of the Council.

4. Affronts to the Counter-Reformation and to Doctrinal Fights

§ 31

Such abhorrence for the militancy of the Church in general – and for the Crusades in particular – is also manifested toward the Counter-Reformation, "condemned" by the progressivists in coherence with this spirit.

---

[54] *Ibid.*, pp. 130-132.

§ 32
In his comments on the first conciliar session, Council chronicler Henri Fesquet is unsparing in offenses against the previous doctrine of the Church. We believe that his considerations are expressive of the Council's *animus injuriandi* since we know that what he reports reflects the opinion of the most enlightened participants at Vatican II. Here we see his outrage over the "age of the Counter-Reformation":

"Following their pastoral and missionary instincts and counting on the support of the Pope, the Bishops refused to be intimidated. At the same time, **certain abstract and scholastic fictions, an intractable fixism, a narrowness of spirit, a lack of concern for the outside world had to give way** before the meaning of History, the 'master of life' (John XXIII), the progress of religious sciences and a concern for entering into contact with 'the others.' Without this effort to adapt to the world, there would have been no *aggiornamento* in the Church – the final end of the Council. Thanks to this effort, however, a new climate could be installed in the nave of St. Peter's …

"It is not an exaggeration to say that Vatican II did away with the age of the Counter-Reformation and its doctrinal harshness."[55]

§ 33
In his commentaries on the schema on Ecumenism (second session), Fesquet offends the Church when he describes her habitual polemical position "as sterile." He also offends her when he pejoratively depicts the general state of affairs before the Council. The following excerpt demands our attention:

"On Monday the assembly will begin to discuss the schema on Ecumenism. It is an event of the greatest importance. In effect, for the first time in History, a Council will address this problem. Doing so, Vatican II realizes the dearest wish of **John XXIII**. During the short years of his pontificate, the late Pope **carried out a silent and truly amazing revolution in this field**.

"The Roman Church abandoned her defensive, polemical attitude, which was fruitless, toward other Christian confessions and entered onto the grand ecumenical road. Before John XXIII, the official position of the Roman Church was for the most part this: to affirm that the Catholic Church was the only authentic Church and to wait until those who had separated from Rome through the course of centuries would return to the orbit of the Papal Church.

---

[55] H. Fesquet, *Le journal du Concile*, pp. 147-148.

"There was not much concern to know if the Catholic Church herself should be reformed to make her features better conform to the Gospel and less hostile toward the separated Christian. Or to consider whether she should give more importance to the common patrimony of all the confessions. Practically speaking, it was the Holy Office that was in charge of ecumenism, and its action consisted principally in warning against the dangers of inter-confessional gatherings.

"With John XXIII, everything changed abruptly. One of the most important acts of this Pope's reign was to create a secretariat for the union of the churches, which took from the Holy Office its exclusive authority over ecumenical matters and gave that task to specialists."[56]

§ 34   Along these same lines, Cardinal Joseph Ritter, Archbishop of St. Louis, added his comment on the schema on Ecumenism:

"This schema corresponds to the *aggiornamento* defended by John XXIII and Paul VI, and it finally tolls the death knell of the Counter-Reformation."[57]

Commenting about the schema on Revelation discussed in the fourth session, theologian Fr. Gustave Martelet, S.J., disciple of Henri de Lubac, said:

"This is a grand text. This schema is essential for our relations with the Orthodox [Eastern Schismatics] and makes reconciliation possible. **I hope that this document at the same time will show the outdated character of the Counter-Reformation and anti-Modernism.**"[58]

§ 35   Fr. Jean-Marie Tillard, O.P., a conciliar expert and a consultant to the Secretariat for the Union of Christians, considered the Catholic reaction to Protestantism a "lack of wisdom" and a "unilateral" action of the Church. He wrote:

"In our studies on ecumenism, it increasingly appears to us that **the explosion of the West against the Reformation,** which has numerous causes, **was largely due to a lack of wisdom on the part of the Church of Rome. She was unable to reconcile the communion of faith with the diversity necessarily born from**

---

[56] *Ibid.*, pp. 331-332.

[57] Joseph Elmer Ritter, Intervention in the Conciliar Hall of November 19, 1963, *in ibid.*, p. 340.

[58] Gustave Martelet, Press statement of October 30, 1965, *in ibid.*, pp. 1025-1026.

sowing the Gospel in different socio-cultural ambiences. One could say that Rome imposed, with the Faith, a 'civilization' and a 'culture.' **Her reaction to the Counter-Reformation ... and her action at the Council of Trent were unilateral,** in the sense of excessively identifying unity with uniformity."[59]

§ 36   Much the same thinking is expressed by Fr. Daniel Olivier, professor at the *Institut Catholique de Paris* and contributor to *La Croix* and *Concilium*. He calls Luther the victim of an insecure and passionate reaction of the Church:

"**Luther,** in addition to the suspicion of heresy of which he **became a victim,** had the misfortune to emerge as a threat to the institution of the Papacy in the Church. Events would later confirm that he did in fact constitute a grave danger to the Primacy. Rome was no longer able to win the respect of all without a fight to uphold it. **The process that opened against him** [Luther] in the spring of 1518 **expressed a reaction of insecurity**. They found it preferable to shut him up rather than run the risk of an anti-papal hurricane. In a context so passionate, the doctrinal debate Luther desired could not fail to seem purely academic."[60]

§ 37   Fr. Boaventura Kloppenberg, O.F.M., a Brazilian *perito* at the Council and author of *The Ecclesiology of Vatican II*, echoes these opinions. For him, the anti-Protestant attitude of the Church was "unbalanced":

"At times **certain emphatically stressed doctrines** (only because they were denied by someone) **led the post-Tridentine Church to liturgically dubious and pastorally problematic practices ... All this produced a Church somewhat unbalanced in emphasizing doctrines and practices**. We were all born ... into this anti-heretical and anti-Protestant Church. We have identified ourselves with her."[61]

In a cordial *tête-à-tête* with Fr. Congar, Fr. Giulio Girardi, former professor at Rome's Salesian University and an early promoter of the Christians for Socialism Movement, describes the Counter-Reformation as detrimental to "fundamental Christian values":

---

[59] Jean-Marie Tillard, "Pluralismo teologico e mistero della Chiesa," *Concilium*, 1984/1, p. 130.

[60] Daniel Olivier, "Perché Luther non è stato capito?" *Concilium*, 1976/8, p. 34.

[61] B. Kloppenburg, *A ecclesiologia do Vaticano II*, p. 13.

"I will distinguish two stages in this decade [1960-1970]: *the first* closed with the Council; *the second* is the post-Council. The characteristic of the first is the idea that the Church can only be Catholic if she is Christian. The second stage is characterized by the idea that the Church can only be Christian if she is human.

"According to the first stage, the Church will only be truly Catholic if she is Christian. **Such a rediscovery of Christian values was a reaction to the hardening that marked the Counter-Reformation and caused it to accentuate the characteristics of the Catholic Church so strongly that certain fundamental Christian values suffered from it.**"[62]

§ 38   During the discussion on the schema on Ecumenism, Bishop Jean Gay of Basse-Terre et Pointe-à-Pitre (Guadalupe), speaking about missionary work, described the effort to evangelize the people as a "sordid fight." These were his words:

"The concrete application of the principles set out in chapter I implies, above all, a renewal of our missionary methods. **What purpose would it serve to increase fraternity between the Bishops and the [non-Catholic conciliar] observers if this noxious competition and sordid fight would continue to reign in the practical life of communities? It is necessary to avoid converting persons who are already Christian** and to direct special attention toward those who still do not know Christ."[63]

§ 39   Analyzing the schema on Religious Liberty in the third session, Henri Fesquet offended the militancy of the Church in History by calling the pre-Vatican II Church an "intellectual tyranny." He said:

"The conciliar debate served to clarify ideas for the Church on this crucial point [the right of persons to adhere to error] in view of her past mistakes. A mortal blow was delivered by Vatican II to the classical doctrine of tolerance.

"**Historians cannot help but note that this doctrinal revolution – for this is what it was – was finally achieved in a not so difficult way. The Council had already marked the end of the Constantinian era and the era of intellectual and spiritual tyranny as seen throughout History with the condemnation of John**

---

[62] Yves Congar and Giulio Girardil, "Dialogue entre les Pères Congar et Girardi - 1960-1970: Dix années décisives pour l'Eglise et pour le monde," *I.C.I.*, January 1,1970, pp. 22-23.

[63] Jean Gay, Intervention in the Conciliar Hall of November 26, 1963, in B. Kloppenburg, *Concílio Vaticano II*, vol. 3, p. 370.

Hus, burned alive in 1415, **the detention of Galileo** (1633), **and other crimes of the Inquisition. More recently, we saw the shocking methods of the Holy Office which, quite literally, tortured so many consciences. These methods rightly invoked the condemnation of the Bishops.**"[64]

§ 40   Fr. René Laurentin, a *perito* at Vatican II, also approved the Council's denial of the Church's past. His appraisal did not lack multiple offenses:

"What was overcome [at Vatican II] **was historical narrowness and stains. Also, the nostalgia of 'Christendom'** with its grandeurs and miseries, as well as **its outmoded political conceptions.** The Augustinian conception of politics died at Vatican II. **So also did post-Tridentine precisions, the harshness of the 19th century, the anxious and desperate battle to defend the remains of the Middle Ages** by attacking the 'modern' ideas head-on: liberty, equality, fraternity, the rights of men. These values, unilaterally understood as dangerous in the 19th century, found their rightful place in schema XIII [*Gaudium et spes*] and others. **Without abandoning the demand of the absolute that inspired the *Syllabus*, Vatican II transcended its suspicions and rigidity.**"[65]

§ 41   We close this Chapter with the words of John Paul II, who judged intolerance to be "a sickness of humanity and the ignominy of the Churches." However, wise intolerance in defense of the Faith is none other than the exercise of Catholic militancy. Thus, John Paul II, directing offenses toward intolerance as a whole, seems to strike at the honor of the Church Militant. On a visit to Poland, John Paul II declared:

"Throughout the centuries, our country was a hospitable house for all its inhabitants. Diverse nationalities, religions and confessions lived here, one alongside another. Poland stands out for its tolerance – rare in Europe – and justly noted by historians.

"In my Message for the celebration of the 24th World Day of Peace, I dealt more amply with the question of religious minorities and confessions on the world scale. **Intolerance, a sickness of humanity and the ignominy of the Churches,** can manifest itself on the part of the stronger, as well as the weaker.

---

[64] H. Fesquet, *Le Journal du Concile*, pp. 491-492.

[65] R. Laurentin, *Bilan du Concile - Chronique de la quatrième session*, p. 365.

[handwritten: There is lack of tolerance by everyone except Catholic Church!]

"For example, lack of tolerance appears where pressure and constraint are applied to 'convert' and, also, where the fundamentalist mentality prevails. Thinking above all about the 'stronger' communities, I wrote: 'However much one loves the truth of his own religion, this does not give any person or group the right to suppress the liberty of conscience of those who have other religious convictions. Nor do they have the right to make them trick their consciences by offering or denying certain privileges and social rights on the condition they change their religion.'"[66]

*[handwritten: but it is our duty to defend the *Faith, teach it, correct in charity]*

[handwritten right margin: christian, Islam, Protestant; Catholics aren't fundamentalists]

The testimonies presented in this Chapter II reveal the hostility nurtured by progressivist theologians against the militant character of the Church. It seems to us that they are an expressive sampling of the whole current of Progressivism, as well as of the spirit of the Council.

[handwritten: They JP II Pvi XXIII didn't realize, they were assuming the opponents position in good faith as a bridge-builder as I did for 30 yrs. to evangelize .... it didn't work! I lost my faith became very codependent + oppressed by others false beliefs — I was too open + naive + not well formed in the Tradition of the Faith. I we little ones aren't theologians ... they hurt us.]

---

[66] John Paul II, Speech in the Lutheran temple of Warsaw of June 9, 1991, "Il dovere de rispondire alla volontà di Cristo esige che restiano saldi sulla via verso l'unità tra i cristiani," *L'Osservatore Romano,* June 10-11. 1991, p. 8.

Chapter III

THE SACRALITY OF THE CHURCH IDENTIFIED AS A STUPID PRETENSION, AND HER DEVOTIONS A MANIFESTATION OF FANATICISM

§ 1   Progressivists manifest a visceral opposition to the solemnity and sacrality of the Church. This attitude received many endorsements at Vatican II. Worthy of note is Paul VI's decision to abandon the use of the *sedia gestatoria*, the papal tiara and the Fisherman's Ring.[1]

---

[1] a. At the solemn opening session of the Council, John XXIII was already paving the way for the gestures of Paul VI. This is how Cardinal Franz König described the ceremony of October 11, 1962: "Inside St. Peter's, John XXIII descended from the *sedia gestatoria*, took off the papal tiara and put on the same miter that all the other Bishops were wearing. No one knew why he did this. Perhaps he wanted to show that it is not the exterior power of the Papacy that is important, but the spiritual" (F. König, interview with Silvano Stracca, "Il Concilio sorpresa per il mondo," *Avvenire*, October 16, 1992).

Since his first audience of November 17, 1958, John XXIII displayed a profound uneasiness with regard to papal pomp and ceremony. His private secretary describes how he tried to avoid the ceremonial and the *sedia gestatoria*:

"Upon entering the Ducal Hall, John XXIII caught sight of the official ceremonial: Prelates of the Antechamber, members of the Noble Guard, the Palatine Guard, the *sedia*-bearers. He turned to me and asked, 'What is this?' Embarrassed I responded, 'It is the preliminaries for the audience.' 'But it is not what I wanted. This is a family meeting.' During the entrance into the Hall of the Blessing, he tried to avoid the *sedia gestatoria*. To be presented to his dear visitors from Bergamo and Venice carried on the shoulders of the young men bearing the *sedia* intimidated him and made him almost sad" (Loris Capovila, "Quelle humour denso di umiltà," *Avvenire*, November 20, 1992).

b. Paul VI had the same distaste for papal ceremony. On November 13, 1964 before the start of a Melkite Eastern rite concelebration, he dismissed the *sedia gestatoria* and walked on foot along the Basilica of St. Peter to the Altar of the Confession. At the end of the ceremony, Cardinal Pericle Felici declared, "The Church is truly the mother of the poor, and the Pope has decided to offer a new witness

§ 2   The famous Pact of the Catacombs,[2] at which 40 conciliar Prelates met in the Catacombs of Saint Domitila, also aimed to abolish important aspects of the sacrality of the Church.

of this by donating his tiara for the benefit of the poor." As Cardinal Felici pronounced these words, the Pope himself placed his tiara on the altar. It was later learned that the tiara had been donated to the Diocese of New York, which sold it to an American museum (cf. H. Fesquet, *Le Journal du Concile*, p. 714).

This gave a powerful impetus to the movement of impoverishing the Church. At a conference in Rome, Archbishop Helder Camara pointed to that gesture as an example to be followed by the whole Church Hierarchy (cf. B. Kloppenburg, *Concílio Vaticano II*, Petrópolis: Vozes,1966, vol. 5, p. 530).

c. In fact, the gesture had important after effects. For example, John Paul I dispensed with the act of coronation of the Pope at his "inauguration" ceremony. Cardinal Suenens relates: "September 3, 1978 saw what was in the past called 'the coronation of the Pope,' which John Paul I transformed into a simple ceremony of pastoral inauguration, officially called the 'solemn Mass marking the beginning of his ministry as supreme Pastor'" (*Souvenirs et espérances*, p. 259).

d. Along these lines, John Paul II abolished the use of the majestic plural (*pluralis maiestatis*) in papal language. Cardinal König observes: "Perhaps we need to be reminded of something: that is, before John Paul II the Pope always spoke using the [majesticl] 'we.' John Paul II began to use the 'I.'" (Franz König, *Il Concilio sorpresa per il mondo*, *Avvenire*, October 16, 1992).

e. The Pope used a ring with an emerald, which received the beautiful name of the Fisherman's Ring. Paul VI abandoned the papal ring and replaced it with a flat ring made of a common gold metal. On it the figure of an angel flying away with the tiara was stamped, symbolizing the flight from pomp and the adoption of poverty. Paul VI gave his former Fisherman's Ring to U.N. Secretary-General U Thant for it to be sold and the money distributed to the poor (Cf. Georges de Nantes, *Liber accusationis in Paulum Sextum,* CRC, St. Parrès les Vaudes, 1973, p. 71; Wigand Sieber, *Katholisch oder Konziliar*, München/ Vienna: Langen Müller, 1978, p. 421; V.A., *La visita di Paolo VI alle Nazioni Unite,* Libreria Editrice Vaticana, 1966 p. 76; H. Fesquet, *Le Journal du Concile*, p. 1036).

Following the example of Paul VI, most of the Bishops also stopped wearing their amethyst rings and adopted Paul VI's plain metal ring.

f. Benedict XVI continued the ban of the tiara and *sedia gestatoria,* refused in his turn to sit on the throne at his papal "inauguration" but restored the use of a gold ring without any precious stone.

[2] a. The Pact of the Servant and Poor Church – or the Pact of the Catacombs, as it is more generally known – was made close to the

end of Vatican II on November 16, 1965, by around 40 conciliar Fathers. These Bishops met at the Catacombs of St. Domitila to sign a semi-secret pact that aimed to do away with riches, pomp and ceremony in the Catholic Church. The names of the Bishops present are not known. Here we cite some of the significant texts from the resolutions made at that gathering:

"We, Bishops meeting at Vatican Council II, after becoming aware of deficiencies in our lives of poverty following the Gospel's teaching ... commit ourselves to the following measures:

"1. We will seek **to live in the ordinary way of our people in matters of housing, food and means of transportation** ...

"2. **We renounce forever wealth and its appearances, especially in clothing** (rich materials and brilliant colors) **and insignias made of precious metals** (indeed, these signs must be evangelical ... **without gold or silver**).

"3. **We shall not own either estates or goods**. ...

"4. Whenever possible, **we will entrust the financial and property management of our dioceses to a commission of competent laymen** ...

"5. **We refuse to be addressed** in speech or writing **by names and titles signifying grandeur and power** (Your Eminence, Your Excellency, Monsignor) ... We prefer to be called by the evangelical name of Father. ...

"6. In our behavior and social relations, **we will avoid everything that can appear to confer privileges, priorities or even a preference to the rich and the powerful** (e.g., giving or receiving banquets, giving them special places in religious services)" (in B. Kloppenburg, *Concílio Vaticano II*, vol. 5, pp. 526-527; See also H. Fesquet, *Le journal du Concile*, p. 1121; *Concilium* 1974/4, pp. 118-120.)

b. At the time of the Pact of the Catacombs, Archbishop Helder Câmara – known as the "red Archbishop" and one of its probable signers – gave a press conference in Rome that had international repercussions. In it, he emphasized the new commitment to poverty:

"We, the Most Reverend Excellencies, have need of a most excellent reform. ...

"To begin with ... we must simplify our dress and way of life. While acknowledging the many beautiful personal and local initiatives [of poverty], as the Council ends the spectacle [of richness and pomp] we present in St. Peter's Basilica on the last day will be the same as it was at the Opening Session. ... Some said that we had no right to give the Pope lessons [on poverty]. But it is Paul VI who gives us lessons, and we who appear a little slow to learn them. I emphasize – for myself and my brother Bishops – his offering of the tiara and the crosier.... a decision Paul VI made that will endure forever. **There are Bishops who would like to be simpler, who**

§ 3

Further, at the Council a considerable number of Bishops' statements encouraged the abandonment of the pomp that traditionally surrounded the episcopal dignity. [3]

---

would like to travel like everyone else, for example, in buses and trains, who would like even to stand in line" (in B. Kloppenburg, *Concílio Vaticano II* , vol. 5, p. 530).

[3] a. With the same spirit that would lead to the Pact of the Catacombs, Bishop Georges Mercier of Laghouat, made this comment:

"Numerous Bishops have already adopted a note of greater poverty and simplicity in their clothing. They could go even further and follow the letter of the Gospel text, 'neither gold nor silver.' Why not apply these words to themselves in their episcopal insignia and have them made of ordinary metal? Doing away with worldly and honorific titles used for Bishops would likewise be a more authentic testimony of their spirit of poverty. ...

"Why should genuflection, outside the Church, still be maintained as a sign of special respect? Still other simplifications can be suggested – in liturgical ornaments, in lifestyle, etc. ... On the eve of the Council (July 7, 1962), Pope John XXIII suggested to the women religious of the whole world that poverty is hardly compatible with 'ostentation in buildings or settings' ... Vanguard Bishops have gone so far as to choose humble dwellings in poor neighborhoods in order to transform their episcopal palaces into schools. How good it would be if such examples would become contagious! ... Shouldn't the episcopal body make a voluntary initiative to strip itself of the exterior signs of riches that still remain and refer to a temporal power that has fortunately passed?" (G. Mercier, Statement about the 'poor Church,' *Equipes Enseignantes*, special issue, 2nd quarter, 1962-1963, in Y. Congar, *Pour une Eglise servante et pauvre*, Paris: Cerf, 1963, pp. 145-146).

b. For Cardinal Joseph Frings, Archbishop of Cologne, the distinctions and honors paid to ecclesiastical dignitaries were nothing but exterior signs that could be eradicated – as had already happened in Communist countries – with no harm to the Church. In a Pastoral Letter, he stated:

"The various exterior signs and ceremonies that spotlighted the Bishop only appeared in Church history at the time of Emperor Constantine, when the honors paid to high officials of the Roman Empire were established and then extended to the Bishops. The Church can be envisaged without these exterior honorific distinctions. In places where persecution rages, she is forced to renounce such distinctions, and this does not harm her interior life" (Joseph Frings, *Lettre Pastorale de Carême*, in *Documentation Catholique*, 1963, col. 463, *in* Y. Congar, *Pour une Eglise servante et pauvre*, p. 147).

c. Bishop Juan José Iriarte of Reconquista, Argentina, wants Bishops to "liberate" themselves from episcopal palaces, miters and the signs of respect and veneration given to them by the simple people of God. In an interview with the French daily *Le Monde*, he stated:

"How difficult it is for us, poor Bishops of the Church of Christ in the 20th century, to pass on this message [of poverty] ... Today this **message is delivered by men of proletarian austerity ... who call each other 'comrade'** and are accustomed to the curt, direct language of their leaders. ... On the other hand, **we Bishops have to convey this message from the heights of marble altars and episcopal 'palaces.' in the incomprehensible baroque style of our pontifical Masses, with our strange miters and the even stranger circumlocutions of our ecclesiastical language.** Furthermore, **we present ourselves** to our people **dressed in purple, in the latest model of automobile or in a first-class train cabin. And these people call us 'Your Most Reverend Excellency' and bend their knees to kiss the stone in our ring!** It is not easy to liberate oneself from this heavy load of history and customs" (J. J. Iriarte, Interview given to *Le Monde*, January 6, 1963, in Y. Congar, *Pour une Eglise servante et pauvre*, pp. 149-150).

d. Archbishop Émile Maurice Guérry of Cambrai views the riches and pomp of Church ceremonies as an "obstacle to evangelization:"

"The second evangelical value: *poverty and simplicity*. How many of those in **the popular masses censure the Church for her ostentatious riches, her pompous ceremonies, her exterior display, the importance she appears to give to prestige, money and the 'classes' – even in her acts of worship!** This also poses an obstacle to the evangelization of the poor and the popular masses. ...

"In certain parishes in France, **a serious effort was made to reveal the true face of a poor and divested Church,** despite all the appearances. But there is still so much to be done in this sense! Today, in the conciliar meetings, moving appeals for poverty and simplicity are resounding. They have found a strong echo in the hearts of the Bishops" (E. Guerry, *Lettre Pastorale*, D.C., 1963, col. 181, in Y. Congar, *Pour une Eglise servante et pauvre*, pp. 147-148).

e. These statements and attitudes opposed to the sacrality of the Church were ratified by the words of Paul VI:

"**The poverty of the Church with the noble simplicity of its forms is a testimony to her fidelity to the Gospel. It is the condition, at times indispensable, to verify her own mission**" (Opening speech to the 2nd General Assembly of the Latin America Bishops Conference, August 24, 1968, in *Insegnamenti di Paolo VI*, vol. 6, pp. 411-412).

f. For more statements during the Council of numerous Prelates and theologians favoring the so-called "Church of the Poor" and calling for

§ 4

With regard to sacrality, the face of the Church was disfigured in this post-conciliar period. The Holy Mass – her principal act of worship – was modified, many ceremonies abolished, and certain devotions undervalued and ridiculed. [4]

Such blows wielded against the sacrality of the Church have been tolerated, if not stimulated and directed, by the highest authorities of the Church.

Let us look at a sampling of excerpts demonstrating the progressivists' *animus injuriandi* directed against the sacrality of the Church in the post-conciliar period.

1. Offenses to the Sacrality of the Church

§ 5

Fr. Peter Huizing, professor at Gregorian University and the University of Nijmegen and a respected canonist who served as a consultant in the preparation of the New Code of Canon Law, attacks the titles always used by the Church. He demands "desacralization" as a necessary component for the reform of the Curia:

"Normally, either personally or as a group, the Pope, a Cardinal or any other member of the Roman Curia does not give the impression of being as holy as, or holier than, any other Christian. In view of this, **the continued use of titles, such as 'Holy See,' 'Holy Father,' 'Sacred Congregation,' 'sacred power,'** and so on, **ridicules and shames the whole community of the Church. It is a stupid pretension.** It is as if a president or prime minister were to have titles such as 'first citizen' or 'father of the nation,' or to claim to have a 'patriotic power.'

"Likewise, **titles such as 'Vicar of Christ' run the risk of obscuring faith in Jesus by effectively identifying the person of**

---

the abolition of ecclesiastical pomp and splendor, see also H. Fesquet, *Le journal du Concile*, pp. 85-87, 102-103., 110, 157-158., 206-207, 309, 374-375, 681, 700, 713-714, 719-723, 1035-1039.; R. Laurentin, *Bilan de la première session*, p. 146, note 28; *Bilan de la deuxième session*, pp. 39, 297-298, note 4; *Bilan de la troisième session*, p. 47, 188-190, 213, 285-286.

[4] In addition to this Chapter, other parts of this Collection deal with abolishing various aspects of sacrality: In this Volulme, Appendix I, Part I, *passim*; Vol. IV, *Animus Delendi I*, Chap. VI.2; Vol. XI, *Ecclesia*, Chaps. III, IV.1. 2 and V. Here we present only what is indispensable to express the spirit of those who promote desacralization.

the Pope as Christ's only personality. A substantial desacralization of the Roman Curia is an essential condition for the reform of the Curia itself. [5]

§ 6

Worthy of note is the outrageous statement of a North American Bishop, who asked not to be mentioned, against the decorum of the Princes of the Church:

"We are dressed like marquises. The only thing missing are the earrings."[6]

Council chronicler Henri Fesquet also makes an offensive critique:

"The description made by Cardinal Felici **of the thousand costumes worn** on the occasion of the public session of October 28 **by all the different categories of Prelates made me think of a high fashion show of churchmen."** [7]

§ 7

Fr. Congar, who played an important role in the adoption of the idea of the "Poor Church" as opposed to the Sacral Church,[8] views the solemn attire, insignia and honors representing the dignity of the Princes of the Church as nothing more than "pretensions of prestige." He states:

"Are there not certain pretensions of a lordly type of prestige in the trappings surrounding the Bishops and the Roman Court: in the dress, insignias, 'retinue,' honors and heraldry? Even though the economic and social structures of Feudalism disappeared, many representations of it remained on the surface, at times even real titles and privileges: above all, the representations that are so natural to carnal man."[9]

---

[5] Peter Huizing, *Vaticano III: una costituzione sulla Chiesa,* in V.A., *Verso la Chiesa del terzo millennio* (Brescia: Queriniana, 1973), pp. 170-171.

[6] H. Fesquet, *Le Journal du Concile,* p. 1035.

[7] *Ibid.,* p. 1037.

[8] Congar's book, *Toward a Servant and Poor Church* [*Pour une Eglise servante et pauvre*], was published in 1963 between the first and second sessions of the Council with the presumed aim of influencing the Fathers to support the desacralization of the Church. The work was dedicated to Cardinal Lercaro, Archbishop of Bologna, a leading proponent of instilling miserablism in the Church. Indisputably, Congar's initiative produced precious fruit for Progressivism. In November 1965 the signers of the Pact of the Catacombs, inspired by Congar's book, gave their document a similar title, calling it: "The Pact of the Servant and Poor Church."

[9] Y. Congar, *Pour une Eglise servante et pauvre,* p. 116.

§ 8

Essentially the same thinking and *animus* opposed to sacrality was adopted by Bishop Émile Marcus of Nantes in his contribution to a collection titled *The Church of the Future*. Bishop Marcus goes so far as to endorse a proposal to "eliminate" God. He affirms:

"Today **we are living in a time of intense desacralization, when man aspires to shape his destiny in a realm other than that of religious rites.** ... The sign of salvation must be presented by the Church, above all, in the sphere of secular life. This sign is the love for the global responsibility of man, who enters the fight in this world in order to give his own meaning to the combat against evil, injustice and suffering. ... **'True faith,'** writes Jeanson,[10*] **'consists in wagering that the human species is capable of incarnating God, achieving Him, eliminating Him as it creates its own humanity.'** To this faith the modern man opposes **'the belief that comes from fear.'** What is certain is that man is called to prove himself here.

"Hence this quest for an evangelization that proceeds from the human, rather than from a whole ritualistic apparatus that contemporary man still uses, but can hardly be taken seriously."[11]

§ 9

As one may recall, among other errors, in the early 1900s Modernist Alfred Loisy was condemned for not admitting that the Church is the Kingdom of God.[12] To avoid incurring a similar condemnation, the progressivists adopted an ambiguous position,[13] one

---

[10*] Francis Jeanson, *La foi d'un incroyant* (Seuil, 1963), p. 183.

[11] Émile Marcus, *O que é evangelizar?*, in V.A., *A Igreja do Futuro*, (Petrópolis: Vozes, 1973), pp. 108-109.

[12] The theses of Loisy and other Modernists were condemned by the Decree *Lamentabili* issued by the Holy Office on July 3, 1907. The thesis that the Church is supposedly distinct from the Kingdom of God was included in that condemnation (cf. DS, 3452).

[13] In his book on *Lumen gentium*, Msgr. Gerard Philips explains Loisy's position: "During the modernist crisis, in one of those famous red booklets (*L'Évangile et l'Église*), A. Loisy launched a grenade that would disturb the sleep of many a dogmatic theologian: 'Jesus preached the Kingdom, but it was the Church that emerged.' To refute him, it was deemed appropriate to sustain that the Church and the Kingdom were fully identical from all standpoints. The text of the Council (Vatican II) took different positions. By (erroneously) placing the two terms in complete opposition, Loisy only saw the 'Church' as an exterior society, effectively devoid of any vitality and eschatological perspective" (Gérard Philips, *La Chiesa e il suo mistero nel Concilio Vaticano II - Storia, testo e commento della Costituzione Lumen gentium,* Milan: Jaca Books, 1982, 2nd ed., p. 92).

that could harbor Loisy's statements as well as the Catholic position –
a not so simple task... Its resolution to the problem was the "Pilgrim
Church," which is not properly speaking the Kingdom, but rather it
contains the Kingdom inchoately: it is on its way to becoming the
Kingdom.

§ 10   Addressing this question of the Church and the Kingdom of
God, Hans Küng states that the traditional teaching – the glorification
of the Church as the Kingdom – is "insupportable":

"Instead of identifying the Church with the Kingdom of God
... what should be emphasized is the difference between the two.
**When that which the New Testament says about the Kingdom
of God is applied to the Church, it is impossible to avoid an
insupportable glorification of the Church**, an ecclesiology of glory
that makes the Church the final object." [14]

§ 11   Fr. Congar sets out general principles that foster the scorn
progressivists have for the sacrality of the Church:

"**The imagination of modern man is stimulated by something other than liturgical mysteries and saint legends.** His imagination even runs the risk of being oversaturated with novels, newspa-
pers, illustrated magazines, cinema, television, and so on... But it finds
an inspiring and wholesome exit when it looks at the infinite perspectives opened by scientific conquests. ... There is little doubt that a new
humanity is called to be born from these new inventions and contemporary achievements. How the horizons have broadened! **This new
man will not be attracted to the Church by means of hagiographic
marvels or brilliant ceremonials** but, rather, by finding in her the
truth of a spiritual relationship of communion with others." [15]

§ 12   Fr. Louis Bouyer, a member of the International Theological
Commission, unsparingly insults the Sacred Liturgy that so splendidly
emits the brilliance of the sacrality of the Church:

"**Yesterday's liturgy was nothing more than an embalmed cadaver. And what is called liturgy today** [before the reforms of Paul VI] **is nothing but a decomposing cadaver.**" [16]

Bouyer goes on to endorse the affronts expressed by Archbishop André Pailler of Rouen:

---

[14] H. Küng, *A Igreja*, vol. 1, p. 135.

[15] Y. Congar, *Pour une Eglise servante et pauvre*, p. 122.

[16] Louis Bouyer, *A decomposição do Catolicismo* (Lisbon: Sampedro,
n.d.), p. 202.

"At the Plenary Assembly of the French Bishops, Archbishop Pailler did not hesitate to courageously and intelligently denounce **the gross errors that pervade religion** in many points, that is, **in precisely those points where one finds a clear survival of paganism and sorcery, making it [the religion] the object of 'scandal and laughter of modern man'**...

"'**Part** ... **of our liturgy continues to ask God for what farmers ask from fertilizers:** a cosmic salvation that makes God supply for our insufficiencies. *Imprimaturs* **are given** in due form **to pictures and booklets promising salvation without any difficulty – in exchange for ritual practices that signify nothing. The holy Mass itself is seen by some as a rite with commercial value. They are futilely trying to sustain the faith of the weak by maintaining these practices. In all of them, religion is at war with faith ... What we want is to see the faith purified of all magical and superstitious expressions and to recognize the** more or less disguised **remains of paganism in such things.**'"[17]

§ 13   Commenting on the Constitution *Sacrosanctum concilium*, René Laurentin uses adjectives such as "magical," "superstitious" and "formalist" to describe the pre-conciliar liturgy. This excerpt draws our attention:

"Even more profoundly, the Constitution on the Liturgy responds to a twofold concern for renewal that is the soul of the schema on the Church. On one hand, this Constitution defines the Church as *people of God*, the community of those who want to live according to the Gospel. On the other hand, it restores the sacramental foundations of the Church.

"This twofold re-valorization gives priority to grace over exterior aspects of the institution, to the ontological over the juridical, to life over a static hierarchy, as a reaction against the restrictive demands of the Counter-Reformation. This is fundamentally the spirit of the Constitution on the Liturgy. Following this harmonious line, **it restores the role of faith**, the living word and, therefore, **the living languages, so disparaged to the exclusive advantage of the rite itself, with the danger of the magical and superstitious deviations that followed.** ...

"What it does is to resuscitate the active and communitarian participation of the faithful in prayer that reunites the Church in Christ.

"**This presupposes the overcoming of formalism and rubricism**. The liturgy must really place the faithful in contact with the

---

[17] *Ibid.*, p. 202.

Word of God, with the salvific events of the history of salvation, so that it restores the central and omnipresent place of the Paschal Mystery of the death and the resurrection of Christ."[18]

§ 14

In the same conciliar document on the Liturgy, Fr. Laurentin analyzes the part pertaining to sacral music. After citing and endorsing the violent attack by composer Igor Stravinsky, he goes on to extend the affronts to much of traditional sacred art. The chronicler makes these remarks:

"The chapter on sacral music [in the Constitution on the Liturgy] keeps Gregorian in its official place, which is important, but it recommends the encouragement of – and not just the tolerance for – introducing the living music of each people and time.

"This twofold recommendation will help to rid us of the banal religious music that lacks both the functional advantages of Gregorian and the relevance of living music. Reacting to these backward and meaningless forms, Stravinsky exploded in an interview granted to Fr. Naspy in August of 1963. He said: '**The present-day music is corrupted, distressing and scandalous** … I would like to have the opportunity to speak about this to the Pope. **I would beg him to get rid of everything: all those idiot conservatives in Rome who have let music become bogged down, the composers who always serve the same tired old clichés. Let the Holy Father free himself from all those idiots – put them all out!**'

"Those are violent words. One can argue about his form. But the man who had this brutal reaction has high qualifications in music and is a recognized authority on this topic. He was referring to religious pieces: the *Pater, Ave,* Mass and psalms. He himself directed the first three in Rome during the Council in the Church of Minerva. His inspiration brought surprising notes of tradition and sobriety. **The violence of Stravinsky's words, however, is no greater than that of the prophets when they perceived a sign of God in their times. What for him is a blaring scandal and for others just a whisper is the debasement and insignificance that corrupt both the human structure and the religious orientation of the symbols so frequently tolerated in the liturgy.**

"**The statues, paintings and images marked by the so-called Sulpician style as well as others diminish the man who enters into contact with them: They inevitably falsify the expression of faith in Christ and the human reality that he came to baptize.**

---

[18] R. Laurentin, *Bilan de la deuxième session,* pp. 244-245.

"What is true for plaster art is also true for music. **It behooves us to exit this infernal cycle that began with the decadence of the Middle Ages.** It is necessary for artists worthy of that name – those who have studied properly and stand in the vanguard of representing the conscience of their epochs and countries – to express themselves with the double authenticity of being men of their time and of the liturgy, which is the place where man encounters God." [19]

§ 15   Speaking in the name of the Vietnamese Prelates, Bishop Paul Seitz of Kontum protested against devotion to images. He said:

"Sacred art should be *ancilla liturgiae* [the slave of liturgy]: paintings, statues, etc. should be means to encourage devotion and piety, and not values in themselves. For this reason, **the whole cult rendered to images as such should be abolished ... because it is superstition or leads to it.**"[20]

From the examples presented in this Item 1, the Reader can judge for himself the *animus injuriandi* of these theologians regarding the sacrality that surrounded the religious devotions and ceremonies before Vatican II.

2. Offenses against the Apparitions and Revelations of Our Lady

§ 16   Devotion to Our Lady is an inexhaustible source of sacrality for the Church.

The spirit of one who has recourse to the Mother of God is permeated with her goodness and supernatural tenderness. We have magnificent reflections of this state of spirit in the prayers *Salve Regina* and *Memorare*.

The Marian devotion of an individual overflows into the life of the family, Catholic schools, pious guilds, fraternities and associations of the faithful who assemble to praise the Most Holy Virgin.

There are also religious Congregations that have sprung up through the centuries whose primary focus is to spread Marian devotion. Priests, Bishops, Cardinals and Popes have consistently stimulated the propagation of the cult of Mary throughout History.

Thus, by both a natural inclination of the faithful and the encouragement of the Hierarchy and Religious Orders, churches were built, Masses instituted, statues enthroned, processions and vigils held,

---

[19] *Ibid.*, pp. 255-257.

[20] Paul Seitz, Intervention in the Conciliar Hall of November 13, 1962, in B. Koppenburg, *Concilio Vaticano II,* vol. 2, p. 156.

feast days celebrated, novenas and litanies said, and so on – all in honor of the Blessed Virgin Mary, Queen of the Angels and the Saints.

As time went by, these excellent acts of devotion gave rise to an extraordinary treasury of sacred art. Literature, architecture, music, paintings, sculptures and statuary instilled a Marian sacrality that perfumed the ambiance of the Holy Church.

Thus, one can state with assurance that devotion to Our Lady is a vital factor that enriches sacrality in the Church, both from the natural standpoint and, most importantly, from the supernatural stance.

Therefore, this Chapter, which deals with the topic of offenses to the sacrality of the Church, will examine offenses made against the Immaculate Virgin and the dogmas related to her.

*

§ 17   Such insults are not without foundation in actions of John XXIII and the Conciliar Fathers. For example, the cool reception this Pontiff gave to the request of Our Lady of Fatima is described in Laurentin's chronicle of the debates about the Blessed Virgin, which took place in the third conciliar session. He wrote:

"On one hand, it would have been desirable to analyze, recall and reinforce the titles and formulas [of Our Lady] in use in numerous papal encyclicals. The Council had the wisdom, however, to leave things as they were. This explains why no speaker proposed – despite certain hopes – to introduce the title of Co-Redemptrix. There was also a desire to renew a solemn consecration of the world to the Immaculate Heart done by Pius XII. **This consecration, about which John XXIII was very discreet and almost reserved,** was an indirect way of honoring the message of Fatima, the source of that consecration."[21]

The same chronicler goes on to describe the exterior cult to Our Lady as "formalism":

"**John XXIII** wanted to promote a renewal of the interior life and **seemed to fear that the exterior brilliance and formalism of certain consecration ceremonies [to Our Lady] would help to make that renewal fall into oblivion.**"[22]

§ 18   Offering a pretext to affront the Virgin, Dom Christopher Butler, Abbot President of the English Benedictine Order, said this about the praise rendered to the Mother of God during the second session of Marian discussions:

[21] R. Laurentin, *Bilan de la troisième session*, p. 39.
[22] *Ibid.*, p. 374, note 4.

"**Attenuating the glory of Our Lady would help the majority of our separated brothers to understand the Church.**"[23]

§ 19   Cardinal Paul-Émile Léger, Archbishop of Montreal, considered devotion to the Blessed Virgin Mary as "sterile affection" and "vain credulity" along with other disrespectful remarks. He says:

"I feel a special difficulty in relation to the title 'mediatrix.' Its exact meaning is very difficult, and, in fact, this word has been interpreted in a great variety of ways. Furthermore, it seems to be frontally opposed to the *unicus Mediator* [Christ as one and only Mediator].

"About the cult to Mary, **I believe that the text proposed to renew Marian devotion will not be strong enough to end all the abuses that the schema wants to repress.** Because, **even though it diminishes the abuses of a sterile affection and a vain credulity, it says nothing expressly about the need to correctly direct the Marian cult. It speaks as if this cult would lead the faithful in and of itself to the knowledge, love and glorification of Christ.** The schema's affirmations are certainly true – but do they not proceed from an excessively theoretical view of things? In fact, **it often happens** – as Cardinal Newman has already noted – **that the Marian devotion of the Christian people is not sufficiently oriented to God or to Christ.**"[24]

§ 20   Many progressivists rise up against devotion to Our Lady and attack it bitterly. In one of his works, *The Word and the Spirit*, Fr. Yves Congar calls the Third Secret of Fatima a "utopia" supported by "fanaticism." He wrote:

"In its form or sense of explaining the future, **prophecy reappears** especially in times of upheaval and historical crisis. The documentation provided by Döllinger[25] illustrates its link to a certain inter-

---

[23] Christopher Basil Butler, Article on devotion to Our Lady, *Il Tempo*, October 28, 1963, in R. Laurentin, *Bilan de la deuxième session*, pp. 285, note 25.

[24] Paul-Émile Léger, Intervention in the Conciliar Hall of September 16, 1964, in B. Kloppenburg, *Concilio Vaticano II*, vol. 4, p. 25.

[25] Johann von Döllinger (1799-1890), along with Johann Adam Möhler, were leaders of the German Romantic School (about Möhler, see Vol. I, *In the Murky Waters of Vatican II*, Chap. IV § 3 Note 5, Chap. VI §§ 4-15). After Döllinger was excommunicated in 1871, he founded the "Old Catholic" sect that denied the dogma of Papal Infallibility. The "documentation" to which Congar refers is found in Döllinger's book, *Der Weissagungsglaube und das Prophetentum in der christlichen Zeit*, published in 1871, the year when Döllinger officially left the Church.

CHAPTER III 105

pretation of History, frequently **with the aim of supporting some national, dynastic, popular, pontifical or spiritual claim.** **Sustained** by fervor and in its extreme **by fanaticism,** it exploits human hope and militancy regarding the future, so that the **imagination constructs its utopias or provides an exit to escape fears, hatreds and political options.**

"Thus stories were born about the Antichrist, a chastisement and the destruction of Rome, or, in a contrary sense, about an angelic Pope, the Muslims and the Holy Land, the end times, etc. **Our own time still resounds with echoes of these affirmations.** Once again there is talk of the 'Malachi Prophecy,' Nostradamus, **the Third Secret of Fatima mobilizing 'blue armies.'"** [26]

§ 21   Fr. Hans Küng also wrote against Fatima. In this text, he accused the three children, as well as Catholics who believe in Fatima, of being Montanists and Joachimists, two different heresies about the end times. He affirmed:

"**As in Montanism, some** post-Tridentine **visionaries were fixed on apocalyptic ideas** (prophecies of the approaching end times, a great war, **an apocalyptic catastrophe or the conversion of Russia). Their devotees were** at the same time **terrified and fascinated** – one of the reasons for their disconcerting success. **Just like the Montanists, the post-Tridentine visionaries** also **presented characteristically rigorous moral demands: a condemnation of the world and a call for extraordinary acts of mortification to avoid chastisements. As in Montanism, in the post-Tridentine visions one finds prophetesses** in action[27] **who are especially concerned with transmitting revelations that announce the future.**

"**As in Joachimism, one finds a mystical interpretation of numbers** and anticipated dates: e.g. **important events that take place on the 13th day of the month ... As in Joachimism, it is often considered necessary to make a new congregation to spread the new ideas ... in which some particular form of piety**

---

[26] Yves Congar, *La Parole et le Souffle* (Paris: Desclée, 1984), pp. 116-117.

[27] Küng clearly alludes to Sister Lucia, one of the three children to whom Our Lady appeared at the Cova da Iria at Fatima in 1917. The seer transmitted two messages of the Virgin to the world and was the custodian of the contents of the third part of the secret of Fatima. The allusion to Fatima becomes even clearer further on in the text, which refers to the 13th day of the month, the day when Our Lady would appear at Fatima.

(an image, devotion or medal) is considered as important as the Word of God witnessed in Scripture." [28]

§ 22

Referring generally to the apparitions of Our Lady, Küng insists it is "fanaticism" that spurs Catholics to believe in apparitions and miracles:

"A specifically **Catholic fanaticism** ... manifests itself in the Church as something 'tamed' and, for this very reason, less dangerous. But in this case it also **calls upon a higher revelation, a new prophecy ... a special revelation that surpasses what was revealed by Christ.** In such circumstances, **these circles of fanatics find a large audience who are much more interested in stories and books about the new 'revelations,' 'apparitions' and 'miracles' than in the original Christian message found in the Holy Scripture.**" [29]

With these examples, the Reader has an idea of the offenses made against devotion to the Blessed Virgin and her apparitions in this disconcerting post-conciliar period, with no sanctions issued against their perpetrators by the constituted authorities.

3. Marian Dogmas: Excrescence, Exaggerations, Triumphalism

§ 23

"The excrescence of Marian dogmas" – this is the outrageous expression, borrowed from the Greek Schismatics, which Hans Urs von Balthasar uncritically uses to refer to dogmas that the Church defined over centuries to establish the doctrine related to the Virgin. That is to say, the magnificent Marian dogmas of the Church would be reduced to an excrescence. Von Balthasar says:

"We understand the well-known principle of Scheeben,[30*] that is, that the mystery of Mary and that of the Church mutually intertwine and illuminate each other in a kind of *pericoresis*,[31] with one having need of the other to be properly situated and focused. ...

"**Not turning away** interiorly **from this** *pericoresis* **is very important to every ecumenical dialogue with the Eastern church,**

---

[28] H. Küng, *A Igreja*, vol. 1, pp. 282-283.

[29] *Ibid.*, p. 281.

[30*] *Handbuch der Katholischen Pragmatik* (Frieburg: Herder, 1954), n. 1819. Matthias Joseph Scheeben (1835-1888) was a German Catholic theologian who wrote a two-volume work, *Mariology.*

[31] *Pericoresis* in theology refers to the internal relationships of the Three Persons of the Holy Trinity.

which does not accept the 'excrescence' of the successive Western dogmas about Mary." [32]

§ 24

Following von Balthasar's line of thinking, Küng points out in a special edition of *Concilium* on the "ecumenical study of Mary" how Vatican II took a stand against the "excesses" of Marian devotion. He contentedly reports the "crisis" this "exaggerated Marianism" is experiencing:

"No Christian Church elevated the figure of **Mary** in such a theological way as the Catholic Church, which established her as part of a certain soteriology.[33] **With the two dogmas of 1854 and 1950,**[34] she also **became associated with papalism and triumphalism.**

"At Vatican Council II (1962-1965), however, **there was open criticism of the excesses of theoretical and practical Marianism.** For intra-Catholic and ecumenical reasons, **John XXIII refused** from the start **to define any new dogma. And after an emotional debate, the Council rejected ... a separate document on Mary** and, instead, incorporated explanations about Mary in the Constitution on the Church **and expressly warned against Marian exaggerations.**

"Anyone who participated in this debate could verify that this exaggerated Marianism, which at the time of Pius XII received its last important expression, **had entered into a crisis. It should surprise** no one that after the Council – except for publications by a few specialists – **books and theological articles about Mary became a rarity, and the broad and extensive Mariological vein seemed to shrivel,** even in Roman Catholic theology." [35]

---

[32] H. U. von Balthasar, *A face mariana da Igreja*, in Wolfgang Beinert, *O culto a Maria hoje* (São Paulo, Paulinas,1979), pp. 318-320

[33] Soteriology (from the Greek *soterion* = salvation and *logos* = study or word) is the theology of Redemption that encompasses three main points: 1. The foundation for Redemption, that is, its necessity; 2. The biblical data or terms usually employed by Scriptures to designate the Redemption; 3. The theological theories by which the Fathers and theologians, interpreting data from the Scriptures, expounded the dogma of Redemption accomplished by Our Lord Jesus Christ.

[34] The two dogmas to which Küng refers are the Immaculate Conception, proclaimed by Pius IX on December 8, 1854, and the Assumption of Our Lady, defined by Pius XII on November 1, 1950.

[35] H. Küng, Editorial "Maria nas Igrejas," *Concilium*, 1983/8, pp. 3-4.

§ 25   Jesuit theologian Fr. John McKenzie, considered by Küng as the "Nestor of American Catholic exegesis,"[36] was a pioneering and outspoken biblical scholar who taught classes at the Universities of Notre Dame, Chicago, Loyola and De Paul. He does not hesitate to state that the dogmas on the Immaculate Conception and the Assumption of Our Lady lack any historical basis in the New Testament. Disdaining the value of Tradition in these definitions, he affirms:

"We are not concerned about the value of tradition in how this term may be interpreted. But it would be pointless to pretend that the critical-historical method of investigation is more favorable toward Tradition than the New Testament. ... **The New Testament does not provide *any historical basis for faith in the Immaculate Conception or the Assumption.* The New Testament does not provide *any basis for belief in Mary as the mediatrix of all graces.*"** [37]

§ 26a   Further on, McKenzie reduces the Most Holy Virgin to a creature "subject to the defects and frailties" of man conceived in original sin. In so doing, he rebels against the dogma of the Immaculate Conception and offends the purity of the Mother of God. Here are his words:

"This brings us to the question of the biblical proofs of the purity of Mary. **The dogma of the Immaculate Conception of Mary was proclaimed without any biblical proof** and, for this reason, is outside our sphere of interest. **The same can be said for belief in her purity. True, she is not described as a sinner, but neither is she described as an example of virtue. We** simply **do not know enough about her to affirm that she was something more than a normal good woman, subject to the defects and frailties of our fallen human nature.** She could also have had those defects and frailties, which – to use Wordsworth's expression – constitute the 'lonely pride of our contaminated nature.' According to traditional belief, Mary could not even grow in her faith ... which seems to reveal some imperfection." [38]

The documents presented in this Item 3 are only some examples of the many we could offer if we were to dedicate ourselves to a special study on this topic.

---

[36] *Ibid.*, p. 5. In Greek mythology, Nestor, the King of Pylos, took part in the War of Troy even though he was already advanced in age. He was regarded as a wise and persuasive counselor.

[37] John McKenzie, "The Mother of Jesus in the New Testament," *Concilium*, 1983/8, p. 18.

[38] *Ibid.*, p. 26.

4. The Virginity of Mary Most Holy Contested [39]

For a Catholic, to question the virginal Nativity of Our Lord Jesus Christ, the *virginitas in partu* [Our Lady's virginity while giving birth to Our Lord] and the perpetual virginity of Our Lady constitute a supreme offense to the Faith. It is even graver because the Church has repeatedly pronounced herself on this matter. [40]

---

[39] The topic of this Item 4 in some way constitutes an exception to the present Volume because it does not deal directly with offenses to the honor of the Church, but with the denial of the virginity of Our Lady – an offense to the Faith and not to the honor of the Church or the Faith. Therefore, the subject is examined under a criterion somewhat different from the others. We introduce it here because it fits well in an ensemble dealing with offenses to the Blessed Virgin Mary..

[40] The virginity of Mary Most Holy has been taught uninterruptedly by the Church. As examples, we will cite some documents of the Magisterium defending this dogma of the Faith:

a. Her Virginity *in genere*:

• In the *Symbol of the Apostles* in its multiple versions: (cf. DS: 10-13, 15-17, 19, 21-23., 25, 27-30, 42, 64).

• In the formula *Fides Damasi* (DS, 72).

• In the *Epistolarum fragmenta ad episcopos orientales* (circa 734) by St. Damascus I (DS, 144).

• In the *Symbol of Constantinople*, promulgated by the Second Council of Constantinople, May to July 30, 381 (DS, 150).

• In the Third Ecumenical Council of Ephesus, *Ep. II and III Cyrilli Episcopus Alexandriae ad Nestorium*, June 22 to September, 431 (DS, 251-252).

• In the *Formula unionis inter Sanctum Cyrillum Episcopus Alexandriae. et Episcopos Eccleisae Antiochenae* of the year, 433, by St. Sixtus III (DS, 271-272).

• In the Letter *Lectis dilectionis tuae* of June 13, 449 to Flavian, Bishop of Constantinople, by St. Leo the Great (DS, 291-292).

• In the Letter *Licet per nostros* of February 13, 557 to King Childebert I, by Pope Pelagius I (DS, 442).

• In the *Symbol* of the Fourth Council of Toledo, opened December 5, 633 (DS, 485).

• In the *Symbol* of the Eleventh Council of Toledo, opened November 6, 675 (DS, 533).

• In the *Symbol* of the Sixteenth Council of Toledo, opened May 2, 693 (DS, 571).

• In the Letter *Ex litteris tuis* of the year 1169, by Alexander III (DS, 748).

• In the Constitution *Cum quorumdam hominum*, of August 7, 1555,

Notwithstanding these pronouncements, some conciliar theologians felt free to dispute this dogma of the Faith. To this effect, they could unfortunately invoke the loophole left in the Dogmatic Constitution *Lumen gentium* [41] concerning *virginitas in partu*.

---

by Pius IV (DS, 1880).

b. Her Perpetual Virginity (*fuit semper virgo*):

• In the *Hermeneia* or *Interpretatio in Symbolum*, initially attributed to St. Athanasius of Alexandria (373) and later to St. Epiphanius (DS, 46).

• In the *Symbol* of St. Epiphanius, Bishop of Salamina (374), in its long formula (DS, 44).

• In the Letter *Licet per nostros*, of June 13, 449, by St. Leo the Great (DS, 299).

• In the Letter *Inter ea quae* of March 26, 521 to Emperor Justinius, by Pope St. Hormisdas (DS, 368).

• In the Letter *Humani generis* of February 3, 557 to King Childebert I by Pope Pelagius I, (DS, 442).

• In the *Symbol* of the Sixth Council of Toledo, opened January 9, 638 (DS, 491).

• In canons 2, 3 and 4 of *Actio V*, of the Lateran Council, October 31, 649 (DS, 502-503).

• In the dogmatic synod Letter *Omnium bonorum spes*, of March 27, 680, addressed to the Emperors by the Council of Rome (DS, 547).

• In the *Symbol* of the Sixteenth Council of Toledo, opened May 2, 693 (DS, 572).

• In the *Symbol* of the Council of Friuli (796 or 797) (DS, 619).

• In the Letter *Congratulamur vehementer*, of April 13, 1053, to Peter, Patriarch of Antioch, by St. Leo IX (DS, 681).

• In the definition against the Albigenses and Cathars in chap. 1, *De Fide Catholica*, of the Fourth Lateran Council, November 11 to 30, 1215 (DS, 801).

• In the profession of faith of Emperor Michael Paleologus to Pope Blessed Gregory X, at the Second Council of Lyons, *Sessio IV*, July 6, 1274 (DS, 852).

• In the Constitution *Cum praeexcelsa*, of February 27, 1477, by Sixtus IV (DS, 1400).

• In the Constitution *Gravis nimis* of September 4, 1483, by Sixtus IV (DS, 1425).

• In the Constitution *Cum quorumdam hominum*, of August 7, 1555, by Pius IV (DS, 1880).

[41] The primary redactor of *Lumen gentium*, Msgr. *Gérard* Philips, states this quite explicitly: "The conciliar text [LG 57] did not avoid the

A. Against *Virginitas in Partu*

§ 27

With regard to Our Lady remaining a virgin during the birth of Our Lord, the progressivists deny the value of Tradition as a source of Revelation. Like the Protestants, they demand eyewitness accounts of the actual parturition of Mary Most Holy. Further, assuming an air of impartiality, they try to overestimate spiritual virginity in order to be able to deny physical virginity, which they distinguish from the former. Finally, they resort to modern science to claim that physical virginity is of no account. Today, they argue, a woman can be made pregnant through artificial insemination and delivered by a caesarean section without breaking the integrity of the hymen, which characterizes virginity.

These statements, all profoundly offensive to the honor of the Immaculate Virgin, are found in the work of Karl Rahner, perhaps the greatest and most accepted theologian of Vatican Council II and the post-conciliar Church. [42]

§ 28

In the text below, Rahner disregards Tradition as a source of Revelation to clearly oppose this dogma of Faith:

---

expression of the Gospel, but pointed out another fact of undeniable importance: 'The Son did not diminish her virginal integrity, but rather consecrated it.' This circumlocution is very simple, and the formula chosen is liturgical and traditional."

He then justifies this choice of words: **"It is known that many questions, especially of late, have been raised about *virginitas in partu* ... One thing is certain: The virginity in question ... is not taught as a personal privilege of Mary"** (Gerard Philips, *La Chiesa e il suo Mistero*, p. 544; the context can be checked in Vol. I, *In the Murky Waters of Vatican II*, Chap. VIII, Item 1, pp. 209-210).

[42] In his book, *The Great Theologians of the 20th Century* (*Os grandes teólogos do século vinte*, vol. 1, p. 95), Battista Mondin comments that Rahner "increasingly appears as the most eminent figure of Catholic theology in the 20th century" who "made a radically anthropocentric vision fitting to modern man." Mondin continues his eulogy: "A theologian of an extraordinarily acute originality (a new Duns Scotus) ... Rahner decisively helped to make Vatican II the Council of dialogue between the Church and the world."

In tribute to the "decisive contribution" made by the German theologian, Paul VI received him in an audience, praising his work at the Council and his theological writings (Cf. Antoine Wenger, *L'Eglise en son tempo – Vatican II – Chronique*, vol. 2, p. 254; H. Fesquet, *Le journal du Concile*, p. 313).

"**The doctrine on *virginitas in partu* must be methodically considered by theology as being only implicitly contained ... in the apostolic *depositum fidei*.** If, however, the content of this doctrine ... cannot be demonstrated with certainty through a dogmatic method, then one must consider only that which, in a process of 'explanation,' can be deduced from the testimonies of apostolic tradition. ... Therefore, **from the apostolic tradition onward, what cannot be proved as implicitly contained in such assertions cannot be proclaimed as obligatory, as binding by Faith.** ...

"**From what has been said, we do not consider this case** [*virginitas in partu*] **to have really happened.**" [43]

In the same work, Rahner again contests Our Lady's virginity during childbirth, and demands eyewitness accounts as necessary for Tradition to be credible. Rahner affirms:

"If it is presupposed that in the apostolic *kerigma* [witness] there were other truths in which the problematic question [of the virginity of Mary] must have been implicitly contained – either because no previous testimonies were found or because they did not exist – then **with what possibility of success and with what right can we presuppose that this apostolic tradition truthfully contained more than what we can read in the totality of Scripture?** ...

"**There is something else that should not be forgotten: dogmatically speaking, an enunciation on this matter by a Holy Father in the middle of the second century would mean nothing for us.** ... **Unless this Pontiff were so kind as to expressly and solemnly declare that this doctrine originated from the Apostles** – which is highly improbable – and has absolute authority for the whole Church, then **one could infer only that this pronouncement is contained in tradition, but not that it belongs with certainty to the *divine-apostolic Tradition*. What definitively matters, however, is the latter.**" [44]

On his 80th birthday, Rahner was honored in an article filled with eulogies in the Vatican's daily *L'Osservatore Romano*. It also reaffirmed his influence in the Council: "The contribution of the Jesuit theologian at Vatican Council II is well-known, especially in the preparation of *Lumen gentium*" (Alfredo Marranzini, "Karl Rahner ha avvicinato la teologia alle necessità spirituali dei contemporanei," *L'Osservatore Romano*, April 6, 1984, p. 3).

[43] Karl Rahner, *Escritos de teología,* vol. 4, p. 197.

[44] *Ibid.*, pp. 191-192.

§ 29   Continuing on, Rahner dares to raise indecorous hypotheses about Our Lady:

"From what we could prudently presume, **a truly explicit apostolic tradition regarding this doctrine is highly improbable. Would it be psychologically probable that Mary would have spoken about the intimate details of her parturition?** ... And **even if she had, we would not know the contents of that report which,** based on her experience, **obviously would have necessarily included the details. When the question of 'how' the parturition took place** is brought up, **the data** are far from uniform and **do not give the impression of coming from an actual report of an eyewitness."** [45]

§ 30   Rahner supports those who, like himself, deny Our Lady's virginity during childbirth and consider this doctrine as nothing more than a kind of symbolic "representation:"

"**This reservation ... of a more recent theology** with respect to classifying and defining the content of that doctrine [of *virginitas in partu*] **is perfectly understandable.** ...

"**Authentic doctrine and its authority do not always and everywhere exist in such a way that the truth to which they refer can be clearly distinguished ... from a certain type of representation."** [46]

§ 31   Along the same lines, we read in the Catechism of the German Episcopate this text that raises doubts about Our Lady's virginity during childbirth. It tries to explain the virginal parturition of Mary as if it were something common, like any other birth, and enhanced by pious interpretations that lack historical evidence:

"**The texts of Matthew and Luke** [on the virginal parturition of Mary] **are not historical narratives** in the modern sense of the term. Certainly we cannot reduce them to sagas or a-historical legends, **but we must understand them as pious and edifying stories (*haggadah*),** which present the tradition of the Old Testament in the light of the fulfillment of the New. The event and the theological interpretation, the narrative and the confession of faith, are intimately linked. **These narratives contain a historical nucleus; nonetheless, we cannot approach them initially as *de facto* historical data,** but must ask how they affirm the faith. This question often presents itself: **Is the theme of the virginal birth just a way to express an affirmation of faith or does it belong to the affirmations of Faith?** ...

---

[45] *Ibid.*, p. 196.
[46] *Ibid.*, p. 185.

"According to John 3:16, parturition with pain is a sign of the profound turmoil in the face of life, a consequence of original sin. However, now that the new [supernatural] life has appeared and the Redemption from the original decay is present, life no longer enters the world with the sign of death and its messenger, pain. The broken creature is entirely regenerated and saved. **The physical process of the birth (of Jesus) is no different.** The whole event, considered as a personal collaboration, is a sign of salvation and the remedy for man. Tradition speaks, then, of the happiness of Mary at the birth of her son."[47]

§ 32   After denying the objectivity of Our Lady's virginity, Rahner goes on to offer a new concept of virginity that would no longer require bodily integrity. Offenses to Our Lady are not lacking in this text:

"One can object that ... the actual parturition of Mary is 'Marian.' It has her personal characteristics, **but this does not mean that it is virginal. This must be answered** with another question: Is it clear what is meant by 'virginal' when the term is applied to parturition? **The presence or absence of pain has nothing to do with the concept of 'virginity' (so we can leave the question open as to whether or not there was pain).** But, as far as the concepts apply, **'bodily integrity' can only be seriously linked to 'virginity' insofar as it relates to the sexual act, but not as related to parturition.**

"Therefore, from the standpoint of a purely conceptual analysis, *virginitas in partu* **is problematic in itself. In any case, what the traditional doctrine presupposes in practice about what took place at Mary's parturition cannot be deduced from this concept ... It can be seen, at best, as an after-the-fact and unfortunate summary of what was said in other places about the event.**

"To say that Mary is 'the Virgin' during the parturition, therefore ... means that the parturition of the holy Virgin was something unrepeatable with regard to the grace of the holy Virgin in her totality, inserted into the history of salvation with a miraculous character."[48]

§ 33   In the above paragraph, Rahner introduces a paradoxical concept: The "holy Virgin in her totality" would not necessarily be a virgin during the parturition. The contradiction is flagrant. Progressivists, however, have an "explanation" for this contradiction. They are

---

[47] *Catechism of the German Episcopate*, in "Catecismos no espelho," *30 Dias*, February 1992, pp. 46-47.

[48] K. Rahner, *Escritos de Teologia,* vol. 4. pp. 203-204.

not referring to Mary Most Holy, who would only be a historical personage, but rather to a "cosmic Virgin," a universal feminine element latent in all of Creation, encompassing it and already existing prior to it.[49]

From this universal feminine element, another element, the "cosmic Christ," made his appearance in History. The entrance of this "cosmic Christ" into History – especially after the resurrection of the historic Christ – supposedly signifies a qualitative leap in the universal process of evolution, which inaugurates the stage where man will overcome death. Soon, according to the progressivist utopia, all of humanity will reach that stage through the mysterious progression of an evolutionary energy immanent in the world. Thus, according to this concept, whether or not the "historic" Mary was a virgin is irrelevant. The person herself was nothing but the veil of a cosmic reality. This is just a quick explanation to enable the Reader to understand what underlies the contradiction in Rahner's text. [50]

§ 34
The next excerpt by Fr. Leonardo Boff fits perfectly with Rahner's, clarifying it in some points and maintaining the same contradictions in others. Assisted by the explanation above, the Reader should be able to follow it without difficulty. We emphasize in bold print the offenses to the Mother of God:

"**The grandeur of Mary does not reside in the fact that she is virgin, but in the fact that she is the *woman*** chosen to receive the Word made flesh in her womb. ... No matter how deeply entrenched in the permanent faith of the Church it is, **the perpetual virginity of Mary does not hold a central place in the hierarchy of truths**. ...

"If God chose the way of virginity and not that of biological sexuality to enter the world, what reasons can be invoked for this *a posteriori*?

"First, we must say that there are no necessary reasons *a priori*. **God could easily have chosen to have an earthly father,**

---

[49] The doctrine of the 'Eternal Feminine' (*das Ewig-Weibliche*, an expression coined by Goethe in the last stanza of his second Faust) is spread by various harbingers of the progressivist current. The following works stand out: *La vie cosmique; Ecrits du temps de la guerre* and *L'Eternel Féminin* by Teilhard de Chardin; *Glaubhaft ist nur Liebe* and *Herrlichkeit* by Hans Urs von Balthasar; *Paradoxe et mystère de l'Eglise* and *L'Eternel Féminin* by Henri de Lubac.

[50] This progressivist doctrine will be studied in Volume VIII of this Collection, *Fumus Satanae*, Chap. I.

who would not have been any kind of rival to the eternal Father. ... Second, the **virginal conception has nothing to do with a negative attitude toward sex**. ...

"Third, **we must definitively abandon the thought of many holy Fathers who believed the virginal birth of Jesus was a necessary condition for Him not to be contaminated by original sin. This opinion exaggerates the biological factor in the transmission of original sin**.

"The reasons for virginity must be sought in Christology and Pneumatology [study of the Holy Ghost], not just in Mariology. Virginity, then, appears as a way to give concrete form to a truth that came into the world with Jesus and by Jesus. In Jesus Christ the apostolic faith discovered the emergence of the new Adam, especially after the resurrection. Finally, a being over whom death no longer holds sway bursts into History. ... God takes the absolute initiative and introduces the beginning of a new humanity ... The virginal conception of Jesus manifests this truth. ...

"Furthermore, the new being inaugurated by Jesus is not a mere continuation of the same creation. ... Instead, it is rupture and protest. It signifies a new and definitive resumption of creation by God. The virginal conception marks this rupture. ...

§ 35   "**The biological aspect of virginity has no human and salvific value as such. Reducing virginity to its merely biological aspect is a sign of a simple mind, a symptom of a weak religious sensibility, indicating the absence of a refined spirit.** The biological aspect is the support, expression and sign of another reality: the bursting forth of a new reality. Quite clearly, virginity is not at the service of its own exaltation, but is totally at the service of Christ and its universal significance."[51]

§ 36   Fr. Karl Rahner endorses the theses of Austrian physician and theologian Albert Mitterer that gave rise to the present day contestation of the traditional doctrine on Our Lady's virginity in childbirth. Already in the 1950s, Mitterer cautioned against emphasizing the physical aspect of Our Lady's virginity and proposed that the dignity of the Son of God or the Mother of God did not demand a miraculous birth. Mitterer claimed the virginity of Mary would not be a biological reality but a simple metaphor. Rahner makes this commentary:

---

[51] Leonardo Boff, *O rosto materno de Deus - Ensaio interdisciplinar sobre o feminino e suas formas religiosas* (Petrópolis: Vozes, 1979), pp. 153-155.

"Mitterer does not endorse what the traditional theory envisions about *virginitas in partu,* but he develops ... a concept of maternity and virginity ... that departs from modern natural sciences. Based on the presupposition ... of maternity and full virginity, **Mitterer** ... **reaches the conclusion that full maternity includes phenomena that theology excludes in the traditional interpretation of *virginitas in partu*: that is, the opening of the mother's birth canal, the breaking of the hymen, delivery pains, etc.** According to him, **full virginity** - therefore also *in partu* - **does not disappear even when these things take place because they have absolutely nothing to do with the concept of physical virginity."**

He continues his endorsement of the same theses: "**Mitterer rightly emphasizes that the absence of these physical phenomena is not an unequivocal sign of virginity.** For example, **in the case of a child engendered by artificial insemination and delivered by a cesarean operation, the mother preserves the signs traditionally attributed to *virginitas in partu*.** Notwithstanding these signs, one cannot say that virginity in fact exists."

Rahner then returns to his central idea: "Accordingly, for Mitterer the miracle of *virginitas in partu* ... does not consist in the concrete way it happened and its consequences, but in the fact that the parturition ... lacked the presupposition it must have in the natural order and whose unmistakable sign normally is the parturition itself: the birth of a child by the work of man. Hence, for Mitterer, ***virginitas in partu* is not an independent phenomenon of itself but the simple application of the doctrine that Mary is 'always a Virgin' to the parturition. ... The traditional meaning attributed to the concept *virginitas in partu* results from a time and culture conditioned to overvalue the hymen,** according to Mitterer. **This threatens true maternity ... and denies the pain [of childbirth]."**

§ 37   In a footnote supporting Mitterer, Rahner asks: "**Can one, without danger of falling into Docetism** [52] **... deny the Child the 'pain' *of being born*?** And, if not, **can one then ... biologically and theologically deny Mary's 'pain' in giving birth** [53] ... which belongs to childbirth in the biological order?" [54]

---

[52] On the position of Docetism in this matter, see excerpt by McKenzie cited in § 43.

[53] On the legitimacy and orthodoxy of the traditional Church teaching on Our Lady's painless delivery, see Pope Alexander III's Letter *Ex litteris tuis* of 1169, (DS, 748).

[54] K. Rahner, *Escritos de Teología*, vol. IV, p. 179.

§ 38
Hence Rahner's affirmation that could be deemed as conclusive of his thinking: **"One should not expect ... that past enunciations [of the Magisterium] on Mary's childbirth to have that kind of indisputable dialectic certainty and absence of mystery that many 'beatos' appear to assume ... regarding a more pious and orthodox theology."**[55]

§ 39
Would theologian Joseph Ratzinger be supporting these theses when he describes the discussion about the virginal birth of Our Lord Jesus Christ as "just a way to evade" the real question? Let the Reader judge for himself:

"Speaking frankly, I consider the dispute today about the virginal birth as just a way to evade the actual question that needs to be addressed: that is, **whether a God who makes himself man can** also be born of the Virgin, and **place in this birth a sign of His unicity.** Is this possible for God to become man?"[56]

§ 40
Theologian Jean Galot, S.J., professor at the Gregorian University, also offends Our Lady with this indecorous statement. He affirms:

"[Mary's parturition] took place in an ordinary way, like all other parturitions. It was a fully physical delivery. Therefore, **Jesus opened the womb of His mother with the spilling of blood that is part of childbirth."**

According to Galot, **"the normal parturition is compatible with the thesis of virginal integrity without corruption or stain ... for parturition as such cannot remove one's virginity because it cannot be identified with a sexual act."** [57]

B. Against the Perpetual Virginity of Mary Most Holy

§ 41
In view of this appalling series of statements by Rahner, it is no wonder that others can comfortably raise the most absurd hypotheses about the virginity of Mary. For example, Schillebeeckx says:

"I believe that **the traditional hypothesis that,** before the annunciation, **Mary had decided to live virginally in marriage**

---

[55] *Ibid.,* p. 203.

[56] J. Ratzinger, *Fé e futuro* (Petrópolis: Vozes, 1971), p. 15.

[57] Jean Galot, *A mulher na obra das salvação* (Ed. Universidade Gregoriana, 1984), in Antonio Socci, "E chegou para Maria o dia do parto," *30 Dias*, November 1991, pp. 66-67.

with Joseph should be dismissed. ... The hypothesis favored by recent Mariologists maintains that Mary did not think about a virginal marriage." [58]

§ 42

Fr. John McKenzie finds an "influence of Gnosticism" in the statement of the dogma of Faith on the perpetual virginity of Our Lady:

"The arguments in favor of *Mary's perpetual virginity* have all been drawn from what has come to be called *ratio theologicae convenientiae* (arguments of theological convenience). In Mariology this kind of argument was summarized by a saying attributed to Duns Scotus: *Deus potuit, decuit, igitur fecit* [God could have done it; it was convenient for Him to do it; therefore, He did it]. I do not know how valid contemporary theologians consider this principle. It certainly appears to establish a *human judgment on what is convenient for God to do*, rather than consider the real events that took place, as a pattern for what happened in History.

"Once [one admits that] the alleged evidence in favor of Mary's perpetual virginity could not *resist the normal historical investigation*, one understands why the first and later believers replaced the lack of proof with theological convenience. It was easy to suppose that the human receptacle that brought forth the Word Incarnate must have been used exclusively for Him and was shared by no other either before or after. It becomes more difficult to claim that this receptacle must be preserved unscathed, since this *implies a veiled supposition that parturition 'damages' the female reproductive organs*. This, in turn, leads to a further insinuation that it is 'better' that these organs never be used for their biological and social end.

"At this point the scholar begins to suspect the possible influence of some form of *Gnosticism*. He need not invoke the *ratio theologicae convenientiae* to know that in early Christianity there were forms of Gnosticism that identified sexuality with sin, and even radical sinfulness. It is known that the belief that Mary conceived Jesus without what for centuries was called the 'stain of carnal intercourse' fits with both Gnostic ideals and the belief that the supreme realization of femininity is the combination of maternity and virginity. One can conclude that *a belief that involves such dubious associations had need of more proof than the affirmation that the conception and birth of Jesus simply*

---

[58] Edward Schillebeeckx, *Maria, Mãe da Redenção* (Petrópolis, 1968), pp. 45-52, in L. Boff, *O rosto materno de Deus*, pp. 155-156.

followed the normal human processes. The prodigy of the birth of Jesus, if one believes what Christians have always believed about it, would be more marvelous if He were born exactly like any other child of a woman. These considerations oblige us to ask if the old arguments of theological likelihood still speak to us with the same cogency as in the past.

§ 43

"Other questions arise when one compares belief in the virginal parturition with other beliefs considered heretical in the early Church. There were various forms of the error called *Docetism*, which denied in various ways the authentic and full humanity of Christ. ...

"The specific form of Docetism to which I refer was the belief that Jesus passed through the body of Mary as if through a tube or canal. The *ignorance of those times about the growth process of the fetus* prevented men of faith from realizing that this belief denied to Jesus the normal processes in the full development of a human being. *In fact what they were saying was that Mary was not the mother of Jesus.* **Perhaps we should ask whether denying Jesus a human father also means denying Him the normal and 'natural' development of a human person. One can ask whether or not the virginal parturition is part of an ancient vision of the cosmos as obsolete as the explicit biblical belief in a geocentric universe."** [59]

§ 44

Rahner adds a word to question the perpetual virginity of Our Lady: **"The doctrine of the integrity of Mary is no more explicit and perceptible in apostolic tradition than the doctrine we are discussing [*virginitas in partu*]."** [60]

C. Doubts about the Virginal Conception of Our Lord

§ 45

Referring to studies by two American Catholic theologians, Fr. McKenzie insinuates in an article in *Concilium* that belief in the virginal conception of Our Lord is not binding by the Faith:

"Certainly, the *virginal conception of Jesus is not on the same historical level as the death of Jesus on the Cross.* The cautious conclusion of [Raymond] Brown[61*] is that a historical and criti-

---

[59] J. McKenzie, "The Mother of Jesus in the New Testament," pp. 23-24.

[60] K. Rahner, *Virginitas in partu, Escritos de teologia,* vol. 4, pp. 205-206.

[61*] Raymond E. Brown, *The Birth of the Messiah* (New York: Garden City, 1977) and Joseph A. Fitzmyer, "The Virginal Conception of Jesus in the New Testament," in *To Advance the Gospel* (New York: Crossroads, 1981).

cal analysis of the texts does not exclude an affirmation of faith that Jesus was virginally conceived. Fitzmyer's equally cautious conclusion expresses a concern to not exaggerate what the texts actually say. **Neither of these scholars ... proposes that the evidence taken from the texts [of the New Testament] obliges a statement of faith in the virginal conception of Jesus.**

"Neither excludes the theory that the *virginal conception* is present in the text *as a theologoumenon* [62] a narrative expressing the belief that Jesus is the Son of God, a theory accepted by some recent Roman Catholic scholars. This idea seems to be supported by the fact that **belief that Jesus was the Son of God is certainly expressed** frequently in the New Testament, especially **in the Gospels** and in Paul, ***without any reference to the absence of a human father.*** This is most apparent in the Gospel of John, whose proclamation of the Only-Begotten admirably fits the pronouncement of the virginal conception. Notwithstanding, John demonstrates no awareness of the virginal conception.

"Summarizing the proofs of the virginal conception taken from the New Testament, one can say that **there were no witnesses of the virginal conception except for Mary and Joseph.** The Gospels of Matthew and Luke not only provide no evidence of the testimony of Mary and Joseph, but give positive indications that they were written without their testimony." [63]

§ 46

Until the beginning of Vatican II, if Catholic theologians had defended theses like the ones set out in this Item 4, they would have been severely censured – suspended from orders, excommunicated or declared heretics. Nothing could be more coherent since they would be denying fundamental dogmas of the Catholic Faith.

After the Council, the very pillars of the Faith were shaken, and no religious authority in the Church showed any special concern to combat these theses or punish their authors. Undoubtedly, this almost universal reaction of the Shepherds, including those in the Vatican, is an expressive example of the tolerance of the spirit of the Council.

---

[62] *Theologoumenon*: theological doctrine that is still not explicitly defined by the official Magisterium and, therefore, is not obligatory for the faithful to believe (cf. K. Rahner and H. Vorgrimler, *Petit Dictionnaire de Théologie Catholique,* Paris: Seuil, 1970, p. 479).

[63] J. McKenzie, "The Mother of Jesus in the New Testament," pp. 20-21.

5. Other Offenses to the Immaculate Virgin

In this Item we will present various other offenses to the honor of the Blessed Virgin that reveal the progressivist desire to discredit the august figure of the Mother of the Savior or to denigrate devotion to her.

§ 47   Some progressivists irreverently imagine "pre-Christian affinities" between the cult to the pagan goddesses of Antiquity and devotion to the Blessed Virgin.[64] In itself this comparison is gravely offensive because it suggests that the cult to the Mother of God would be nothing more than a new rendition of the cult to the pagan deities.

The offense becomes graver, however, when one considers that the worship paid to some of these goddesses – such as Aphrodite, Venus, Astarte and Ishtar – was made in sexual orgies. To think that devotion to the Virgin Mary could be "particularly related" to such pagan divinities ceases to be a simple injury and becomes an audacious blasphemy.

Let the Reader judge, for example, what the theologian of Salamanca Fr. Luis Maldonado writes:

"**Mary is particularly related to the goddesses Cibeles** (Phrygia), **Demeter** (Eleusis), **Artemis** (Ephesus), **Isis** (Egypt), **Aphrodite** (Greece) and **Venus** (Rome) … **whom, it seems were honored as** *mater dolorosa, stella maris, regina coeli,* **etc., in addition to being considered virgins and mothers. Their more ancient predecessors appear to be Inanna of Sumeria, Ishtar of Babylonia and Astarte of Canaan.**"[65]

Fr. Leonardo Boff also affirms that early devotion to Our Lady had pagan origins:

---

[64] Cf. Luis Maldonado, *Introducción a la religiosidad popular* (Santander: Sal Terrae, 1985), pp. 72-74.

[65] *Ibid.*, p. 72. In a note, Maldonado repeats the same idea, referring his reader to other authors who defend that thesis: "That the cult to goddesses has influenced Marian devotion is affirmed by Loisy, Norden, Dibelius and others. One can consult the following works: Jean Daniélou, *Le culte marial et le paganisme*, in H. de Manoir, ed., *Maria*. Paris, 1949, vol. 1, pp. 161-189; G. van der Leeuw, *Fenomenologia de la religion*, Mexico, 1964, pp. 9-91; L. Boff, *El rostro materno de Dios*, Madrid: Paulinas, 1979, pp. 259-281; F. Heiler, *Die Frau in den Religionen der Menschheit,* Berlin, 1977; E. O. James, *The Cult of the Mother-Goddess*, London, 1959; E Neumann, *Die grosse Mutter,* Zurich, 1956; Erich Fromm, *Psicoanálysis de la sociedad contemporánea*, Mexico, 1956."

"It is known that in the early Christian culture **many black statues of Isis with her son Horus seated on her lap were venerated as being the Virgin Mary with her Divine Son. Various Catholic sanctuaries to the 'black Virgin' seem to harken back to the cult transposed from Isis**: the black Our Lady of Einsiedein in Switzerland, the black statues of Montserrat in Barcelona, Orleans and Marseilles, the black Virgin in the north rose window of the Cathedral of Chartres and another one in the underground crypt of the same cathedral, the one in Rocamadour (France), the Virgin of Czestochowa of Poland or Our Lady of Aparecida [Brazil]. **Isis, as well, was called the 'goddess of ten thousand names.'**"[66]

§ 48   For Fr. McKenzie, Our Lady in traditional Marian devotion would be "a fictional, plastic figure," "a legend," a product of the dominant classes of society:

"**The real Mary or the historical Mary is** at least **as intangible as the real or historical Jesus**, but not exactly for the same reasons. Genuine historical evidence about Mary is so scarce and weak that it would impose an embarrassing silence on historians if they were dealing with any other figure. **We know as little about Mary as we know about the mother of Abraham Lincoln**, who – according to one story – would have observed that everything he was he owed to his angelic mother. Jesus never even spoke like this about Mary according to the accounts. **But this left the imagination of Christians totally free, unrestrained, without the reins of historic facts.**

"**The Mary of legend, art, poetry, hymns and even Christian theology is a fictitious figure.** I am not sure that it can be affirmed that the Mary of faith is as important as the Mary of history. *Faith in Mary in traditional Christian devotion is faith in something that is not true.* ... Every symbolism presupposes that one should believe in the reality that is being symbolized. **But what would be the reality expressed by the art, hymns and legends of traditional Marian devotion?** ...

"*The Mary of traditional devotion is a plastic figure.* **This figure seems to have been invented to meet the needs of the epochs that created it, above all, the 10th to 17th centuries.**

"We could venture a bit further to affirm that **these were the needs of the dominant classes of Christendom, which were the patrons of the art and literature of those centuries.**"[67]

---

[66] L. Boff, *O rosto materno de Deus*, p. 243.

[67] J. McKenzie, "The Mother of Jesus in the New Testament," pp. 26-27.

§ 49

For Leonardo Boff, presenting Our Lady in the elevated position of Queen of Heaven and Earth, adorned and swathed in the splendors of her royalty, would be a "mythification" of Mary. According to the theologian, it is necessary to de-mythify Mary Most Holy, presenting her – under the pretext of historical fidelity – with "callused hands," a "face marked by a hard life" and "thick feet." Boff says:

"Mary would have appeared like so many other women of Galilee, just as her Son looked like the other men of his area ... **When we consider Mary in the symbolic records**, rarely do we see this humble historical situation: **rarely do we find her hands callused by work, her face marked by the dignifying signs of a hard life, her feet thick from standing on them for so long**. What we see in the symbolic Mary is a beautiful damsel crowned with jewels and gold, dressed in brocades and silks, her hands delicate, her skin treated, her face transfigured. What symbolic grandiloquence should exalt is her exceptional lack of brilliance, and not hide it. To the contrary, **we mystify Mary and make ourselves victims of confusing her historical dimension with the symbolic one**. The faithful who kneel before her statues should be able to see beyond the symbol and know the history of that singular woman of our world who lived her life like all women."[68]

§ 50

It is not a far distance to go from demystifying Our Lady by exaggerating a prosaic vision of her, as we saw in the text above, to actually blaspheming her. Taking this step with impunity is Karl-Josef Kuschel, professor at the Institute for Ecumenical Research of the University of Tübingen and director of the Catholic Theological Faculty in the same city. He does not hesitate to transcribe – and endorse – highly offensive excerpts from German literature against the Virgin of Virgins. Among others, he cites the poem *Maria* by Bertolt Brecht,[69] who scripts this allusive description of Christ's birth:

"The night of **her first parturition**
Was cold. But in later years
She forgot that completely:
Her concern was for the frost on the windows and the smoking chimney,
And the disgust she felt while expelling the placenta in the morning.

---

[68] L. Boff, *O rosto materno de dios,* pp. 258-259.

[69] Bertolt Brecht, a well-known German author and playwright, was a Communist with anarchist tendencies (cf. *Der Kleine Brockhaus,* Wiesbaden, 1961, vol. 1, p. 169).

But above all she forgot the bitter shame
Of not being alone -
So typical of the poor.

It was principally for this reason
That many years later
This turned into the party where
The whole lot was there.

The rough conversation of the shepherds was silenced.
Much later, in history, they were transformed into kings.
The wind, which was very cold,
Was presented as if it were angelic songs"[70*]

§ 51   After citing this poem, Kuschel comments:

"The text continues, driven by the discrepancy *between what actually was and what came to be*, the discrepancy between the Christian idyllic vision that would portray Bethlehem 'much later' and the historic reality that tells us what really took place: A woman – Mary is her name – brought to light a Son in miserable circumstances.

"The one present there is **not some Madonna, nor the mother of God, nor the queen of heaven, but a concrete, historical woman who became a mother for the first time**. The criticism is present when he speaks of the 'disgust she felt while expelling the placenta,' her 'shame,' the poverty of the shepherds and the cold. History and history of influence, image and counter-image are presented in a critical tension."[71]

What these authors feel free to say is a consequence of what Fr. Hans Küng calls the "unmasking" of a "spurious Marianism," an action that was initiated, according to him, to favor ecumenism with the Protestants:

"The Council accepted a large part of the topics presented by the reformers: ... "The reform of popular piety, ... a final end to the medieval system of indulgences – to which the Lutheran Reform is closely linked, the reform of the fasting prescripts. ... **It also unmasked the dangers of a spurious Marianism, lacking biblical immediacy and Christocentrism. Vatican II clearly limited it, above all, by not accepting a special Marian schema and not**

[70*] Bertolt Brecht, *Weihnachtsgedichte*, in *Gesammelte Werke* (Frankfort, 1967), vol. 3, pp. 122-125.
[71] Karl-Josef Kuschel, "Maria e a literatura," *Concilium,* 1983/8, pp. 124-125.

including this topic in the schema on the Church, a fact that in practice has already had immense, positive results. Nor did it arrive at any new Marian dogmas."[72]

§ 52   Leonardo Boff presents a "subversive" Mary, which would be the true interpretation of the spirit of the *Magnificat*. Referring to the Latin American countries, he affirms:

"It is from these depths that one can hear the clamor of the oppressed people, crying out for liberation. The poor Lazaruses of today beg and insistently beat on the door of the rich modern Epulons, asking for only one thing: to be men. They were considered not to be human, they implored to be men. The Churches understood their messianic mission to be in solidarity with those who have no voice and their spokesmen. ...

"In that sound-box, **we hear the prophetic hymn of the Virgin Mary with all its challenging, prophetic, subversive and liberating content.** Mary's ears are not just open to the message of heaven; she has one ear open to God and the other completely open to the clamors of her oppressed Jewish people."[73]

§ 53   A meek and non-subversive Mary would be the product of the "exploitation of the *macho* power." Invoking the authority of Paul VI, Boff defends this thesis:

"**There was an exploitation of Mariology in the sense that it was advantageous to the *macho* power: to present Mary only as a meek woman who says yes (*fiat*), who resigns herself to do the will of God, who hides herself in her domestic duties in modesty and anonymity**. What is forgotten is a whole other dimension recalled in the encyclical of Paul VI: 'Mary of Nazareth was far from being a timidly submissive woman or one of an abstract piety; on the contrary, she was a woman who did not hesitate to assert that God avenges the humble and the oppressed, and removes the powerful people of this world from their thrones (cf. Lk 1:51-53) (*Marialis cultus*, n. 37).'

"Mary emerges not only as a model for women, but for every male or female disciple of the Lord, including those involved in works of liberation and achievements of justice."[74]

---

[72] H. Küng, *Veracidade*, pp. 118-120.

[73] L. Boff, *O rosto materno de Deus*, pp. 199-200.

[74] *Ibid.*, pp. 45-46.

§ 54   Fr. Leo Alting von Geusau, a theologian from the Low Countries, founder of the Center of Dutch Documentation (DOC) and later of IDOC International, is a specialist on ecumenism. He objects to applying the titles of "co-redemptrix" and "mediatrix" to Our Lady:

"It is possible to attribute the title of co-redeemer and mediator to certain beings because of their participation in the unique redemption and mediation of Christ. **The danger exists, however, that** in this last case and above all **with regard to Mary, the terms 'co-redemptrix' and 'mediatrix' suggest a kind of parity [with Christ].**[75] In any case, **these words constitute a source of misunderstanding.** For this reason, perhaps it is better to translate them in a less ambiguous form and change the terminology ... to 'New Eve' and 'Mother of the faithful.'

"On this topic, **one should note that Pius XII and John XXIII consciously avoided the use of the word 'co-redemptrix,'** thus clearly expressing that the Magisterium is cautious in this respect. The reason for such reluctance probably comes from the objections raised by theologians about the term. Consequently, **it is very doubtful that the 'dogma' of 'Mary, mediatrix of all graces' can be promulgated in the near future.**"[76]

§ 55   To close this series of offenses to Our Lady and objections to her devotion, let the Reader consider a commentary on Fr. Teilhard de Chardin by Cardinal de Lubac:

"**Solidly well grounded, Fr. Teilhard de Chardin did not run the risk of falling into the deformations of a Marian cult whose roots,** more or less hidden, **would be independent of the Mystery of Christ.** A keen observer, **he feared not** the development [of Marian doctrine], but rather **a certain 'uncontrollable**

---

[75] The fears of Fr. Von Geusau were certainly not shared by St. Pius X, who, on the occasion of the 50th anniversary of the proclamation of the dogma of the Immaculate Conception, spoke about Our Lady as the mediatrix of all graces in his Encyclical *Ad diem illum* of February 2, 1904. He based himself on two Doctors of the Church: "If, therefore, Christ is the source ..., Mary is the aqueduct' (St. Bernard, *Sermo in Nativitate, Beatae Mariae Virginis: De acquaeductu*, n. 4, in PL 183, 440), or the neck that links the head to the body' (cf. St. Bernardino of Siena, *Quadragesimale de Evangelio eterno,* sermon 51, a. 3, c.1)" (DS 3370).

[76] Leo Alting von Geusau, *Alcune idée sulla mariologia attuale*, in V.A., *I grandi temi del Concilio* (Rome: Paoline, 1965), p. 500.

growth' of the 'Marian,' a danger to what he called 'the Christic ensemble.' Undoubtedly he was reluctant in the face of certain exuberant forms of Marian fervor."[77]

The diverse offenses presented in this Item 5 strike at the honor of the Mother of God and are quite expressive of the *animus injuriandi* that characterizes the spirit of the Council.

6. Affronts to Devotion to the Saints [78]

§ 56

We cannot fail to mention the Saints, members of the Church Triumphant. Through their intercession, graces fall constantly over the children of the Church Militant. These graces – of truth, goodness and beauty – give the faithful, even in this "valley of tears," a foretaste of the glory in which the Blessed dwell. In recognition of these graces, the Church Militant elevates to the Saints prayers and ceremonies of devotion. These solemnities also serve to make the earthly Church in some way a prefigure of the celestial Church.

Thus, in this *sacrum convivium* of graces and protections falling downward from Heaven, and homage and petitions soaring upward from earth, the sacrality of the Church increases, the atmosphere of religiosity becomes more intense, the spirit of Faith assumes more vigor, and the Catholic sense finds its natural atmosphere. To maintain the sacrality of the Church, therefore, it is very important to have devotion to the Saints.

These principles are well-known to the progressivists who, in their visceral anti-sacral *animus*, launch themselves against cults and devotions to the Blessed in Heaven.

§ 57

For Urs von Balthasar the teachings of traditional piety drawn from the lives of the Saints – for example, the mystical doctrine of the *Interior Castles* of St. Teresa of Avila, to which he makes a disdainful allusion – would only be the "rubbish," "discarded tinfoil" and "old, rusty sardine cans" left over from a picnic, whose true purpose would be to deviate the sinner away from Christ.

---

[77] Henri de Lubac, *L'éternel féminin – Etude sur un texte du Pére Teilhard de Chardin* (Paris: Aubier/Montaigne, 1968), pp. 211-212.

[78] Given the large quantity of texts against Our Lady, the Reader can well imagine that the conciliar progressivists did not spare the other Saints of the Church in their affronts. To prevent this present Volume from becoming too long, we will present only a few examples of the offenses to the Saints. Should it be necessary, much more could be written on the topic.

This is what von Balthasar says when, referring to the Heart of Jesus in his typical metaphorical style, he pictures ascension to love for Christ as climbing a savage mountain:

"What a blessed jungle your love is! No one will ever be able to subdue you ... I had fully equipped myself with maps and measuring devices [to find the mountain of the love of Christ]. I knew by heart the twelve degrees of humility, as well as the seven ramparts drawn around the castle of the soul. On many mountain peaks I saw little flags and signals set up, and on the side of that mountain red and blue markings told me that many climbers had already passed by there. **Certain camp sites were littered with 'instructions for the Holy Life,' as if with discarded tinfoil or empty cans of sardines.**

"As time went on, I lost the habit of paying any attention to this familiar rubbish. It only struck me that they became more and more sparse, **and they appeared to be old and rusty and on the verge of becoming a part of the wilderness itself, lost as they were in the thick forest and tangled branches.**[79]

"And all those who tried to exorcize you [jungle of the love for Christ] and destroy your charm seemed childish and silly. And I felt an irritation rising up in me against them [the traditional methods of piety], because they were seducing the souls of those who could have understood your magic, o savage place!"[80]

§ 58 Fr. Rahner proposes that the Saints would not be models of the supernatural life. Their mystical lives would be no more than natural psychological or para-normal experiences. Commenting on Rahner's views, Jesuit Harvey Egan observes:

"For terminological reasons, **Rahner would reserve the word 'mysticism' for only these pure and intense psychological experiences of our graced orientation to the God of love. The difference, however, between the mysticism of the saints and the less explicit form of ordinary Christian life is not a super-**

---

[79] The reader will have noticed the confused metaphors in the literary style of von Balthasar. In the same metaphor he imagines a tropical jungle and a bare mountain. 'Little flags,' 'red and blue markings' placed on the peaks and sides of the mountains can only be seen from afar on the bare mountains and not on the mountains covered with jungles.

[80] H. Urs von Balthasar, *Le Coeur du monde*, pp. 221-222.

natural difference. The difference belongs to the 'natural order of psychology and para-psychology'"[81]

§ 59   Fr. Maldonado singles out the prophets and missionary Saints of the Church as being "intolerant" and "fanatical":

"Certainly **Yaweh's monotheism**, as an expression of absolute perfection and purity, **presents itself** at times through the length of History **as a supreme form of intolerance and fanaticism**. But it seems that **it was the prophets who did the most to introduce similar attitudes into the Israelite religiosity. Both the prophets and missionaries ... were examples of an unparalleled intolerance or the worst kind of absolutism, which caused so many persecutions, religious wars, inquisitions, etc.**"[82]

§ 60   Addressing the "Church of love" and its relations with the hierarchical Church, von Balthasar unjustly accuses St. Peter of being "the greatest of sinners." Fr. O'Donnel, summarizing the book *Casta Meretrix*[83] of von Balthasar, writes:

"The Church of love obeys the hierarchical Church. The supremacy is conferred to **Peter** in John 21, but the one chosen to be the universal pastor **is himself the greatest of sinners**."[84]

§ 61   The French Dominican Yves Congar considers that St. Thomas Aquinas – without a shadow of a doubt one of the most brilliant stars in the firmament of Catholic apologetics – would have had an ecumenical mentality:

"**St. Thomas** died at age 49 (like St. Dominic). And he **spent his whole life looking for texts, constantly informing himself, in order to dialogue with the heretics of his time.**"[85]

In an interview with the Author of this Volume, Congar returned to the same idea about St. Thomas. He stated:

"During his life, **Thomas of Aquinas was incredibly curious about everything – in making dialogue with different cur-

---

[81] Harvey D. Egan, *What are they saying about mysticism?* (New York/Ramsey: Paulist Press, 1982), p. 101.

[82] L. Maldonado, *Genesis del Catolicismo popular – El inconsciente colectivo de un proceso histórico* (Madrid: Cristiandad, 1979), p. 122.

[83] This work will be analyzed in the Appendix I of this Volume.

[84] John O'Donnel, "Man and Woman as '*Imago Dei*' in the Theology of Hans Urs von Balthasar," *Clergy Review* (London) n. 78, 1983, p. 124.

[85] *Jean Puto interroge le Père Congar*, p. 40.

rents of thought. ... A dialogue of discussion! **But what a surprising openness to Arabs, Jews, the followers of Maimonides**, etc!"[86]

§ 62

In his turn, Hans Küng considers the great Doctor of the Church St. Robert Bellarmine a "victim of a restrictive non-biblical conception of the Church:"

"In the definition of what the Church is, **the New Testament prevents us from including at will too many elements and conditions. Otherwise we can become victim to a restrictive non-biblical conception of the Church, as it happened, for example, with Bellarmine, who, in his definition of the Church, inserted the condition of submission to the Papal Primacy, thus refusing to logically acknowledge even the Orthodox Churches as Churches.**"[87]

§ 63

Also worthy of note are the inexplicable criticisms that then Cardinal Ratzinger made about the venerated apostle of Vienna, St. Clement Marie Hofbauer:

"Thus we come to another man who was also an adversary of Sailer, as well as Wessenberg: **Clement Marie Hofbauer, the Bohemian apprentice to a baker who became a saint. Certainly this man in many aspects was vile, even somewhat reactionary.**"[88]

§ 64

Küng could not resist making an offensive criticism of the cult to the Saints in general, considering that it fostered the paganization of the Faith. He also shows himself favorable to the Protestant notion that Christ can be the only mediator between God and man. He says:

"It is obvious that **in all these 'revelations,' 'apparitions' and 'miracles,' Christ himself only rarely appears. He passes to a secondary plane to give way to the 'saints,'** oftentimes a founder of a new order or congregation ...

"**How many Catholics have there been** since the Council of Trent **who run after each new 'revelation' – often imagined or fraudulent! They read grand books about new promises and avidly listen to the most recent narratives of miracles**, but how many have never in their whole lives read the Sacred Scripture at least once from beginning to end?

---

[86] Yves Congar, interview granted to the Author in Paris, February 19, 1983.

[87] H. Kung, *A Igreja*, vol. 2, p. 45.

[88] J. Ratzinger, *Fé y futuro*, p. 74.

"How many Catholics in post-Tridentine times **have preferred all types of prayers, novenas and devotions to saints, rather than participation in the Eucharistic banquet! For those devotees, Christ in practice abdicated His function as sole mediator between God and all men!** Despite all their apostolic zeal – many times admirable – and all their efforts, **there is the imminent risk of a dangerous decentralization and paganization of the Christian faith, all the more dangerous in that it is often imperceptible** and well-intentioned."[89]

*

§ 65   Certainly it is not misplaced to insert here some offenses made against the practice of indulgences and devotions that carry special blessings for the Catholic faithful. Paul VI asked the *Sacra Penitenciaria*[90] to present a document to reform the indulgences at the Council. Commenting on that document, Fr. René Laurentin attacks indulgences as an encouragement to "fetishism":

"The document joins in the dispute about special privileges granted to religious orders, confraternities and associations. It made the indulgences uniform and suppressed the monopoly of 'indulgenced objects.' It reduced the use of those objects and established that they – scapulars, medals, belts, cords, Crusader rosaries or St. Brigid beads – should be considered as no more than blessed objects and link the indulgences only to the value of the private initiative of the faithful who venerate, carry or use such objects. It did away with 'indulgenced objects' as such in order to give more value to personal acts of the faithful.

"It abolished the 'objects blessed by the Pope or by a Bishop.' Further, no faculty or privilege was mentioned to distinguish one Bishop from another on these grounds, including the Major Penitentiary and the Pope himself (and this last point seems to have been

---

[89] H. Küng, *A Igreja*, vol. 1, pp. 281-282.

[90] The Apostolic Penitentiary is the organ of the Holy See with the competence to distribute indulgences and privileges. Other duties of this Roman Dicastery included regulating when Bishops can deal with heretics; issuing norms for Mass stipends, fasting and abstinence, and restitution for confiscated Church property. It is also the final appeals court for decisions of the Roman Rota in cases of marriage and the legitimation of children and resolves excommunications regarding the election of the Pope and absolution for cases of conscience.

desired by Paul VI in person). **In summary, the document reacted to a formalism that very easily slips into fetishism** and to powerful material interests."[91]

Further on, he describes indulgences as a pastoral and theological problem that is finally being resolved:

"In conclusion, what happened at the Council with regard to indulgences was not surprising. By thus focusing the conciliar reflection on this question – which for many years was surrounded by a conspiracy of silence – a pastoral and theological problem inevitably came to light.

"It was a pastoral problem because, as Cardinal König showed ... **there is,** on one hand, **a category of Christians who frequently earn indulgences in a too formalist if not superstitious way** and, on the other hand, enlightened Christians who ignore or despise them."[92]

*

This Chapter III thus offers the Reader a sample of the *animus injuriandi* of various theologians who attack the sacrality of the Church.

Furthermore, as we saw, this de-sacralization seems to be fully coherent with the ideal of the "poor Church" desired by John XXIII and Paul VI and adopted by Vatican II.

*   *   *

---

[91] R. Laurentin, *Bilan de la quatrième session*, pp. 144-145.
[92] *Ibid.*, pp. 150-151.

Chapter IV

THE CHURCH CONSIDERED NOT JUST HOLY, BUT ALSO A PROSTITUTE AND A SINNER [1]

§ 1

Running parallel to the History of the Catholic Church, a river flows whose waters are currents of thought and movements that deny her sanctity.[2] Such waters have turned pitch black from the hues of the various heresies that have flowed into them. The Catholic Church, these heresies claim, sinned insofar as she became the owner of lands and material properties – sacred buildings, educational institutions, hospitals, objects of worship, art, piety and so on – and thus became powerful. They clearly advocate a "miserablist" Church which would supposedly better reflect the evangelical ideals.

Accusing the Catholic Church of sin, they hurl insults at her, comparing her to a prostitute who sold her honor for riches. Hence in some sects we find that they associate the Church with indecorous figures that easily surpass the limits of decency, showing how the hatred of the heretics devised her in order to please the wretched vulgarity of the crowds they attract. There are other sects, however, that claim to be cultured and scholarly. They jumble together passages of Ezekiel, Isaiah and the Apocalypse that refer to prostitutes in attempts to find a foundation for their insults through a typically impassioned exegesis bereft of intellectual merit.

It is not surprising that heretics think and say such things. As the Latin maxim says, "*Ossa decent fortes magnis canibus*" [Strong bones for big dogs].

§ 2

Progressivists have adopted this twofold accusation: *first,* that the Church is a sinner because of her properties and power, and *second*, that this supposed sin is tantamount to prostitution. But they give some twists to this accusation, which at times increase the gravity of

---

[1] Two cumulative aspects should be distinguished in this topic: *first,* the offense that it represents to the honor of the Catholic Church, which we will examine here, and *second,* the ecclesiological discussion about the possible sinfulness of the Church, which will be studied in the Appendix I of this Volume and in Vol. XI, *Ecclesia*, Chap. IV.

[2] To avoid fastidious repetition of the same sources, the basis for this statement and other assertions presented in this Chapter without accompanying proofs can be found in the Appendix I of this Volume and in Vol. XI, *Ecclesia*, Chap. IV.

the offense, and at other times prevent an immediate identification with heretics of the past. Such twists include the following:

> *First*, progressivists point to not only the Church's material power,[3] but also her juridical and institutional power as sinful. This alleged sin – which they call Pharisaism – consists of making the observance of laws and the juridical system ends in themselves.[4] Another sin would be to remain with the doctrinal forms of the past, which they call the "sin of the Synagogue," or the absolutization of outdated forms.[5] Yet another sin for which the Church should do penance would be exercising her militant character by combating error, evil and those who are evil.[6] Therefore, today's progressivists attribute to the Church a much broader range of sins than the heretics who preceded them.

---

[3] Cf. Y. Congar, *Pour une Église servante et pauvre*, pp. 107-123; see also Chap. III and the Appendix I in this Volume.

[4] Cf. Y. Congar, *Vraie et fausse Reforme dans l'Eglise* (Paris: Ed. du Cerf, 1950), pp. 152-154,155-170. In this Volume see Chap. V.

[5] Cf. *ibid.*, pp. 152-154.,170-195. In this Volume see Chap. VI.

[6] a. At the end of the fourth and last conciliar session on December 4, 1965, Paul VI addressed the non-Catholic observers during a liturgical ceremony in the Basilica of St. Paul Outside-the-Walls. He asked pardon for the "non-Christian" conduct the Church supposedly exercised in the past:

"Far from raising a sentiment of envy in us, this [the 'Christian treasures of high value' that belong to the schismatic confessions] augments the sense of fraternity in us and the desire to reestablish the perfect communion desired by Christ. And it leads us to discover still other positive consequences on the pathway to peace: **We have recognized certain faults and certain common sentiments that were not good. For these we have already asked pardon of God and of you. We have discovered their non-Christian roots, and, on our part, we have proposed transforming them into sentiments worthy of the school of Christ: We renounce the offensive polemic based on preconceptions, and we no longer are concerned about a vain prestige.**

"Instead we seek to keep in mind the exhortations repeated by the Apostle upon whose tomb we find ourselves this evening: 'I fear that there may be among you quarreling, jealousy, outbursts of anger, factions, slander, gossip, arrogance and disorder' (2 Cor 12:20). We want to reinstate relations that are human, serene, benevolent and confident" (Allocution at the ecumenical ceremony at St. Paul Outside-the-Walls of December 4, 1965, in B. Kloppenburg, *Concílio Vaticano II*, vol. 5, p. 484).

b. Three days later on the vespers of the closing of the Council, Paul VI published the Brief *Ambulate in dilectione*, directed to the Greek Schis-

§ 4   *Second*, like certain heretics, they attribute sinfulness not only to churchmen but to the very essence of the divine institution.[7]

§ 5   *Third*, in an attempt to escape the imputation of being heretics, progressivists admit the sanctity of the Church. But they also affirm – in dialectic opposition – her supposed sinfulness. They say either that the Church is holy and sinful at the same time or, in a more radical fashion, that she is both chaste and a prostitute. They fail to explain how this contradiction in terms would be possible. They simply present the contradiction in a dialectical form, perhaps in the hope that by some prestidigitation worked by Hegelian dynamism, the thesis and antithesis will be transformed into a new synthesis.

The novelty of characterizing the Church as holy and sinful, as chaste and a prostitute, is not in presenting her as holy and chaste,

---

matics with the intent to lift the excommunication that, since the 11th century, fell over the followers of Focius and Cerularius, even though they had manifested not the least repentance for their errors. The text was read by Cardinal Bea, president of the Secretariat for the Union of Christians. Paul VI was present on the dais at the reading; at his left was Meliton, the schismatic metropolitan of Heliopolis and head of the delegation sent by Athenagoras to the Council.

We present here two significant paragraphs from that papal Brief:

"Once again we are reminded of the sad events which, in the wake of many dissensions, led to strife between the Churches of Rome and Constantinople in 1054. ... Things reached such a point that the Papal legates pronounced a sentence of excommunication against Michael Cerularius, Patriarch of Constantinople, and two other churchmen. ...**But now that times and minds have changed, we are very happy indeed to find that our venerable brother Athenagoras I, patriarch of Constantinople, together with his synod, are united with us in desiring that we be joined by charity**, 'the pleasant and healthy bond of minds.' ...

"And so, being anxious to make further progress along a road of brotherly love that leads to perfect unity, and to remove obstacles and shackles, in the presence of the Bishops gathered together in the Second Ecumenical Vatican Council, **we declare that we greatly regret the words and deeds that were said and enacted at that time and that cannot meet with our approval. Furthermore, we wish to erase from the memory of the Church and remove from its midst the sentence of excommunication then pronounced, and to have it buried in oblivion**" (Brief *Ambulate in dilectione* of December 7, 1965, *in ibid.* p. 489).

On the nullity of this lifting of this excommunication see Vol. V, *Animus Delendi II*, Introduction Note 22b.

[7] Cf. Karl Rahner, *La Chiesa peccatrice nei decreti del Vaticano II* (Rome: Paoline, 1968), pp. 452, 465, 477. See also Item 2 of this Chapter.

since these were always considered integral aspects of the Catholic Church. The novelty is the introduction of the supposed aspects of sinfulness and prostitution. One can see, therefore, that the use of this dialectic opposition is a trick to assert sinfulness in the very definition of the Church. It is a new presentation whose ultimate goal is to re-establish the old insults and errors of the heretics.

§ 6   *Fourth*, like the heretics, progressivists went to the Old and New Testaments to find references to prostitutes or the symbol of prostitution in order to express the apostasy of the Jews, and they then applied them to the Holy Catholic Church. In the Old Testament they especially like to exploit the marriage of the Prophet Osee with a prostitute, as well as excerpts from Ezekiel, Isaiah and Jeremias. The episodes of Tamar and Rahab also serve their purposes.

In the New Testament they emphasize the episodes of the adulterous woman whom Our Lord saved from being stoned, the repentant Mary Magdalene, and the prostitute of the Apocalypse, also symbolized by Babylon. In this regard, the similarity of progressivists to heretics could not be greater. But the former seem to surpass the latter in their obsession with erotic themes, giving them a central place in the life and history of the Church.

§ 7   *Fifth*, the progressivists embarked on a whole exegesis of Patristics on the aforementioned biblical texts. Based on this study, they compose and decompose texts at will with the aim of giving respectability to their thesis of a Church that is holy and sinful, chaste and a prostitute.[8]

From this we can see that the progressivist onslaught to have the Catholic Church presented as sinful and a prostitute is a broad-ranging assault. To our knowledge it is the most organized and articulated effort ever undertaken in History on this topic, even when compared to the heresies of the past.

Having set out this general overview, let us go on to look at some texts that offend the honor of the Catholic Church.

---

[8] The following explanation of Von Balthasar is an expressive example of this progressivist "exegesis" which "breaks down" the thinking of the Fathers and Doctors of the Church in order to construct a new ensemble – different from the intention of the Church Fathers – that serves their purposes. He states:

"What has been said so far teaches us to have a critical view of theological tradition from the end of the first century up to our days, without rejecting its totality. What we must do is not only order its affirmations on a scale of values, but break them down in order to recompose them in a new way" (H. U. von Balthasar, *Mysterium Paschale*, in *Mysterium salutis*, vol. III/6, p. 107).

1. The Note of Prostitution Supposedly Present in the Essence of the Church

§ 8

In the 1950s Fr. Hans Urs von Balthasar published the work *Casta Meretrix*, in which he tried to prove that the blasphemous affront made by Luther, Zwingli and Hus – who called the Catholic Church a prostitute – would be objective. For this perfidious purpose, he used many sophistic arguments and deceitful interpretations. Here we present the fundamental passage from his book, in which he clearly affirms that the figure of the prostitute defines the Catholic Church:

"The figure of the prostitute [*forma meretricis*] ... is so appropriate to the Church that it ... defines the Church of the New Covenant in her most splendid mystery of salvation. The departure of the Synagogue from the Holy Land to be among pagans was an infidelity of Jerusalem, the 'opening of her legs in every road of the world.'

"But this same movement, which takes her to all peoples, is the mission of the Church. She must unite and merge herself with all peoples, and **this new apostolic form of union cannot be avoided."** [9]

For a Catholic priest to express himself with such indecency regarding the Holy Church is truly shocking! His statement is such an affront to the Catholic Church, that one could say that it surpasses even the *animus injuriandi* of the past heretics.

§ 9

In his writings on the Apocalypse of St. John, the heresiarch Martin Luther constantly employed the expression *"rote Hure von Babylon"* (the red whore of Babylon) to insult the Catholic Church.[10] In so doing, he was but repeating similar offenses flung by heretics who preceded him and paved the way for his revolt. For example, the 12th century Waldensians used to say *"Romanam Ecclesiam esse meretricem Babylon, et omnes ei obedientes damnari"* (The Roman Church is the prostitute of Babylon, and all who obey her are damned).[11] In the 14th century, the Fraticelli sect contended that *"quod*

---

[9] H. U. von Balthasar, *Casta Meretrix*, p. 267.

[10] Cf. Martin Luther, *Ausgewählte Schriften*, ed. by Karin Bornkamm and Gerhard Ebeling (Frankfort: Insel Verlag), vol. 3, p. 63; Hellmut Diwald, *Luther - Eine Biographie*, (Bergisch Gladach: Gustav Lübbe Verlag, 1982), p. 155.

[11] Stephane of Bourbon, *Tractatus de haeresi*, col. 1779, *in* H. U. von Balthasar, *Casta Meretrix*, p. 269.

Ecclesia Romana facta est meretrix et ad hoc ut possit melius fornicare, transivit ultra montes" (The Roman Church has become a prostitute and, in order to better fornicate, traveled beyond the mountains – that is, beyond the Alps – to Rome).[12]

§ 10   In these blasphemies of past heretics, there does not seem to be a special concern to define the Church as a prostitute in her essence. But von Balthasar – whom John Paul II made a Cardinal in 1988 – does precisely that...

As if this were not enough, the author goes on to claim that on the Cross Our Lord fulfilled the "prostitution" of the Old Testament, which he sees as synthesizing the relations of the Chosen People with God. He reaffirms, once again, that the "new Daughter of Sion," that is, the Church, would also be a prostitute.

He pretends that since "prostitution" in the Old Testament is the "shame" of God and the Cross is the "shame" of Our Lord, then the Church in her relations with Him "sinks into the madness of the Cross" and assumes the role of prostitute in the New Testament... Although his text is subtle and not perfectly clear, the offenses to the Holy Church, Our Lord and God the Father are blatant. Von Balthasar says:

"The Old Testament mystery of the prostitute[13] **is superseded by that of the cross, which takes every mystery to its end and fulfillment – just as the shame of the daughter of Sion in the Old Testament** (especially in Osee) **properly fell on the betrayed God-Husband (like *Dieu cocu*).**[14] Also, as in Ezekiel

---

[12] Statement of the *Fraticelli* offensive to the Church, *in* Felix Vernet, entry *Fraticelles*, in DTC., vol. 6, col. 780.

[13] Commenting on the relations between God and the Chosen People, the author explains his central idea of the Old Testament as "mystery of the prostitute": "A new dimension is opened with the prophets, especially Osee. By ordering him to seek out a prostitute, marry her and beget children of the prostitution upon whom the shame of their mother would fall, God wants to give an unheard-of meaning to his relations with the people: **What exists is no longer the juridical relations of an earthly wife with her celestial Lord, but the loving relationship of a God-Husband humiliated by the betrayal of a woman.** In His ire, God discovers His 'shame,' but, **He ends by marrying the prostitute, justifying her and changing the name of her children, thus revealing the 'frailty' of his love"** (H. U. von Balthasar, *Casta Meretrix*, p. 195).

[14] We ask the Reader to excuse the low level into which our analysis must descend in order to understand progressivist blasphemies. Our

when **Sion** is invited a last time to profoundly repent of its shameful sin, it then **participates in some way in the ignominy of God, which was definitively assumed and mysteriously borne on the cross by the Church** and by redeemed humanity. We see this also in how the Church, at depth, can no longer consider her own ignominy except in her crucified Lord and insomuch as the Lord ... permits her to see it.

"**In its deepest and most characteristic core, the prostitution of the new Daughter of Sion sinks into the simple 'madness of the Cross.'** ... Jerusalem besieged by the kings of the world, stripped by them of her garments and ornaments, exposed to mockery, is finally torn to pieces and cast into the fire: in the end this Jerusalem is found nowhere but on the cross. This is the way that Christians are exhorted to take upon themselves the dishonor of Jesus and to abandon the old Jerusalem."[15]

§ *11*　Von Balthasar pretends that this notion of a prostitute as a symbol of the Church is an underlying concept in Origen's writings. **He affirms that Origen admits "the idea of the fundamental identity between the celestial bride 'without stain or** blemish' (Eph 5:27) **and the decadent sinner** who weeps at the rivers of Babylon."

He continues: "**A sinner, she awaits the Savior since the beginning of History**, and when He appears, she prostrates herself to anoint his feet. **Her penitence earns her the admirable destiny of Rahab the sinner**, because, writes Origin, 'No one can be deceived in this regard: Outside Rahab's house, that is to say, outside of the Church, there is no salvation.' She is the only way that leads to heaven. **But would she already here [on earth] be totally pure and spiritual, like the Gnostics or Montanists would like? Origin ... knows fully well that sin is always in the interior of the Church ... Because the sin of just one member stains the whole body and, therefore, Christ himself.**"[16]

---

study is made with the sole aim of defending the honor of God and the Church. The French term *cocu*, which von Balthasar unceremoniously uses referring to God in his relations with the Church, translates to 'the cuckolded God,' meaning a man betrayed by an unfaithful wife (Cf. M. Bescherelle, *Dictionnaire National*, Paris: Garnier-Frères, 1871, vol. 1, entry *cocu*). That a theologian praised by John Paul II and Benedict XVI as a model for priests (cf. Chap. I, § 3, Notes 4-7) should refer to God in this undignified way is undoubtedly an expression of the spirit of the Council and the *animus injuriandi* of Progressivism.

[15] H. U. von Balthasar, *Casta Meretrix*, pp. 204-205.

[16] H. U. von Balthasar, *Parole et mystère chez Origine* (Paris: Cerf 1957), pp. 82-83.

§ 12

In another work, von Balthasar's central thesis regarding the Old and New Testaments appears again: God behaves like the lover of a prostitute-wife, who represents the Chosen People in the Old Testament and the Church in the New. Let the Reader gauge the gravity of this offense:

"The existential initiation to this whole existence is the Old Testament, the history of the relations between Israel and a God who not only performs 'great deeds' from on high on behalf of His Chosen People, thus revealing himself as the true **God** in the face of the impotent gods of other peoples, but **takes His historic alliance with them [the Israelite people] seriously and acts like a deceived and humiliated lover when faced with the perjuries of His beloved wife, who behaves like a prostitute** (Ez 16:23). As the Lord, He must threaten her with punishment and judgment; but **as her lover, He cannot help but show, even in His extreme abjection, His 'frailty of love.'** For He does not abandon His wayward wife, but seeks her out to make a New Covenant with her, promising her an eternal reconciliation."[17]

It is difficult to imagine a broader usage of the figure of a prostitute. In the Old Testament, it would supposedly express the archetype of God's relations with His Chosen People – marriage with a prostitute. In the New, it would allegedly reflect the very essence of the Church.

The boldness of von Balthasar's insults would make the heretics themselves blush...

§ 13

Leonardo Boff also employed the expression *casta meretrix* in his controversial book *Church: Charisma and Power*, prompting Cardinal Ratzinger to silence him in 1985 for one year with a tenuous and ambiguous censure.[18]

In an interview with the German magazine *Der Spiegel,* Boff speaks about the meeting he had with Ratzinger. Let us stress that this meeting, during which Cardinal Ratzinger "severely" censured Fr. Boff, is the only face-to-face encounter between the two. Boff reports the meeting.

"*Der Spiegel*: So was anything said about the process?

---

[17] H. U. von Balthasar, *De l'Intégration - Aspects d'une théologie de l'Histoire* (Bruges: Desclée de Brouwer, 1970), p. 79.

[18] On the mildness of this censure, see Vol. V, *Animus Delendi II*, Introduction, Note 9 o-p; In this Volume II, Introduction § 19, Note 10; Vol. I, *In the Murky Waters of Vatican II*, Chap. I, Note 12; Vol. IV, *Animus Delendi I*, Introduction §§ 26-27, Note 11.

"Boff: Yes. Ratzinger said, 'You do not need to read your report to the end. I consider all the pages as having been read. Choose a few important points.' So, **I took** two very controversial points: the tension between the Church of Rome and other Christian churches and **the question of the Church as *casta meretrix*, a chaste prostitute, a topic I dealt with in my book.**

"*Der Spiegel*: **What do you mean by that?**

"Boff: **The image is not mine. It is often used to describe the duplicity of the Church: During the day she lives chastely and at night she dedicates herself to prostitution. Christ attempts to purify her, perhaps through the theology of liberation. Ratzinger commented: 'Naturally, this can also be very pharisaic to regard others in this way.'** I answered: 'I do not exclude myself from this criticism.'"[19]

§ 14   The only criticism reported by Boff, therefore, is that the then Prefect of the Sacred Congregation for the Doctrine of the Faith ignored his accusation of the Church as *casta meretix* and remarked on the possible "pharisaism" of Boff in imagining himself and Liberation Theology as being purer than the other members of the Church. It is as if Cardinal Ratzinger said, "You are being too proud."

Someone could contend that the expression *casta meretrix* was also included in the Cardinal's criticism. If in fact he considered that there were doctrinal errors and offenses in the expression *casta meretrix* as employed by Fr. Boff, we can only wonder why he never criticized Cardinals von Balthasar and de Lubac for their similar use of the term.[20] Why was no censure made of these two theologians, who – along with Cardinal Ratzinger himself and John Paul II – constituted a homogeneous group of thought and action that provided the intellectual and political underpinning of the *Communion and Liberation* movement?[21]

---

[19] Interview granted to B. Kraatz and M. Müller under the title "Die Kirche ist eine keusche Hure," *Der Spiegel*, September 17, 1964, pp. 149-151.
[20] Other excerpts from the works of de Lubac can be found in Item 3 below.
[21] *Comunione e Liberazione* (Communion and Liberation - CL) was established between 1968 and 1969 by the Milanese priest Luigi Giussani as a lay movement in line with the thinking of Vatican II. By a pontifical decree of February 11, 1982, the *Fraternity of Communion and Liberation* was officially recognized by the Church (cf. Fausto Perrenchio,

Since von Balthasar often uses the expression *casta mere-trix* and de Lubac endorses it, why did Ratzinger ignore their affronts to the honor of the Church? Or did Cardinal Ratzinger only caution Fr. Boff to be prudent and avoid using the expression at that time? If so, did he agree with that concept but find it inadvisable to use it at that moment? There are no clear answers to these questions.

In conclusion, we can only ask: What could be a greater affront to the honor of the Holy Catholic Church than the infamous affirmation that in her very essence she would be a prostitute?

2. Sin Would Be Present in the Essence of the Church

§ 15

In his work, *The Sinner Church in the Decrees of Vatican II*, Karl Rahner refers to sinfulness as being part of the essence of the Church. This is highly offensive to the sanctity of the Spouse of Christ – and substantially no different from the statements made by von Balthasar that we analyzed in Item 1.

In this first excerpt Rahner affirms that the "sinful element" of the Church's members enters her very essence:

"Allusion is frequently made to the sinful element from which the Church originated [that is to say, the Gentiles] ... **The**

Communione e Liberazione, in Agostino Favale ed., *Movimenti ecclesiali contemporanei*, Rome: LAS 1982, p. 378).

Cardinal Ratzinger, admired by CL members, placed great hopes in the organization (cf. *Rapporto sulla Fede – Vittorio Messori a colloquio com Joseph Ratzinger*, Milan: Paoline, 1985, p. 41). The same can be said of Hans Urs von Balthasar, who co-authored with Msgr. L. Giussani a work on the spirituality of the lay movement titled *L'impegno del cristiano nel mundo - Già e non ancora*. It was Cardinal Ratzinger who celebrated the funeral Mass of its founder Msgr. Giussani in Milan on February 24, 2005, and gave the homily.

However, CL received its greatest support from John Paul II, with whom the movement enjoyed "most cordial" relations since the beginning of the 1970s. *"Noi ciellini* [we members of CL]..."*, the Pope is supposed to have once said, implying that he considered himself one of the CL. Paul VI also encouraged the movement (Cf. "Perché affannarsi tanto? E cosí semplice obblidire al Papa," *Jesus*, Milan, June 1985, p. 69).

Members of Communion and Liberation are in charge of important activities such as the Istra Institute and the Jaca Book publishing house, both based in Milan. They also directly or indirectly run the magazines *Communio* and *CSEO, 30 Giorni,* and *Traces,* the movement's monthly magazine. Those publications count on the collaboration of numerous Prelates and highly placed Vatican personages.

question falls on the men who form and officially represent the Church and, therefore, play a profound part in the very essence of the Church."[22]

The thesis that the Church is a sinner in her essence reappears in the same work:

"She **[the Church] would** not really **be** the People of God, but **merely an abstract entity with an almost mythological character, if one were to suppose that the sinfulness of her members did not involve herself as well.**"[23]

Commenting on *Lumen gentium*, in which he played an important role, Rahner says:

"In fact, **the Constitution understands *in practice* that the Church is a sinful Church, and not just that sinners ... exist in her.** It avoids the expression 'Sinful Church,' but **the substantial reality, the fact that the Church ultimately shares the guilt for the sins of her members, comes through quite clearly.**"[24]

Thus, according to Rahner's reliable testimony, Vatican II would have endorsed this offense made to the holiness of the Church.

§ 16

Cardinal Yves Congar affirms that evil is linked to the very essence of the Church. Presenting his thesis, the French Dominican appeals to Hans Küng for support:

"From this historicity of the Church and those concrete realities that transcend her history comes a mixture of the pure and impure, the luminous and the uncertain, the evangelical and the 'carnal.' **We can affirm with Hans Küng that the 'evil essence' is mixed into the good essence of the Church.** There is nothing more traditional than the theme of the temptations and vices of the Church, of her reforms, of her historical faults, of the weaknesses that mar her

---

[22] K. Rahner, *La Chiesa peccatrice nei decreti del Concilio Vaticano II*, p. 452.
Not to betray the context, we add here that Rahner contradicts himself on the same page, affirming, "This [sin] regards the men of the Church (and, therefore, not properly the Church as such) since one can say that the immaculate purity of the Church ... is never placed in doubt."
We omitted it because the excerpt quoted in our text corresponds to others that follow it which affirm the opposite. Why Rahner included this prudential nuanced disclaimer here, when this is not what he normally defends, is a question open to speculation.

[23] *Ibid.*, p. 477.

[24] *Ibid.*, p. 465.

life. It is the fatal consequence of her being a society constituted by men and existing in its historicity." [25]

§ 17   Fr. Joseph Ratzinger also seems to deny the sanctity of the Church and identify her essence with the sinner. He writes:

"One must not distinguish too carefully between 'the Church' and 'the men in the Church.' **The immaculate character of the Church, which can thus be abstractly distinguished, does not have any real historical meaning.** The Church lives in men – in this time and in this world. She lives in a truly human way, notwithstanding the divine mystery she contains in herself. Also, **the institution as such bears the weight of humanity; the institution is affected – from the human point of view – by her difficult role of being the rock of scandal."** [26]

§ 18   Later, as Cardinal Prefect of the Congregation for the Doctrine of the Faith, Ratzinger further explains his thinking, making it clear that he considers that the note of sin exists in the essence of the Church. He states:

"The idea of the Body of Christ developed in the Catholic Church with the meaning that the Church presents herself as 'the Christ who continues to live on earth.' She is described as the Incarnation of the Son that will continue until the end of time. This raised the opposition of the Protestants, who saw this as an insupportable identification of the Church with Christ, an identification in which the Church, so to speak, would adore herself and consider herself to be infallible.

"Some Catholic thinkers, without reaching this point, also began to conclude that this formula would attribute a definitive character to every ministerial word and action of the Church, which would make any critique of her seem an attack on Christ himself, thus forgetting her human element. For this reason, it is necessary for the difference between Christ and the Church to become clearly manifest, that is to say, that **the Church is not identical to Christ but is different from Him. She is the Church of sinners, which incessantly needs to purify and renew herself. Thus, the idea of 'reform'** – which could not develop easily in the notion of the Body of Christ – **became a decisive element of the concept of People of God."** [27]

---

[25] Y. Congar, *Église Catholique et France moderne*, pp. 16-17.

[26] Joseph Ratzinger, *Il nuovo popolo di Dio* (Brescia: Queriniana, 1971), p. 282, *apud* José Gonzalez Ruiz, "Lettera aperta al Cardinal Ratzinger," *Adista*, January 19-21, 1987, p. 11.

[27] J. Ratzinger, "La eclesiología del Vaticano," *Iglesia-Mundo* (Madrid), October 1986, p. 19.

§ 19 Fr. André Liége describes the "sin of the Church" in an offensive way, as the Reader will see. Not insignificant is his duplicitous spirit when, in the very act of accusing the Church and listing her "sins," he declares that he does not want to accuse or denounce... These are his words:

"But what is this sin [of the Church]? Without preparing a libel for a public accusation, it is easy to highlight its more frequent expressions: the discrepancy between her words and actions; **the immunity of her supposedly divine behavior; her lack of courage to speak out against disorders in society; her misuse of ceremonies and words that have become routine and insignificant**; her pretension to have a power without function; her closing off into an ecclesiastical universe; her distrust of the spirit of research; **her complicity with the forces of wealth and power of the world; the laziness of her faith; her lack of pastoral imagination; her mediocre expressions of religious practice**; her distrust of human liberty; **her lack of sincerity in extra-ecclesial encounters and dialogue; her fear of internal contestation**... Without the intention to denounce, it would not be difficult to continue this woeful list."[28]

§ 20 A violent critique against the "sin" of the Church is also found in the Jesuit organ, *La Civiltà Cattolica*. The accusations are placed on the lips of the average Catholic of the 1960s. However, the magazine places no restrictions on the accusations and gives its immediate endorsement. The editorial makes numerous offenses:

"For this reason, the Church today – affirms the Catholic of the 1960s and 1970s – should place herself in their school [of the 'others' who were previously despised by the Church: non-Catholics, non-Christians, the lay world] and review her whole past, which is far from being 'glorious.' This is because even though in the first three centuries the Church may have lived according to the ideal of the Gospel, **in all the others she strayed far from the purity of the evangelical message. Thus, in the formulation of dogmas and in theology, she was inspired more by Greek philosophy than by Sacred Scripture. In legislation, she came to be guided more by Roman Law and medieval decretalism than by the Gospel.** In her relations with the world, she behaved more as an heir of Constantine than as the 'sign' of the Son of man, who lived poor and died on the Cross.

---

[28] André Liégé, "A Igreja diante de seu pecado," in V. A., *A Igreja do futuro*, pp. 120-121.

"The Church sinned, falling into rationalism, juridicalism and authoritarianism so that, instead of fostering charismas, she suffocated them. Instead of being the place of liberty, she was the place of law and constraint. Instead of proclaiming the word of God and its mystery, she proclaimed human words, a theology made by man by means of his poor reason. Above all, the Church sinned by 'constantinizing herself,' that is by becoming an enormous structure of power – both political and ecclesiastical – with everything 'demonic' that 'power' naturally contains, since by its nature power is oppressive, tending to make man a slave, subjecting him to a sub-human or, at best, an infantile condition.

"Today, the Church should assume a position of penance before these sins, asking pardon of God and of men, in particular, of the 'poor,' whom she principally offended because she was sent to announce the Good News to them, and she failed to do so!"[29]

The Church is a sinner! These echoes of the sinister affronts of Luther were heard again at Vatican II and are repeated today by significant representatives of the Church.

3. 'A Holy and Sinning Church,' a Mitigated Version of the 'Chaste Prostitute'

§ 21

Today we often hear terms like "Church of saints and sinners," "Church of the elect and sinners," the "holy and sinning Church," *Ecclesia sancta et simul semper purificanda* (a holy Church constantly being purified). When one encounters such contradictory expressions without knowing what we have been presenting in this Chapter, it is normal to become perplexed. In any case, as one analyzes them, the suspicion grows that those who employ such expressions are trying to avoid some bolder formula that they dare not put in writing.

Based on the analysis previously presented, we can affirm that the underlying thinking behind those various expressions is the one that links together the virgin and the prostitute that would exist in a Church living in constant dialectical antagonism. The formula they are avoiding, therefore, is that of *casta meretrix*.

§ 22

This is confirmed by Cardinal de Lubac, once under suspicion of heresy by the Holy Office and today lauded as a great and "moderate" theologian. Here are some excerpts from his *Catholicism*, a book that was condemned before the Council:[30]

---

[29] Editorial "Dal 'trionfalismo' al 'complesso d'inferiorità," *La Civiltà Cattolica,* October 3, 1970, p. 4.

[30] De Lubac himself admits this in an interview with the Italian monthly *30 Giorni,* July 1985, p. 11. See Introduction Note 15c.

"**The single image of the bride evokes two opposed visions**, both founded on Scriptures and both frequently portrayed: **on one hand, the wretched being on whom the Word took pity and whom he came to save from prostitution by His incarnation; on the other hand, the new Jerusalem**, the 'bride of the Lamb,' who came down from heaven from God: the daughter of strangers or the daughter of the King. **On one hand, we have an assembly of sinners**, a mixed herd, wheat gathered with the straw, a field with chaff growing in it: *corpus Christi mixtum*, the ark that shelters both pure and impure animals. **On the other hand, we have an immaculate virgin**, mother of saints, born on Calvary from the pierced side of Jesus, **or else from the very Assembly that she has made holy:** *Ecclesia in sanctis, Virgo mater.*"[31]

Further on, de Lubac says: "**The foreign women, the slaves, the sinners present a particularly eloquent picture of the face of** *Ecclesia ex gentibus* [Church of the Gentiles]. There is Jael, the pagan woman from whose hands victory came [32]... **There is Rahab ... Finally, there is the prostitute whom the prophet Osee was ordered to marry. ... This last type of symbol,** one of the most constantly elaborated, **is at the same time one of the most important.**"[33]

De Lubac concludes by reaffirming the notion that both the adulterous women and the upright ones are symbols of the Church:

"**Mary Magdalene,** the Samaritan and **the woman taken in adultery are, in their conversion** and each in their own way, **the** *Ecclesia ex gentibus* ... **whereas the mother-in-law of Simon Peter** [who was an upright woman] **symbolizes,** in her cure, **the** *Ecclesia ex circumcision* [Church of the Circumcision]"[34]

John Paul II endorses the same thesis in the excerpt below:
§ 23   "**The Church is certainly holy,** as we profess in the Creed; **nonetheless, she is also a sinner,** not as the body of Christ, but **as a community made up of sinning men.**"[35]

---

[31] Henri de Lubac, *Catholicisme – Les aspects sociaux du dogme,* Paris: Cerf, 1968, pp. 43-44.

[32] Jael called into her tent the Canaanite general, whose king had attacked the Hebrews, hid him and fed him after he fell asleep she killed him by driving a tent peg through the side of his head (Cf. Judges 4:17-22).

[33] H. de Lubac, *Catholicisme*, pp. 154-155.

[34] *Ibid.*, 162-163.

[35] John Paul II, "Riflessioni sul grand giubileo dell'anno duemila," n. 7 , in "La nave di Pietro fa rotta verso il duemila," *Adista*, May 28, 1994, p. 7. Regarding the insufficiency of the argument in the cited excerpt, see the Appendix I §§ 104-115 of this Volume.

§ 24 Although avoiding an in-depth explanation, Fr. Congar also speaks of a saintly and sinning Church, calling it an "enigmatic combination":

"Christianity is the union of God and man, a union ... that has a special note of *presence*. 'Christianity is the apprenticeship of divine nature in man.' **'The Church is the incarnation in our sinful flesh.' She is the union of two realities, God and man ... the Church of saints, the Holy Church of sinners. All the light in this enigmatic and difficult combination comes from Jesus Christ."**[36]

§ 25 What Congar finds enigmatic and difficult to say, Küng affirms openly. He goes straight to the point with a single stroke of the pen:

"There are not ... two Churches, one holy, descending from heaven, and the other sinful, rooted in the earth. It is *one single* Church, *holy and sinful at the same time*, a *casta meretrix*,[37] as it has often been called since Patristic times, consonant with the images of the Old Testament. **Sanctity and sinfulness are two aspects of the same Church."**[38]

Küng quotes the Constitution *Lumen gentium* to corroborate this thesis: "'**The Church, embracing in its bosom sinners, at the same time holy and always in need of being purified** – *sancta simul et semper purificanda* – **always follows the way of penance and renewal'** (LG, n. 8)."[39]

Then, he hurls new insults at the Church: "Despite all her experiences of the manifestation of grace ... **the Church can never present herself as** a self-justified caste or **class of the pure and holy.** She can never presume that evil exists only outside of herself ... **In her there is nothing perfect** or free from danger, **nothing imperishable and certain, nothing, therefore, that is not in permanent need of correction and perfecting ... Such a Church knows that she does not have to put on a show of high morality before the world."**[40]

---

[36] Y. Congar, *Eglise Catholique et France Moderne*, pp. 123-124.

[37] In Appendix I, §§ 65-91,we will show that this reference to the Church Fathers is without foundation.

[38] H. Küng, *A Igreja*, vol. 2, pp. 104-105.

[39] *Ibid.*, p. 106.

[40] H. Küng, *A Igreja*, vol. 1, pp. 145-146.

We see, therefore, that von Balthasar, de Lubac, Congar and Küng all agree in applying the concept of *casta meretrix* – either directly or indirectly – to the Holy Church. Vatican II also indirectly endorses this thesis by admitting its essence in the formula *Ecclesia semper reformanda*.[41]

4. History Allegedly Symbolized by the Union of God with a Prostitute

§ 26

In another context, Fr. Edward Schillebeeckx, O.P., a theologian whose contributions to Vatican II made him known throughout the world, deals with the "nuptial conception" of History. He presents the marriage of Osee with the prostitute as the habitual model of the relationship between God and the Chosen People in the Old Testament:

"Once the symbol of matrimony is used to express God's love for Israel, the purely allegorical moral meaning [of this relation] becomes obsolete. **What exists is a concrete, earthly marriage uniting two Israelites, Osee and Gomer** [the prostitute]; **it is a very specific union that becomes the** *symbolic and prophetic form* **which properly expresses the historic dialogue of love between God and His people.**"[42]

Further on, Schillebeeckx reaffirms this notion: "This dialogical meaning of matrimony has ... such a profound evocative power that conjugal life becomes the prophetic way that most clearly expresses the encounter of the Chosen People with their God. Furthermore, **a specific conjugal life, that of Osee and Gomer, becomes**

---

[41] Two Vatican II documents refer to this concept:

The first is the Dogmatic Constitution *Lumen gentium*, which states: "The Church, embracing in its bosom sinners, **at the same time holy and always in need of being purified** - *sancta simul et semper purificanda* - **always follows the way of penance and renewal**" (n. 8).

The second is the Decree *Unitatis redintegratio,* which affirms: "**Christ summons the Church to continual reformation** as she sojourns here on earth. **The Church is always in need of this**, insofar as she is an institution of men here on earth. Thus if, in various times and circumstances, **there have been deficiencies in moral conduct or in Church discipline, or even in the way that Church teaching has been formulated,** ... **these can and should be set right** at the opportune moment" (chap. II, n. 6).

[42] Edward Schillebeeckx, *Le Mariage - Realité terrestre et mystère de salut* (Paris:Cerf, 1966), vol. 1, p. 95.

the symbolic and prophetic form of the dialogue of love between God and His people."[43]

This idea of a marriage with a prostitute is not exclusive to the Old Covenant, according to Schillebeeckx. That same marriage would continue after the coming of Christ. This is what the theologian claims, again referring to the case of Osee:

"**The coming of Christ primarily confirms that first significance of matrimony,** the place it occupies in the world order: From now on it is necessary to live the conjugal life 'in the Lord.'"[44]

This notion – union with a prostitute – is repeated throughout Schillebeeckx's work when he refers to relations between Christ and the Church:

"The Jews and pagans constitute the Church ... It is the action of Christ that must make a Church out of this humanity. **The union in 'only one flesh' in matrimony** – a fundamental affirmation of faith in God the Creator – **was already employed in the Old Testament as a means to reveal the divine covenant of grace.** St. Paul continues along the same line and discovers the mystery of Christ and His Church ... **Christ, the lover ... is proposed to man as an example to follow in married life ...**

"The sacramental character of matrimony becomes clear through concepts already present in the Old Testament and re-read in the New in the light of Christ, by virtue of the unity of the mysteries of creation, covenant and redemption in the history of salvation. **One must understand the continuous development of the idea of union of life ('only one flesh') in Genesis** (Creation) ...

"**This continuous use of matrimony as a symbol** and as a translation of the union of grace between God and men – and even more, this way of making the alliance known through a specific union and in it, **as in the case of Osee – reveal,** by their very usage, **a new dimension and depth of earthly reality.**"[45]

In this statement we find a simple summation of his thinking: "**Osee ... is the principal witness of the Revelation of the Covenant in terms of married love.**"[46]

We can see, therefore, that progressivists interpret union with a prostitute as the model for all of History. Not only does such thinking reveal an offense to the Church, the Word Incarnate and the Eter-

---

[43] *Ibid.*, p. 337.

[44] *Ibid.*

[45] *Ibid.*, pp. 127-128.

[46] *Ibid.*, p. 85.

nal Father, but also a veritable erotic obsession that pervades the writings of these harbingers of Vatican II theology.

5. Relations between Christ and the Church Would Be Based on the Sexual Act

§ 28 While not explicitly calling the Church a "prostitute," but probably supposing her to be such, Hans Urs von Balthasar launches a new type of insult. He imagines the holy relationship between Our Lord and the Catholic Church as sexual relations.[47] And he descends into such inappropriate details that one cannot but consider them grave offenses to the honor, purity and decorum of the Church.

Especially worthy of note is the erotic character that von Balthasar imparts to legitimate and current expressions in the mystical-symbolic language of the Church, traditionally understood in their chaste meaning. The Swiss theologian writes:

"Just as the Son behaves to some extent **in a receptive and feminine way in relation to the will of the Father, so also the Church and the Christian behave in relation to the life of the Son. The spilling of this 'semen of God'** (I Jn 3:9)[48] **into the bosom of the world is the most intimate happening in History. But generation and conception take place each time in an attitude of abandonment and a supreme darkness.** The absence of

---

[47] A scholar who has studied von Balthasar's intellectual work is of the same opinion regarding his emphasis on sexuality and use of explicit terms. John O'Donnel makes this general summary:

"Even a casual reading of Balthasar's corpus reveals his preoccupation with the sexual dimensions of the divine and human encounter. Perhaps at first one is struck by the vivid directness of some of the language … and one begins to ask oneself whether sexual metaphors are deliberately intended. A greater acquaintance with the texts convinces one that they are. Moreover, the reader comes to see that Balthasar's understanding of sexuality is central to his vision and sheds light on every facet of his theology: Christology, pneumatology, sacraments, Church, states of life, creation and eschatology.

"As Medard Kehl notes, 'The theme masculinity-femininity (understood as opposition between the forming activity and the passive receptivity, but ordered to the fruitfulness which encompasses both in their union) is doubtless a central thought-form in the theology of Balthasar'" (J. O'Donnell, "Man and Woman as '*Imago Dei*,'" p. 117.

[48] The Latin word *semen*, in the expression *semen ipsius* of the *Vulgate*, is generally translated as seed. In French – used by the author – it translates to *sémence de Dieu*; in German, *sein Same*; in Portuguese, *semente de Deus*. Nevertheless, in the context in which von Balthasar uses the term, its unequivocal meaning is semen, sperm.

all calculation belongs essentially to this 'plenitude of the times' ... It is precisely in the center of masculine reason, which projects its action with a creative spontaneity, that a feminine mystery secretly reigns."[49]

The theologian – known for his obsession with interpreting theology by using the model of the sexual act – continues to refer to a mysterious "bodily union" of humanity with God. In the text below, he imagines the relations between God and the Church – as well as the relations between God and the faithful soul who receives a grace – as a sexual act.

§ 29

Here one is not certain whether he is referring to the Church as the Spouse of Christ or to the hypostatic union or to the Holy Eucharist or, perhaps, to the three together. As one can see, the text is filled with paltry sensuality:

"The 'bodily' union of mankind with the living God is manifested – an extraordinary thing! - through the symbolism of *eros*, as a fulfillment of what was said in the *Canticle of Canticles*: existence considered as nuptials.

"The Church and the soul that receives the semen of the Word and of spiritual truth can only receive it in an attitude of feminine openness and availability, which does not become annoyed, does not close herself or become ruffled, does not make herself rigid or make any virile reaction, but gives herself in darkness, receives in darkness, bears in darkness, without knowing what and how much she received and gave birth to."[50]

§ 30

He returns to this indecent image, this time to imagine the Church being born from the pierced side of Our Lord, like the conquest that a man of the world would make of a woman of a frivolous life.

As he writes on, von Balthasar distorts the sublime phrase of Our Lord in the Garden of Olives: "The spirit indeed is willing, but the flesh is weak" (M. 26:41) to signify that the Divine Master had a carnal "weakness" for the Church, for whom He would have a carnal attraction.

In the text there is a certain confusion regarding the use of the expressions "my flesh" and "my body." According to von Balthasar, at times Christ applies them to the flesh of His own body and, at other

---

[49] Hans Urs von Balthasar, *Théologie de l'Histoire* (Paris: Plon, 1960), 2nd ed., p. 144.

[50] *Ibid.*, p.145.

times, to the Church. In the latter case, he makes an implicit mention – erotically interpreted – to the passage in St. Paul where the Apostle says that the spouses are only one flesh (Eph 5:31). Von Balthasar writes:

"It is with you, my Body, that I continuously wage the great, apocalyptic battle. Whatever remains far from me and from my heart is nothing but inert flesh, lost in itself. But I do not find it difficult to save this flesh because it puts up no resistance and lets itself in due time be brought into the flock. **But this [my Church, my Spouse] that lies closer to me, however, that has been initiated into my mystery and belongs to my body,** perceiving the throbbing of my Heart from within, **this thing has received the Spirit** and is, therefore, awake and able to freely choose. **And for the first time it truly knows the meaning of sin.**

"Thus, I am threatened within my own Body; the mortal enemy waits in ambush within myself. I have suckled a snake at my breast, a worm that does not die. In this, too, **I have become like you. For just as temptation rises within you from your own flesh, so also the deepest threat assaults me from my own flesh.** The spirit is docile and strong, but the flesh is weak; **and where the spirit touches the flesh, it is vulnerable and comes to terms with the flesh's weakness. It is a borderline where the spirit has always betrayed itself, giving in to itself. For if the spirit had nothing of the flesh, how could it come to form only one being with the flesh?**

"It is there where I, the strong God, have betrayed myself to you – my Body, my Church – and where I did this I became weak. There and there alone could I receive the mortal wound. **There I fell, I surrendered to the temptation of loving a body *within my own Body* (for who can hate his own flesh?). There I gave in to the temptation of delivering myself to the mysterious chaos of a body, of plunging below the shiny surface of the flesh.** ...

"**Just as you passionately, with throbbing heart, cross over temptation's boundary, so also have I, fully conscious of the danger, crossed over the boundary of the flesh with quivering heart.** I dared to enter the body of my Church, the mortal body that you are. ...

"**And so, from now on we are no longer two, but only one flesh that loves itself ... For your sake I became weak, since I could only experience your being in weakness. No wonder you realized your advantage over me and took my nakedness by storm! But I have conquered you through my weak-**

ness, and my Spirit has tamed my unruly and recalcitrant flesh (never has a woman made more desperate resistance!). In order to seal my victory and exploit my triumph, I have branded a mark upon you with a red-hot iron, O my flesh, a mark of my own carnal weakness.[51] The mark of my love is now in your sin. Never again will your sinful battle against me be anything other than the long wrestling of love. ...

"It is precisely because you – O unfortunate one! – knowingly sin against love that your sin is imprisoned in my love. And because it is I, at the same time Spirit and Love, who am the battlefield between God and the world, the battle is already and eternally won in me. **Our always unhappy covenant, our bloody-wedding ... is already, here and now, the immaculate bridal bed of divine love."**[52]

The expressions used in these texts are so crude and so undoubtedly offensive to the virginal purity of Holy Church that any comment seems superfluous.

*

In view of what has just been expounded, the Reader can gauge well the *animus injuriandi* of important conciliar theologians against the sanctity and purity of the Mystical Spouse of Christ.

*   *   *

---

[51] In this passage, von Balthasar is probably referring to the old practice in France of branding prostitutes with a hot iron as a measure to suppress the prostitution trade and to punish those engaged in it (Cf. *Grand Dictionnaire Universel do XIXe siècle*, Paris: Larousse: 1875, entry *Prostitution*, vol. 13). The same iron was applied on adulterous women. In the New England States this custom was also in force in the colonial period (Cf. Paul Bourget, *Outre-Mer*, Paris: Plon-Nourrit, 1894, vol. 1, p. 139).

[52] H. U. von Balthasar, *Le Coeur du Monde*, pp. 211-213.
The explanation of how the sexual union of Christ with a "sinner" who deserved to be "branded with a red-hot iron" can form an "immaculate nuptial bed" was already stated in Item 1 of this Chapter and will be expounded in greater length in the Appendix I. It is the theory of the *casta meretrix*.

Chapter V

THE CHURCH SEEN AS
PHARISAIC AND NARCISSIST

Whenever possible, we have tried to associate the offenses progressivists make against the Catholic Church with the theories they are spreading. We do this in an effort to explain such theories or, at least, to present them in a coherent background that sheds light on the objective of the attack represented by the offense.

In this Chapter,[1] it will be more difficult to closely relate the offenses to the underlying themes because of various difficulties, such as the broadness of the offenses and their multiple meanings.

§ 1

Among the important works that influenced conciliar changes is the book by Fr. Yves Congar, *True and False Reform in the Church*, published for the first time in French in 1950. As far as we know, in it he coined the epithet "pharisaism," a term that came to be used frequently against the Church.[2] The French Dominican applies "pharisaism" quite broadly: It refers to everything that leads the Church to

---

[1] This also occurs in Chapters VII and VIII; Chapters VI, IX, X and XI will follow the initial criteria.

[2] It would seem that in his coining of the expression "pharisaism" Congar drew his inspiration from Erasmus of Rotterdam, a Dutch Renaissance humanist and precursor of Protestantism. The term was later employed by conciliar theologians.

Congar says: "The reform of Erasmus essentially consisted in denouncing 'Judaism' in the state in which the Church found herself in his time. That is to say, he considered that the simple and spiritual attitudes of the Gospel had been invaded by all sorts of obligations – worse than those of the Jews – and that exterior practices were meticulously fostered by monks or persons of the Roman court whom **he called 'the Pharisees.' Erasmus touched on a real problem ... the problem of Catholicism** in his time. Almost everywhere the pastoral spirit was obfuscated, smashed by lordliness. The evangelical spirit was crushed by the excrescences of a piety inherited from the epoch of the *flamboyant* [the gothic]. The 'faith' was smashed by 'religion,' and the latter by 'practices.'" (Y. Congar, *Vraie et fausse reforme dans l'Eglise*, pp. 160-161).

Congar's reforming stance, therefore, appears to take the reform of Erasmus as one of its models. This leads us to suppose that the term "pharisaism" was inspired by the Flemish humanist.

commit the "sin" of considering the means of carrying out her mission as the ends. The ensemble of means that help her to spread the Gospel of Christ, which leads to "sin," is called the "system" by Congar.

§ 2   The "system," as he understands it, is the visible aspect of the Church: her structure of power, government, jurisdiction and honor, her magisterial body with its academies and universities and their indispensable tool, the scholastic method. It also includes her juridical and punitive apparatus, along with their corresponding consultative, legislative and executive organs. Further, the "system" also includes the body of dogmatic and moral doctrine, canon law, liturgical rubrics and customs. Finally, it encompasses all the pious practices – the cult of relics and the Saints, pilgrimages, fasting, abstinence, indulgences, and so on. All this would supposedly constitute the ecclesiastical "system" or "clerical apparatus," that allegedly causes the Catholic Church to turn preponderantly to the means – the seeking of power, riches, honors and glory – and thus deviate from her end.[3]

§ 3   Lambasting "pharisaism," Congar asserts: "The danger becomes even more acute when the Church, having become a reputable institution in society, enjoys honors, riches, material advantages and the capacity to influence. For then people run the risk of joining her not to find Christ but, rather, success – personal success or the success of their group. The danger reaches its apex when, not content with enjoying the favors of [the temporal] power, the Church herself assumes power and governs, as was the case in the Middle Ages under the hierocratic regime of Christendom."[4]

§ 4   Therefore, one can see that the sobriquet "pharisaism" can refer to any of the visible characteristics of the Church in the whole "system." If this meaning were to be admitted, all the Chapters of this Volume – from II to X – would be included under this one affront of calling the Catholic Church "pharisaic." It would be the *major* offense that would encompass all the others. The amplitude of the concept covered by this affront caused the *first difficulty* we encountered in making the offense fit the concept.

Nonetheless, after studying the origin of this expression, it seems to us that Congar's usage is somewhat exaggerated and theoretical. In current language, when someone is called a "Pharisee," it means he is a hypocritical person pretending to be virtuous or even holy. This meaning is well-founded: The increpations of Our Lord to

---

[3] Cf. *ibid,* pp. 150-170.

[4] *Ibid.,* p. 165.

the high priests of His time usually begin by emphasizing their hypocrisy: "Woe to you scribes and Pharisees, you hypocrites..."[5]

Thus, some progressivists insult the Church in this sense by calling her "pharisaic," meaning hypocritical. Others, however, will use the term as a synonym of "pretentious" or "vain." Further, there are others who understand the word 'pharisaic' as a synonym of "arrogant" or "insolent," or who adopt fourth and fifth analogical meanings that may not correspond with the others.

§ 5   The problem of harmonizing these various usages with the one applied by Congar constitutes the *second difficulty* in finding a consistent framework of thought for the offense.

Similar difficulties were likewise encountered with respect to some of the principal offenses analyzed in the Chapters that will follow. For example, when progressivists insult the Catholic Church by calling her "sclerotic," some are referring to her traditions, others to her structure, still others to her mentality. When they offend her by calling her the "opium of the people," some aim generally at the Gospel's message of salvation, others specifically target the truths of the Faith, while yet others merely address theoretical teaching.

One can see, therefore, that the *animus injuriandi* of progressivists goes beyond the boundaries of balance and coherence to become the confused tumult of a rabble, goaded on by hatred, clamoring from various standpoints for the condemnation and destruction of the Holy Church.

§ 6   Given such confusion, it appeared to us that the best method to adopt for this and other Chapters is to group together the vaguely similar insults and present them in their multiple meanings without exhaustive background explanations. We believe that the offenses as such will offer expressive examples of the *animus injuriandi* that moves the progressivist conciliar current.

*

§ 7   For Progressivism, as we have seen, the Church is sinful.[6] Nothing in her is integrally holy and perennial; everything must be continuously reformed. This is the concept of *Ecclesia semper*

---

[5] Cf. Mt. 23:13-15, 23-33; Lk 12:56, 13:15; Mk 7:6.
[6] See Chap. IV of this Volume.

reformanda,[7] an old Lutheran notion that was adopted in the documents of Vatican II.[8]

Following this logic, any affirmation of the sanctity of the Church is "hypocritical," and any manifestation of her perennial character – immutable dogmas, a fixed liturgy, centuries-old traditions that settled into practices and customs, etc. – is a "pharisaic" attempt to present her as perfect in order to permit her to evade a continual reform and to conceal her egotistic interests.

Or, if one adopts the meaning proposed by Congar, then the whole ecclesiastical "system" or "clerical apparatus" would be a powerful means to promote the "sin of pharisaism" in the Church. It goes without saying that this is different from the concept the Church always had about herself.

§ 8   Should evidence be needed, it would suffice to consider this testimony of Hans Küng, in which the opposition between the two ecclesiological concepts clearly appears. He lashes out at the Church with several insults, "pharisaic" among them:

"In comparison with the post-tridentine Church of the Counter-Reformation, Vatican Council II represents ... a 180 degree turn in its fundamental characteristics. Doubtless, it is the same Church that must continue to be herself. Nonetheless, **it is a new Church that surged from Vatican Council II.** What counts are her fundamental tendencies. ...

"For example, **that epoch** – the time of the post-tridentine Counter-Reformation – **was marked by introversion, with the Catholic Church turned in on herself; now, there is an opening to others. In that epoch, there were condemnations and excommunications of those with other beliefs; now, there is dialogue with them. In that epoch, there was the rejection of any serious official self-criticism; now, there is the confession of guilt** and

---

[7] The expression *Ecclesia semper reformanda*, of a clearly Lutheran inspiration, was used in the 19th century by Antonio Rosmini, who wrote various works fraught with theological errors, 40 of which were condemned by a Decree of the Holy Office on December 14, 1887 (cf. DS, 3201-3241).

[8] The conciliar documents are reproduced in Chap. IV, Note 41. Bishop Hans Martensen of Copenhagen shows that, in addition to the Lutheran claim for a constantly reforming Church, the Council accepted several other "demands" of the heresiarch from Wittenberg (cf. "Declaração da comissão mista católico-luterana sobre o V centenário de Martinho Lutero," in *SEDOC* 16, Petrópolis, March 1984, cols. 839-840). The text of Bishop Martensen can be found in Volume III, *Animus Injuriandi II*, Chap. I.1.b).

various errors **by the Pope and the Council. In that epoch, there was the idealistic affirmation of an unstained and unmarred Church; now, there is the demand for sweeping reform and renewal.**

"**Then, there was the pharisaic demand for the return of heretics and schismatics; now, there is the ecumenical movement** with our brothers in Christ and the other Christian churches and a practical realization of their concerns. **Then, there was an arrogant isolation regarding the modern world; now, there is a clear dialogue with the modern world** and those outside the Church. **Then, there was praise intoned for a monolithic ecclesiastical unity,** for the power and cohesion of the Catholic body; **now, there are demands for leaving the ghetto and razing her many bastions. Then, there was admiration for the robust and tight juridical structure and the strong organization** of the Catholic Church; **now, there is a reaction against her legalism** and a demand for her to be more spiritual.

"**In that time, there was the** personal **cult of Church dignitaries** of all degrees; **now, there is a rising opposition to clericalism and a demand for fraternity among all with the ecclesial office, viewed as a service** rendered to brothers. **In that time, the Church was adored as a divine-human being,** the result of the perfect synthesis between heaven and earth, identified with the kingdom of God; **now, triumphalism is criticized,** and a Christian realism is presupposed that looks at the Church as an entity made up of men and sinners, as people of God on pilgrimage through the darkness of sin and error, on the way to the coming kingdom of God." [9]

Theologian Joseph Ratzinger showed his disapproval for the "pharisaism" of the Church in 1969:

§ 9

"**Who could doubt that the danger of pharisaism, of** *qumranism*, **also exists in the Church today? Did not the Church try to construct her own small world, thus losing the possibility of being the salt of the earth and light of the world** in her exaggerated movement of flight from the world since Pius IX? Isolation in her own small world – a reclusion that has lasted long enough – cannot save the Church. Nor is it proper for a Church whose Lord died outside the gates of the city. ... 'Outside' – facing the doors defending the city and the sanctuary – is the place of a Church that wants to follow the crucified [Christ]." [10]

---

[9] H. Küng, *Veracidade*, pp. 112-113.

[10] J. Ratzinger, *Il nuovo popolo di Dio*, p. 298, in J. Ratzinger, *Il nuovo popolo di Dio*, p. 298, in Gonzalez Ruiz, "Lettera aperta al Cardinal Ratzinger," p. 5.

§ 10   For his part, Bishop Boaventura Kloppenburg affirms that to love the immutability of the Holy Church is "pharisaism":

"Churchmen are always subject to the great temptation of fixing the Church in a concrete and victorious type of incarnation, of perennializing her in that form even when previous circumstances have ceased to exist, or of trying to replicate her exactly as she was, even in new situations. **This is the fixism that leads to formalism, legalism and juridicism, to a dangerous kind of pharisaism, to the ghetto.**

"The day the Church considers herself ready, complete, finished, unchangeable, immutable and definitively structured in her institutions and laws, she would cease to be leaven, light and salt; she would cease to be the universal sacrament of salvation and to fulfill her essential mission ... and **she would commence her actual infidelity.** Always unfinished, always on the way, always tending toward consummation ... always in a world that passes and changes – the Church must always be *in fieri*, always in continuous progress (UR, n. 6A)."[11]

§ 11   Listing some of the progressivist victories achieved at Vatican II, chronicler Henri Fesquet applies the epithet "pharisaism" to preconciliar Catholicism. We refer to this paragraph:

"Without denying the purest part of her tradition, the Roman Church renounced her notion of having the monopoly on truth. She rendered generous homage to the truths contained in other religions – all of them – starting with her sisters, the non-Catholic Christian confessions. In less than four years, Rome entered through the front door into the ecumenical concert, from which she was tragically absent. **Today the other churches can no longer censure Catholicism for its arrogance or its pharisaism.**"[12]

Msgr. Gérard Philips, who was the final redactor of the Dogmatic Constitution *Lumen gentium*, the principal document of Vatican II, explains the intentions that inspired it:

"Catholic sinners are not declared superior to the righteous who are non-Catholic. **Such a statement would be** to prefer appearance to the reality of grace, and would be **the canonization of pharisaism as an ideal of life.** The Council certainly does not assume such an attitude and carefully avoids giving Catholics any occasion for vanity."[13]

---

[11] B. Kloppenburg, *A eclesiologia do Vaticano II*, p. 97.

[12] H. Fesquet, *Le journal du Concile*, p. 1124.

[13] G. Philips, *La Chiesa e il suo mistero nel Concilio Vaticano II*, p. 178.

§ 12   When Msgr. Philips describes the idea that the Catholic sinner is more than the non-Catholic righteous man as "pharisaic," he directly contradicts the traditional teaching of the Church.[14]

---

[14] The solution to the question of how a Catholic sinner is superior to a non-Catholic righteous man is not difficult, even though progressivists contest or confuse the topic in order to open the way for ecumenism.

a. As St. Robert Bellarmine teaches, "The true Church is the community of men united by the profession of the true Christian Faith and by the communion of the same Sacraments under the government of legitimate shepherds and, principally, the one Vicar of Christ on earth, the Roman Pontiff" (cf. *De conciliis et Ecclesia,* book 3, chap. 2, in *Opera omnia,* Palermo/Naples/Paris: Pedone Lauriel, 1872, vol. 2, p. 75).

The great Doctor of the Counter-Reformation goes on to draw consequences from this definition regarding those inside or outside the Church: "By virtue of the *first part* [of the above definition], all infidels are excluded, both those who have never been in the Church, like the Jews, Turks and pagans, and those who were in her bosom and later fell away, like the heretics and apostates. By virtue of the *second part,* catechumens and those who are excommunicated are excluded, since the former are not admitted to the Sacraments and the latter are excluded from them. By virtue of the *third part*, the schismatics are excluded, those who have the Faith and Sacraments but are not subject to the legitimate shepherd. ... All others, however, are included, even if they are reprobates, criminals and the impious" (*ibid*).

b. Since mankind was elevated to the supernatural order by the Incarnation and Redemption of the Divine Word, natural justice no longer sufficed; it was necessarily superseded by supernatural justice, lest it become meaningless or false.

True supernatural justice exists only in the Holy Church, for the reasons expounded by St. Robert Bellarmine. Therefore, all those who know the Church and reject her are excluded from this justice.

As a consequence, the category of the righteous who are outside the Church is reduced to two types: *first*, those who live in regions so primitive and inaccessible that they have never heard about the Holy Church and the Catholic Faith and who follow only natural law and are faithful to it; *second*, those who are in a process of conversion from false religions or paganism to the Catholic Church and are thus moving toward supernatural justice.

c. The generic comparison of a righteous man outside the Church with a sinner inside her would be like comparing a healthy unborn baby with a sick adult man. The former still is not born and unable to be in communion with the Church; he has a preparatory, embryonic life. The latter lives in communion with her, but he is sick due to his sin, and his communion with the Church is deteriorating.

Let us now look at different standpoints of this comparison between the Catholic sinner and the righteous man outside the Church that can be made:

* *From the standpoint of communion with the Church*: The Catholic sinner is superior because he has a true communion with her, since he did not deny the Faith or submission to the Supreme Pontiff, nor is he barred from the Sacraments. Whereas the non-Catholic righteous man is not truly in communion with the Church but is only oriented toward the Faith; neither has he submitted to the Pope, nor can he frequent the Sacraments.

* *From the standpoint of participation in sanctifying grace*: The Catholic sinner **no longer has** sanctifying grace, but he participates in the exterior elements of supernatural life, i.e., he can assist at Mass and acts of worship or piety, which are powerful vehicles of graces that are accessible only to Catholics. The non-Catholic righteous man **still does not have** sanctifying grace, but only a medicinal grace, and does not participate in the exterior elements of supernatural life. In this regard, therefore, the former has more conditions to return to the state of sanctifying grace than the latter has to attain it.

* *From the standpoint of charity or correspondence to divine grace*: A comparison is practically impossible here since the action of grace and the response of individuals differ in every case and belong to the mystery of the relations between God and each man – *de internis nec Ecclesia*. Therefore, it can be that a non-Catholic righteous man is a furnace of love of God – like Augustine after he left Manichaeism but still was not baptized – and have greater charity than the average Catholic sinner. Or the Catholic sinner can become a model of repentance, stricken with sorrow and, moved by love, willing to atone for all the evil he has done – like a Mary Magdalene, who far surpassed the normal non-Catholic righteous man.

Therefore, analyzed under these various prisms, the Catholic sinner is more than the non-Catholic righteous man, save for the case, indiscernible to man, of the latter having more charity than the former.

d. By branding this serene and balanced position as "pharisaism," progressivists reveal their denial of the traditional teaching of the Church that salvation is found only in her bosom (cf. DB, 2, 14, 39-40. 246, 423, 430, 468-469, 570b, 714, 999, 1473, 1613, 1696, 1677, 1716, 1954, 2199, 2319). Only those who assume the error that there is salvation outside the Church can imagine supernatural justice in those who belong to false religions, know about the Holy Catholic Church and are not moving toward conversion to her.

e. We suggest, in addition to these explanations, the reading of Vol. V, *Animus Delendi II*, Part II, Chap II §§ 1-6, which carefully analyzes an important progressivist sophism that favors ecumenism. This sophism is based in large part on the emotional and doctrinal exaggeration of the existence of righteous men living outside the Catholic Church.

§ 13

Hans Küng affirms that it is "pretentious" for the Catholic Church to identify herself with the Church of Christ. Once again the insult of "pharisaism" is brandished:

"With her great pretension of identifying herself [with the Church of Christ], does this single Church ... do justice to the other Christian churches whose baptisms – and, therefore, insertion in the Body of Christ – cannot be contested, as well as many other things? ... **Does she not imagine herself to be too important, pharisaically presenting herself as so self-assured** and conscious of her own justice and so little inclined to penance? ... **To pretend to be the whole** – when the truth is that the whole results from the integration of the parts – **is to become guilty** in a new way **of perpetuating the division."**[15]

§ 14

Fr. René Laurentin criticizes the position of the Church on marriage and birth control, branding those moral norms as "pharisaism":

"To the measure that this [moral] formalism is established in the Church, it allows no place between the pharisaic satisfaction of having fulfilled the law and despair, between revolt and laxity. We must overcome this dilemma by better situating the duty of fecundity within the ambit of the whole life of the couple. A simple abstract consideration of the materiality of each act runs the risk of being insufficient."[16]

§ 15

Fr. Peter Huizing, S.J., professor of Canon Law at the University de Nijmegen, dean of the Canon Law Department of Gregorian University and a consultant to the Pontifical Commission that wrote the new Code of Canon Law, also offends the Church by calling the celibacy requirement for priests "hypocritical":

"The way of linking the mission to govern in the Church to the juridical obligation of celibacy is unrealistic and frequently hypocritical. The way of dealing with married priests is positively anti-Christian."[17]

§ 16

The Vatican organ *L'Osservatore Romano* published a critique by William May, a member of the International Theological Commission and professor of Moral Theology at Catholic University in Washington, of the book by Austrian moral theologian Fr. Bernhard Häring, *Pastoral on Divorce*. In this work, Häring accuses the Church

[15] H. Küng, *A Igreja*, vol. 2, p. 39.

[16] R. Laurentin, *Bilan de la troisième session*, p. 205.

[17] P. Huizing, "Vaticano III: una costituzione sulla Chiesa," in V.A., *Verso la Chiesa del terzo millennio*, p. 169.

of "pharisaism" in the application of her moral laws. We transcribe the words of May on this point:

"**The author** [Häring] presents himself as one who only wants to show the mercy and love of Christ; in fact, however, he **ends by presenting the teaching and praxis of the Church as a legalist and pharisaic betrayal of the Gospel of love and mercy of the Lord.**"[18]

*

In addition to the adjective "pharisaic," so frequently used to offend the Church, the epithet "narcissistic" is also hurled at her by some progressivists.[19]

§ 17

Speaking before 223 theologians from all over the world assembled in Brussels in 1970 for the first congress of the magazine *Concilium*, Fr. Antoine Vergote, professor at the University of Louvain, accuses the Church of having a "narcissist" superiority complex:

"In her way of thinking, speaking and acting, **the Church is excessively prone to present her message as a totalitarian system** and as a single block. She does not leave enough room for those who are outside or moving along the borders of the Creed. We exclude not only those whom we call heretics, but, by our behavior, we tend to alienate all those who do not completely adhere to our Faith. **This false self-assurance keeps us isolated in a narcissistic superiority.**"[20]

---

[18] William E. May, "Le opinioni di P. Bernhard Häring sulla pastorale dei divorziati risposati," *L'Osservatore Romano*, March 6, 1991, p. 2.

Häring's work is entitled *Pastorale dei divorziati. Una strada senza uscita?* (Bologna: Dehoniane, 1990).

May's criticism of his insult of "pharisaism" is the only one of which we know that has been published by an organ linked to the Holy See.

[19] The term narcissism refers to a mixture of vanity and egoism. According to Greek mythology, Narcissus was a handsome youth who, seeing his reflection in a pool of water, fell in love with himself. Unable to catch his own reflection in the waters to consummate his love, Narcissus pined away and changed into the flower that bears his name (cf. *Enciclopedia Universal Ilustrada*, entry Narcisism, Bilbao/Madrid/Barcelona: Espasa Calpe, 1930-1956, vol. 37.

[20] Antoine Vergote, "La presenza della Chiesa nella società di domani – Riflessioni bibliche," in V.A. *L'Avvenire della Chiesa – Il libro del Congresso* (Brescia: Queriniana, 1970), p. 171.

§ 18   In his commentary on the fourth conciliar session, Fr. Laurentin considers that even the Church's self-examination in rendering an account of her mission has the "bad smell of narcissism." He states:

"The Constitution *Lumen gentium* expounded the structures and internal life of the Church. It found its way in the wake of the question insistently placed [at the Council] in 1962 by Msgr. Huyghe and taken up by Cardinal Montini and, afterward, by others: 'Church, what do you say about yourself?'

"This preliminary question in itself had something of the bad smell of narcissism. But the Church, departing from the words of Christ – 'Go and teach all nations and baptize them' – could only give one response: I am, for God and for the world, a servant of God called to give God to the world and the world to God so that, in one same movement, God is recognized and the world saved."[21]

§ 19   In another context – wholly metaphysical – von Balthasar applies the term narcissism to the Christian mystery, this time, however, in an awkward laudatory fashion. He pretends that **"the Christian mystery is that of 'Narcissus fulfilled.'"**[22]

According to him, every man should reach Christ through self-contemplation, like the legendary Narcissus, who contemplated his image in the waters. For von Balthasar, "transcendence toward the Ideal makes the Ideal ... immanent in us." [23]

§ 20   In essence, what Fr. Congar qualifies as "ecclesio-centrism" is no different from the term "narcissism" applied to the Church. He states:

"The most unpardonable sin is, then, 'ecclesio-centrism,' where the Church is preoccupied above all with herself, her growth and her unity, instead of being concerned with service for the growth and unity of men."[24]

*

---

[21] R. Laurentin, *Bilan de la quatrième session*, p. 71.

[22] Cf. H. U. von Balthasar, *Parole et mystère chez Origène*, p. 30.

Von Balthasar borrows the expression "Narcissus fulfilled" from the German poet Rainer Maria Rilke, to whom he gives credit in a footnote. However, he does not explain how and by whom Narcissus was fulfilled.

[23] *Ibid.*

[24] Y. Congar, *Èglise Catholique e France moderne*, p. 63.

Here we close this sample of the *animus injuriandi* displayed toward the Church by various expressive conciliar theologians, who brand her as pharisaic, hypocritical and narcissist.

*   *   *

Chapter VI

THE CHURCH BRANDED AS TYRANNICAL, ABSOLUTIST AND USURPING

§ 1

In this Chapter we will present texts reflecting the *desire to offend* turned mainly against the principle of authority in the Church. They reveal the profound egalitarian spirit of their authors as well as their revolt against the Spouse of Christ in her hierarchical character.

According to the teachings of the New Testament, the Papal Magisterium, St. Thomas Aquinas and other authors, the best reflection of God in Creation is the hierarchy of beings.[1] Consequently, the already serious progressivist offenses against the hierarchical character of the Church increase in gravity.

---

[1] In the New Testament, see: Mt 25:14-30; I Cor. 20:28-31;

In the Pontifical Magisterium, see: Pius VI, *Decretal Letter to the Cardinal de La Rochefoucauld and the Archbishop of Aix-en-Provence* of March 10, 1791, in Pius VI, *Pontificis Maximi Acta* (Rome: Typis S. Congreg. de Propaganda Fide, 1871), vol. 1, pp. 70-71; Leo XIII, Encyclical *Quod apostolici muneris* of December 28, 1878, in AAS, vol. 11, p. 372; Encyclical *Rerum novarum* of May 15, 1891, in AAS, vol. 23, p. 657; St. Pius X, Apostolic Letter *Notre charge apostolique* of August 25, 1910, in AAS, vol. 2, pp. 613-615.; Motu proprio *Fin dalla prima* of December 18, 1903, (Petrópolis: Vozes, 1959), p. 23; Pius XI, Encyclical *Divini Redemptoris* of March 19, 1937, in AAS, vol. 29, p. 81; Pius XII, Allocution to the Patriciate and Roman Nobility, Radiomessage of January 5, 1942, in *Discorsi e Radiomessaggi*, pp. 347-348; Allocution to the Patriciate and Roman Nobility of January 5, 1942, *in ibid.*, p. 347-348; Allocution to the Patriciate and Roman Nobility of January 19, 1944, *in ibid*, p. 181; Radiomessage of Christmas 1944, in AAS, vol. 6, p. 239; John XXIII, Encyclical *Ad Petri cathedram* of June 29, 1959, in AAS, vol. 51, pp. 505-501; John Paul II, *Allocution to the youth in Belo Horizonte*, of July 1, 1980, in *Todos os pronunciamentos do Papa ao Brasil*, (São Paulo: Loyola, 1980), p. 34.

In St. Thomas Aquinas, see *Summa Theologiae*, I^a, q.47, a.2; q.50, a.4; q.96, a.4; *Summa contra Gentiles*, II, 45; *De regimine principum*, book 1, chap. II, in *Opuscula philosophica* (Turin/Rome: Marietti, 1954), pp. 257-358;

St. Dyonisius Aereopagita, *La hierárchie céleste*, (Paris: Cerf, 1970), chaps. I, 2-3; II; St. Francis de Sales, *Traitè de l'amour de Dieu*, in *Oeuvres completes* (Paris: Vivès, 1866), vol. 1, p. 321.

In other authors, see: Joseph-Thomas Duhamel, *Lettre pastorale* (Ottawa), 5th series, n. 2, pp. 40-42.; Plinio Correa de Oliveira *et alii*, *Agrar-*

Given the extension of the topic, the progressivist revolt against the hierarchical character of the Church and the ecclesiastical Hierarchy will not be dealt with exclusively in this Chapter.

§ 2

The first injurious salvoes come from Congar, praised by Paul VI as one of the theologians who most contributed to the preparations for Vatican II: [2]

"In him [the Word Incarnate] God revealed himself as a servant, as one who gives love, thus breaking the chain of needs and interests. The saints are the only true Christians: 'Our Church is the Church of Saints.'

"The Church was not always so. She is not sufficiently so ... **She stores her treasure in vases soiled with dirt and at times her hands are filthy**. Although she has a message of truth and liberty, it happened that **she was tyrannical and enslaving**. Collectively, **she played the role of** what would be for individuals **an oppressive sentiment of guilt**." [3]

§ 3

Antoine Vergote, professor at the University of Louvain and a member of various scientific associations, including the Freudian School of Paris, speaks in a similar vein:

"In her way of thinking, speaking and acting, the Church is too inclined to present her message as a totalitarian system and as a single block." [4]

---

ian Reform - A Matter of Conscience, in collaboration with A.C. Mayer, G.P. Sigaud and L.M. Freitas (São Paulo: Vera Cruz, 1960), pp. 64-65; Plinio Correa de Oliveira, *Revolution and Counter-revolution,* pp. 41-46; *A Igreja ante a escalada da ameaça comunista – Apelo aos Bispos silenciosos* (São Paulo: Vera Cruz, 1976), p. 25; *Sou católico: posso ser contra a reforma agrária?* in collaboration with C.D. Campo (São Paulo, Vera Cruz, 1981), pp. 80-82; "Projeto de constituição angustia o País" in *Catolicismo* (extra edition), October 1987, p. 187; *Nobility and the Traditional Analogous Elites in the allocutions of Pius XII to the Patriciate and the Roman Nobility* (Porto: Livraria Civilização ed., 1993), pp. 223-225)

[2] In his journal of the Council, Henri Fesquet writes: "The Pope [Paul VI] just recently stated in one of his private audiences (this is fact, not rumor): 'Rev. Fr. Congar is one of the theologians who contributed the most to prepare Vatican II and whose thinking is the most acted upon by the Council Fathers.' In saying this, Paul VI did nothing more than recognize an obvious truth" (H. Fesquet, *Le journal du Concile,* p. 280).

[3] Y. Congar, *Église Catholique et France moderne,* p. 171.

[4] A. Vergote, "La presenza della Chiesa nella società di domani," in V.A., *L'Avvenire della Chiesa - Il libro del Congresso,* p. 171.

§ 4

Bishop Gerald Huyghe of Arras, France, strikes at the whole hierarchical structure of the Church at the third session in the Conciliar Hall:

"Authority and institutions are necessary, but they should be oriented to foster communion among persons and to the possession of truth. Before inviting the world to dialogue, **the Church must reform her customs, institutions and laws that present themselves – in every level of the Church hierarchy – like a blind and dominating authority** rather than like a dialogue of charity."[5]

§ 5

Hans Küng, whom the former Archbishop of Cracow Cardinal Karol Wojtyla called an "eminent theologian" who "played an extraordinary role" in preparing the Council,[6] assails the "oppression" of the Church:

"**Not everyone** who knows something about the concrete life of the Church **realizes how much truth there is in the accusations against the 'institutional Church,' which incessantly tramples men underfoot, showing neither pity nor mercy, injuring them and almost crushing them.**

"**Wouldn't it be possible to produce innumerable examples of this** also in our 20th century? This is even if we omit the most famous 'cases' of **the anti-modernist question** or, in the pontificate of Pius XII, **the question of worker priests, the purge of the theologians of France**, etc. – all victims of the ecclesiastical inquisition in the 20th century.

"This is not to mention still many other things that show the continuation of the Roman inquisitorial spirit after the Council. **Who does not recall** the countless demotions and transfers, prohibitions to write and speak ... **the hardly democratic practice of naming Bishops and priests for ecclesiastical posts,** and so on?

"But, in addition to this, who can forget what has happened to the laity: **the suppression of free expression, the painful situation in marriage processes, the useless imposition of burdens, ecclesiastical mandates, decrees, institutions and harsh or sibylline answers to so many vital problems regarding** Catholic schools, **conjugal morality and ecumenical cooperation?**"[7]

---

[5] Gerard Huyghe, Intervention in the Conciliar Hall of October 27, 1964, in B. Kloppenburg, *Concílio Vaticano II*, vol. IV, p. 249.

[6] Cf. M. Malinski, *Mon ami Karol* Wojtyla, p. 180; text cited in the Introduction, Note 14o, of this Volume.

[7] H. Küng, *Veracidade - O futuro da Igreja*, pp. 103-105.

§ 6

Küng continues such offenses in his work *The Church*:

"It is precisely **the Church who must permanently convert and renew her message to the world – in a constant metanoia – in order to receive the Kingdom of God** that is to come. ... She should not place herself in an ascetic isolation from the world, but rather be obedient, in love, to the will of God in the world's daily life, not by fleeing from the world, but working for it. ... As if the Church could present her own liturgical, dogmatic and juridical laws and her own prescriptions, traditions and customs as commandments of God. ...

"**A Church that**, in this end of time, **forgets to whom she owes obedience, usurps command for herself, becomes sovereign and presents herself as a highborn lady, enslaves and enchains herself.**" [8]

Once again, Küng attacks: "**Will the Church be credible? Will she really be able to help man reach an authentic Christianity and humanism? There are those who say that she stands before a great obstacle, referring not to the Church as a community of persons and believers, but as an institution, an institutional system,** an institutional structure. **This Church would be ceaselessly and unscrupulously sacrificing truth to the benefit of ecclesiastical authority** – which could never be insulted or endangered – by handing over the people to the institution.

§ 7

"**This Church would be less concerned about announcing the Gospel and the well-being of men than about her antiquated, sclerotic institutions, her obsolete constitutions removed from reality, her hyper-civilized authority, her dead system. The consequence is** uncertainty, fear, **terror, the enslaving of men by an intolerant institutional regime that is ultimately indifferent to the concrete needs and concerns of the real man,** at depth, **a regime devoid of love.** A more recent example ... is her position on the birth control question, where truth was undoubtedly sacrificed for the prestige of the ecclesiastical magisterium, and the need of men was set aside to safeguard the institution. ...

"**It is impossible to find a sufficient biblical basis for what is called the 'Roman system'** ... **imagined as liturgical, theological and administrative juridicism and centralism ... and as the authoritarianism, absolutism and imperialism of the Roman curia.**" [9]

---

[8] H. Küng, *A Igreja*, vol. 1, pp. 147-148.

[9] H. Küng, *Veracidade - O futuro da Igreja*, pp. 94-96.

Traditional theology is part and parcel of the "Roman system." So Küng also turns against it, both in this excerpt and in his book, *Infallible?*

§ 8

In the following text, Fr. Yves Congar also attacks the juridical structure of the Church. He makes frequent offenses to her honor. He begins by labeling her structure as "juridicist" and "moralist," only to end by calling her a "tyrant" and "narrow-minded." In Congar's book that calls for a poor and servant Church, one reads:

"Her juridicism in theology, ethics, liturgy, etc. defines the unequivocal and strict conditions for every single thing that exists to bear its name, be valid, or fulfill an obligation. This is the attitude that **dominated and did so much damage, especially in the liturgy. In this sphere, it favored a scrupulous and hardly spiritual instinct** of the past by which man was interested only in the rite, in the material aspect of his obligation, and not in the profound personal action of one who, much more than satisfying an obligation, participates with the 'heart.' That is to say, people were interested in the minimum legal conditions necessary to show that they were following the law – at least its letter and authority – but not the real sense of things. ...

"In all these cases, we find a transformation of the living spiritual reality, interior quality and engagement of persons into 'things.' A whole study would have to be made about **this process of degradation in the pastoral, which so easily risks being transformed into research on how-tos and pastoral letters about 'things'** ...

"It would also be the case to speak about 'moralism,' defined as follows: 'Moralism begins when the action is considered more important than the inspiration that gave rise to it.'[10*] In this way **good and sin are,** so to speak, **separated from the particular living person who practices them ... in order to be considered as things defined by a completely exterior criteria**. ... The reaction of orthodoxy followed these same lines: It valorized partial aspects of the hierarchy, almost reaching the point of seeing the Church only as a society where some command and others obey; above all, it exalted authority. It considered the Church from the vantage point of her rights and powers that structured her as a society. In summary, it viewed the Church as a juridical subject of authority and rights. ...

[*Unfehlbar?*]. His criticisms of "Roman" theology were warmly applauded by Cardinal Ratzinger (cf. Joseph Ratzinger "Contradições no livro *Infalível* de Hans Küng," in V. A., *O problema da infalibilidade*, coord. by K. Rahner, São Paulo: Loyola, 1976, p. 101). The mentioned text is cited in Chap. VIII.1 NOte 3 of this Volume.

[10*] A. N. Bertrand, *Témoins*, p. 59, in Andre Lalande, *Vocabulaire technique et critique de la philosophie* (Paris, 1960).

§ 9

"In these observations there is absolutely nothing of opposition between the Church of charity and the Church of law: **There is only a historical description of a certain invasion, evident to us, of representations and, at times, actual practices of juridicism. This is a critique of a certain way of envisaging and presenting the Church**, whose parcel of truth should be conserved, but **whose tyrannical and narrow-minded predominance must be denounced as a malady**, from which today's Church is notably being rapidly cured."[11]

§ 10

Congar boldly returns to attack the "pyramidal" and "mechanical" structure that he says exists in the Church: "**The institution runs the risk of becoming an absolute in itself, thanks to a clerical and pyramidal ecclesiology, in some ways soulless and mechanical.**"[12]

§ 11

Expressing a similar view, Johann Baptist Metz, a principal exponent of "political theology," says:

"In Catholicism there is a kind of constitutive mistrust of grace as freedom. For this reason, **the sensory aspect in Catholicism also often appears as very bleak, sacramentalist and ritually rigid, extremely monolithic and pre-fabricated, as if it had nothing to do with the spontaneity and liberty of man.**"[13]

§ 12

Considering the advantages the Decree *Christus Dominus* offered the progressivist current, Laurentin disdainfully attributes a "spirit of caste and domination" to a considerable part of the Church. He states:

"The decree innovates on a topic that was a candent matter for more than one thousand years and seemed untouchable: the problem of the exemption of religious orders (that is, their independence in relation to Bishops.) This privilege [of exemption from episcopal jurisdiction], necessary to safeguard the internal authenticity of religious life, has a complex and tense past. It was granted for the first time in 628 by Honorius I to the Monastery of Bobbio. It was extended in the next century, and only at the end of the 10th century did it pass to France. It then applied to isolated monasteries in the countryside.

"The conflict started a little later when the mendicant religious, likewise exempt, established themselves in the cities. A reciprocal cold

---

[11] Y. Congar, *Pour une église servante et pauvre*, pp. 103-105.

[12] Y. Congar, "Os grupos informais na Igreja," in Afonso Gregory, *Comunidades eclesiais de base - Utopia ou realidade* (Petrópolis: Vozes, 1973), p. 141.

[13] Johann Baptist Metz, *Más allá de la religión burguesa - Sobre el futuro del Cristianismo* (Salamanca: Sígueme, 1982), p. 58.

war started. Thus, the Lateran Council (1215) reserved the right of vicars of parishes to hear confessions – and barred the religious orders from it! But the promoters of radical centralization – those who distrusted the Bishops and tried to diminish them – developed exemption in the opposite sense.

"At Vatican II, the spirit of caste and domination was overcome. The climate of an encompassing charity and the desire to subordinate everything to the kingdom of God permitted this situation of conflict and rivalry to evolve into a situation of understanding and cooperation."[14]

§ 13

Among the offenses made by Maximus IV against the Church, we find the excerpt below, where he also indirectly qualifies her as "absolutist." The Melkite Patriarch affirms:

"These are no longer the times of the Middle Ages. **The age of childhood is passed**. Today the world requests – with tenacity and virility – the recognition of human dignity in all its plenitude and the social equality of all classes. ... Very well! We can no longer impose laws on this world without showing their positive significance and wisdom. And does not the state of soul of **today's society** perhaps **call for a revision of the presentation of our moral teaching? In fact, this teaching, principally since the 16th century, adapted itself too much to the legalism and immaturity of a closed, absolutist society. Present day teaching is still too marked by the legalism of a superseded epoch** totally steeped in Roman Law."[15]

§ 14

"Authoritarian theology" is another depreciative expression used by conciliar theologians to attack the hierarchical Magisterium of the Church. In this sense, we present an excerpt from Fr. Chenu as he offends Scholasticism:

"**An instrument of this authoritarianism in theology was St. Thomas [Aquinas]**. In July 1914 ... **the Congregation in charge of teaching upper-level theology** had just published a list of 24 theses that were considered a summary of the teaching of St. Thomas. **It wanted to impose acceptance of these 24 theses on all the doctoral candidates in theology**. In order to receive the doctoral title and thereby teach in the Church at this level, the candidates had to accept these theses. **I view this as one of the most irritating**

[14] R. Laurentin, *Bilan de la quatrième session*, p. 241.

[15] Maximus IV, Intervention in the Conciliar Hall of October 27, 1964, in B. Kloppenburg, *Concílio Vaticano II*, vol. 4, p. 244.

abuses of the magisterial power of the Church, which introduced this kind of coercion even into the scholarly elaboration of theology." [16]

§ 15   Discussing the topic of culture in the Constitution *Gaudium et spes* during the third conciliar session, Bishop Léon Elchinger of Strasburg attributed "dogmatic imperialism" to the teaching of the Church:

"It would be advisable for the schema to set forth how the Church fulfilled her role regarding the cultural problem through various practical and positive ways. ... We should recognize our weakness and seek means to amend ourselves. **Isn't the Church too inclined toward a so-called dogmatic imperialism**, an attitude that makes us judge any scientific advancement too precipitously, as if our faith gave us the guarantee of omniscience and infallibility? ...

"Today we must have a more open mentality and a more benevolent attitude toward secular and religious cultural movements. ... **An intelligent pastoral must be drawn up to correct dogmatic imperialism** and not allow the legacy of the past to prevent the Church from looking toward the future."[17]

§ 16   The consideration of the Faith as a conjunct of supernatural and metaphysical truths – as the Church always understood it before Vatican II – is accused of being a caricature. It is Congar who makes this offense in the form of a question:

"Can the 'Faith' be turned into adhesion to a system of transcendental metaphysical statements, hovering over the history of men without truly penetrating it? ... **Limited to this, faith would be a guarantee of order, but would run a great risk of being an ideological cover for a fixed hierarchical order. Have we drawn a caricature? We hope not. But hasn't a certain religion without reference to human history and without a dimension of hope given the pretext for such a caricature?**"[18]

§ 17   Metz adopts the same line of thinking as Congar and Chenu:

"Even the **Bishops and the theologians can easily become the mandarins of a Church which**, under the mantle of neutrality

---

[16] *Jacques Duquesne interroge le Père Chenu,* pp. 30-31.

[17] Léon Arthur Elchinger, Intervention in the Conciliar Hall of November 4, 1964, in B. Kloppenburg, *Concílio Vaticano II,* vol. 4, p. 288.

[18] Y. Congar, *Un people messianique,* pp. 192-193.

and, therefore, of 'political innocence,' **promotes a well-known Integralism** and gives stability to political alliances without taking into account suffering and actual oppression."[19]

Bishop Kloppenburg is also strongly offensive:

"**The colonialist, imperialist and dominant mentality** that some centuries ago took over Western Europe also **sullied the Church.** Vatican II is an attempt to purify her of this stain. **She is Catholic *de jure*; we hope she will start to be Catholic *de facto*.**"[20]

Fr. Jean-Pierre Jossua, O.P., dean of the Dominican center Le Saulchoir and a follower of Chenu and Congar, writes:

"A formula by Yves Congar affirms, 'All are enlightened and active.' This would refer to the fecundity of reflection as well as the formulation of the Faith. **Absolutized, the idea of a professional theologian is blasphemous: They would be specialists on God in Christianity!**"[21]

One tactic typical of Fr. Congar is to take three steps forward and one backward. He advances with the most radical progressivists, then later backs up a bit, giving some small reverence to the very principle he is combating – in this case, the hierarchy – so that he can appear impartial or somewhat conservative. He thus aims to protect his flanks, left exposed by his quick advance.

This tactic is clearly seen in the text below. After violently attacking the superiority of the clergy over the faithful, Congar refers in a positive way to the hierarchical Church. He does not explain, however, how his previous attack would not collide with the anti-egalitarian character of the Church. In the resulting confusion about what the French Dominican actually believes, one thing is patent: He managed to take two steps forward in the destruction of the Church.

19

Notwithstanding his tactical subtleties, the outrageous character of his language is striking:

"**We have** – implicitly, unavowedly, and even **unconsciously – the idea that 'the Church' is made up of the clergy, and that the faithful are only the beneficiaries or the clientele. This horrible notion** is inscribed in so many structures and customs that it **seems natural and unchangeable. It is a betrayal of the truth.**

---

[19] J. B. Metz, "Sulla presenza della Chiesa nella società," in V.A., *L'avvenire della Chiesa,* p. 138.

[20] B. Kloppenburg, *A eclesiologia do Vaticano II*, p. 124.

[21] Jean-Pierre Jossua, *Dalla teologia al teologo, in* V.A., *L'avvenire della Chiesa*, p. 78.

There is still much to be done to de-clericalize our conception of the Church – without, of course, affecting the hierarchical structure – **and to make the clergy fully aware of their position as member-servants.**"[22]

§ 20   Addressing the same topic, Cardinal Julius Döpfner, one of the four moderators who presided over the sessions of the Council, attacks the "pre-conceived authority" of priests and calls the priestly dignity, derived from participation in the Sacrament of Orders, a "professional mask." The Cardinal says:

"The forms of priestly life are deeply marked by an obsolete class consciousness that no longer accords with the social evolution of the modern world. ... On a large scale, **the clergy still survives as a 'class' in a totally anachronistic way. Today's priest must take into account that the *pluralist society*, with its universal leveling in public life, recognizes ... only what is legitimized by personal service and not by belonging to a class.** In the eyes of modern society, the priest's authority is no longer founded first of all on sacramental ordination and its special dignity; above all, they want to see the priest's personality and his activity as a member of modern society in the 'free competition of professions.'...

"Simply put ... the demands of our time can be expressed in this way: **The priest must be a man among men. ... He cannot count on a pre-conceived authority but must create his position by his personal activity** ... and by the effort that is indispensable today in any profession. **For many of us this will be a true liberation, to know that we are considered as men by those around us, instead of hiding behind a 'professional mask.'"** [23]

§ 21   A similar position is expressed in a report by the Mixed Theological Group, composed of Catholic theologians and Protestant pastors, presented at the end of the Congress of the Secretariat for Ecumenical Activities. This conference took place in Trent from July 31 to August 7, 1976, and was presided over by Msgr. Luigi Sartori, at the time president of the Association of Italian Theologians. The report stated:

---

[22] Y. Congar, *Pour une église servante et pauvre*, pp. I35-137.

[23] Julius Döpfner, *La Chiesa vivente oggi* (Bari: Paoline, 1972), pp. 472-474.

"The Church can never dispose of the gifts of God. She cannot act as if she owned them or like an autonomous arbiter, let alone as if she had a despotic ownership over them." [24]

*

Such are the offenses delivered and spread by various conciliar and post-conciliar theologians, which reflect the *desire to offend* the Catholic Church, especially her hierarchical character. Such a mentality is necessarily a component of the spirit of the Council.

*   *   *

---

[24] Mixed Theological Group, "La presidenza nell'Eucaristia," in V.A., *Il regno di Dio che viene - Atti della XIV sessione di formazione ecumenica organizzata dal Segretariato Attività Ecumeniche (SAE),* Trent, July 31 to August 7, 1976 (Turin: Elle Di Ci, 1977), p. 361.

Chapter VII

THE CHURCH SEEN AS STERILE, SCLEROTIC [1] AND THE OPIUM OF THE PEOPLE

Unfortunately, the list of offenses against the Holy Church is a long one. Nevertheless, it is indispensable to know it in order to gauge the extent of the hatred for her and the ardent desire for her auto-demolition. Thus, one can determine the mentality of those who influenced Vatican Council II or played an important role in its application.

§ 1   By fully weighing the gravity of these outrages, and in particular by considering them as a whole, the Reader will in some way participate in the present-day Passion of the Church, analogous to that of Our Lord. By rejecting such affronts, he can make reparation for the injustices being committed against the Immaculate Spouse of the Lamb of God (cf. Apoc 21:9).

This Chapter will present the injuries of those who compare the Church to a barren old woman and consider her an archaic and sclerotic institution that only serves to anesthetize those who follow her. The Church, in their opinion, is the "opium of the people."

§ 2   In the frontispiece of a book on the future of the Church by various authors, including Fr. Chenu, one reads this description of the Church as a barren old woman, which parodies the text of Isaiah (54:1-3):

> "How often the Lord caused His heralds to be born, giving joy to barren women.
> **The whole Bible speaks of this humor of God …**
> **Such is the Church: the old woman who at times seems doomed to sterility.**
> **But she will have the last laugh, for she will conceive …**
> **Although it shall be amid great pain."** [2]

§ 3   In his contribution to the work, Pierre Eyt, a member of the International Theological Commission, rector of the well-known

---

[1] Sclerosis is from the Medieval Latin *sclirosis*, a hardening; here it refers to a lack of adaptation to progress and innovation within an institution or organization.

[2] Anonymous, "O riso de Sara ou a paixão da Igreja que concebe," in V. A., *A Igreja do futuro*, p. 7.

Institut Catholique of Paris and later Archbishop of Bordeaux and a Cardinal, explains how this "sterility of the Church" should be understood:

"It seems to us that – in what historian Lucien Febvre called her 'time of stagnation' – the Church as a communitarian institution of faith, **stably established her structures, conceived as definitive and destined to continue on without change. Likewise, we feel that in this frozen atmosphere, traditions played a determining role."**[3]

He continues: "Until recently, **the preponderance of archaism in the Christian mentality was expressed by many intellectual and practical attitudes**, and, in the eyes of many, **the faith and everything connected with it was becoming,** so to speak, **a 'place' of non-change, fixism and repetition** in a world that was increasingly understood as coming-into-being! What must be recognized is that this coming-into-being was not valued by the Church. She believed it to be superficial or meaningless. For this reason, **the faith appeared as a factor of resistance to change and of nostalgia for the 'time of stagnation'** when the Church extended her structures and dominated the future of the world! *Stat crux dum volvitur orbis*. [The cross stands still, while the world turns around it].

"In this crucial matter ... **the Council and *Gaudium et spes* have brought us to a *point of no return*,** even if numerous vestiges of the old mentality can still be found." [4]

§ 4   Referring to the teaching of theology in the pre-conciliar period, Fr. Chenu irreverently calls it "sterile":

"The teaching of theology was lamentable in the seminaries as a whole and even in Catholic institutes. There were certainly some persons who attempted various breakthroughs, but they were under suspicion. **Many abstract, sterile truths were taught, as if faith were an object to be possessed.** The whole effort of research and innovation were atrophied to the benefit of affirmations and repetitions. ...This de-humanization, which lasted almost up to the Council, explains the present day crisis in the priesthood." [5]

Referring to the teaching prior to the Council, Fr. Jean Danielou, S.J., calls it "mummified." His view is summarized by a journalist in these words:

---

[3] Pierre Eyt, "Igreja e mutações sócio-culturais," *in ibid.*, p. 16.

[4] *Ibid.*, pp. 16-17.

[5] *Jacques Duquesne interroge le Père Chenu*, p. 42.

"**Danielou**, who in 1946 published an essay on the present day orientation of religious thought, **fires point-blank at the official theology. He criticizes the Church's dissociation from contemporary culture as 'outside reality and dead theoretical speculations.' What remained fixed in academic formulas and lost contact with the movement of philosophy and science, he called a 'mummification of thinking.'**

"**The way out of that process of sclerosis that struck the Church is indicated by the return to the sources** (the Bible, Church Fathers, liturgy) **and by contact with the modern philosophies** (Marxism, Phenomenology, Existentialism) in order to confront the concrete problems of man." [6]

§ 5   Considering the changes made by the Council, Fr. Jean Cardonnel, O.P., speaks offensively against the Church:

"**What is Vatican II? It is the promise of a rupture with the past, with what is sclerotic, with what was repeated a thousand times in words and actions** regarding the Good News, which etymologically means the Gospel." [7]

§ 6   Melkite Bishop Edelby of Antioch, a major figure at the Council, made various offenses against the Catholic Church in a particularly tactless conciliar intervention. The topic under discussion was the schema that came to be the Constitution *Dei Verbum*. These were his words:

"The timidity of this paragraph is explained by **the difficulties of the Latin Churches in extracting themselves from the post-Tridentine atmosphere. The time of controversy with Protestantism has passed**; it was always strange for the Eastern Church, as for the new Churches of Africa and Asia. **This obsession must end definitively** so that we can enter completely into the mystery of the Church. **For this schema is dealing with the whole Church, and not subtle, sterile scholarly debates**.

"Certainly, the reformers opposed Scriptures to the Church, but this was because **the Latin Church**, in which they were born, **allowed the authentic sense of Tradition to become atrophied,** a tradition that the East and West had shared during the first millennium.

---

[6] Jean Daniélou, Criticism of Church teaching before the Council, in H. de Lubac, interview granted to Marco Politi, "Irrequieto ma ubbidiente," *Il Messagero*, February 2, 1983, p. 3.

[7] Jean Cardonnel, "Talk with Fr. Cardonnel," *Historia* (Paris), October 1982, p. 96.

By separating itself from its Eastern sources, the Latin Church ended in the sterility of the 16ᵗʰ century and the false problems that entangle us, in particular those regarding the interpretation of Scripture."[8]

Speaking in the Conciliar Hall, Bishop Elchinger of Strasburg likewise offended the Church as being "immobilized and sclerotic":

"The Church herself should be the source of life. **She must overcome every type of immobilization, sclerosis and conformist emptiness in her institutions and her faithful.**"[9]

In an overview on the first conciliar session, Fr. René Laurentin offensively qualifies the Church as "sclerotic":

"Such are the perspectives that have opened inside the Catholic Church. **The different points considered** – adaptation in tradition, diversification in unity, restoration of the collegial episcopate – **all aim at one same thing: to remedy her scleroses**.

"**The Church of these last centuries at times brought to mind an aged organism whose brain,** although still intact and working, **was poorly informed by the senses, thus causing very slow and flawed reactions.** An effective contact between the center and the periphery, between Rome and the Episcopate, should condition the future dynamics of the pastoral adaptation installed by Vatican II to definitively restore the youth of the Church, which, according to John XXIII, is the objective of the Council." [10]

§ 7

Further on, he comments on the intuition of John XXIII: "We needed the prodigious instinct of the old peasant of Bergamo [John XXIII] to introduce this renewal that we are seeing into the somewhat **sclerotic organism of the Roman Church**." [11]

Laurentin praises the Constitution *Sacrosanctum Concilium* as providing a remedy for a "sclerotic Church": "In short, **that Constitution would make the official Prayer**, the essential prayer **of the Church, leave a deplorable situation, a sclerosis that deeply paralyzed her for more than 10 centuries**."[12]

---

[8] Neophytos Edelby, Intervention in the Conciliar Hall of October 5, 1964, in B. Kloppenburg, *Concílio Vaticano II*, vol. 4, p. 112-113; see also V.A., *A Igreja Greco-Melquita no Concílio*, pp. 43-44.

[9] L. Elchinger, Intervention in the Conciliar Hall of October 21, 1964, *in ibid.*, vol. 4, p. 209.

[10] R. Laurentin, *Bilan de la première session*, pp. 88-89.

[11] *Ibid.*, p. 116.

[12] R. Laurentin, *Bilan de la deuxième session*, p. 243.

Also dealing with liturgy, Fr. Chenu violently offends the Church while justifying the intention of one of his fellow progressivists: "**Fr. Duployé wanted to get out of the liturgical filthiness in which we found ourselves.**"[13]

Msgr. Johannes Wagner, adviser for the Congregation for Divine Worship, insults the Church with these words: "**Passing through the authentic trial that the Council proved to be, the Church became immune from the dangers of her fossilized liturgy.**"[14]

§ 8   Making a general assessment of the Council, Laurentin affirms: "Vatican II, a pastoral Council, paradoxically became the Council of a doctrinal renewal. The theologians found an unprecedented audience there: 'a Council of specialists,' it was called at the very first session – with a somewhat critical note because it was too much so. This could be explained by a historical situation.

"**For centuries theology had been in a process of sclerosis. It progressively lost contact with its sources and life itself to become a collection or system of theses.** In the shadows, the persistent work of frequently unknown theologians remedied this situation. Vatican II decisively legitimized the achievements of that current which returned to both the sources and the living reality of salvation."[15]

Parallel to the general meetings of the Council, an intense intellectual activity was taking place in Rome – conferences, interviews, manifestos, petitions – which often received widespread media coverage. For example, this was how the conferences of the 'Red' Archbishop of Brazil, Helder Câmara, managed to achieve broad repercussions.[16]

§ 9   In a similar way, Fr. Jacques Loew, O.P., founder of the leftist Worker Priest Movement, announced a concurrent conference as the fourth conciliar session unfolded, thus aiming to influence the Decree *Presbyterorum Ordinis* then under discussion. We follow the narrative of Fesquet, who describes the influence of this meeting at which Loew calls the Church "sclerotic." The journalist from *Le Monde* writes:

---

[13] *Jacques Duchesne interroge le Père Chenu*, p. 92.

[14] Joannes Wagner, "La nueva litugia," in V.A., *La reforma que llega de Roma*, p. 43.

[15] R. Laurentin, *Bilan de la quatrième session*, p. 369.

[16] Cf. H. Fesquet, *Le Journal du Concile*, pp. 744-748, 1092.

"On Thursday night, Cardinals Tisserant, dean of the Sacred College, Richaud, Archbishop of Bordeaux, Martin, Archbishop of Rouen, Roy, Archbishop of Quebec, around 30 conciliar Fathers [Bishops], Mr. Brouillet, ambassador of France to the Holy See, and numerous clerics and laymen filled the basement hall of the Church St. Louis of the French to listen to Fr. Loew, a Dominican priest who had been a cargo worker on the docks of Marseille as one of the first French priests to share the fate of manual workers.

"That conference, which had significant value at that moment when the Council was studying the priesthood, was followed with the greatest attention. The priest made almost no allusion to the manual work of the priests, but his whole exposition energetically called for the Church to find efficient means to diminish the gap that separated her from the masses.

"With his direct language packed with metaphors he learned from his fellow workers, Fr. Loew evoked the absence of God in the contemporary world, 'an absence which, according to Léon Bloy, became one of the attributes of God.' The major part of the exposition explained why and how it was indispensable for Catholicism to eliminate everything that could impede the word of God from reaching our contemporaries.

"'**We must extricate our faith from its sclerotic casing,**' he said. '**Many things entangle us. It is as if the mystery of faith were crushed by casuistry. People are suffocated.** Problems replace great certainties. We must re-find the grand axes of faith. *Aggiornamento* in itself is not sufficient. It is necessary to make the primordial truths shine. Conversion can only come from that.'" [17]

§ 10   Fr. Bernard Sesboüé, S.J., a member of the International Theological Commission, writes for several progressivist French theological magazines. He believes that for many, including himself, the Church has become "outdated" and her teaching "sclerotic," as one can read in his book *The Gospel in the Church*, which he gave the Author of these lines during their meeting in Paris on February 21, 1983. In it, we find this description of the Church:

"By definition the Gospel is good news, a force of life, an explosion of novelty ... For many, however, **the Church is** something totally different: A **majestic but outdated institution turned toward a past seen as obsolete, she offers a rigid, sclerotic teaching.**

---

[17] Jacques Loew, Lecture given in Rome on October 22, 1965, *in* H. Fesquet, *Le Journal du Concile*, p. 998.

She has a constant suspicion toward everything that is unsettling and new. In addition, **she purports to exert her power over consciences; her dogmas are obligatory and her moral teaching coercive.** **From this to conclude that there is nothing else to be expected from an institution where the Gospel is … truly 'alienated,' there is just a step.**" [18]

§ 11   Another member of the International Theological Commission, Brazilian Bishop Boaventura Kloppenburg, O.F.M., was a conciliar *perito* and author of a chronicle of Vatican II. He does not hesitate to insult the Church; he calls her perennial teaching nothing more than a "sterile paralysis." The theologian says:

"One cannot help but be impressed at how easily Vatican II overrode certain positions of Trent that seemed definitive. We have here a beautiful example and a precious lesson for the future. **Our position before the Magisterium – even the Supreme Magisterium** – in Ecumenical Councils **neither can nor should always be one of pure and simple acceptance,** repetition and fixation. … The Councils did not say everything definitively, nor always in the best way. **We cannot transform theology into a passive and subservient repeater of dogmas that were formulated in the past. That would be a sterile paralysis.**" [19]

§ 12   René Laurentin, also hurls the insult of "paralysis" at the pre-Vatican II Church: "**Taking steps forward in relation to Vatican I, which was dominated by a perspective bogged down in paralysis,** the Constitution *Dei Verbum* proposes a theology of the development of dogma."[20]

§ 13   Along these lines, Von Balthasar endorses strong offenses he made in an early writing. An interviewer for 30 *Giorni* reminds the theologian of a preface he wrote to the published letters of a university colleague:

"*Question:* Later, in your high-school and university years, you met the young Joseph Rast. After his premature death, you published his letters. In it I found a preface in which you wrote: 'He – Joseph Rast – made a choice, completely overcoming through his whole trajectory the **overly stagnant, putrid, arid and hypocritical waters of Catholicism.**' Is this an image of Catholicism that you have also experienced?

---

[18] Bernard Sesboüé, *O evangelho na Igreja - A tradição viva da fé* (São Paulo: Paulinas, 1977), pp. 15-16.

[19] B. Kloppenburg, *A eclesiologia do Vaticano II*, p. 223.

[20] R. Laurentin, *Bilan de la quatrième session*, p. 277.

"*Answer:* It is a somewhat strong expression. But he [Rast] had a penetrating gaze. He was completely oriented toward an existential and ultimate cultural decision. He wanted to renew Swiss Catholicism."[21]

§ 14

Writing on the need for the Church to adapt to the demands of modern youth – symbolized by the May 1968 revolt at the Sorbonne – Fr. Congar describes the criticisms he imagines exist in the minds of the youth. The Dominican considers that the Church appears "insignificant" and useless, offering only "sterile words." Here is Congar's description:

"J. L. Barrault gives testimony ... to a quite generalized attitude today, and not just among the youth: Yes to Jesus, but no to the Church. No to [administrative] apparatus, to authority. ... The expressions are innumerable, but they agree with the analyses and diagnoses: There is a rejection of what has been done, a rejection of imposed norms, in the final analysis, a rejection of forms. Some will go so far as to say: 'The important thing in life is to be able to do what one wants, what one feels like doing.'

"Many appreciate certain authentic values: peace, the equality of men, scientific and technical efficiency ... the liberties of a democratic type. But they do not think that the doctrinal system the Church proposes, especially the language of her institutions and her practice, shares these vital values. **So the Church appears to them as insignificant. As for the rest, no one needs her to live these values and promote them efficaciously because it is nothing more than repeating sterile words.**" [22]

§ 15

The author goes on to affirm that the "sterile words" attributed to modern youth are those of Scholasticism:

"The amazing change in the world imposes on the Church a no less amazing effort of revision and renewal. ... **Many of the *representations* of the Faith can no longer be accepted and, therefore, can no longer be proposed in the terms, categories and framework bequeathed to us by Scholasticism**, the apologetics of the 18th and 19th centuries, and the scholastic teaching and preaching common at the beginning of this century." [23]

§ 16

To illustrate his affirmation that the Church cannot be immutable and should always be *in fieri,* evolving, Kloppenburg cites – with an obvious endorsement – the "prayer" of an author condemned

[21] E. Koller, "Cento domande a von Balthasar," interview granted to E. Koller, in *30 Giorni,* July 1984, p. 12.

[22] Y. Congar, *Église Catholique et France moderne*, p. 52.

[23] *Ibid.,* p. 53.

by the Church, Josef Dillersberger. In it, the latter criticizes the "old things" of the Church and longs for their destruction:

"In an article in the magazine *Concilium*, Prof. Skydsgaard [the Danish pastor who represented the World Lutheran Union as an observer at the Council] recalls the text of an article published in 1931 by the then young Josef Dillersberger ... which was written as a prayer for the renewal of the Catholic Church. In it Dillersberger implores the Holy Spirit, the 'tempestuous breath of God,' to act soon and renew everything:

"'But where art Thou here on earth? They say that Thy Church is filled with Thee. **But everything in her is so still, so silent, even somewhat dead!** *Two-thirds cadaver* was the judgment of a Communist in the Soviet Union. ... **In Thy Church,** Lord, **everything is already so old!** In her the old things are worth much, much more than the new! **Any innovator** among us **is taken for a heretic!** ... In Thy Church ... any novelty is immediately met with the greatest suspicion and mistrust ... Spirit of the Lord, who loves new things, when wilt Thou renew the face of Thy Church? **When wilt Thou show us what of the old can and must disappear?** ... It suffices for Thee to will it, and Thy **tempestuous breath will blow away everything old and all will be new!** ... **Unleash hurricanes in Thy Church!** Renew her face! Unfurl once again the banners of freedom upon the children of God!'

"Skydsgaard then notes that after these lines were published, the author was almost immediately suspended from his academic teaching post by the Pontifical Congregation of Studies, and that only recently was he reinstalled." [24]

§ 17   Chronicler Laurentin describes the Church as burdened by "carapaces" and "archaisms," as he closes his narration of the second conciliar session. He says:

"Today Vatican II is at a crossroads [of History]. The early success of the liturgical reform, which is beginning to be applied, should not make us forget the essential part of the work still to be done. Even so, there is no danger of failure, and the progress achieved in the course of one year is manifest: Decisive elements of the program were unveiled by Paul VI and essential points of the conciliar work were established or are in the process of being established. **The Church shook off certain carapaces and archaisms**. Gestures and actions that would not have seemed possible a year ago have multiplied. The

---

[24] B. Kloppenburg, *A eclesiologia do Vaticano II*, pp. 97-98.

trip of Paul VI [to Jerusalem] and his meeting with the patriarch Athenagoras is just one particularly impressive example."[25]

Assessing the first conciliar session, the same author disparagingly calls the Church before Vatican II a "lethargic organism":

"That all the Bishops of the whole world have actually gathered together is a fact of incalculable importance. ... **This meeting of the scattered organs of government of the Church makes one think of a lethargic organism whose vital connections were all reestablished, suddenly reactivated.** This phenomenon took place on various levels. Each Bishop renewed his insertion into the Church as a whole. Each regional or national Episcopate found occasion to make contacts, unprecedented in number, as in intensity and duration. The Episcopal Conferences acquired a new cohesion. Some took form and others were purely and simply founded, like the Italian Conference, for example."[26]

§ 18

Along these lines, Bernard Sesboüé not only calls the teaching of the Church and her traditions "vile" and "unbearable," but also brands her dogmas as "taboo points." In his work *The Gospel in the Church*, he writes:

"The emphasis of present day thinking is that 'progress' has made us wiser and more powerful than our parents in confronting the world and ourselves. ... **There is something vile in the complication of 'traditions'** that necessarily multiply in every human community. **Hasn't time managed to free us from a prison that became unbearable, even though an almost iconoclast courage was needed to do so?**

"**Likewise, in the language of the Church, the lure of the Gospel was subtly transformed into an austere body of 'doctrines,' an armor that became increasingly heavy** as the centuries passed. **What was simple and joyful became complicated and obscure; what was living ceded way to an increasingly abstract and intellectualized teaching.** ... The official teaching of the Church became a part of this, and **doctrinal development crystallized into a certain number of 'taboo' points called** *dogmas*."[27]

*

---

[25] R. Laurentin, *Bilan de la deuxième session*, p. 270.

[26] R. Laurentin, *Bilan de la première session*, p. 60-61.

[27] B. Sesboüé, *O Evangelho na Igreja*, pp. 16-17.

§ 19   There is no small number of theologians – among whom we choose four of the most expressive – who have recognized certain criticisms of the Church made by Communists as true and just. They consider the Catholic Faith and teaching as presented before Vatican II to be the "opium of the people," an insult flung by Marx against religion.[28] To avoid such criticism, religion should take up the banner of class struggle.

The first progressivist theologian we will look at is Fr. Marie-Dominique Chenu, a pioneer in the "opening" to Communism and one of the four theologians who maintained contacts with Marxists at the time of the Council.[29] Chenu says:

"It is also necessary to be extremely sensitive to everything that is lived, sought and achieved in the community, in its concrete commitments. I would dare to say that in this communion and quest, **the theologian is not situated on the side of the institution, which always considers it difficult to remove itself from an abstract discourse, where the words of the Gospel end by being an opium.**"[30]

§ 20   This same presupposition is adopted by Fr. Karl Rahner, a theologian often praised by the post-Conciliar Pontiffs and official organs of the Vatican.[31] In order not to be the "opium of the people,"

---

[28] Marx's oft-quoted line reads as follows: "The struggle against religion is, therefore, indirectly the struggle against the world whose spiritual aroma is religion. Religious suffering is, at one and the same time, the expression of real suffering and a protest against real suffering. Religion is the sigh of the oppressed creature, the heart of a heartless world, and the soul of soulless conditions. **It is the opium of the people**" (Karl Marx, *Contribution to the Critique of Hegel's 'Philosophy of Right,'* Cambridge: University Press, 1970, p. 131).

[29] Chenu explains: "Since the Council expressed the desire for the Church to dialogue, four editors of *La Nouvelle Critique*, a doctrinal magazine of the Communist Party, invited four theologians to regular meetings at which I, along with Fr. Congar, participated" (*Jacques Duquesne interroge le Père Chenu*, p. 167).

[30] *Ibid.*, p. 21.

[31] On the eulogies of Paul VI for Fr. Rahner's work, as well as the prestigious audience the Pontiff granted him during the Council, see A. Wenger, *L'Église en son temps,* vol. 2, p. 254; B. Mondin, *Os grandes teólogos do século vinte,* vol. 1, p. 98; H. Fesquet, *Le journal du Concile,* p. 313.

On the support of Paul VI and John Paul II for Rahner, as well as an article in *L'Osservatore Romano,* see in this Volume: Introduction, Note 14k, o, t: Chap III Note 42.

the Church would have to halt her civilizing work and "keep the mortal wound of society open," which appears to mean that the Church should stimulate class struggle. Rahner says:

"The mediation of Christian salvation is, therefore, **the exact opposite of an analgesic (an 'opium of the people'): In fact, it must keep a wound that is mortal open.** It is precisely for this reason that the mediation of salvation must remain conscious of itself: It cannot betray its nature. **It cannot give the impression of wanting to prepare a 'better world' (like a paradise) in this life before death."** [32]

§ 21

After statements like these by Chenu and Rahner, it should come as no surprise that they were followed by others with clearly revolutionary and Marxist tendencies. Such is the case of Küng and Metz, whose texts are quoted below.

In an article that asks what the Christian message really is, Fr. Hans Küng responds with a Marxist interpretation of the Gospel:

"Faith in the Crucified [Christ] makes man so free regarding law that he becomes capable of renouncing a right without giving anything in return. ... It makes man so free that in the social struggle for power, he becomes capable of using power to his own detriment, to favor another. ... The Christian message, for example, the words of the Sermon on the Mount, confirmed by the life and death of Jesus, are not meant to create some new law or install a new legal system. They are meant to free man before the law. ...

"Such a message does not become the opium of a false consolation. In a much more radical way than anywhere else, it leads toward life on this earth and tries to change this world where there is the danger of employers oppressing workers, institutions crushing people, systems annulling freedom, and power suppressing the law." [33]

§ 22

Fr. Johann Baptist Metz preaches a revolutionary theory that he calls "subversive memory." According to this concept, faith is authentic only when it upsets the established order or authority. [34] This is the "memory" to which he refers:

---

[32] Karl Rahner, *Abbozzo di una antropologia teologica, in Chiesa, uomo e società* (Rome/Brescia: Herder/Morcelliana, 1970), p. 27.

[33] H. Küng, "Qual è il messaggio cristiano?"- in V.A., *L'avvenire della Chiesa*, pp. 122-123.

[34] On the "subversive and liberating memory" of Johann Baptist Metz, see his talk at the International Congress of Theologians promoted by *Concilium* magazine in 1970, in which he develops his ideas on this topic (Cf. "Sulla presenza della Chiesa nella società,"in V.A., *L'avvenire*

"This understanding of faith would no longer propose a dead, authoritarian faith. For this reason, it would no longer raise the suspicion of being only a faith of children or of truly being the 'opium of the people.' This understanding of faith would consist above all in attempting to develop Christianity itself as a dangerously liberating and redeeming memory of Jesus Christ with regard to present-day society and its systems." [35]

In another work on the presence of the Church in society, Metz insists that the Church must free herself from her regular acts of worship, which act as an "opium of the people":

"It is in action that prayer is freed from the suspicion of being a pure 'opium of the people' or the thought that the invoked name of God is nothing but a magic formula to reach an anonymous destiny [heaven], where all human hope of freedom is finally shipwrecked. The spirituality of a liberated freedom, therefore, cannot be reduced to simple acts of worship, isolated and removed from the conflicts and oppressions of our daily social environemnt. This road to the purely cultish Church is frequently recommended today, above all in intellectual circles. I, on the contrary, consider it an erroneous road, which would end in an esoteric Church of cult, thus transformed into the 'opium of the intellectuals.'" [36]

Once again, Metz insists on the need for the Church to change in order not to be the "opium of the people":

"If the Church manages to make this change of positions [from 'Church for the people' into 'Church of the people'], she will be able to testify with special credibility to the fact that even in a life lived under the sign of oppression, she can instill an invincible hope and promise that cannot be substituted by a representation or considered the opium of the people." [37]

*

della Chiesa, pp. 129-131). See also "Redenzione ed emancipazione," in V.A., Redenzione ed emancipazione (Brescia: Queriniana, 1975), p. 177.

[35] J. B. Metz, "La 'teologia política' in discussione," in V.A., Dibattito sulla 'teologia política' (Brescia: Queriniana, 1972), p. 261.-

[36] J. B. Metz, "Sulla presenza della Chiesa nella società," p. 139.

[37] J. B. Metz, "Per una Chiesa rinnovata prima di un nuovo concilio," in V.A., Verso la Chiesa del terzo millennio, p. 129.

Here we close our exposition of offenses directed toward the Catholic Church that consider her sclerotic, sterile and the opium of the people. We believe that this sample reveals quite well the *animus injuriandi* of the spirit of the Council.

*   *   *

Chapter VIII

HERESIES AND PAGAN ERRORS
ATTRIBUTED TO THE CHURCH

Among the multiple offenses progressivists direct at the Church, we find a series that attributes heresies to her. Some consider the Church *in genere* as heretical; others accuse her doctrine of being Monophysitist, Pelagian, Docetist, Jansenist, and so on.

The bad faith and hatred of those who make such affronts to the Church is particularly striking from two standpoints:

§ 1 *First*, such offenses are generally pronounced by the same progressivist theologians who foster ecumenism with false religions.

Thus, while admitting all kinds of real heresies in their relations with these sects, they unjustly impute fictitious heresies to the Church. If their criticism of the Church were made in good faith, how could they accept the heresies of false religions? If there is good will in their dialogue with these false sects, how could they censure the Church at the same time? One sees, therefore, that the progressivists who promote ecumenism and accuse the Church of harboring heresies are doubly fraudulent.

§ 2 *Second*, in order to declare the existence of a heresy it is necessary to have a criterion of judgment, which normally is orthodoxy. Now, orthodoxy is found only in the Holy Church, which conserves the treasure of Faith pure and whole. Heresies are real insofar as they move away from the true Faith. When progressivists attribute heresy to the true Faith, to be consistent they must be taking another faith as their point of reference. This new faith, however, is rarely mentioned, and when it is, it is only fragmentarily. They fail to present it in its totality, probably out of fear that it would be condemned as heretical.

Thus, by branding the Holy Church as "heretical," progressivists either are giving vent to an irrational and blasphemous hatred or they are inspired by an unstated doctrine that, in fact, really appears to be heretical.

In short, they are either irrational and blasphemous, or fraudulent and probably heretical.

Notwithstanding such considerations, we will go on to show the *animus injuriandi* of various progressivist theologians whose opinions are expressive of the spirit of the Council.

1. Heresies Are Attributed to the Church

§ 3   Fr. Mario von Galli, a collaborator of the Swiss Jesuit magazine *Orientierung* and author of a chronicle on the Council, implicitly denies the Faith of the Catholic Church and insults her by stating that the treasure of the Faith – exclusive to the Catholic Church – "is perhaps poorer" in her than in any other religion, and that she cannot be called the one true Church. He states:

> "This religion of Christianity, called the only true religion, is inexorable with regard to Jesus Christ and cannot be separated from Him; but as for the rest, **it is perhaps the poorest of all the religions.**" [1]

§ 4   Cardinal Congar comments on the "ecclesiological heresy" that would supposedly exist in the Catholic milieu:

> "Our friend Dom Clément Lialine (+1958), who had a very profound sense of the Church and an enthusiasm for the Encyclical *Mystici Corporis*, would speak of **the 'ecclesiological heresy,' judging that so much is spoken about the Church that Jesus Christ can be forgotten.**" [2]

§ 5   What follows are various texts by Fr. Hans Küng, an author praised by Cardinal Joseph Ratzinger [3] and considered an "eminent

---

[1] Mario von Galli, "La relación con las religiones mundiales," in V.A., *La reforma que llega de Roma*, p. 202.-

[2] Y. Congar, *Un people messienique*, p. 32, note 8.

[3] Commenting on Küng's book *Unfehlbar? Eine aufrage* [*Infallible? An Inquiry*], Cardinal Joseph Ratzinger stated in 1971: "A predominantly critical article should not, however, ignore the positive side of Küng's book. This can be clearly deduced from all that we have said before, when we affirmed that he opened for discussion – explicitly and unequivocally – problems that need to be reformulated. He denounced obscurities in the historic and systematic structure of Catholic theology, which in fact have persisted and until now have generally been avoided and not confronted head-on" (cf. J. Ratzinger, "Contradicões no livro 'Infalivel'? de Hans Küng," in V. A., *O problema da Infalibilidade*, p. 93.

Further on, the Cardinal praises Küng's view of theology: "I want to emphasize again that I decidedly agree with Küng when he makes a clear distinction between Roman theology (taught in the schools of Rome) and the Catholic Faith. To free itself from the constraining fetters of Roman Scholastic Theology represents a duty upon which, in my humble opinion, the possibility of the survival of Catholicism seems to depend" (*Ibid.*, p. 101).

theologian" by Cardinal Karol Wojtyla. [4] Here he makes grave offenses against the Mystical Body of Christ. At the same time, he clearly
considers heretical sects as legitimate daughters of the Catholic Church:

"The daughters have a fear of being absorbed. … **For them,
this mother [the Catholic Church]**, despite her incontestable grandeur and historical experience, **not only has become old and sluggish, backward and vile in spirit, but also confused and dispersed. Her gaze seems to have become blurred**, precisely toward what is essential and decisive. **Her faith has become too superstitious, her love too legalist, and her hope too earthly.** For
her daughters, she is not the same as she was at the beginning. …

"**But what this mother can never deny**, despite all the
bitterness, complaints and harsh judgments, **is that she is the mother
of these daughters**, all so different from one another and, frequently,
not so similar to her."[5]

§ 6   The same author imagines that the Church would not have the
right to deny the criticisms of heretics since she also would be "filled
with encrypted heresies":

"**What would be the justification for the Church if she
did not seriously face the appeal to self-criticism, reform and
renewal according to the Gospel when a heresy appears?** … At
the beginning of any discussion with the followers of the heresy, there
must be the recognition that *each* **Christian in the Church is poten-
tially a heretic, that the Church is filled with 'encrypted heresies.'**"[6]

§ 7   Küng insists on this same offensive thinking, trying to equate
the Holy Church, pure and immaculate, with the errors of heresy:

"**For the Church is formed the same way … as the heresies**, by human persons and sinners. **In the Church there has always been**, along with hidden treasures, **much rubble and, at times,
even garbage**. Alongside her wisdom **many errors have appeared**;
alongside unmet demands, **sins and vices have also existed**."[7]

The theologian goes to the extreme of saying that in the Holy
Church nothing is perfect: "The Church can never imagine evil, sinful-

---

[4] Cf. M. Malinski, *Mon ami, Karol Wojtyla*, p. 189, text on the Introduction Note 14o of this Volume.

[5] H. Küng, *A Igreja*, vol. 2, pp. 76-77.

[6] *Ibid.*, vol. I, p 356.

[7] *Ibid.*, p. 354.

ness and the emptiness of God only outside of herself. **For there is nothing in her that is perfect.**"[8]

He also denies the Church as the only true Church of Christ. Attacking this dogma in a disrespectful way, he makes a doctrinal error and also insults the honor of the Holy Church:

"We cannot become so enamored with our Church that we fail to note the existence of other churches which, just like her, **also claim to be the true Church of Christ and, from many standpoints, actually have more right to claim this than we do.** That is, to the degree that **these churches listened more attentively to the Gospel and fulfilled the evangelical message with greater fidelity!"** [9]

§ 8

In conferences transmitted by Vatican Radio, Fr. Germano Pattaro, professor of theology and ecumenism at the Seminary of Venice, seems to consider the Catholic Church an accomplice – at the least – of what he calls a sin against the Holy Spirit. At the same time, he admits heretics and schismatics as authentic Christians who belong to the true Church of Christ. He affirms:

"The geography of the Church shows in a surprising way the state of division in which Christians find themselves. This is unnatural, because the will of Christ for the Church is something different. ... The express will of Christ demands unity as the defining element of his Church. For this reason, Christians must compare their behavior with the will of Christ and accept the diagnosis of sin that falls upon them, because every division is a manifest violation of Christ's mandate for the Church. Consequently, it is rightly said that **the state of separation in which Christians find themselves is a sin against the Spirit**, prevents the preaching of the Gospel, gives scandal to the world and makes a mockery of the will of the Lord." [10]

Up to this point, we have shown progressivist attacks that attribute heresy to the Church herself. Now we will present examples of conciliar and post-conciliar authors who attribute various heresies to Catholic doctrine.

---

[8] H. Küng, *Veracidade*, p. 30.

[9] H. Küng, *A Igreja*, vol. 2, p. 48.

[10] Germano Pattaro, *Riflessioni sulla teologia post-conciliare* (Rome: A.V.E., 1970), pp. 99-100.

Monophysitism [11]

§ 9   The first affront comes from Fr. Chenu, one of the inspirers of the proposal to adapt the Church to the modern world, which found voice in Vatican II's *Message to the World* as well as the Pastoral Constitution *Gaudium et spes*. Chenu attributes to the Church a Christology contaminated by "Monophysitism:"

"Over the centuries, Christian 'spirituality' ... if not in theory, at least in mentality and behavior, almost always tended to admit – more or less consciously – the existence of a certain region of the soul superior to the body that is the meeting place with God, characterizing an a-temporal relationship with Christ inside **a more or less monophysitist Christology.**" [12]

§ 10   Msgr. Luigi Sartori, then president of the Association of Italian Theologians, accused the Christology of the Church of being "inclined toward Monophysitism," that is, her own divinization:

"Notwithstanding the equilibrium of the dogma of Chalcedon, which recognized the humanity of Jesus Christ without prejudice to His divinity and vice-versa, **the Christology that became consolidated preponderantly in the sentiment and life of the Church over the centuries was more inclined toward Monophysitism**, which made it difficult to think about the true and full humanity of Jesus. The *model of Christ [forma Christi]* that seems to have principally inspired the structure of the Church was that of the *glory of His Resurrection [gloria resurrectionis]*. The *Kingdom of God* – even when it was accomplished through the mediation of the *Kingdom of Christ* – frequently came to be a justification for the *Kingdom of the Church*." [13]

---

[11] **Monophysitism** (from the Greek *monos* meaning 'one,' and *physis* meaning 'nature') is a heresy from the 5th century that claimed Our Lord Jesus Christ had only one nature, the divine and not the human. Progressivists accuse traditional Catholic Christology and ecclesiology of being Monophysitist because of the adoration and supreme veneration they give to Our Lord and the Church. According to the followers of Progressivism, more importance should be given to the "human" aspects of Christ and the Church.

[12] Marie-Dominique Chenu, "The History of Salvation and the Historicity of Man in the Renewal of Theology," in V. A., *Theology of Renewal - Renewal of Religious Thought* (Montreal: Palm Publishers, 1968), vol. 1, p. 165.

[13] Luigi Sartori, "Regno di Dio e Chiesa," in V.A., *Il Regno di Dio che viene*, p. 36.

§ 11   Kloppenburg explicitly states that to consider the Catholic Church as divine would be "Monophysitism:"

"A *supernaturalist Monophysitism* claimed that Christ's human nature was absorbed by His divine nature. Analogously, the **ecclesiological Monophysitism imagines a confusion or absorption of the human elements of the Church by her divine elements** ...

"In particular, it is pious persons who sincerely and devoutly adhere to the Church in this way ... who have a monophysitist tendency to embellish the Church with an aura of the divine, exalting everything that exists in the Church as if it were divinely perfect ... and stressing the sublimity, indefectibility and sanctity of the Church. ... These persons are now scandalized by the reform movement [of the Council]. ... For them the Church, her Liturgy, her Canon Law, her Papal Documents, and even her Latin, were all untouchable, holy and sacrosanct. **Now, this monophysitist faith is beginning to waver.**" [14]

§ 12   The attribution of "Monophysitism" to the Church also comes from the pen of Rene Laurentin as he extols the fruits of the Council:

"If Vatican II fulfils its promises, it will undoubtedly appear in the eyes of History like the first stage of a rediscovery of the Holy Spirit. Many indications already show that the new phase of ecclesiology has taken that route. The Christocentrism of the present-day ecclesiological movement tends to flow into a Pneuma-centrism [centrism of the Holy Spirit] that will complete it. **Thus it will overcome the temptation toward a certain Monophysitism of the mystical body,** that is to say, a tendency to diminish the personality of the members of this body, of which Christ, the Divine Person, is the head. Instead a new value will be fully given to the personal reality of the members of this body and the bond of Love that joins them in unity."[15]

§ 13   Commenting on conciliar documents that consider the Church in need of permanent reform,[16] Austrian theologian Ferdinand Klostermann offends the Church by suggesting that until Vatican II, the Church would have been "monophysitist." The reason would be that up until then she did not sufficiently consider the human element that constituted her:

---

[14] B. Kloppenburg, *A eclesiologia do Vaticano II*, pp. 47-48.

[15] R. Laurentin, *Bilan de la quatrième session*, p. 367.

[16] Cf. LG 8; UR 6.

"**Only such a Church** [*semper reformanda*] **can have the possibility of – and even the necessity for – a reform of structure, and not be conceived as monophysitist, spiritualist or angelic. She also takes seriously her human, social element**, and, therefore, the temporal and mutable element that is in continuous interdependence with the world, and even with sin. In this way, the structures of the Church can change, because the men who constitute her and guide her change, and because the world changes – the world in which the Church is necessarily inserted. Thus, even the Church structures should change, because sin exists in this Church."[17]

§ 14

The Congregation for the Doctrine of Faith published its *Observations* to a statement released by the Second International Anglican-Roman Catholic Commission (ARCIC-II). In it, the following paragraph stands out, in which that Congregation admits the existence of "Monophysitism" in the pre-conciliar ecclesiological position:

"It is true that **the Council**, although insisting on the specific nature of the Church, **wanted to correct what one can call a certain ecclesial 'Monophysitism' by discretely setting up a guard against an excessive assimilation of the Church to Christ**. She is the spotless Spouse purified by the spotless Lamb (LG 6), but she is also constituted by men and, in this regard, 'is summoned by Christ to that continuous reform which, as a human and earthly institution, she is always in need' (UR 6)."[18]

Pelagianism[19] and Jansenism[20]

§ 15

Fr. Josef Fuchs, S.J. is a well-known moral theologian and professor of the Pontifical Gregorian University. In an interview with the Author of these lines, he said that in the last centuries Church doctrine had taken on a naturalist tendency that generated a spirituality with a Pelagian tendency, since it considered that man did not need grace to become holy. According to Fr. Fuchs, all men – and not just

---

[17] Ferdinand Klostermann, "Princípi per una riforma di struttura della Chiesa," in V. A., *La fine della Chiesa come società perfetta* (Verona: Mondadori, 1968), p. 245.

[18] Congregation for the Doctrine of the Faith, "In margine alle osservazioni sul documento dell'ARCIC-II," *L'Osservatore Romano,* November 20, 1988, p. 8.

[19] **Pelagianism** is the doctrine of the heretic Pelagius in the 4th and 5th centuries that denies original sin and the consequent corruption of human nature (cf. *Catholic Encyclopedia*, NY: Encyclopedia Press, Inc., 1913, entry Pelagianism).

[20] **Jansenism** is the doctrine of Cornelius Jansen (1585-1638), a Dutch theologian who – against the teaching of the Magisterium – exagger-

Catholics – are "impregnated with grace." This was his statement that affronts the Church:

"The concept of God, of grace, took on something of Pelagianism in the last few centuries." [21]

§ 16   In his turn, Msgr. Philippe Delhaye, secretary of the International Theological Commission, contends that the sexual morality taught by the Church from the 17th to 19th centuries had traits of Jansenism:

"The Church is giving a greater welcome to sexuality. ... This is the reason why John Paul II speaks often about the youth and the Gospel in his many talks on marriage and sexual life. ... **The Church is turning her back on certain Jansenist interpretations. One can say that the 17th, 18th and 19th centuries were Jansenist centuries as far as the teaching on sexuality is concerned.**" [22]

Docetism [23]

§ 17   In this testimony of Chenu, he describes the spirituality of the Church as "Docetist:"

"In opposition to **an unconscious Docetism that was nurtured for a long time [in the Church],** that is to say, **an a-temporal, abstract and a-cosmic 'spirituality,'** [today] there is interest in the historic and concrete humanity of Christ that leads us

---

ated the doctrine of St. Augustine on grace. It emphasizes a Calvinist predestination, denies free will and maintains that human nature is incapable of good. This doctrine was influential in France in the 17th century. One of Calvin's main followers became Pasquier Quesnel, who preached that the action of grace was irresistible (cf. Bernardino Llorca, *Manual de Historia Eclesiastica*, Barcelona: Labor, 1942, pp. 680-684; *Catholic Encyclopedia*, entry Jansenism).

[21] Josef Fuchs, Interview granted to the Author, Rome, February 4, 1983.

[22] Philippe Delhaye, Interview granted to the Author, Louvain-la-Neuve, Belgium, February 28, 1983.

[23] **Docetism** (from the Greek *dokesis*, "appearance") was a heresy of the 2nd and 3rd centuries which affirmed that Our Lord's physical body was an illusion, as was His Crucifixion. That is, Christ only *appeared* to have a physical body and to have died, but in reality He was incorporeal, a pure spirit, and could not physically die. Thus, Our Lord would have descended from Heaven with only the appearance of a body, passing through the womb of Mary without taking on anything from her body, as water passes through a canal (cf. Bernardino Llorca, *Manual de Historia Ecclesiastica*, pp. 680-684; *Catholic Encyclopedia*, entry Docetism).

to rediscover man as a partner of God in the history of the world. 'Since God made himself man, man comes to be the measure of all things' (Karl Barth)." [24]

§ 18   Alberto Franzini's doctoral thesis at Gregorian University was recommended to the Author of this Work by Cardinal Alfons Maria Styckler. Commenting on the Constitution *Dei Verbum*, Franzini makes it clear in it that he considers that the notion of Revelation prevalent in the Church up until the Council had traces of Docetism:

"By reaffirming the total truth of the mystery of the Incarnation, **the Constitution** [*Dei Verbum*] not only **wanted to eliminate all traces of Docetism,** but to reinforce the concrete character of biblical revelation before any other religion or revelation." [25]

Nominalism [26]

§ 19   Insulting the Latin Catholic Church, Melkite Archbishop Edelby calls her mentality "nominalist":

"**It is necessary to do away with the too juridical and even nominalist mentality into which the** reformed and **Latin Catholics have closed themselves.** It was that mentality which, already in the Middle Ages, opposed the consecration to the *epiklesis*.[27] It was that mentality which, even recently, considered the

---

[24] M.D. Chenu, "The History of Salvation and the Historicity of Man," p. 166.

[25] Alberto Franzini, *Tradizione e Scrittura - Il contributo del Concilio Vaticano II* (Brescia: Morcelliana, 1978), p. 269.

[26] **Nominalism** is the philosophical doctrine which considers that abstract, universal concepts and general ideas do not exist except in name. They are mere verbal designations, serving as labels for a collection of things or a series of particular events. It affirms that only the individual external object is concrete and real. The concept only exists in the intelligence.

In the Middle Ages the principal nominalists were Roscelin of Compiègne, Abelard and William of Occam. The most important of those who opposed Nominalism were St. Anselm, William of Champeux and St. Bernard. Nominalism is inseparable from an empiricist theory of knowledge. Hume, Condillac, Stuart Mill, Taine and Spencer are all nominalists (cf. *Nouveau Larousse illustré – Dictionnaire universel encyclopédique*, Paris: Larousse, vol. 6, entry Nominalism, p. 402; B. Llorca, *Manual de historia eclesiastica*, p. 426; *Catholic Encyclopedia*, entry Nominalism).

[27] *Epiklesis* (Latin *invocatio*) is the name of a prayer that occurs in the Eastern liturgies after the words of Consecration, in which the celebrant prays that God may send down His Holy Spirit to change the bread and

primate and collegiality as separate realities. It is still this mentality that reappears, juxtaposing Scripture and Tradition. But the question is badly formulated. What must be done is to return to the mystery of the Church, the essence of this Council."[28]

Deism [29]

§ 20

In his memoirs, Cardinal Suenens describes his time as a seminarian, judging the ecclesiastical ambience of the 1920s as "deist":

"In that epoch, we were still in a 'deist' type of spiritual climate: The Trinity had very little relation to life, and the Holy Spirit disappeared in God in a kind of anonymity as a consequence of the theological explanations of the time."[30]

2. Pagan Errors Are Attributed to the Church

It is not enough that certain Conciliar Fathers and theologians assert that the Church was infected with the heretical errors. Some important thinkers who exerted great influence during and after the Council ventured even further, suggesting that the Catholic Church – up until the Council – would harbor pagan elements that must be eradicated.

---

wine into the Body and Blood of His Son. This form has given rise to one of the chief controversies between the Eastern and Western Churches, as the Eastern Schismatics believe that the *Epiklesis*, and not the words of Consecration, is the essential form – or at least the essential complement – to operate the Transubstantiation (cf. *Catholic Encyclopedia*, entry Epiklesis).

[28] N. Edelby, Intervention in the Conciliar Hall of October 5, 1964, in B. Kloppenburg, *Concílio Vaticano II*, vol. 4, p. 113; R. Laurentin, *Bilan de la troisième session*, p, 100; V.A., *A Igreja Greco-Melquita no Concílio*, p. 44.

[29] **Deism** is the doctrine of those who, basing themselves exclusively on rational grounds, without reliance on any revelation, religious authority or holy text, admit the existence of a supreme being whose nature remains undetermined (cf. Paul Foulquié, *Dictionnaire de la langue philosophique*, Paris: Presses Un. De France, 1962, entry Déisme; *Catholic Encyclopedia*, entry Deism).

[30] L. J. Suenens, *Souvenirs et espérances*, p. 24.

Sado-Masochism [31]

As we have already noted, one of the most influential progressivist mentors of Vatican II was Fr. Yves Congar, made a Cardinal by John Paul II in 1994. In his book *The Catholic Church and Modern France*, he resorts to an imaginary dialogue between a "moderate" and a "radical" progressivist.

In a noteworthy dialectics, he expresses, through the words of the radical progressivist, the boldest positions without indicating whether he supports or condemns them. He then smoothes over the radical position with the words of the "moderate," again without saying whether he endorses such opinion. We are, therefore, left hanging in the air, not knowing precisely what Fr. Congar thinks. This tactic has a Hegelian tone, whereby one could suppose that the position of the French Dominican would be that of an imponderable synthesis between the two "opposed" positions.

For the goals of this Study, we will consider that Fr. Congar's position is, at the least, that of the "moderate." Even as such, the latter virtually accepts the radical's criticism that the Holy Church would be sado-masochist, as we can see below:

"X [radical]: The Church attributes a kind of value to suffering as such. **She is sado-masochistic.** She poured ashes on all human joys. She placed crosses everywhere. It is not without reason that in the minds of the people priests are related with death.

"Y [moderate]: One would have to see when this started to happen and determine whether it was something cultural. The first Christian centuries spoke of death in terms of birth, peace, life, release. ... Recently the [Holy Week] black cloths and silver tears [on the statues] have been suppressed." [32]

---

[31] **Sadism** is the sexual perversion that consists in taking pleasure by inflicting harm on others, which can reach the point of death. **Masochism**, its counterpart, is the sexual pleasure obtained from receiving the sadistic punishments. In psychology, **Sado-masochism** is either the combination of sadistic and masochistic perversions in the same person, or the practice – often followed by morbid sexual actions – in which one partner adopts a sadistic role and the other a masochistic one.

[32] Y. Congar, *Église Catholique et France Moderne*, pp. 211-212.

Stoicism [33]

§ 22

Fr. Schillebeeckx, a theologian who played an active role during the Council, considers Patristic theology a tributary of "stoic thinking." He implies that by deeming sexual relations legitimate only for procreation in matrimony, Catholic Morals would also be "stoic":

"Although the Patristic theology attempts to give a biblical or Christian vision, **it cannot be denied that it does so by using Hellenistic concepts and**, principally in the first centuries, **concepts borrowed from the Stoics. ... From this mentality comes the thinking that to seek pleasure or any other thing that can obscure the use of reason is a diminution of human dignity and is, therefore, sinful.**

"This mentality explains the repulsion of Patristic theology for a concretely lived sexuality because of the orgy-like nature of the sexual act and the inevitable eroticism inherent to it, an element that we consider an instrument of the gift of love, a profoundly human gift of the spouses. ...

"Like the Stoics, priests also accepted the medical opinion of the time, which affirmed **that the sole end of sexual relations is procreation**. But the priests never established the morality of sexual life based on the biological end of the sexual organism. ... This biological end is never presented as a moral norm. The fundamental presupposition remains: Sexual union is *essentially* an act of procreation. Hence, sexuality is unknown in its essence, as when the procreation element is excluded or the sexual act is required at moments when effective procreation is in fact impossible." [34]

§ 23

For authors Flick and Alszeghy there would be "stoicism" in the Catholic teaching that instructs the faithful to be conformed to the adversities of life:

"The exhortations of the Fathers of the Church to face all adversities with serene patience are often expressed in a language that doubtlessly is influenced by that of the Stoics."[35]

---

[33] **Stoicism** is the philosophical school that shows a great indifference toward everything that affects the senses, an indifference that reaches the point of denying pain and suffering (cf. P. Foulquié, *Dictionnaire de la langue philosofique*, entry Stoïcisme).

[34] Edward Schillebeeckx, *Evolução e mudanças nas concepções cristãs do matrimônio*, in V.A., *Direitos do sexo e do matrimônio* (Petrópolis: Vozes, 1972), pp. 34-37.

[35] Maurizio Flick and Zoltán Alszeghy, *Il mistero della croce - Saggio di teologia sitematica* (Brescia: Queriniana, 1978) p. 262.

Dualism or Manichaeism [36]

§ 24

Under a different guise, the thinking of Schillebeeckx is assumed by Fr. Antonio Hortelano, professor of Moral Theology at the Alphonsian Academy in Rome. He sees Christianity intoxicated by a "morbid dualism":

"The social and ethical confinement of sexuality comes from very remote times. ... Such control is frequently transformed, however, into a morbid dualism. ...

"Christianity reacted vigorously against the dualist excesses. ... Nevertheless, despite this, it did not manage to free itself completely from the dualist intoxication. This explains to a great extent the modern sexual revolution." [37]

§ 25

Bishop Kloppenburg uses empty slogans to offend the Church:

"A great deal of dualism as well as too much separation existed in the Church-World relationship. A classical example is the theory of the Two Cities of St. Augustine, which had tragic consequences. It is absolutely necessary to avoid dualism."[38]

§ 26

John Paul II often attributed "Manichaeism" to traditional Catholic Morals. For example, during a series of talks on the "theology of the body," he says:

"Today let us return to the classic text of the chapter V of the Letter to the Ephesians, which reveals the eternal sources of the Covenant in the Father's love and at the same time the new and definitive institution of that Covenant in Jesus Christ.

"This text brings us to such a dimension of the 'language of the body' that it could be called mystical. It speaks of marriage as a 'great mystery' – 'This is a great mystery' (Eph 5:32). This mystery is fulfilled in the spousal union of Christ the Redeemer with the Church, and of the Church-Spouse with Christ ... and it is definitively carried out in eschatological dimensions.

---

[36] **Dualism** is the philosophical and religious doctrine that explains the origin and nature of the universe as the action of two opposed essences or two opposed principles. Dualism affirms that good and evil eternally fight between themselves in a battle that was already installed in the creator of the universe. The principal system of thinking that defends this false dualism is **Manichaeism**, and often these two terms are considered synonymous.

[37] Antonio Hortelano, "Rivoluzione sessuale e famiglia," *Concilium*, 1984/3, p. 100.

[38] B. Kloppenburg, *A ecesiologia do Vatican II*, p. 89.

"Nevertheless the author of the Letter to the Ephesians does not hesitate to extend the analogy of Christ's union with the Church in spousal love … to the sacramental sign of the matrimonial pact between man and woman. He does not hesitate to extend that mystical analogy to the 'language of the body,' reread in the truth of the spousal love and the conjugal union of the two.

"We must recognize the logic of this extraordinary text which radically frees our way of thinking from elements of Manichaeism or from a non-personalist consideration of the body. At the same time it brings the 'language of the body,' contained in the sacramental sign of matrimony, nearer to the dimension of *real sanctity*."[39]

Positivism [40]

§ 27   Fr. Chenu, an early promoter of the historical method whose work was condemned before the Council, calls the immutable foundation of theology in the Church the "follies of a pseudo-evangelical positivism":

"World solidarity and the diversity of civilizations form an admirable picture in the laborious genesis of a 'human community' and a kind of challenge to the Catholicity of the Church, long confined – including her theology – to the West. A theologian finds in these themes something like a second inspiration of the transcendence of the Word of God. These themes are many of God's 'signs of the times' written in the secular realities.

"Doesn't such a historicity destroy the speculative construction of theology, or at least reduce it to a very artificial superstructure? **The follies of a kind of pseudo-evangelical Positivism could lead**

---

[39] John Paul II, General audience of July 4, 1984, "Il 'grande mistero' dell'amore sponsale," *L'Osservatore Romano*, July 5, 1984, pp. 1, 4.

For other references John Paul II makes to Manichaeism in traditional Catholic morals, see: General audience of October 15, 1980, "Valori evangelici e doveri del cuore umano," *L'Osservatore Romano*, October 16, 1980, pp. 1-3.; General audience of October 22, 1980, "Realizzazione del valore del corpo secondo il disegno del Creatore," *L'Osservatore Romano*, October 23, 1980, pp. 1-2.

[40] **Positivism** is the philosophical and scientific perspective which holds that the only authentic knowledge is the one based on sense experience and positive verification. This school was founded in the 19th century by Auguste Comte, who saw the scientific method as replacing metaphysics and despised all research about first and final causes as futile (cf. Aurélio B. H. Ferreira, *Pequeno dicionário brasileiro da lingual portuguesa*, Rio de Janeiro: Civ. Bras., 1968, entry Positivism).

us to fear that this should happen. But let us leave them to deal with their own failure." [41]

§ 28   Hans Küng also spares no injurious criticisms against the traditional teaching of the Church, labeling it "dogmatic positivism," "arbitrary" and "biased." Küng affirms:

"Dogmatic positivism considers the official Church documents – and even Revelation – as the beginning and the end of theology, its alpha and omega. Thus it transforms, for example, the *Enchiridion* of ecclesiastical definitions, the Denzinger of 1854, into an unquestionable code that essentially frees the theologian from any critical doubts about the foundation, leading him to a *sacrificium intellectus* [the abdication to use his own intellect]. This neo-Scholastic 'Denzinger-theology' in fact transforms Denzinger into a schema to synthesize all of dogmatics. Based on prescribed – or proscribed – propositions, it constructed a long roster of theses representing a highly arbitrary and biased selection, presented as if it were the message of the Old and New Testament." [42]

*

The Reader has, therefore, in this Chapter more examples of what leading progressivist theologians say and think about the doctrinal purity of the Church. They reveal the new winds that were unleashed with Vatican II.

*   *   *

---

[41] M.-D. Chenu, "The History of Salvation and the Historicity of Man," p. 163.

[42] H. Küng, *Veracidade*, p. 150.

Chapter IX

DEVOTION TO THE POPE LABELED
'INSUPPORTABLE PAPOLATRY'

Progressivism is not only opposed to this or that point regarding the institution and doctrine of the Holy Catholic Church. It is viscerally opposed to the whole Catholic way of being, as well as to the Church and the Faith as a whole.

This antagonism finds a prime representative in one of the harbingers of conciliar theology, Fr. Yves Congar. He was praised and honored by Paul VI numerous times [1] and helped to write ten of the 16 schemas of the Council. [2]

§ 1   Referring to his collaboration in the Constitution on the Church, *L'Osservatore Romano* opines:

"Fr. Congar made a number of extremely relevant contributions to the writing of the conciliar Constitution *Lumen gentium*: the distinction between the ministerial priesthood and the 'hieratic' priesthood, the relationship between the priests and the Bishops, the [role of] Councils in Church life, the relationship between the Church and the State, and the salvation of those who do not belong to the Mystical Body of the Church." [3]

Congar also received the Christian Unity Award in recognition for his theological contributions to the ecumenical movement and Catholic theology. The award was bestowed on the 20th anniversary of the Vatican II Decree *Unitatis redintegratio*.[4] Much could be written to demonstrate the great esteem that the French Dominican enjoys at the Vatican.

§ 2   It is disconcerting for a Catholic, after considering this theologian's great prestige and renown, to find in his writings bold offenses against the Papacy and the devotion the Church has always paid to the Vicar of Christ. "Insupportable papolatry" are his words – included in the title of this Chapter – that refer to the traditional Catholic respect for the Papacy and devotion to the Pope. He states:

---

[1] Cf. H. Fesquet, *Le Journal du Concile*, pp. 280, 297, 998.

[2] Cf. A. Woodrow, "A Rome: Trente théologians du monde entire pour acomplir le Concile," p. 9.

[3] "Conferito a padre Yves Congar il premio per l'unità dei cristiani," *L'Osservatore Romano,* November 28, 1984, pp. 1, 5.

[4] *Ibid.*, p. 5.

"I have already told you, **one must not fall into this insupportable 'papolatry' from which we have suffered so much until recently. ... It is especially necessary to unblock the myth of infallibility.**"[5]

Further on, the same author states:

"**It is absolutely evident that the Papacy as it is today and as seen in History ... is a creation of History.** What, then, does the faith oblige of me on this point? For the *braves gens*,[6] it is simple: The Pope said it, therefore it is true. I will not disturb them, but I cannot adopt this simplistic position. Many cases – from the distant past to contemporary times – prove that the question is less simple than that." [7]

§ 3   In addition to describing devotion to the Pope as a kind of idolatry, "papolatry," Congar brands it "adulation":

"**When Pius IX went through the difficult period when the Pontifical States were suppressed** – becoming 'the prisoner of the Vatican!' – **a veritable adulation for the Pope developed in Rome.** The papal Zuaves [an infantry regiment] who met with death during the siege of Rome ... were considered as true martyrs. ... Thus, **a type of unconscious papolatry developed. In my *dossier* I have truly terrible facts along this line.** Publishing them would make no sense at all; today these things would no longer be considered a position of truth or of courage. **One simple example ... it was common to refer to the 'three white things' - the Host, the Virgin and the Pope!**" [8]

Congar goes on to tell interviewer Jean Puyo how Paul VI honored him by receiving him three times in private audiences. According to the theologian, "papolatry" came to an end with Paul VI:

"At the end of the first session of the Council, when the Fathers went to St. Peter's Square to receive the blessing of John XXIII, who was already sick, I was standing next to the obelisk in the square, not far from Cardinal Montini. I went over to see him, and we exchanged a few words. In particular he spoke to me about Fr. de Lubac.

---

[5] Y. Congar, *Jean Puyo interroge le Père Congar*, p. 213.

[6] A French expression that translates literally as 'the brave people,' but which is commonly used in progressivist jargon to refer sarcastically to those whom they consider simpletons.

[7] Y. Congar, *Jean Puyo interroge le Père Congar*, pp. 229-230.

[8] *Ibid.*, p. 116.-

"After he became Pope, he received me three times in private audiences in his library. The last meeting was in November of 1973. He wanted the two of us to be photographed together. ...

"Puyo - A climate of freedom?

"Congar - Absolutely.

"Puyo - **Still some vestige of papolatry?**

"Congar - **None.**" [9]

§ 4   André Frossard, a well-known progressivist writer and member of the prestigious French Academy, called the devotion of Catholics for the Papacy "idolatry:"

"Understood in its strictly religious sense, the expression 'sovereign pontiff' emits an odor of persistent paganism. During my trips to Rome I often have occasion to pass in front of the obelisk on the Piazza Montecitorio, which bears an inscription in honor of Augustus: *pontifex maximus*. From this distant past derives the fact that **the words 'supreme pontiff' conceal the risk of idolatry, into which many generations of Catholics have fallen. This was in the times when the ceremonial demanded a succession of genuflections before a person who seemed to be more than human.**"[10]

§ 5   Indignation against the Papacy bursts not only from the pens of Congar and Frossard, but also from highly placed Hierarchs. During the Council, the Melkite Patriarch of Antioch, Maximus IV, censured the enthusiastic veneration of Catholics for the **primacy of Peter. He called it a "sickening insistence on recalling this truth and isolating it as if only the Pope existed."**[11]

§ 6   Before Vatican II started, the same Maximus IV gravely offended the institution of the Papacy in a note to the central preparatory commission. He stated:

"One can ask why the Theological Commission and, with it, certain theologians, are trying to make the Council enunciate **excessive principles in praise of the Pope.** Today there are certainly people in the Catholic Church who only want to see in Catholicism its head: the Pope. **From one exaggeration to another, they end by dragging the Church into 'papolatry,' which is not an imaginary**

---

[9] *Ibid.*, p. 118.

[10] André Frossard, "Cos'é un Papa?" *L'Osservatore Romano*, March 23, 1989, p. 3.

[11] Cf. H. Fesquet, *Le Journal du Concile*, pp. 139-140; R. Laurentin, *Bilan de la première session,* p. 50.

danger. They make the Pope out to be not the father, the humble and devoted pastor, the eldest brother concerned with the honor and apostolate of his brothers, **but rather an ecclesiastical replica of the Roman Caesar. An old subconscious imperialism is driving them, and they seem to find in the papacy a fulfillment of their dreams of universal dominion."**[12]

§ 7   Likewise offensive – in this case against the doctrine rather than honor of the Church – was the criticism of the Archbishop of Baltimore Lawrence Joseph Shehan, spoken in the Conciliar Hall on October 11, 1963: **"One can never conceive of papal infallibility without the consent of the Church or against it."** [13]

On February 22, 1965, Paul VI raised both Patriarch Maximus IV and Archbishop Shehan to the Cardinalate...

§ 8   At the 31ˢᵗ General Meeting of the Council, Bishop Emiel-Jozef de Smedt of Bruges harshly attacked the principle of hierarchy in the Church. He also warned against "papolatry" present in devotion to the Pope and affirmed that it must end:

"One should note that hierarchical power is only something transitory. It belongs to the time of terrestrial pilgrimage. ... The people of God exist permanently; the ministry of the hierarchy is a passing situation. ... **When we speak about the Church, we should be careful not to fall into a type of hierarchicalism. It is necessary to avoid every appearance of clericalism, bishopolatry or papolatry.** Because what always prevails is the people of God. To these people of God ... the hierarchy should render its humble services so that the people of God may grow and reach its perfect age, the plenitude of Christ."[14]

§ 9   During the second session of the Council, Msgr. Neophytos Edelby, titular Archbishop of Edessa, gave a lecture in one of the halls of St. Agnes Church in Rome. In his talk, among other insults, he accused the Church of having "a morbid obsession with the Primacy of the Pope." These were his words:

"The Western Church is still very clerical in her thinking and behavior. She takes a view that is different from ours [the Eastern

[12] Maximus IV, Note to the preparatory commission of Vatican II in May 1962, in V. A., *A Igreja Greco-Melquita no Concilio*, p. 96; cf. pp. 67, 100.

[13] Lawrence Joseph Shehan, Intervention in the Conciliar Hall of October 11, 1963, in H. Fesquet, *Le Journal du Concile*, p. 225.

[14] Emile de Smedt, Intervention in the Conciliar Hall of December 1, 1962, in B. Kloppenburg, *A eclesiologia do Vatican II*, pp. 239-240.

Catholic rite]: She holds that **Christ established Peter as supreme chief, a type of Roman Emperor in a cassock**; afterwards, He gave him collaborators and subjects – the clergy and the faithful. It is the opposite for us in the East: that is, first of all Christ chose the faithful, to whom the right of receiving the Gospel belongs; afterwards, He gave them the Apostles, and, finally, so that this group would remain coherent, He chose a head for it.

"In modern Catholic opinion, there is a kind of morbid obsession with the Primacy of the Pope. A prayer of exorcism would almost be needed. To say that the Pope is God on earth is a blasphemy. The Sovereign Pontiff is surrounded by an obsequious respect that has nothing evangelical about it. Let us return to the Gospel. **Everything else is worldliness that should not exist.**"[15]

§ 10 Drawing a fanciful distinction between infallibility and "infallibilism,"[16] the Jesuit magazine *La Civiltà Cattolica* boldly insults devotion to the Pope on the pretext of criticizing the excesses of "infallibilism." In an editorial under the responsibility of Fr. Gianpaolo Salvini, the magazine claims such devotion is related to the "exaggerations of papolatry and a servile byzantinism."

"Infallibilism is a psycho-sociological attitude not that much different from the servility typical of the courtesan mentality, which, like an excrescence, springs up outside the pure doctrine of the personal infallibility of the Pope. Even if at times, for contingent reasons, it was able to play an apologetic role, let it be said frankly that **it was the effect and cause of that ecclesiastical pyramidism that saw the proliferation of the exaggerations of papolatry and the servile spirit of byzantinism.**"[17]

§ 11 Congar tries to ignore the mission of the Pope as Sovereign Pontiff and King, reducing his role to nothing more than a symbol of unity. His preeminence would exist only to fulfill the need that the faithful have to be represented. The French theologian calls manifestations of enthusiasm for the Vicar of Christ "excesses – mediocre from every point of view":

"The Pope is an organ [the head of the body of the Church] on the highest level and in the highest degree. Theology proposes the

---

[15] N. Elderby, Conference in Rome of October 24, 1963, in H. Fesquet, *Le Journal du Concile*, p. 273.

[16] This sophism was analyzed in Vol. I, *In the Murky Waters of Vatican II*, Chap. X § 50.

[17] Editorial, "Il Ministero del Papa dopo i due Concilii Vaticani," *La Civiltá Cattolica*, November 2, 1985, p. 127.

theory. The faithful sense this. When they come to Rome, they want to see the personified image of the unity of the Body of Christ. One cannot understand **this kind of devotion, which has had**, let us say it frankly, **its excesses – mediocre from every point of view** – if one does not recognize on the one hand, the living value of a symbol and, on the other, the traditional sense of representation." [18]

§ 12   Another leader at the Council, Cardinal Julius Döpfner, echoes the words of Congar both in substance and form. To him, devotion to the Pope and the Church derives from a "romanticism" that generates a "blind love" that "makes no sense" at this stage of the Church's evolution. Döpfner writes:

"**There was a time when many of us had a completely a-critical and truly blind love for the Church.** I recall, for example, some pontifical ceremonies before 1933 ... that had **an atmosphere where the Holy Father**, the supreme head of the Church, **stood before us without any shadow of criticism** as the one who sustains and protects the whole Church. **Certainly all this was linked at times to some sort of Romanticism.** We were inclined to assume an indignant apologetic attitude the moment anyone said anything against the Church ...

"**But at the Council the Church herself began to exercise self-criticism. She made her confession** with respect to her past behavior. Also **a suspicion** – engendered by the atmosphere of the time – **entered the people of the Church**, a frequently **serious suspicion about the Church and her leader.** In the end, **the Pope came to be criticized as naturally as a parish priest or school headmaster is criticized.** At times one almost has the impression that people are ashamed of the Church. Some even consider being called Catholic a constraint.

"Even so, **I think that this is an inevitable transition.** Here also it is necessary ... to see where this evolution is ultimately leading. I repeat – knowing that I run the risk of being misunderstood – that **it makes no sense at all to want to return to the time of blind love for the Church.** Today we need an *enlightened love.* ... Such a love, which has become more mature, must also become spontaneous." [19]

§ 13   One sees that restrictions regarding the Papacy and offenses against it characterized the spirit of important personages who played a decisive role at Vatican II. Accordingly, it comes as no surprise to find Fr. Hans Küng, also a Council *perito*, fearless of any sanctions as

---

[18] Y. Congar, *Église Catholique et France moderne*, p. 97.
[19] J. Döpfner, *La Chiesa vivente oggi*, pp. 152-153.

he calls the Papacy an "absurd" institution that stands in the way of ecumenism:

"The fact that the service of Peter ... has become a gigantesque and apparently **immovable, insurmountable and inevitable bloc** that bars the way to a reciprocal understanding of the Christian churches **is an absurd situation**, which will never be properly understood by one who is convinced of the usefulness of Peter's service." [20]

§ 14

Küng goes on to praise John XXIII for having ended the "spiritual dictatorship" that allegedly existed in the Church:

"In the final analysis, what characterized Vatican II was its attentive consciousness of problems related to community, communion, collegiality, solidarity and service. **This consciousness contrasts with the mentality that dominated at Vatican I ... which was one of lordly absolutism** ... and, finally, with the style of governing of Popes such as Pius X with regard to the 'modernists' and Pius XII in his treatment of theologians, Bishops and especially worker priests.

"John XXIII was the first to take a definitive change of direction, realizing a new ideal. ... **He did not conceive of the primacy as the power of a spiritual quasi-dictatorship to be exercised over his spiritual subjects,** but rather as a discreet and humble service rendered in obedience to the true Lord of the Church for the benefit of his brothers, be they Catholic or not." [21]

§ 15

The author then violently criticizes Vatican I and Pius IX, whom he accuses of being despotic and disloyal. He says:

"The Papacy of Vatican Council I did not change the pattern of its predecessors from the Middle Ages with regard to awareness of its spiritual dominion: **Not only did it praise a collection** on the *Romanus Pontifex* **that reproduced false bulls** as if they were authentic documents of the Papacy; **not only did it call for the suppression of the Papal States sacrilegious,** appealing to the sacred and invulnerable property rights of the Apostolic See; **but principally because,** at that Council **Pius IX identified himself with Church tradition and because he stigmatized representatives of the opposition [that is, the liberals] as his enemies and imposed his personal thinking on the Council through morally questionable means.** The difference between that Pope [Pius IX] and those of Vatican II is evident."[22]

---

[20] H. Küng, *A Igreja*, vol. 2, p. 300.

[21] *Ibid.,* p. 280.

[22] *Ibid.,* p. 304.

§ *16*

Fr. Chenu concurs with Fr. Küng in his censure of the combat waged against the enemies of the Papacy. He attacks St. Pius X and endorses the criticism of the Modernists of that time, who called his condemnation the "white terror":

"Pius X and those around him reacted very strongly against what was called Modernism, a global term difficult to define. One can well understand this defensive reflex: **The Church's life was threatened. But she folded in and closed herself off; she condemned and bludgeoned to such an extent that people spoke about the 'white terror.'** The person who directed this policy was Cardinal Merry del Val, the Secretary of State, who had the confidence of Pius X. A great mind, but expressly reactionary." [23]

§ *17*

A curious coincidence is the fact that the communists criticize precisely the same points in the Church and the Papacy that are attacked by the progressivists. And, like the latter, the communists were jubilant at the arrival of John XXIII and Paul VI. The comments in the text below are by a communist, Cesare Luporini, published in the magazine *Rinascità,* and compiled by the progressivist Fr. Philippe de la Trinité, O.C.D.:

"The recent 'order of the day' in the Catholic Church is 'to make herself the Church of dialogue ... with the modern world' – 'not only in the formal way that she has more or less always followed (in order to primarily repulse and condemn the world in an insistent and exterior way), but also in an effort to find ground for a positive relationship.'

"'This has already been clearly codified, in a certain way, in the orientation given by the reigning Pontiff Paul VI in his first Encyclical *Ecclesiam suam* of August 6, 1964.' 'The old condemnations are formally renewed,' but **Paul VI** evokes *Pacem in terris* and **does not lose hope that one day the Communist Movement will enter into a positive dialogue with the Catholic Church.**

"In the final account, 'it is naturally very easy to emphasize the aspect of stopping or braking instead of **the great opening and impulsion of the last phase of Pope John's pontificate,'** but **if one considers the 'Manichaeism of the Encyclical *Divini Redemptoris* by Pius XI and the spirit of Crusade and excommunication that animated his successor, the distance from then to now appears abyssal.** Something irreversible seems to have taken place, not without repercussions on the doctrinal plane.'"[24]

---

[23] *Jacques Duquesne interroge le Père Chenu*, pp. 29-30.

[24] Cesare Luporini, Statements to *Rinascità*, March 27, 1965, pp. 5- 6, in P. de La Trinité, *Dialogue avec le Marxisme?*, pp. 128-129.

With this, one sees that the *animus injuriandi* of many progressivist theologians is also turned against the Vicar of Christ, the Lord of the Church and Column of the World. Further, by means of indirect and poorly veiled attacks, they also assault papal infallibility, a fundament of the Faith and voice of the Holy Ghost. Therefore, this ensemble of offenses undoubtedly constitutes an important element to characterize the spirit of Vatican II.

*   *   *

Chapter X

THE LANGUAGE AND THINKING OF THE CHURCH CONSIDERED ESOTERIC AND INCLINED TO MYTHS

The language and thinking of the Church in her Ordinary Magisterium have always been clear and accessible throughout the centuries. Nonetheless, in progressivist circles today there are many who claim that her language and thinking are esoteric, confused and unable to be proved. This statement is offensive in its form, and unjust and arbitrary in its substance – especially since the conciliar language is in principle ambiguous[1] and its thinking "mysterious" and ambivalent, as we have seen [2] and will continue to see. [3]

Below we offer a sampling of excerpts from theologians approved by the present conciliar Hierarchy who claim that the language of the Church up until the Council was esoteric and her thinking confused.

1. The Language of the Church Thought to Be Esoteric

§ 1

Defending the modern terms adopted by the conciliar documents Msgr. Luigi Sartori, then president of the Association of Italian Theologians, calls the immutable words of traditional theology "esoteric":

"*World* is undoubtedly the key term in this matter [the culture of the modern world]. And *Gaudium et spes* gives a varied and ample description of this word, not only to recover the complexity of biblical language as such, but also to be better disposed for a dialogue with contemporary culture.

"One then observes how many new words (new at least in their semantic value) have entered the vocabulary, such as civilization, culture, progress, autonomy and, above all, history.

"Also, **old words** – such as 'nature', 'person' and 'liberty' – **that in the esoteric usage of our classical theology had been consecrated with precise, immutable meanings ... in the lan-**

---

[1] Cf. Vol. I, *In the Murky Waters of Vatican II*, Chap. I, *passim*; Chap. III, *passim*.

[2] Cf. *Ibid.*, Chap. VII, §§ 2-8; Vol. XI, *Ecclesia*, Chap. I §§ 129-186.

[3] Cf. Vol. VIII, *Fumus Satanae, passim*.

guage of Vatican II are almost always employed with the meanings they have in modern linguistic usage." [4]

§ 2
Elsewhere in that work, Sartori returns to the same notion of
the "esoteric inaccessibility of the language of theology" before Vatican
II, invoking principles of the Constitution *Gaudium et spes* to support his thinking:

"It is this dialogue[5] that in a certain sense epitomizes all the
others: from the dialogue that goes on inside the Church to the one
with our separated brethren and, finally, to the one with all believers in
God.

"Thus, what became important for the language of the Church
is her *capacity to understand* all of humanity (rather than just make
herself understood). **This is the total victory over the esoteric
inaccessibility of the language of theology and that of the announcement of the faith.** The search for the greatest possible 'com-
municability' requires the language of the Church to let itself be shaped
also by the language of contemporary culture." [6]

§ 3
Jesuit René Marlé, professor at the Institute Catholique de
Paris, editor of *Études* and *Recherches de Science Religieuse* and a
contributor to *La Civiltà Cattolica*, thinks that the traditional language of the Church could no longer be assimilated by the people and
became "strange" and "dead."

Fr. Marlé exposes his thinking gradually: He begins by saying
that children cannot assimilate the Church language; then he goes on
to affirm that their parents also have the same difficulty. Finally, he
concludes that the traditional language of the Church lies outside of
"what is relevant in the normal life of men." Here are some excerpts
from his article:

"I insist that children are not the only ones who make the
creation of a new language of the faith necessary. **If the old language can no longer be assimilated** ... it is because in the world in
which they live – and **often first of all in the family** – such language [of the pre-Vatican II Church] gives the impression of

---

[4] Luigi Sartori, "Il linguaggio del Vaticano II," in V. A., *Il linguaggio teologico
oggi* (Milan: Ancora, 1970), pp. 262-263.

[5] The dialogue to which Sartori refers is "that higher disposition to en-
gage in a 'mutual exchange' in its relationships with men and the world,
that is, in giving and receiving in the spirit of humility and charity, of
poverty and obedience" (*ibid.*, p. 254).

[6] *Ibid.*

being a strange idiom, above all, a dead language. It still circulates here and there, like old coins or banknotes that cause one to ask if they are still in use. But this coin [language] is minted in a way that no longer has relevance in the normal life of men; above all, in their daily 'commerce,' they no longer recognize its content. And some even ask themselves if this coin still retains any value at all today."[7]

§ 4

Further on, the Jesuit attributes "magic" and vacuity to the meaning of the word grace:

"And the beautiful word 'grace' – isn't it easily linked to some ethereal or magical meaning? Not to speak of the very idea of God, which is the object of continual denials and about whose content a consensus is always problematic."[8]

Then Marlé returns to insult the traditional language of the Church:

"A language is dead not only because it is no longer spoken by human lips and survives only in texts; rather, it is dead because the whole system of life and existence to which it referred no longer exists. Such a death seems to have struck, at least in part, the language that until today served to announce the Faith."[9]

§ 5

Describing the positions of the traditionalist and progressivist currents in the discussions on the Constitution *Dei Verbum* at the Council, Fr. René Laurentin discredits the traditional thinking of the Church. In his critique, he describes it as out of touch with reality and "esoteric":

"In the first perspective [the traditionalist position], there is a risk of a rationalism of the faith: The mystery is transformed into a problem, the doctrine into a system. At the end of the process, the person is absorbed by this closed doctrine. He goes so far as to forget to confront it with either the sources – certain texts of Scripture and certain recent exegetics do not fit into the system – or the concrete realities. Because human problems and data in fact are even more incommodious (thus the judges of Galileo were not very open to his scientific argumentation).

"In short, an excessive spirit of system led to a rupture with the sources and with human life. These two ruptures are correlated.

---

[7] René Marlé, "Nuovo linguaggio della fede?" *La Civiltà Cattolica,* June 5, 1971, p. 440.

[8] *Ibid.*, p. 440-441.

[9] *Ibid.*, p. 443.

They caused a propensity to esotericism. Forcefully, by the very nature of things, two categories of believers were established: the theologians, the pure ones who have the true doctrine, the doctrine in itself, and the faithful for whom the coin of adaptations and accommodating transitions was minted, that is, those who were open to the superstitious tendencies of a certain popular piety."[10]

§ 6   In a general appraisal of the first session on this Constitution, Laurentin refers again to the "esotericism" of traditional thinking:

"That idea ... which was believed to be Catholic, that system which seemed able to be proposed to the applause of the universal Church, was nothing but a bizarre or esoteric creation."[11]

§ 7   The same author then accuses the Church of "verbalism," an abundant use of words that have little meaning:

"If the Church presents herself now under more modest appearances, if she no longer presents herself as one who always has an immediate answer to everything, she also appears as more serious before God and man, closer to the visible and invisible realities. **If she lost a certain type of certainty and self-assurance,** she developed the sense of work and research, and, **in part, she freed herself from a verbalism that discredited her before the eyes of the more demanding."[12]**

2. The Thinking of the Church Would Be Based on Unprovable Myths

§ 8   It is well known that Karl Rahner was a disciple of existentialist philosopher Martin Heidegger. In the last phase of his lucubration, Heidegger ended by defending his so-called "transcendental ontology," a philosophical system not so different from the Pantheism typical of German Idealism.[13] In a similar way, after having long defended his celebrated "transcendental anthropology," Rahner ended by considering it just a means to synthesize Modern Philosophy in order to transmit it to future generations. He believed that in times to come there would be a new transcendental anthropology that would identify itself with the most advanced form of German Idealism.[14]

---

[10] R. Laurentin, *Bilan de la première session*, pp. 32-33.

[11] *Ibid.*, p. 62.

[12] R. Laurentin, *Bilan de la quatrième session*, p. 366.

[13] Cf. Volume VI, *Inveniet fidem?* Chap. III §§ 61-124.

[14] Rahner writes: "One could perhaps argue that the epoch to which this transcendental anthropology is linked – 'modern times' – is over or in its

§ 9   Speaking on this topic, Rahner takes the opportunity to label the perennial theology of the Church with derogatory epithets such as "pre-theological figurations," "ideological poetry," and "improvable myths." He says:

"**Without a transcendental ontology** of the subject,[15] a theology of grace as well as **theology** in general **is stuck in an ensemble of pre-theological figurations** and is not a valid option for a transcendental experience. And yet this option has become indispensable today, when **theology must face the question of modern**

---

decline. This diagnosis is perhaps correct. Philosophies, however, do not change like fashions, but abdicate in favor of a new philosophy of a new era, and thus their most characteristic values are saved. ...

"This [modern] philosophy is perhaps on its way out; but it is necessary at least to synthesize it if theology is to truly respect the spirit of the period that *will follow* modern times. This makes all the more sense since the philosophy of the future – corresponding to tomorrow's social organization – will undoubtedly be rooted in part in German Idealism (perhaps leftist Hegelianism and its criticism of ideologies). Even if the themes of this next philosophy should be called hope, society, a criticism of ideologies, a new form of liberty with different social bonds, an experience of God lived by man in his effort to realize himself, etc., the theme proper to philosophy will still be man: His mysterious essence in itself still needs to be studied.

"Therefore, considering the form philosophy will take in the future, today's and tomorrow's theology are obliged to orient themselves toward a transcendental anthropology" (K. Rahner, "Théologie et anthropologie," in V.A., *Théologie d'aujourd'hui et de demain,* Paris: Cerf, 1967, pp. 112-113).

[15] It would be a mistake to imagine that in his reference to "ontology," Rahner is adopting an Aristotelian-Thomistic conception of ontology, which is the part of philosophy that studies the nature of being as such. For Rahner this makes no sense at all. He does not consider the category of essence in philosophy, that is, the study of being in Catholic ontology. He considers only the category of existence, that is, the category of experienced realities. In this he adopts the terminology of Heidegger, which distinguishes the '**ontic**' sphere – related to experienced phenomena – from the '**ontological**' sphere – related to what a man thinks about observed phenomena (Cf. Paul Foulquié, *Dictionnaire de la langue philosophique*, Paris, 1962, entry *Ontologie*, B.3.4; Volume VI, *Inveniet Fidem?* Chap. III §§ 194-221). The 'ontology' to which Rahner refers is, therefore, existentialist.

Thus it makes sense that Rahner attacks Catholic Theology, which is based not on experiences but on data from Revelation.

man by asking itself whether, when speaking of 'divinization,' 'filiation,' 'inhabitation of God,' etc., it is not appealing to ideological poetry and improvable myths." [16]

A theologian whose writing is famous for its lack of clarity,[17] Karl Rahner judges himself entitled to criticize the supposed "confused" thinking of the Church:

> "Who has not had the impression that the New Testament – and even more so our Scholastic Dogmatics – constitutes a confused and complicated system of assertions, an incredibly complex ensemble of formulas, opinions, relationships, distinctions and movements of thought with contradictory and often difficult to harmonize orientations, whose synthesis generates even more complicated distinctions?" [18]

§ 10   Fr. Chenu believes Thomism was used as an instrument of power and finds it humorous to identify it as "orthodox" in that sense. What he clearly insinuates is that what the Holy Church proposes as orthodox is nothing but a façade to hide deceitful interests, which is an offense to the orthodoxy of the Magisterium and an affront to the Church. Before Vatican II, he was admonished for this thinking and obliged to retract it. But in the post-conciliar Church, he unabashedly reaffirms those same propositions in an interview with Jacques Duquesne:

> "But the offices of the Curia continued their work without paying attention to the drama of men ... It was a sign of the error of their theology, closed in their idea of orthodoxy. For them **Thomism had become a super-orthodoxy** ... Some time after that, **I wrote that to make Thomism an 'orthodoxy' was the worst disgrace that could have befallen St. Thomas.** The humor of my statement was quite misunderstood in Rome, where they attributed my words to mean that St. Thomas was not orthodox. In the process made against me, I had to sign [a declaration] recognizing that St. Thomas was orthodox!

---

[16] K. Rahner, "Théologie et anthropologie," pp. 109-110.

[17] Along with many others, Fr. Congar testifies to the role Rahner played at Vatican Council II: "When it started, he was not part of the Theological Commission. I remember meeting Fr. Tromp one day in the elevator and telling him: 'It's a shame that Rahner is not part of the Theological Commission!' He answered: 'Do you understand anything Rahner writes? In Latin he is perfectly clear; in German I have more difficulty [understanding him]'" (*Jean Puyo interroge le Père Congar*, p. 131); cf. Vol. VII, *Destructio Dei*, Chap. II.2.A:b, Note 1.

[18] K. Rahner, *Teologia e Bíblia* (São Paulo: Paulinas, 972), p. 96.

"*Question*: Was it your book *Une école de Théologie: le Saulchoir* (*Le Sauchoir: A School of Theology*) that earned you a first condemnation?

"*Response:* Yes. ... What I want to say is that **I was reacting spontaneously against this way of manipulating Thomism as an instrument of power.**" [19]

§ 11 Commenting on the schema on Revelation, René Laurentin criticizes the horizons of the Scholastics as being "narrow" and "outdated":

"**The theses of the Scholastics became outdated,** but the essential was redeemed ... in its full value. There are two ways of transcending the perspectives of the Scholastics. ... One is to reduce the opinions to a common denominator, which brings a poor and insignificant result. The other is to return to the irrefragable data of Revelation, which the Scholastics broached differently, and to consider them in their full dimension. Then, **the narrowness of the Scholastics and their theories is overcome.**"[20]

§ 12 Further on, he returns to the attack:

"**Revelation is not just composed of pronouncements.** It is an ensemble of words and actions; it is the very person of Jesus Christ, our Savior. **Thus it is much more than the abstract, Scholastic and lifeless conception, which presented Revelation as a collection of truths as if they were geometry theorems.**"[21]

§ 13 As he praises the final text of *Dei Verbum*, Laurentin accuses the pre-conciliar doctrine on Revelation of being "rationalist":

"**The first chapter** [of *Dei Verbum*] **liberates the notion of Revelation from the narrow confines in which a certain theological rationalism tried to imprison it, as if God would have limited himself to revealing a collection of abstract truths.** The document restores the vital and salvific dimension of Revelation."[22]

§ 14 Commenting on the Decree *Presbyterorum ordinis*, Laurentin offends the traditional theological conception of the priesthood:

"It is a fact that **the theology on this topic found itself in a state of underdevelopment; even worse, it was formed by a lot of grime that had hardened during the last centuries.**"[23]

---

[19] *Jacques Duquesne interroge le Pére Chenu*, pp. 32-33.

[20] R. Laurentin, *Bilan de la troisième session*, p. 90.

[21] *Ibid.*, pp. 91-92.

[22] R. Laurentin, *Bilan de la quatrième session,* p. 276.

[23] *Ibid.*, p. 245.

§ 15   Fr. Jean-Pierre Jossua, rector of the Dominican Faculty of Le Saulchoir, considers "useless" an orthodoxy that claims to be immutable: One can surmise that Jossua's words counted on the tacit agreement of 223 theologians from around the world who had gathered in Brussels to hear him speak on the 5th anniversary of *Concilium* magazine. In that talk, he said:

"It is the Church that gauges charism and theme. ... She does this so that – through **her diverse formulations** which **render as useless the orthodoxies that call themselves immutable** – the rule of faith, born from the first biblical expression and applied by the Church, maintains the balanced proportions and the fidelity to the entire mystery." [24]

§ 16   Hans Urs von Balthasar, for his part, believes that theology lost its "primitive" and "naïve" character only after Vico and the impious Voltaire offered their contributions by presenting a history of secular civilization:

"**Voltaire and, shortly before him, Vico went beyond this meaning of history marked by a primitive theology by presenting a history of secular civilization, of humankind in general.** Only then did the history of the world emerge from the history of salvation, drawing important contributions from it. For the historical course of Christian salvation broadened to become a general, natural course of history, considered as the 'education of the human race' or simply as faith in a secular progress.

"**From the theological standpoint, one should not lament this secularization too much because the old, naïve identification of the history of salvation with the history of the world was a usurpation by the religious sphere**. But what happened in the history of humanity from Adam to Abraham [the period reported by Genesis] in a non-theological sense can be called an 'evolution' that became increasingly lively. It was only then, when the distinction between the two 'evolutions' was clarified, that one could significantly explain the theological meaning of extra-biblical history." [25]

§ 17   In another work, after praising the theology of the "death of God" that caused a scandal in the 1970's, von Balthasar claims that the Scholastics were wasting their time with futile questions. An example of such a "futile question" would be the consideration of the humanity and divinity of Our Lord during His death...

---

[24] J.-P. Jossua, "Dalla teologia al teologo," in V. A., *'Avvenire della Chiesa*, p. 83.

[25] Hans Urs von Balthasar, *De l'Intégration*, p. 124.

Von Balthasar affirms:

"In any case, **the 'death of God'** during the *triduum mortis* [three days between the death of Jesus Christ and His Resurrection] **is the highest object of an authentic theology, which has no time to waste with futile questions.**" In a footnote, he observes, "**We can only lament that Scholastic theology considered it less important to speculate on the meaning of Holy Saturday, and instead occupied itself with the specious action and futile question of determining if and how Christ continued to be man and God during His death.**" [26]

§ 18

Canadian Fr. Bernard Lonergan, who is considered by many to be the greatest theologian of North America and one of the great theologians of the 20th century,[27] affirms that traditional theology is an "old cloak" that can no longer be patched with new cloth, "an old wineskin" into which new wine should no longer be poured. He states:

"I have been speaking of our renewed theology and now I must add that **a renewed theology needs a renewed foundation. The old foundations are no longer valid.** But we absolutely cannot go forward without foundations. So **new foundations – and , I say, a new type of foundation – are needed to replace the old ones**. ...

"**The old foundations are no longer useful.** In saying this I do not mean that they are no longer true – they are as true now as they ever were. I mean that they are no longer appropriate. **I am simply recalling that one must not patch an old cloak with new cloth or put new wine in old wineskins.** One kind of foundation suits a theology that aims at being deductive, static, abstract, universal, equally applicable to all places and all times. **A quite different foundation is needed when theology turns from a deductive to an empirical approach, from the static to the dynamic, from the abstract to the concrete, from the universal to the historical totality of particulars**, from invariable rules to intelligent adjustment and adaptation."[28]

§ 19

In a lecture broadcast by Vatican Radio, Fr. Germano Pattaro, professor at the University of Venice, affirmed that the thinking of

---

[26] H. U. von Balthasar, "Mysterium Paschale," in V. A., *Mysterium salutis*, pp. 35-36.

[27] Cf. B. Mondin, *Introduzione alla teologia* (Milan: Massimo, 1983), p. 373; *Os grandes teólogos do século vinte*, vol. 1, p. 269.

[28] Bernard Lonergan, "Theology in its New Context," in V.A., *Theology of Renewal*, vol. 1, pp. 41-42.

Scholasticism had become "burdensome" and "psychologically dishonest":

"The absence of a more attentive historical fidelity has made the teaching of this theology [Scholasticism] abstract and remote. Confined to the resonances of pure thought, it became rationally burdensome and psychologically dishonest." [29]

*

The excerpts presented in this Chapter show how the animadversion of various progressivist theologians is also turned against the immutable character of theological teaching, and especially against Scholastic Theology. This opposition is, then, yet another note indicating the spirit of the Council.

*   *   *

---

[29] Germano Pattaro, *Riflessioni sulla teologia post-conciliare*, p. 37.

Chapter XI

THE CHURCH'S SEPARATION FROM THE WORLD WOULD MAKE HER A SECT, A GHETTO, HER RELATION WITH IT, SCHIZOPHRENIC

With regard to Church-world relations, the offenses can be classified as two types: *first*, those concerning the Church's position of separation from the temporal sphere, and *second*, those concerning the relations of the spiritual and temporal spheres.

1. A Sect and Ghetto Church

§ 1   The *aggiornamento* of John XXIII and the opening of Vatican II toward the modern world, characterized by the Pastoral Constitution *Gaudium et spes,* unleashed a cyclone of affronts in many ecclesiastical milieus. The whole past attitude of the Church toward the modern world was criticized in a highly offensive way.

As we have seen,[1] the Church for wise reasons had always been extremely vigilant in regard to the world. She had been particularly on guard against the modern world, born from the errors of the Enlightenment, Deism, the French Revolution and Liberalism.[2]

At the Council, however, previous doctrinal condemnations were, for all practical purposes, considered nonexistent.[3] For "pastoral" purposes,[4] the world was considered as if there were no original sin; pantheistic philosophies that tried to explain it were regarded as respectable viewpoints; its egalitarian and socialistic tendencies were accepted as a "sign of the times," and its immorality was viewed as a demand of modern man.[5]

§ 2   Promoters of this suspicious *aggiornamento* faced, however, a formidable barrier, represented by the consistent and continuous teaching of 2,000 years of the Catholic Magisterium.

---

[1] Cf. Vol. I, *In the Murky Waters of Vatican II*, Chap. IX §§ 57-66.

[2] This is expounded in Vol. V, *Animus Delendi II*, Part I, First Premise.

[3] Cf. Vol. I, *In the Murky Waters of Vatican II*, Chap. I, Note 14; Vol. V, *Animus Delendi II*, Part I, Second Premise.

[4] Cf. Vol. I, *In the Murky Waters of Vatican II*, Chap. VI §§ 34-133.

[5] The Reader can find the proof for these statements in Vol. VI, *Inveniet Fidem?*, Chap. III §§ 125-172; Vol. V, *Animus Delendi II*, Part I, First Premise; Chap. I *passim*

Among the ploys used to overturn that barrier, a cyclone of insults was unleashed against the Holy Church that called her a sect and a ghetto for maintaining a cautious vigilance toward the world for so long a time. By raising this tumult, progressivists hoped to intimidate the faithful, pressuring them to adhere to the revolutionary modern world and preventing them from having recourse to the perennial teachings of the Church.

§ 3   In the case of relations between the Church and the world, the enormous quantity of texts and the relevance of the offending authors lead us to ask whether this attack was prompted by more than just connivance or acquiescence with it by the leaders of the conciliar Church. Indeed, it could well be that those authors received an order from high ecclesiastical circles to produce this cyclone of affronts.

We invite the Reader to judge for himself whether this appraisal is well-founded.

*

First, however, we must briefly examine the gravity of the offense of calling the Church a sect.

§ 4   The notion of sect implies two meanings. *The first*, when applied to the Church, derives not so much from its etymology [6] as from a strange concept the progressivists have about the vitality of the Church. According to this thinking, the Catholic Church should be called a sect whenever she is cut off or separated from something more ample and vital than herself. Removed from this life-giving sap, she would tend to wilt and die.

---

[6] The word **sect** comes from the Latin noun *secta,* from the verb *sequi* (to follow, to accompany). Today's gamut of meanings of sect has been influenced by a commonly made confusion with the etymologically unrelated Latin word *secta,* from the verb *secare,* to cut. (Cf. *Catholic Encyclopedia*, entry Sect and Sects; Wilhelm Bartz, *Sekten heute - Lehre, Organisation, Verbreitung*, Fribourg in Breisgau: Herder, 1967, p. 11; John Carrol, "*Secta,*" in *Dictionarium Morale et Canonicum*, ed. by Pietro Palazzini, Rome: Officium Libri Catholici, 1968, p. 252, in V.A., '*Brainwashing': A Myth Exploited by the New 'Therapeutic Inquisition,'* New York: The American Society for the Defense of Tradition, Family and Property, 1985, p. 42).

Nonetheless, progressivist authors continue to apply the incorrect meaning of "cut off" or "separated" to the word sect when they launch offenses against the Catholic Church or the conservatives. Employing this meaning, Fr. Chenu calls Cardinal Louis Billot "sectarian – in the etymological sense of the word" (Cf. p. 237 of this Volume).

What would be the source of life for the Church? Some Readers might think those authors would be referring to the supernatural life of the Church. This is not so. The attention of progressivists is not turned toward supernatural life. For them, the source of this mysterious vitality, from which the Church is cut off, is the world and humanity. Thus, they deny – either implicitly or explicitly – that the Church is the closed garden of Faith, the exclusive fountain of all truth: "*hortus conclusus, fons signatus*" (Cant 4:12). Instead, they affirm that the world and humanity possess, in themselves, an immanent religious energy that is capable of communicating life, even to the Church. And if the Church is not disposed to receive it, then she is cut off from that vital source: She becomes a sect.

§ 5   The *second meaning* of sect is one that has become more common in current language. It maintains the essential notion of the first meaning – separation from the world – but is turned more toward the way such a separation takes place. What causes this separation of the Church from the world would supposedly be fear or radicalism. The progressivists who employ this meaning also consider the Church a sect.

Separation from the world, according to them, results from a lack of courage to follow the challenging new trends of modernity and generates those faithful who remove themselves from the world to unite in a small group with its own life. In this case, "sect" becomes synonymous with "ghetto" – persons who have removed themselves from the rest of society. Another accusation made against this separation is that it would be a manifestation of pride or radicalism. Progressivists generally do not attribute eccentricity – common to so many sects that proliferate today – as a cause for the Church's separation from the world.

One sees, therefore, that calling the Church a "sect" in either of the two senses constitutes a very grave offense.

The following texts, which call her a sect, use the word at times in the first meaning and at times in the second.[7]

---

[7] The "opening" of the Conciliar Church involves two simultaneous stages: an opening to the world, a process called "secularization," and an opening to the other religions, the much trumpeted "ecumenism." Both processes will be studied in detail in Vol. V, *Animus Delendi II*. The Catholic Church has always conceived her mission as being opposed to both of these "openings" (see Vol. I, *In the Murky Waters of Vatican II*, Chap. IX).

With the aim of combating this centuries-old "closed" mentality of the Holy Church, progressivists attack her, calling her a sect. In coherence

A. Background Criteria

§ 6   The principal criterion used for accusing the Church of being a sect is separation from the world, according to Fr. Antoine Vergote, professor at the University of Louvain. In a talk at the 1970 Congress in Brussels promoted by the magazine *Concilium*, he points to the underlying cause for such separation as her denial of revolutionary liberty and equality:

"The Church is in some ways marginal in the ethical sphere. We can affirm that the two great ethical axes of contemporary humanity are liberty and justice in equality. Liberty is conceived as promoting freedom of expression and creativity and is sought by means of revolt against any form of coercion. Justice is seen as abolishing any vestige of aristocracy or feudalism that remains in society. To provide equal conditions for all individuals and peoples constitutes the fundamental initiative that mobilizes the highest ethical energies. **I will not insist on the past and present guilt of the Church. We are unanimous in pronouncing her guilty for her past and in lamenting that a certain sectarian and conservative attitude has greatly distanced the Church from these two ethical movements that have shaped our civilization.**" [8]

§ 7   Another criterion is found in a statement of Bishop Boaventura Kloppenburg, who judges that the unity of the Church centered in Rome was the principal cause for the Church becoming a "ghetto":

"**Everything was excessively centralized in Rome** to the detriment of the salvation of souls and pastoral action. **This increasingly led to a pernicious uniformity, a sterile rigidity and a sinful Pharisaism, and it was the principal cause for the ghetto to which the Church had reduced herself** and that we must leave at all costs." [9]

§ 8   Msgr. Philips, the main redactor of *Lumen gentium*, clearly attributes the origin of the Church's *aggiornamento* toward the modern world to John XXIII:

---

with this strategy, they call the Church a sect or a ghetto either when she refuses to open up to the world or when she balks in the face of ecumenism.

Accordingly, we will present in this Item 1 excerpts that offend the Holy Church by calling her a sect or a ghetto from the standpoint of secularization and ecumenism.

[8] A. Vergote, "La presenza della Chiesa nella società di domani," in V.A., *L'avvenire della Chiesa*, p. 164.

[9] B. Kloppenburg, *A eclesiologia do Vaticano II*, p. 178.

"He [John XXIII] summarized his plan [to adapt the Church to the demands of our time] with the word *aggiornamento*. **His very clear intuition that the Church is certainly not in tune with the modern world** and is suffering from a delayed growth **made him not hesitate to take the initiative of inviting the Church** to reflect upon her urgent duties and **to liberate herself from the isolation in which she threatened to close herself.**" [10]

§ 9

Cardinal Congar says something similar about the role of John XXIII in saving the Church from a "ghetto" situation:

"**After the red and yellow lights, the traffic signal turned green with the Council of John XXIII,** and the currents in the Church began to fill. The Rhine did not need to flow into the Tiber, to use an expression of Ralph Wiltgen. **Instead of establishing herself as a ghetto, it sufficed for the Church**, the people of God on its way along the pathway of men, **to resume a full dialogue with the world.**"[11]

Therefore, according to these progressivist authors, to avoid being a sect the Church would have to unite with the world, assimilate its liberal-anarchic principles of abolishing all coercion, adapt herself to egalitarianism, do away with any aristocratic or feudal vestiges and, further, eradicate her "pernicious uniformity" – which made Rome her center. This movement to abandon the "sectarian position" was initiated by John XXIII.

B. Progressivists Consider the Catholic Church a Sect and a Ghetto

Below are a number of texts – all of them offensive to the Church – which affirm that the Catholic Church was a sect and a ghetto up until Vatican Council II: [12]

a. John XXIII

§ 10

According to the chronicle of the Council by Henri Fesquet, the Pontiff who convened the Council expressed the desire for the great assembly to be "a current of fresh air" in the Church. On another

---

[10] G. Philips, *La Chiesa e il suo mistero*, p. 13.

[11] Y. Congar, *La crisi nella Chiesa e Mons. Lefèbvre* (Bresica: Queriniana, 1976), p. 61.

[12] The excerpts in this Letter B will be presented in the order of the importance of the various authors (although we do not claim that this order is beyond dispute, especially with regard to those of lesser renown). In these texts the Reader will find the Holy Church accused of being a sect and a ghetto.

occasion, he said: "**It is necessary to leave our ghetto**; we have other things to do than to throw stones at Communism."[13]

b. Benedict XVI

§ 12   As Prefect of the Congregation for the Doctrine of the Faith, then Cardinal Joseph Ratzinger, wrote in *L'Osservatore Romano*:

"In this context one can understand the hope that was linked to the announcement of the Council. **Finally, all mediocrities, limitations and fears, which were generated at the time of the 'ghetto,' could be abolished in order to achieve a new liberty and generosity of the faith, and to re-enter the cultural flow and fuse with it. At that time it looked possible to surmount the separation between the Church and society, raze barriers and build a Church living in the world, and the world with her.**"[14]

c. CELAM (Latin American Bishops Council)

§ 13   In the conclusions of the 1968 Medellin Conference in Colombia, where support was given to Base Christian Communities and the Liberation Theology propounded by Gustavo Gutiérrez, the Latin American Bishops affirmed:

"This [traditional] religiosity – more cosmic in nature, where God is the answer to all of man's questions and needs – can enter into a crisis, and, in fact, it has already begun to do so as it faces the scientific knowledge of the world that surrounds us.

"**This religiosity places the Church before the dilemma of continuing to be the universal Church or becoming a sect** and, therefore, not incorporating into herself those who do not express themselves with this type of religiosity. **Since she is a Church and not a sect, she must offer her message of salvation to all men**." [15]

d. Karl Rahner

§ 14   Rahner makes it quite clear that, if the Church follows the path set before Vatican II, she will become a "ghetto" and a "sect":

"This ['secularized'] world is pluralist in its conceptions and composed of men among whom **no single individual controls the**

---

[13] H. Fesquet, *Le Journal du Concile*, p. 44.

[14] Joseph Ratzinger, "Papa mariano, esecutore fedele del Concilio Vaticano II," *L'Osservatore Romano*, October 16, 1992.

[15] CELAM, *A Igreja na atual transformação da América Latina à luz do Council - Conclusões de Medellin* (Petrópolis, Vozes,1980), p. 90.

totality of knowledge or culture ... which can only happen in society as a whole. Despite the considerable increase of education among the masses, despite the information explosion, despite the power of the communications media, society has become more confused and less tractable than ever before and no longer sees where the future is leading. In short, society is less integrated, with all the consequences this implies for the individual and for society itself.

"Whence a totally new task arises for the Church in regard to herself. ... **It is not a question for her to re-transform this secular, pluralist world into the homogeneous society of another age, which brought for the Church her own integration. If the Church were to try to do this** – and the temptation is always present and strong – **she would make herself a ghetto and would tend ... to transform herself into a 'sect.'**" [16]

§ 15   He also asserts that to follow a single, universal theology would lead to a sectarian Church:

"Although one must try to speak *only one* language, to mutually understand one another, to reciprocally translate theologies in their plurality, this effort in fact has its limits today. **To try to achieve an absolutely homogeneous theology**, equally accessible to every theologian ... even if it were successful, **would only lead to the theology of a small sect, which could no longer speak with the world that surrounds it**." [17]

e. Marie-Dominique Chenu

§ 16   Fr. Chenu, who played an influential role in the adaptation of the Church to the modern world, accuses the great Thomist theologian Cardinal Louis Billot of being "sectarian":

"In another domain, that of theology, someone who played a strong role was a professor at the Gregorian [University], Fr. Billot. Pius X named him Cardinal to show his great confidence in him. Billot ... was a first class theologian, but he had closed himself in one sector of theology, imperiously ignoring all the others. **Entrenched in one sector, he became sectarian in the etymological sense of the word.**" [18]

---

[16] K. Rahner, "Theological Reflections on the Problem of Secularization," in V.A., *Theology of Renewal,* vol. 1, pp. 173-174.

[17] K. Rahner, *Magistero e teologia dopo il Concilio* (Brescia: Queriniana, 1967), p. 33.

[18] *Jacques Duquesne interroge le Père Chenu*, p. 30.

f. Hans Küng

§ 17
With his characteristic hostility toward the pre-Vatican II Church, the theologian refers to her as a "ghetto":

"The Church cannot 'solve' the great problems of the world: hunger, the demographic explosion, war ... What she can do - we will say it plainly - is to place herself at the service of the world ...

"The Church is at the service of the world when she *unites herself* with the world ... She cannot seek refuge away from the world in a ghetto and live her life in splendid isolation."[19]

g. Johann Baptist Metz

§ 18
The disciple of Karl Rahner agrees with his mentor that the traditional orthodoxy of the Church is "sectarian":

"Next to this danger of losing her identity by undertaking an energetic adaptation [to the world] is the danger of losing her identity through a passive adaptation, which is less noticed by today's world but must be seen at all costs if one is seeking the road for the Church and society of today and tomorrow. **It is the danger of the Church herself becoming a sect in the theological sense; it is the danger of adopting a traditionalist orthodoxy proper to a sect and a sectarian mentality turned toward itself inside the Church."** [20]

h. Luigi Sartori

§ 19
In the two excerpts below, the ex-President of the Italian Association of Theologians insists that the modern Church must flee the "ghetto" mentality of the past:

* "Not only is it important that, from *Pacem in terris* onward, the Church obliges us to observe the signs of the times, to seek them out and discern them, but it is important also that some signs of the times have already been identified; we have made a discernment. This signifies that it is not enough to have a simple theoretical enunciation that only serves to theatrically declare, 'We Christians are also interested in History. ... **We are not closed off in a ghetto ... We are not egocentric.'"** [21]

---

[19] H. Küng, *A Igreja*, vol. 2, pp. 329-330.

[20] J. B. Metz, "Sulla presenza della Chiesa nella società," in V.A., *L'avvenire della Chiesa,* p. 143.

[21] Luigi Sartori, "Spirito Santo e storia - Testimonianza cattolica," in V.A., *Lo Spirito Santo pegno e primizia del Regno* (Turin: Elle Di Ci, 1982), p. 78.

* **"Assimilating the ecumenical method includes the Gospel's commitment to 'be against', to be against all the 'againsts'**: that is, against war, discrimination and idolatries, and not against other persons. In fidelity to the New Testament, **this method includes inserting oneself into a community and fleeing the ghetto temptation."** [22]

i. Louis Bouyer

§ 20   Fr. Louis Bouyer, a member of the International Theological Commission, endorses the words of journalist Henri Fesquet here:

"Speaking very plainly, a very credible commentator on the Council addresses this topic [whether Catholicism is dead]: **'Will the Roman Church, which had gradually assumed the appearance of a sect and seemed to have no interest in the modern world except to anathematize it, insert herself once again into the fabric of the history of men,** stimulating and transforming her effort in order to construct a less narrow, less sectarian, less compartmentalized, less hostile, less unjust and more humane world? ... Vatican II opened the way. And now that the conciliar plow has passed, the turned ground – silently but ardently – awaits the seeds that have to be sown.'" [23]

j. Antoine Vergote

§ 21   The professor at Louvain University and co-founder of the Belgian School of Psychoanalysis believes the Church took the form of a "sect," but now she must re-examine her position of isolation to become a dynamic part of the modern world:

"Because of this profound transformation of spirit ... the Church became marginalized in our culture. ... **If the Church were truly marginalized ... she would take on the appearance of a sect. She would look like a group of marginalized persons, who for psychological and sociological reasons, excluded themselves from a creative civilization. The process that defines a sect is well known: On the margins of civilization and situated outside of it, the sect sets itself up against society and develops an attitude of disdain and self-defense, which adds nothing to the culture and destroys its own truths.**

---

[22] L. Sartori, in Lucia Posio, "L'attenzione su...," *Notizie Ecumeniche* (Bollettino di Collegamento e d'Informazione dei Giovani S.A.E., Resoconto del I Convegno Nazionale Giovani S.A.E.), n. 6, November 1983, p. 4.

[23] L. Bouyer, *A decomposição do Catolicismo*, p. 216.

"It is an undeniable fact that in a certain sense the Church has become marginalized. As a consequence, she has often assumed a sectarian attitude (with regard to science, philosophy and politics). ... Today what we desire is precisely that the Church re-examine her criteria for her relationship with the world and realize that her attachment to these false criteria regarding her presence in it will effectively make her marginalized in the full sense of the word." [24]

k. Norbert Greinacher

§ 22   The German professor of practical theology at Tübingen and proponent of Liberation Theology affirms that the Church should re-define herself as Church-community and abandon her "ghetto":

"Still to this day the Church finds herself in this phase of development characterized by laicization, secularization and apostasy, and one can ask what sociological configuration the Church will assume in today's and future society. We offer a brief response, referring to the concept of *Church-community*. This is characterized by an unrestricted acceptance of the principle of free will. 'Christianity will be transformed from a traditional and hereditary Christianity into a Christianity of free choice.' [25*] Even though it will represent a minority in a laicized and secularized world, **the Church-community will be characterized first of all by an opening to this world rather than by isolating herself in a kind of ghetto."** [26]

l. Leo von Geusau

§ 23   The Dutch theologian who played an active role at Vatican II considers the pre-conciliar doctrinal "system" not only obsolete, but also a "ghetto":

"Any attempt to establish a secure system based on human certainties with claims to attain eternity, thus capable of conditioning or channeling the salvific action of God – be it individual or collective – always runs the risk of becoming the denial of the call of God. One may say that the starting point of the call of God ... is the solidarity of the whole human race, which tends, in an absolute way, toward universality. ...

---

[24] A. Vergote, "La presenza della Chiesa nella società di domani," in V.A., *L'avvenire della Chiesa*, pp. 162-163.

[25*] K. Rahner, "Il significato teologico della posizione del cristiano nel mondo moderno," in V.A., *Missione e grazia* (Rome, 1967), 11-67, p. 44.

[26] Norbert Greinacher, "Aspetti sociologico dell'autorealizzazione della Chiesa," in V.A., *Chiesa, uomo e società*, Rome/Brescia: Herder-Morcelliana, 1970, p. 72.

"The times in which we live seem to demonstrate more clearly than ever how the old Judaism or a ghetto Christendom failed to understand this fundamental point** when they accepted every pretext to be exclusive." [27]

m. Boaventura Kloppenburg

§ 24

In the three excerpts below, the Franciscan theologian relies on Council documents to demand that the Church leave the "ghetto":

* "New junctures (or new signs of the times) require new formulas, including in the field of dogma. For this reason, the Church – in order to be able to fulfill her mission – 'has the duty of scrutinizing the signs of the times' (GS, 4a); and theologians and pastors must 'hear, distinguish and interpret the many voices of our age' (GS, 44b). ... **To simply condemn such efforts ... and comfortably and intransigently attach oneself to formulas taken as definitive ... can be the easy way, but it means being in a ghetto**, and making the Church unable to be the 'universal sacrament of salvation' that she wants to be and that she should be (LG, 48b, 129; GS, 45a, 342; AG, 1a, 862; 5a, 871)" [28]

* "New problems, new investigations, new ways of expressing the ancient deposit. This is what we have today. **We cannot simply shut our eyes and ears to avoid seeing or hearing the signs of the times and close ourselves off as a 'little flock' in a kind of ghetto** that confidently reaffirms formulas of times past, and piously insists on practices that sprang up in circumstances that no longer exist. **We would be traitors to our mission.**" [29]

* "It is necessary to insist with the words of the Council: The Christian faithful gathered together out of all nations into the Church 'are not marked off from the rest of men by their government, nor by their language, nor by their political institutions,' and so they should live for God and Christ in a respectable way their own national life' (AG, 15f). **This is the definitive condemnation of 'Christendom' and of the eternal temptation to form ghettos. It is not the mission of the Church to build, in the world of men, a world apart from it, with a Christian form of government,** its own political party and its own schools."[30]

---

[27] L. Alting von Geusau, "La Chiesa, 'scandalo' del mondo," in V.A., *La fine della Chiesa come società perfetta*, pp. 165-166.

[28] B. Kloppenburg, *A eclesiologia do Vaticano II*, pp. 65-66.

[29] *Ibid.*, p. 99.

[30] *Ibid.*, pp. 91-92.

n. Tommaso Federici

§ 25   The professor at the Pontifical Liturgical Institute pretends that Christendom was locked in "a ghetto." He refers to the Constantinian period of the Church as the time that begins with the exit from the Catacombs (313 AD) after the Edict of Milan of Emperor Constantine up until Vatican II:

"In that [Constantinian] period, **there was the greatest possible decadence of Christianity, still excessively 'European.'** In general **it remained closed in a ghetto where pride and triumphalism prevailed.**" [31]

o. George Maloney

§ 26   According to the founder of the John XXIII Institute for Eastern Christian Studies at Fordham University, today the true Christian is obliged to leave the "ghetto" inside which the Church had locked him in order to become a citizen of the universe:

"**A Christian** who is deeply rooted in the person of the one and triune God sees – through contemplation – the power of Jesus Christ acting in the lives not only of Christians, but of all human beings, independent of culture or religion. He **becomes a citizen of the whole universe. He breaks the ghetto notions that determined how Jesus Christ should and must act in His universe** in order to see Him in a constant process of unfolding the universe toward its plenitude by means of the basic goodness that exists in human beings.

"Through technology, he begins to see that God is promoting a cosmic consciousness in the minds of all men in every corner of the universe. Psychologically, such Christians no longer live in their particular village, city or nation, but they begin to think as citizens of one single, gigantesque 'global village.'" [32]

p. Avery Dulles

§ 27   The American Cardinal and famous Jesuit scholar criticizes the traditionalist position against ecumenism as "sectarian":

"In some [progressivist] ambiences, the good name of ecumenism has been obfuscated by a strong tendency to level all dif-

---

[31] Tommaso Federici, "Religione e religioni oggi," in V.A., *Incontro tra le religioni* (Verona: Mondadori, 1969), pp. 16-17.

[32] George Maloney, "A oração e o divino pessoal," *Concilium*, I977/3, p. 118.

ferences and seek agreement at the cost of compromise. Reacting to such excesses, **some have felt justified to return to a rigid and pleasing sectarian position.**"[33]

q. Henri Desroche

§ 28

The ex-Dominican who founded the Sociology of Religion Association also considers the Church as a kind of sect:

"The Christianization of philosophy into a *theology* is not possible without a certain theologization of Christianity. ... Or, according to the diagnosis of Troeltsch, **a sect is perhaps nothing but the latent protest of the evangelical or apocalyptic kingdom against the established Church; order is perhaps nothing but the *churchification* of a *sect* ...** Or, as many will say, the canonization of saints according to the established nomenclatures is not possible without a self-canonization of our own criteria of prestige." [34]

r. Henri Fesquet

§ 29

As he summarizes the consequences of the Council, the chronicler of that event clearly draws a line between two eras in the Church: the traditional pre-conciliar era when the Church was like a "sect" closed in a "ghetto" and the new emerging era of openness to the world and other religions:

"At the end of the Council in Rome, the convergence of the living forces of Christianity [Catholics, schismatics and heretics] becomes increasingly clear, awaiting a time to come when there would be a convergence of the living forces of all the great religions.

"The time was ripe for this. For, humanly speaking, **the Catholic Church seemed condemned to be a sect, had she not energetically opted for a triple re-awakening: intellectual, spiritual and pastoral.** For a sharp observer, the process of divorce between the Church and the world today seems to have halted. With the condition, however, that Vatican II cannot in any case or any realm be considered a simply provisory – albeit prestigious – parenthesis in the history of Catholicism."[35]

§ 30

Still summarizing the effects of the Council, he says:

---

[33] Avery Dulles, "Ecumenismo: problemi e possibilità per il futuro," in V.A., *Verso la Chiesa del terzo millennio*, p. 121.

[34] Henri Desroche, "Sciences des religions et théologie chrétienne," in V.A., *Bilan de la théologie du XXe.siècle*, vol. 1, pp. 228-229.

[35] H. Fesquet, *Le journal du Concile*, p. 1034.

"Vatican II is now over. John XXIII, who convoked it, is dead. But both remain so alive in the memory that there is little room for nostalgia as we reach the end of 1965, which will remain in History as the date that divided two very different eras of Christianity. The more time that passes, the more this paradoxical truth lived at the Council will become apparent: discontinuity in the continuity of the Church.

"It was during Vatican II that Rome truly entered into the 20th century, simultaneously appraising the backwardness of the Church and the effort of *aggiornamento*. In effect, **the Council did away with the feeling that the Catholic Church – although scattered throughout the world – was similar to a sect:** a Western religion linked in practice to the Greco-Roman civilization, **a religion of the developed countries that was exceedingly alienated from the great currents of History, contemporary thought and the pressing concerns of the men of our days**.

"The Council, so to speak, knocked down the walls of the 'Catholic' citadel, and let the 'fresh air' from outside enter, according to the image of John XXIII." [36]

This is a sampling of texts calling the Holy Church a sect and a ghetto that clearly offend her from the standpoint of her separation from the world. Given the large number of representative Prelates and theologians with this *animus injuriandi*, we believe it reflects well the spirit of the Council.

2. The Church-World Relations before Vatican II Is Called Schizophrenic

§ 31

Behind their insults, we see that what many progressivists are defending is an indiscriminate "opening" of the Church to the world. This, however, does not reflect their entire doctrine. They further deny that any difference should exist between the spiritual and temporal spheres – the Church and the world. We will analyze this position in another Volume of this Collection. [37] Here we cite, as a single example, a particularly offensive statement [38] that considers the distinc-

---

[36] *Ibid.*, p. 1118.

[37] Vol. V, *Animus Delendi II*, Part I, *passim*.

[38] What follows are other works that express the same doctrine – doing away with the distinction between the Church and the world – although with different emphases and nuances, depending on the author defending this thesis:

Antonio Acerbi, *Due ecclesiolgoie* (Bologna: Dehoniane, 1975), p. 360; Hans Urs von Balthasar, *Abbattere i bastioni*, pp. 97-98, 107, 113-114,

tion between the Church and the world – a doctrine preached by the Magisterium for centuries – to be the result of a mental imbalance, a schizophrenia, which is a psychotic disorder where a person suffers hallucinations of living two simultaneous and different lives. [39]

143; "Eschatologie," in V.A., Questions théologiques aujourd'hui (Paris: Desclée de Brouwer, 1965), vol. 2, p. 278; De l'Intégration, pp. 136-137; "Mysterium Paschale," in V.A., Mysterium Salutis, vol. 3, 6, p. 106; Théologie de l'Histoire, p. 164; Gregory Baum, 'La presenza della Chiesa nella società di domani," in V.A., L'avvenire della Chiesa, p. 151; Rocco Buttiglione, Il pensiero di Karol Wojtyla, p. 245; Marie-Dominque Chenu, "The History of Salvation and the Historicity of Man in the Renewal of Theology," in V.A., Theology of Renewal, vol. 1, p. 160; Jacques Duquesne interroge le Père Chenu, p. 78; "La Chiesa e il mondo," in V.A., I grandi temi del Concilio, pp. 833-835; Yves Congar, Eglise Catholique et France moderne, pp. 231-233; "Le rôle de l'Église dans le monde de ce temps," in V.A., L'Eglise dans le monde de ce temps, vol. 1, p. 314; Pour une Église servante et pauvre, pp. 132-133; "Salvación y liberación," in V.A., Conversaciones de Toledo - Teología de la liberación (Burgos: Aldecoa, 1973), p. 202; "1960-1970: Dix annés décisives pour l'Église et pour le monde," I.C.I., January 1,1970, pp. 23-24.; Christian Duquoc, "Um paraíso na terra?" Concilium, 1979/3, pp. 88-89.; Pierre Eyt, "Igreja e mutaçöes sócio-culturais," in V.A., A Igreja do futuro, pp. 17-19.; Maurizio Flick and Zoltán Alszeghy, Il mistero della croce, pp. 42-43; Leo-Alting von Geusau, "La Chiesa 'scandalo' del mondo," in V.A., La fine della Chiesa comme società perfetta, pp. 156-158; Ferdinand Klostermann, "Princípi por una riforma di struttura della Chiesa", in V.A., La fine della Chiesa comme società perfetta, p. 245; Hans Küng, A Igreja, vol. 1, pp. 135-136, 181-182; vol. 2, p. 190; Veracidade, p. 155; Jacques Mouroux, "Situation et signification du chapitre I: Sur la dignité de la personne humaine," in V.A., L'Eglise dans le monde de ce temps, vol. 1, p. 252, Germano Pattaro, "Regno di Dio e 'ideologie'," in V.A., Il regno di Dio che vienne, pp. 270-272; Gérard Philips, La Chiesa e il suo mistero, p. 479; Paul Poupard, "Le radici cristiane dell'Europa," L'Osservatore Romano, December 19, 1984, p. 5; Karl Rahner, "Theological Reflections on the Problem of Secularization," in V.A., Theology of Renewal, vol. 1, p. 186; Luigi Sartori, "Regno di Dio e Chiesa," in V.A., Il regno di Dio che vienne, p. 38; Edward Schillebeeckx, Cristo sacramento dell'incontro con Dio (Rome: Paoline, 1970), pp. 252-253; "Les sacraments, organes de la recontre de Dieu," in V.A., Catholiques et protestants (Paris: Seuil, 1963), p. 240; Antonie Vergote, "La presenza della Chiesa nella societá di domani," in V.A., L'avvenire della Chiesa, p. 170.

[39] Although in non-technical language this is the concept employed by Hans Küng in the cited text, we are aware that in fact schizophrenia is not limited to this symptom alone. If a more precise definition were

§ 32
The excerpt below is by the conciliar *perito* Fr. Hans Küng:

"The new sincerity and veracity does not stop at the doors of the Church because of the simple fact that **all the members of the Church are also men of the world, increasingly less disposed to divide their existence between the Church and the world in a schizophrenic way. There can be no doubt that precisely on this point the Catholic Church was assisted** – perhaps more than we imagine – **by Vatican Council II.**" [40]

With this last example of an offense against the traditional relationship between the Church and the world, the Reader has elements to judge the results of conciliar tolerance toward such affronts, so deleterious for the honor of the Church. Both the offenses themselves and this tolerance are expressive of the spirit of the Council.

*   *   *

---

required from a medical point of view, one would say that schizophrenia (from the Greek *schizein* = to cut, divide + *phrein* = soul, spirit) is a mental disorder of a psychotic nature whereby the patient turns to his own, interior, imaginary world (autism) and increasingly withdraws from the real, exterior world, causing a division in his own personality.

[40] H. Küng, *Veracidade*, p. 7.

CONCLUSION

§ 1
We believe it has been established that innumerable conciliar and post-conciliar theologians, many of them leading mentors of Vatican II, are surprisingly hostile to the Holy Church. Hence, the title of this Volume: *Animus Injuriandi.*

It is difficult to deny that such offenses reflect a state of mind, a mentality that clashes in every possible way with the true *sentire cum Ecclesia.*[1]

§ 2
Unfortunately, it is also difficult not to think that such Prelates and theologians, given their importance and number, have received a "green light" – an expression of Fr. Congar[2] – to proceed with such a bold and broad onslaught as the one exposed in this Volume. That is to say, they have been permitted to continuously and methodically offend the Holy Church "from the sole of her foot to the top of her head" (Is 1: 6).

§ 3
Therefore, given the tolerance the conciliar Popes have shown toward such offenses, and given the coherence of such affronts with the progressivist interpretation of the documents of Vatican II, we cannot fail to consider the *animus injuriandi* expounded in this Volume as one of the most remarkable expressions of the spirit of the Council.

§ 4
The animosity that steeps their spirits, the gravity of the offenses, the ingratitude of these members of the Church who are still in some way her sons, the grandeur and majesty of the victim under attack – the Church herself – bring to mind the divine figure of Jesus Christ, His hands bound, His divine Person covered with insults and scorn, His head crowned with thorns, His sacred body scourged.

---

[1] *Sentire cum Ecclesia* generally translates as 'to feel with the Church.' St. Ignatius of Loyola established rules for this way of thinking with the Church. As those rules became increasingly famous, so also did the expression *sentire cum Ecclesia.*

[2] Cf. Y. Congar, *La crisi nella Chiesa e Mons. Lefèbvre*, p. 61.

Against Him also priests and doctors rose up, provoked by the highest officials of the Jewish synagogue.

§ 5   And from the depths of this tragic picture, a voice reaches the ears of the faithful in a sublime echo of the centuries-old liturgy of the Passion, the voice of the One who was Just above all the just, the voice of the spotless Lamb, who poignantly asks: "*Popule meus, quid feci tibi?*" [3]

* * *

---

[3] From the refrain of the Reproaches of the Good Friday liturgy: "O my people, what have I done to thee?"

APPENDIX I

THE ROLE OF VON BALTHASAR'S *CASTA MERETRIX* IN THE MULTI-CENTURY ONSLAUGHT OF MISERABLISM IN THE CHURCH

If the Reader tries to argue with a progressivist about the offenses presented in this Volume, especially those referring to the sacrality and sanctity of the Church, he will generally encounter an obstacle.

§ 1 The progressivist will certainly present this line of reasoning:

1. In the Church, there have always been sinners, be they among the faithful or the Hierarchs. There were even Popes who sinned and were publicly recognized as sinners. Therefore, History tells us that there are sins in the Church. Consequently, one may say that in her very nature the Church is sinful.

2. We also find evidence of many sins in the Old Testament, and God Himself, through the mouths of the Prophets, rebuked Israel innumerable times. Referring to the whole Chosen People, God compared them to a prostitute.

3. Thus, both in the Old and the New Covenants, the ensemble of faithful – that is, the Synagogue and the Church – can be symbolized by a prostitute.

4. Further, it is common to find that the Church Fathers used such symbols in relation to the Church.

5. Therefore, one can legitimately uphold that the Church is a sinner and that the prostitute is a proper symbol for her.

6. The recognized theologian Cardinal Hans Urs von Balthasar demonstrates exactly this thesis in his book *Casta Meretrix*.

7. By adopting the notion of a sinful Church, Vatican Council II only gave its blessing to an ancient tradition.

An expressive example of this argumentation is an excerpt from an article by Fr. John O'Donnel, S.J., published in *The Clergy Review*: [1]

---

[1] The article "Man and Woman as *Imago Dei* in the Theology of Hans Urs von Balthasar" was sent to the Author of this Volume by Fr. Edouard Hammel, S.J., professor of Moral Theology and then Vice-Rector of Gregorian University, to help to clarify the two conversa-

§ 2   "But Balthasar (at least in theory) is not unrealistic. Proof of this is found in his extensive essay on the Church as *casta meretrix*. In this essay of over 100 pages, **Balthasar draws upon all the resources of his patristic learning to show that the Church is not only to be imaged as the virgin, mother, bride and dove, but also as the harlot. Vatican II in its document on the Church stressed that the Church in her pilgrim condition will ever stand in need of purification. This is, no doubt, a language evocative of the Reformation. In this essay Balthasar argues that, although Luther's diatribe against the Roman Catholic Church as the whore of Babylon may strike us as scandalous, nevertheless this line of thinking is not new ...**

"The Fathers of the Church did not hesitate to use the analogy of the Old Testament in which God took to Himself an adulterous bride in the way Osee, under divine command, took Gomer to himself and remained faithful to her in spite of her adultery. In the same way the Church of Christ is made up of pagans whose principal sin is idolatry, the worship of false gods, which the Old and New Testaments often speak of as adultery. But just **as the Canaanite harlot Rahab received the soldiers of Joshua in her home** and was saved by her faith in Yahweh, **so the Church is made up of pagan gentiles** who are saved by their faith in Christ. Thus **the Church, who was once a harlot, has now become** by the grace of Christ **a chaste virgin**. But she must always be mindful of her past lest she surrender her new-found dignity and return to her former prostitution.

§ 3   "But **is this prostitution just a thing of the past? Is the** Church, who was once a harlot, now the bride without spot and wrinkle? **Or is it the case that the Church is both harlot and virgin, *casta meretrix*? Balthasar believes that we must indeed affirm both the immaculate sinless character of the bride and the permanent infidelities which blemish her in her pilgrim state."[2]**

---

tions they had in Rome on this and other topics (February 2 and March 7, 1983). He would seem to endorse this line of thinking. Fr. Hammel participated in the writing of *Gaudium et spes* and was also a member of the International Theological Commission (ITC); in 1975 he was placed in charge of the Pontifical Commission for the Rights of Women.

[2] John O'Donnel, "Man and Woman as *Imago Dei* in the Theology of Hans Urs von Balthasar," *The Clergy Review*, n. 78, London, 1983, p. 122.

Faced with this argument, our Reader could become uncomfortable and uncertain about how to respond.

To make it easier for him to answer, we decided to add this Appendix to Volume II of this Collection, which will analyze the symbol of the prostitute and the problem of a "poor Church," or a "miserablist Church."

*

§ 4   This Appendix I does not pretend to exhaust the topic of the supposed peccability of the Church[3] and of an imaginary peccantness, or sinfulness, that would exist in her very essence (n. 1 above). We intend to deal with such matters in greater detail in Volume XI of this Collection.[4]

Nor do we intend to directly address how the Council blessed the thesis of the sinning Church (n. 7 above). This matter will be discussed in more detail also in Volume XI.

Our goal here is to situate the theme of the work *Casta meretrix* in a historical context and to present a refutation of it.

In so doing, we believe we will be providing the Reader with arguments to counter the objections above, as well as offering him a concrete example of the fraudulent character of the progressivist argument.

*   *   *

---

[3] We adopt the word **peccability** here to mean the possibility of sinning. The term **peccantness** or **sinfulness** is understood as the actual existence of sin, with the consequent atmosphere of disorder that it creates, making the sinner prone to commit other sins.

[4] Vol. XI, *Ecclesia*, Chap. IV.

Part I

A Miserablist Church – Doctrinal and Historical Overview

§ 5   As we have seen in this Volume, the progressivist current – stimulated by the examples of John XXIII and Paul VI – clearly intended to do away with the sacrality of the Catholic Church in the name of the "evangelical ideal" of a "poor Church." [5] We also saw that their accusation of "sinner" hurled at the Church is based on the presumption that the "sin" of the Church is to have power and riches.[6] From these notions, one can infer that for the Church to cease being a "sinner," "pharisaic" and "carnal," she would have to rid herself of her wealth and structure, her "system."[7] In other words, it becomes more or less explicit that she should be transformed into a type of invisible or ethereal Church, a pneumatic Church. She would become what could be called the "miserablist Church."

1. The Miserablist Position and the Catholic Position

§ 6   When it comes to the accusation of *casta meretrix* translated into the question of whether or not the Church should have riches, pomp and a visible structure, we see that the progressivist current appears to proceed from an immense black river, partly subterranean, that flows parallel to the history of the Church.[8]

§ 7   From the early times of the Church, this river began to form by a confluence of sects that claimed the Church was strictly spiritual. Thus they denied that she had the characteristics of a visible society composed of men and, as such, could own and manage property, land and wealth. By advocating a so-called evangelical poverty, these sects opposed the pomp and solemnity of her acts of worship and the beauty of her sacred buildings, which have always been a characteristic of the sacrality of the Church.

§ 8   Revealing a radically egalitarian nature, these sects denied the legitimacy of the visible characteristics of the Church's power to govern, teach and sanctify. In other words, they rebelled against the establishment of papal power as a monarchy and the bishops' power as an aristocracy. Likewise, they opposed the prerogatives of such powers

---

[5] Cf. Chap. III, Notes 1, 2, 3, §§ 1-4; Chap. IV, *passim.*

[6] Cf. Chap. V, §§ 1-7.

[7] Cf. This "system" was described by Fr. Y. Congar in Chap. V §§ 1-4.

[8] In Section I.2 below, we list the principal sects and major figures that adhered to this current of thought.

– the governmental, juridical and legislative bodies equipped to exert vigilance and punishment, as well as their corresponding executive organs. Similarly, they called for the abolishment of the monarchical and aristocratic system of teaching in the Church, through which she distributes the treasures of the Faith and truth. For the same reasons, the hierarchy of orders was also combated and condemned as an evil.

§ 9

As a consequence, such sects opposed the Church having any influence whatsoever in temporal life, either in the culture of peoples or in their civilization. Even more exasperating for them was her influence over the State whereby she oriented it on the path of the Catholic Faith and Christendom.

§ 10

Notwithstanding, the Holy Church followed a direction diametrically opposed to the one desired by these sects and organically established herself as a triple monarchy – of government, teaching and sanctification. This triple monarchy was founded on three different counts of papal power:

• By virtue of the *potestas vicaria*, the power that Our Lord granted St. Peter (Mt 16:19, Jn 21:15-17), the Pope is the absolute monarch of the Church by divine mandate;

• By virtue of the *potestas ex pacto*, the power vested in the Pope by those who make a vow of obedience to him, that is, the whole Hierarchy and the secular and regular Clergy,[9] he is the absolute monarch by contractual delegation;

---

[9] **Regarding the secular clergy**: At their ordination, priests make a solemn promise of obedience to the Supreme Pontiff and to their Bishop (cf. John Paul II, *Código de Direito Canônico de 1983*, can. 273; note to can. 273 by Jesus S. Hortal in the official edition of the National Conference of Brazilian Bishops, São Paulo: Loyola,1983, p. 123; *Codex Iuris Canonici* of 1917, can. 127; Arturo Alonso Lobo, "Comentários al libro segundo del CDC," in V.A., *Comentarios al Codigo de Derecho Canonico* (Madrid: BAC, 1963), vol. 1, pp. 417-419.

In his turn, when the Bishop is consecrated, he takes an oath of fidelity to the Holy See (cf. John Paul II, *Código de Direito Canônico* of 1983, can. 380; *Codex Iuris Canonici* of 1917, can. 332 § 2; F. Claeys-Bouuaert, entry 'Evêques,' in *Dictionnaire de Droit Canoique*, vol. 5, col. 577).

Regarding the regular clergy: The *1917 Code of Canon Law* affirmed: "All religious are subject to the Roman Pontiff as their supreme Superior, whom they are obliged to obey also by reason of the vow of obedience" (can. 499, § 1). Renowned authors such as Fr.

- By virtue of the *potestas domestica* or *potestas dominativa*, the power a father has over his family or a lord over his household, the Pope is a feudal monarch by the natural order of things.[10]

§ 11   Thus established on the firm rock of the Papacy, the Holy City became powerful, important and glorious before the temporal Kingdoms and the Empire and, consequently, fulfilled the words of the Prophet:

"Arise, be enlightened, O Jerusalem: for thy light is come, and the glory of the Lord is risen upon thee ... and the Nations shall walk in thy light, and Kings in the brightness of thy rising. Lift up thy eyes round about and see: all these are gathered together, they are come to thee: thy sons shall come from afar, and thy daughters shall rise up at thy side.

"Then shall thou see and abound, and thy heart shall wonder and be enlarged, when the multitude of the sea shall be converted to thee, the strength of the Nations shall come to thee. The multitude of camels shall cover thee, the dromedaries of Madian and Epha: all they from Saba shall come, bringing gold and frankincense: and skewing forth praise to the Lord. All the flocks of Cedar shall be gathered together unto thee, the rams of Nabaioth shall minister to thee: they shall be offered upon My acceptable altar, and I will glorify the house of My majesty" (Is. 60:1-7).

§ 12   Therefore, the Church is a *societas perfecta,* that is, she is a visible society, which in her own sphere pursues an absolute and supreme good, possessing all the means to achieve her end. She is also sovereign: Her supreme authority is subject to no other power, with the triple power to legislate, judge and punish.

§ 13   However, the State is also a *societas perfecta*. Thus, the organic development of Church-State relations made it necessary to clarify which of the two powers – the Church or the Empire – should

---

Gerardo Kindt, C.S.S.R., defend that the religious is subject to the Pope and owes him obedience on two counts: the power of jurisdiction and the vow of obedience (cf. *De potestate dominativa in religione,* Bruges/Paris/Rome: Desclée de Brouwer, 1945, pp. 166-167, 202, 210 note 67, 218, 263-264, 327-330).

The *1983 Code of Canon Law,* however, does not affirm that obedience to the Supreme Pontiff is owed by virtue of the vow, but limits it to what is set out in the respective Rules of the Orders or Congregations (cf. John Paul II, *Code of Canon Law,* can. 590; note 1).

[10] For more on the distinction between the three powers described in the text, see Vol. XI, *Ecclesia,* Chap. I. §§ 87-92.

have primacy. The key figure who resolved this dilemma was the great St. Gregory VII. In the realm of principles, he settled the question with his famous *Dictatus Papae;* [11] in the realm of facts, the question was resolved by the historic episode at Canossa where the Empire, represented by Henry IV, subordinated itself to the Church. More than 200 years later, Pope Boniface VIII reaffirmed the doctrine of *Dictatus Papae* in more general terms in the Bull *Unam Sanctam.* [12]

---

[11] Of the 27 propositions in St. Gregory VII's *Dictatus Papae,* these are the ones defining the supremacy of the Sovereign Pontiff over all temporal powers:

"n. 9 - That all princes shall kiss the feet of the Pope alone;

"n. 11 - That his name is unique in the world;

"n. 12 - That it may be permitted for him to depose emperors;

"n. 19 - That he himself must be judged by no one;

"n. 27 - That he may absolve subjects from their oath of fidelity to wicked rulers (Cf. Augustin Fliche, "La réforme grégorienne et la reconquête chrétienne (1057-1123)," in Augustin Fliche and Victory Martin, *Histoire de l'Église depuis les origines jusqu'à nos jours,* Paris: Bloud & Gay, 1946, vol. 8, p. 80).

[12] In the Bull *Unam Sanctam* Boniface VIII established the supremacy of the spiritual over the temporal power:

"We are informed by the texts of the Gospels that in this Church and in her power are two swords, namely, the spiritual and the temporal. For when the Apostles say: 'Behold, here are two swords' (Lk 22:38]), that is to say, in the Church, since the Apostles were speaking, the Lord did not reply that there were too many, but sufficient. Certainly the one who denies that the temporal sword is in the power of Peter has not listened well to the word of the Lord commanding: 'Put up thy sword into thy scabbard' (Mt 26:52). Both, therefore, are in the power of the Church, that is, the spiritual and the temporal sword: The latter is to be administered for the Church, and the former by the Church; the former by the hands of the priest, and the latter by the hands of kings and soldiers, but at the will and accord of the priest.

"However, one sword ought to be subordinated to the other and temporal authority should be subjected to spiritual power. For since the Apostle said: "There is no power except from God and the things that exist, are ordained by God' (Rom 13:1-2); they would not be so ordained if one sword were not subordinated to the other, and if the inferior one, as it were, were not led upwards by the other. For, according to Blessed Dionysius, it is a law of the divinity that the lowest things reach the highest places by intermediaries. ...

"Hence we must recognize very clearly that the spiritual power surpasses in dignity and in nobility any temporal power whatever, as

So, by means of these two great Popes, the Church reached the apogee of her earthly glory. The Vicar of Christ came to be recognized by the whole world not only as the Monarch of the Church, but as the supreme arbiter of Christendom and the temporal sphere in general.

§ 14

Thus, the power of the keys was fixed and blessed for all times. The papal symbols were established in consonance with this doctrine: The Pope's triple-crown rests on the gold and silver keys that cross each other. With the gold key the Pope directly opens and closes the whole spiritual sphere. With the silver key, he indirectly opens and closes the temporal sphere. This is undeviating Catholic doctrine.

§ 15

Nevertheless, for the miserablist current, the fact that the Church possesses both spiritual and temporal powers signifies the very height of her prostitution. And the two Pontiffs of *Dictatus Papae* and *Unam Sanctam* represent the very embodiment of her sin. It is certainly for this reason that in the *Divine Comedy*, Dante places Pope Boniface VIII in the deep layers of Hell,[13] to the great relish of certain contemporary theologians.[14]

---

spiritual things evidently surpass the temporal. ... It belongs to the spiritual power to establish the temporal power and to pass judgment if it is not good. Thus is accomplished the prophecy of Jeremiah concerning the Church and the ecclesiastical power: 'Behold today I have placed you over nations, and over kingdoms,' and the rest.

"Therefore, if the temporal power err, it will be judged by the spiritual power; but if a minor spiritual power err, it will be judged by a superior spiritual power; but if the highest power of all err, it can be judged only by God, and not by man, according to the testimony of the Apostle: 'The spiritual man judged of all things and he himself is judged by no man' (Cor 2:15). (Bull *Unam Sanctam* of November 18, 1302, in Marie-Hippolyte Hemmer, "Boniface VIII," in *DTC*, vol. 2, cols. 999-1000).

[13] In *The Divine Comedy,* Dante Alighieri spares Pope Boniface VIII no insults and incriminations. The Italian version we used, prepared by Cesare Gàrboli, following Scartazzini and Vandelli, is based on the text of the Dante Society (Turin: Giulio Einaudi, 1954, p. XXX). The comments between brackets are from the explanatory footnotes of these highly regarded Dante scholars.

a. Among Dante's tirades against Boniface VIII, we chose these excerpts:

• St. Peter from Heaven denounces Boniface VIII for turning Rome into a place of carnage and corruption, a veritable sewer:

"He [Boniface VIII] who on earth usurps that place of mine,

that place of mine, that place of mine which now
stands vacant in the eyes of Christ, God's Son.
He has turned my sepulcher [the city of Rome,
where Peter is buried] into a sewer
of blood and filth, at which the Perverse One [Lucifer]
who fell from here takes great delight down there [in Hell]
  (*Paradise,* canto XXVII, 22-27).

• Beatrice comments to Dante about Boniface's successor, Pope Clement V. She predicts he also will shortly be damned to Hell, thus stuffing Boniface VIII deeper down into Hell:

"But God will not permit him [Clement V] to stay long
in the Holy Office [of Vicar of Christ]: He shall be thrust down
where Simon Magus pays for his guilt, and he [Clement V]
shall stuff the Alagnese [Boniface VIII] deeper down! [into
the cave of Hell where the Simoniacs are]"
  (*Paradise,* Canto XXX, 145-148)

• Other excerpts can be found in *Hell,* canti XIX, 52-57, XXVII, 40-136, especially 67-70 and 85-89; *Paradise,* canto XVII, 49-51.

b. The similarity between the thinking of the Florentine poet and those of the miserablist current is not limited to insulting Boniface VIII, but also includes attacking the temporal possessions of the Church.

• Dante thus refers to the Donation of Constantine, the lands given to the Pope by Constantine in the 4th century, which would have introduced wealth to the Church, as a great evil:

"O Constantine, what evil did you sire,
not by your conversion, but by that donation
which the first wealthy Pope [St. Sylvester] got from you!"
  (*Hell,* canto XIX, 115-117)

• In *Purgatory,* when Beatrice points to the chariot, which symbolizes the Church, the Poet imagines St. Peter criticizing the donation of temporal goods (the feathers of the eagle) which St. Sylvester received from Constantine (the eagle)

"Once more the eagle swooped down through the tree:
this time into the framework of the chariot [the Church]
to leave some of its golden feathers there.

Like sorrow pouring from a grieving heart,
a voice from Heaven said: 'My little ship,
O what ill-fated cargo you bear!"
  (*Purgatory,* Canto XXXII, 124-129)

• Other stanzas that make the same criticism of the Church's wealth can be found in *Purgatory,* canto XXXIII, 31-63; *Paradise,* canti IX, 112-142, especially 127 to the end; XVIII, 115-132; XX, 55-60; XXI, 127-135; XXII, 76-90.

c. In other passage, Dante uses the figure of the prostitute to refer to The Roman Curia, which would have sold herself to the King of France, Philip the Fair (the giant), in exchange for lucrative alliances. The kisses of the two represent their mutual temporal interests. That relationship changes, however, when the Holy See is transferred to Avignon, the giant's flight with the transformed chariot (the Church) upon which the prostitute is seated:

> "Seated thereon, securely, as if in a fort
> high on a hill, I saw an naked prostitute
> casting bold, sluttish glances all around.
> And next to her I saw a giant standing at her side,
> To prevent anyone from taking her from him,
> From time to time the two of them would kiss.
> But when she turned her roving, lustful eyes
> on me, her lover in a fit of rage
> beat her ferociously from head to foot
> Then, furious with jealousy, the giant
> ripped loose the monster [the transformed chariot],
> dragging it away
> far off into the woods, until the trees
> blocked from my sight the prostitute and that strange beast"
> (*Purgatory*, Canto XXXII, 148-160).

• See also *Hell*, XIX, 57, where Dante accuses Boniface VIII of making the Church a prostitute; and in verses 106-111 he accuses her of 'playing whore with the kings' of this Earth.

[14] This satisfaction with Dante's Poem is expressed by von Balthasar in his study on *Dante*, inserted in his book *The Glory and the Cross:*

"Dante's criticisms of the medieval Church that became worldly are unending. From the height of the Empyrean, Beatrice and [St.] Peter launch their censures against this dissolute Church, and, in a terrible image, **the poet sees the glorified Peter suddenly become incandescent with rage and fulminate against the 'infamous' Boniface VIII, who has turned the Apostle's tomb into a sewer of blood and excrement.** All Heaven takes on the same angry red color, Beatrice grows pale, and the spheres are darkened because **'the Bride of the Lord' has become a venal whore who can be bought with gold"** (H. U. von Balthasar, *La gloire et la Croix - Dante*, p. 337).

It seems that von Balthasar either erred or was too hasty in attributing the adjective "infamous" to Boniface VIII in his reference to that passage of the *Divine Comedy* (Cf. *Paradise*, canto. XXVII, 22, 27). In the stanza in question, according to the mentioned Dante scholars, the "infamous one" to which von Balthasar refers (from the Italian *perverso,* better translated as 'perverse one' in English) refers to Lucifer rather than Boniface VIII.

Similarly, it is misplaced to call the Church "a venal whore who can be bought with gold," because in the canto referenced by von Balthasar, we find only these words – attributed by Dante not to the Church but to St. Peter:

> "The bride of Christ was not nourished on blood
> that came from me, from Linus and from Cletus [Popes who succeeded Peter],
> to be used to buy gold,
> but rather to live content in this delightful life [of paradise]
> (*Paradise*, canto XXVII, 40-43).

In the excerpt above of verse 42, "*per essere ad acquisto d'oro usata*" – "to be used to buy gold" - von Balthasar translated this phrase as if it said "in order that she be bought for gold." The scholars that we are following, however, recommend the translation we provide. Further, Dante does not use the words "venal whore" that von Balthasar deceptively inserts into his citation.

It is curious that von Balthasar, "the most learned man of his time," according to Cardinal de Lubac (cf. *Paradoxe et mystère de l'Église*, p. 184), failed to capture the exact meaning of various texts in Dante's famous Poem and did not bother to inform himself on such important points. Instead, he precipitously attributes such affronts to a Pontiff and the Church.

Interpreting Dante, Von Balthasar returns to the assault against the Church's power and riches:

"Peter reproaches the Popes for their ambition and thirst for honors which divide the Church and for their abuse of the power of the keys by means of centuries-old wars and excommunications for political ends. He also censures them for their simony. **They [the Popes] deliver the Bride of Christ to adultery; they turn her into the whore of Babylon, and permit the kings of the earth ... to fornicate with her.**

"Once purified by his confession ... **Dante receives the task of observing the full horror of Church history ... thus viewing the gradual transformation of the pure Bride into the *Magna Meretrix*.** Further, in Paradise Peter solemnly tells him to make heaven's wrath known on earth, and he adds: 'Do not hide what I myself hide not.' Besides the Popes, he does not spare the bishops and the whole clergy; which he places in Hell among the hypocrites, the avaricious and the homosexuals" (H. U. von Balthasar, *La Gloire et la Croix - Dante*, p. 337).I

Here again we find some mistakes on the part of von Balthasar:

In his eagerness to prove that "the Popes deliver the Bride of Christ to adultery," he again makes an error of interpretation. In the original text, we read:

2. The Principal Miserablists from the Early Church to Vatican II

§ 16   Through the course of History, heretics professing different errors have flowed into the miserablist current. At the time of the Apostles, there were the Nicolaites[15] and Martius of Ponto;[16] in the second century, Carporates and Epiphanius.[17] The next century saw the Manicheans;[18] in the 6th century, the communist-style teachings of Mazdak in Persia came to light;[19] later, there was Paulicianism in Ar-

---

"But the Vatican and every sacred place
in Rome which marked the burial-ground
of the army who follows Peter [the martyrs]
shall soon be free of this adultery [of profanation]"
(*Hell*, canto IX, 139-141).

Von Balthasar appears to have understood "the army who follows Peter" as being composed of Popes and not of the martyrs, as scholars Garboli, Scartazzini and Vandelli assert. Also, von Balthasar's interprets the "adultery" as a sin of the Church, when it is actually the profanation of the martyrs' relics. Once again, his assault against the Popes and the Church here is baseless.

• In the lines of *The Divine Comedy* cited by the theologian in footnotes, we did not find the expression "whore of Babylon" which he attributes to the Poet.

• Equally imprecise is his referral to the *"magna meretrix"* [great whore]. In fact, the lines in question are in *Purgatory,* canto XXXII, 148-160, which we cited in Note 13c above. There, the "prostitute" of verse 149 and 160 is not the Church, but refer to the Roman Curia seated on the chariot, which represents the Church at the time when the Papacy was moved to Avignon.

There are, then, six serious errors of interpretation accompanied by unfounded offenses in just these two excerpts of the theologian...

Continuing on in that text, Von Balthasar clearly asserts his support of the Poet's position: "**His [Dante's] wrath ... is neither sectarian nor heterodox ... It springs only from the loving zeal of a Christian layman**" (*ibid.*, p. 338).

[15] Cf. Igor Chafarevitch, *Le phénomène socialiste* (Paris: Seuil, 1977), p. 28.

[16] Cf. Juan Bautista Weiss, *Historia Universal* (Barcelona: La Educación, 1927), vol. 4, p. 147.

[17] Cf. I. Chafarevitch, *Le phénomène socialiste*, p. 29.

[18] Cf. Gustave Bardy, entry "Manichéisme," in DTC, vol. 9, cols. 1859, 1861, 1867; J. B. Weiss, *Historia Universal,* p. 167.

[19] Cf. G. Bardy, "Les Églises de Perse et d'Arménie au VIe. siècle," in V.A., *Histoire de l'Église*, vol. 4, p. 497.

menia, Licaunia and Frigia.[20] The 9th century saw the rise of the icono-
clasts Claudius and Agobard, who were Bishops of Turin and Lyons
respectively.[21]

§ 17

Multiple Gnostic sects of a socialist-communist character bur-
geoned in the Middle Ages, including the 10th century sect of the
"Friends of God" in Byzantium and the "Dragovitsna church" in Bul-
garia,[22] both predecessors of the Cathar movement. The Cathars in
turn spread all over Europe, dividing and subdividing into multiple
denominations. For example, in France the Cathar movement included
Henrique de Lausanne, Eudes de l'Étoile, Peter of Bruys[23] and the
"Poor Men of Lyons"[24] founded by Peter Waldo.[25]

These Waldensians, along with the Albigensians, were supported by Nicetas of Constantinople, the "pope" of the Cathars,[26]
who was vigorously combated by St. Dominic.

In the Low Countries, this movement was represented by
Tanchelin,[27] Lambert the Stutterer, and the sect of Publicans or
Populicans.[28] In Italy, the Cathar movement spawned the *Communelli*
and the *Communiati*,[29] the penitential order of the *Umiliàti* that included Hugh Speroni,[30] Arnold of Brescia,[31] the *Patarini* of Lom-
bardy,[32] the "Apostolic Brethren" of Segarelli and Dolcino,[33] and the

---

[20] Cf. R. Janin, entry "Pauliciens," in DTC, vol. 11, cols. 56-58.

[21] Cf. I. Chafarevitch, *Le phénomène socialiste*, p. 92.

[22] Cf. Raymond Foreville, "Les grands courants hérétiques et les
premières mesures générales de répression," in V.A., *Histoire de
l'Église,* vol. 9/2, pp. 330-332.

[23] Cf. Augustin Fliche, Raymond Foreville & Jean Rousset, *Du premier Concile du Latran à l'avènement d'Innocent III, in ibid.*, vol. 9/1,
pp. 92-99.

[24] Cf. *Enciclopedia Universal Ilustrada,* entry "Fraticelos," vol. 24, p.
1150.

[25] Cf. R. Foreville, *Les grands courants hérétiques,* p. 342.

[26] *Ibid.*, pp. 337-338.

[27] Cf. B. Llorca, *Manual de Historia Eclesiastica,* p. 414.

[28] Cf. R. Foreville, *Les grands courants hérétiques*, p. 336.

[29] Cf. F. Vernet, entry "Communistes," in DTC, vol. 3, col. 596.

[30] Cf. R. Foreville, *Les grands courants hérétiques*, p. 341.

[31] Cf. A. Fliche, R. Foreville & J. Rousset, *Du premier Concile du
Latran*, pp. 330-332.

[32] Cf. R. Foreville, *Les grands courants hérétiques*, p. 341.

[33] Cf. I. Chafarevitch, *Le phénomène socialiste,* pp. 61-63.

Fraticelli,[34] who had the firm support of Michael de Cesana and William of Occam.[35] Marsilius of Padua – who inspired a Florentine revolution against papal authority in favor of the sovereignty of the people – defended doctrines similar to those preached by Protestantism and the French Revolution.[36] In some verses of *The Divine Comedy,* Dante defends principles analogous to those of the miserablist current.[37]

In various regions of Germany, Belgium, France and Spain, John Oliva spread certain apocalyptic ideas of Joachim de Flora, along with a strong dose of the quietist mysticism. Oliva's adepts took up the name Beghards and Beguines.[38]

§ 18

Also merging into the miserablist current were heretics and sects that preceded or continued the Pseudo-Reformation, such as Wycliffe in England at the end of the 14th century,[39] John Hus and the Thaborites in Bohemia at the beginning of the 15th century,[40] Savonarola[41] and Campanella[42] in Italy, Luther[43] and the Anabaptists

---

[34] *Enciclopédia Universal Ilustrada,* entry "Fraticelos," vol. 24, p. 1150. The miserablist theory of this sect is explained by F. Vernet: "There are two churches, one Roman, carnal, rich, stained with crimes; the other – theirs – is spiritual, poor, holy, the only true church which was dear to the Sicilian group of Henry of Ceva" (entry "Fraticelles" in DTC, vol. 6, col. 780),

The *Fraticelli* were condemned by John XXII's Constitution *Gloriosam Ecclesiam* of January 23, 1318 (Cf. DR, 484-490).

[35] Cf. B. Llorca, *Manual de Historia Eclesiastica,* p. 500.

William of Occam and Michael of Cesena upheld that Our Lord Jesus Christ and the Apostles lived in such an extreme state of misery that they did not own what they used for their daily needs. This position was condemned as heretical by Pope John XXII in the Constitution *Cum inter nonnullos* of November 13, 1323 (Cf. DR, 494).

[36] Cf. Pierre Virion, *Le mystère de Jeanne d'Arc et la politique des Nations* (Paris: Tequi, 1972), pp. 45-47.

[37] See the passages of *The Divine Comedy* cited in Note 13, above.

[38] Cf. *Enciclopédia Universal Ilustrada,* entry "Fraticelos," vol. 24, pp. 1150-1151.

[39] Cf. B. Llorca, *Manual de Historia Eclesiastica,* p. 501.

[40] Cf. *Ibid.,* pp. 502-503; I. Chafarevitch, *Le phénomène socialiste,* pp. 43-45.

[41] Cf. Marcel Maxime Gorce, entry "Savonarole," in DTC, vol. 14, cols. 1219, 1229.

[42] Cf. I. Chafarevitch, *Le phénomène socialiste,* pp. 105-107.

[43] At the Diet of Worms (1521), the Papal Nuncio accused Luther of adopting old heresies: "For the most part, your ideas are those of the

of Thomas Münzer in Germany,[44] the English and German Lollards,[45] and the English *Ranters*, *Diggers* and *Levelers* in the 17th century,[46] and so on.

With the vigorous reaction of the Counter-Reformation, the religious effects of this miserablist current diminished, even though its notorious influence can still be found in the sect of the Moravian Brothers.

§ 19   The waters of this same miserablist river – transforming its principles of religious poverty into politico-social ideals and acting in the temporal sphere – flowed into the upheavals of the French Revolution and the failed Communist experiments of Babeuf. A little later the utopian Socialism of Saint-Simon and Charles Fourier merged into that current, followed soon after by the so-called scientific Communism of Marx.

§ 20   In some aspects, the romantic movement of the 19th century helped give continuity to the miserablist current. Thus we find Victor Hugo presenting as a model for Bishops a certain Msgr. Bienvenu, a character in *Les Misérables,* who divests himself of the Episcopal Palace and the magnificent life of a Prince of the Church with its pensions to live sparsely in a poor abode.[47] Lamennais, a convergence point for various revolutionary tendencies, was also no stranger to the miserablist current.[48] In the late 19th century, the Modernist move-

---

Beghards, the Waldensians, the Poor Men of Lyons, the Wycliffites and the Husites" (L. Keller, *Johann von Staupitz und die Anfänge der Reformation*, Leipzig, 1888, *in ibid.*, p. 87).

[44] Cf. I. Chafarevitch, *Le phénomène socialiste,* pp. 53-54.

[45] Cf. *Ibid.*, p. 55; Rení Hedde, entry "Lollards," in DTC, vol. 9, cols. 910-925.

[46] Cf. I. Chafarevitch, *Le phénomène socialiste,* pp. 56-59.

[47] Cf. Victor Hugo, *Les Miserables,* vol. 1, pp. 25-84.

[48] We refer especially to the doctrine of Lamennais in *La censure de Toulouse*, proposition 49: "When this happens (when the Roman people break the last link by which the head of the Church still binds a remnant of political society to the pontifical cross: *Paroles du Globe*); when this happens, will you not believe that this is progress? (n. 83, January 7, 1831, col. 6)" (in A. Fonck, entry "Lamennais," in DTC, vol. 8, col. 2512).

In their miserablist longings, "Lamennais and his friends went so far in their dream of emancipation [freeing the Church from any favor received from the State] that they exhorted the Church to abandon her grand cathedrals, considered 'temples of the State,' and to transport their altars to the farms" (cf. Robert Havard de la Montagne,

ment, which installed itself in the Church with certain romantic assimilations, ardently defended the miserablist ideals.[49]

§ 21   Less than two generations passed between the condemnation of Modernism and the first manifestations of Progressivism. In the 1930s, with progressivists installed in key posts, the "social movement" gained ground in the Church. The "rights of the poor" were hypertrophied, while charity and mercy atrophied. After the Second World War, the worker-priests set a model for the future. Initially, their promoters were condemned; a little later, however, several of these worker priests were rehabilitated and played key roles as *periti* at the Council. [50]

Histoire de la Démocratie Chrétienne de Lamennais à George Bidault, Paris: Amiot & Dumont, 1948, p. 29).

It is expressive of his miserablist tendencies that, among Lamennais' last wishes, was his instruction to be buried in as simple a wood coffin as possible in a common grave (Cf. J. Lucas-Dubreton, *Béranger - La chanson, la politique, la société*, Paris: Hachette, 1934, p. 259).

[49] See Antonio Fogazzaro, *Il Santo* (Milan, 1907), in which he criticizes ecclesiastical pomp, honor and riches (pp. 222-223.), exalts the "poor Church" (p. 303) and emphatically counsels the Pope to leave the Vatican (p. 224).

See also the anonymous work, *The Plan of the Modernists* [*Il Programma dei Modernisti*] (Turin: Fratelli Bocca, 1911). It condemns ecclesiastical riches "that cloud the correct vision of things"; the political responsibilities of the Church; her system of governance described as "small and decrepit noble oligarchies which, in exchange for a little pomp, impose customs in open contrast with the tendencies of the world"; her power – "a sterile force that notwithstanding haughty appearances ... executes a work that delays the progress of society." The text extols the "evangelical ideal" of the "poor Church": "The Church must know how to be that great force of moral elevation that she was in her less wealthy but more efficient times, above all in her early times. Then her history, which today is on a descending trajectory, will receive a powerful impulse toward a new ascent" (pp. 124-126),

[50] Fr. Marie-Dominique Chenu, inspirer of the worker-priests movement and one of the mentors of "opening" the Church to the world at the Council, testifies: "It was only a few years later, with the shock of the Council, that the situation would change. Cardinal Liénart brought to the great assembly some priests from *Mission de France* and several worker-priests, who then played the role of qualified and consulted *periti*" (*Jacques Duquesne interroge le Pére Chenu*, p. 160).

§ 22   At the beginning of Vatican II, John XXIII moved the Church
closer to the ideals of the miserablist current when he expounded his
aim: "It is necessary to shake off the imperial dust that has gradually
accumulated on the throne of Peter since the time of Constantine."[51]
Paul VI continued that trend when he stopped using the Triple Crown
and sold it to give the money to the poor.[52] During the Council, the
"Pact of the Catacombs"[53] was made; in it the Prelates promised to
abolish the "sin" of the Church: riches, pomp, solemnity and sacrality.
The "Poor Church" was inaugurated.

In parallel, the Council's official documents echoed the
Lutheran principles of *Ecclesia semper reformanda* and the believer
as *simul justus et peccator*.[54] The Church began to ask forgiveness
for her 'sins'...[55] The notion of a "Sinning Church" was introduced.[56]

---

[51] Cf. Y. Congar, *Le Concile au jour le jour - Deuxième session* (Paris:
Cerf, 1964), p. 44.

[52] At the end of a concelebrated Mass in the Greek Melchite rite at
St. Peter's Basilica, Cardinal Pericle Felici stated: "The Church is
truly the mother of the poor, and the Pope decided to give a new
testimony of this by donating his triple-crown for the benefit of the
poor." As these words were spoken, Paul VI went to the altar and
placed the symbol of his spiritual and temporal royalty on it. That
triple crown was later sent to the Archdiocese of New York for a
public viewing, where the faithful were exhorted to make contributions for the needy. It was then purchased by an American museum
(Cf. H. Fesquet, *Le Journal du Concile*, 713-714).

[53] See Chap.III § 2 Note 2 of this Volume.

[54] These ideas of Luther were adopted in two of the most important
documents of the Council. The Dogmatic Constitution *Lumen gentium* states: "The Church, however, clasping sinners to her bosom,
**at once holy and always in need of purification, follows con-
stantly the path of penance and renewal**" (n. 8). The Decree
Unitatis redintegratio, on ecumenism, affirms: "Christ summons the
Church as she goes her pilgrim way to that **continual reformation**"
(n. 6).

[55] For example, the request for forgiveness addressed to heretics and
schismatics in the Decree *Unitatis redintegratio*: "The words of St.
John hold good about sins against unity: 'If we say we have not sinned,
we make him a liar, and his word is not in us' (I Jn. 1:10). So, **we
humbly beg pardon of God and of our separated brethren**" (n. 7).

[56] Commenting on *Lumen gentium*'s adoption of the notion of "sinning
Church," Karl Rahner says: "In practice, the Constitution knows that
the Church is a sinning Church, and not only that sinners ... exist in

§ 23   "Poor Church," "Sinning Church" – the Conciliar Church seemed only a step away from fully embracing the ideals of the miserablist current, which considers the characteristics that make her a *societas perfecta* as prostitution.

All that remained was to actually brand the Church with the infamous label of prostitute – as Luther and his predecessors had done – since the fundamental thinking of the miserablist current appeared to have been virtually accepted.

That last step was taken with the work *Casta Meretrix*[57] by Hans Urs von Balthasar, which says that the Holy Catholic Church is, in her very essence, both chaste and a prostitute.[58] More than just the expression of one theologian's thinking, von Balthasar's book aims at legitimizing the boldest goals of the miserablist current through the centuries. For this reason, it merits our close attention.

*   *   *

---

her. It avoids the expression 'sinning Church.' But the substantial reality – that is, the fact that the Church is guilty for the sins of her members – comes across quite clearly" (*La Chiesa peccatrice nei decreti del Concilio Vaticano II*, p. 465; see also pp. 458-478).

[57] The work *Casta meretrix* was published before Vatican II in 1961, but only became popular after the conciliar documents adopted the notion of the "sinning Church."

[58] In Notes 72, 157 below, we present the excerpts in which the author makes this statement.

Part II

ANALYSIS OF THE WORK *CASTA MERETRIX*

1. Limits of this Analysis

§ 24

In our study of the work *Casta Meretrix*, we noted that von Balthasar made many unfounded historical, exegetic and doctrinal generalizations when presenting his thesis. Thus, our analysis will expose the inaccuracies contained in these generalizations upon which von Balthasar based his conclusions. It seems to us that the simple exposition of these lacunae invalidates his thesis.

Since von Balthasar claims to present "a purely historical work,"[59] this refutation will principally examine the symbol of the prostitute as a historical symbol. We will not analyze its mystical, allegorical or artistic applications.

When von Balthasar's generalizations refer to Patristics – the works of the early Church Fathers – we will not examine the sources cited. We will suppose that von Balthasar faithfully reproduced the excerpts he quoted. We leave to others the task of checking those excerpts with the originals. Perhaps such a comparison would reveal further inaccuracies regarding the context and the original intent of the Fathers.[60]

2. Objectives of the Book *Casta Meretrix*

§ 25

The **principal objective** of the work *Casta Meretrix* is to legitimize the statement that the Church in her very essence is a prostitute.

In order to do that, von Balthasar presents the "prostitute aspect" of the Church alongside her "holy aspect." She could be defined not only as "holy" or as a "sinner," but simultaneously as "holy *and* a sinner," "chaste *and* a prostitute." Therefore, according to him, there is a contradiction in the essence of the Church.

---

[59] H. U. von Balthasar, *Casta meretrix* (Brescia: Morcelliana, 1969), p. 193.

[60] This is not just a vague suspicion, but is based on an express intent of von Balthasar. Indeed, in § 35, we cite him affirming that the works of the Church Fathers and Doctors should be read with a critical spirit in order to be "decomposed," and then "recomposed." This leads us to question whether he faithfully transcribed the excerpts and used them in their proper contexts.

Here is the first passage where von Balthasar manifests his intention:

"That Luther dared to compare the Roman Church to the whore of Babylon sounds like an atrocious blasphemy to us. However, it was not he who invented this expression, which we find already in Wycliffe and Hus. However, not even their language is completely new; it is a severe simplification and exaggeration of a very ancient *theologumenon* [theological hypothesis], whose first source is the judgments of God, the betrayed Husband, on the great prostitute Jerusalem in the Old Testament, and the way the New Testament utilized these primary texts of the Old Testament.

"That the Church of Christ is very distinct from the unfaithful Synagogue, that at least part of her being is perfect purity and immaculate fidelity, no believer or Christian theologian (not even Luther) put in doubt. However, to affirm that she must be *only* this and that, as the concrete Church of *these* believers, she cannot be anything else, could be an *a priori* hasty denial, since it was admitted without hesitation in other Christian epochs."[61]

Further on, after explaining and citing a passage from Dante, referring to a poem by Savonarola and quoting an excerpt from William d'Auvergne, von Balthasar more precisely defines the main goal of his work:

"Even though such texts do not have the value of a decanted theology, they strongly encourage the discussion of the theological question of whether the Old Testament affirmations about the great prostitute, Jerusalem, can still in some way be applied in the New Testament. But, can any *theologumenon* about the ancient people of God be considered totally obsolete and irrelevant to the new people, rich only in historical interest, especially if it is so significant and central?

"Departing from the impossibility of such a hasty dismissal, Erich Przywara wrote his brilliant Theology of the Hour titled *Old and New Covenant*. In the following pages we intend to make a much more modest work, that is, to draw together some materials (by no means all!) from theological tradition which demonstrate how in the New Testament this idea [the Church as a prostitute] remains alive among great theologians. ... Without jeopardizing the immaculate character of the Church, her holiness and indefectibility, another reality must be taken into account, one that cannot be merely excluded."[62]

---

[61] *Ibid.*, p. 189.

[62] *Ibid.*, pp. 193-194. The explicit affirmation of prostitution in the essence of the Church appears in texts quoted in Notes 70, 72, 157.

§ 27

As he presents his aim – to legitimize the notion that the Church is in her essence a *chaste prostitute* – von Balthasar unceremoniously enters into a contradiction. In fact, if the Church is pure in her essence, how could she also be essentially sinful? Nowhere in his work do we find an explanation for this contradiction. It is accepted as a *Dasein*, a fact to be admitted without any proof.

It seems to us that by assuming this contradiction, von Balthasar adopts the dialectic and evolutionist method of Hegel, according to which a thesis and an antithesis that clash and struggle for some time will necessarily generate a synthesis. So, the concept of a chaste Church – defended by Catholics – clashing with the concept of a prostitute Church – defended by heretics – , would have generated the progressivist concept of the Church as *chaste* and a *prostitute*, the synthesis of the two previous positions...

§ 28

The **secondary goal** of von Balthasar's work is to provide progressivists with the arguments they need to defend this thesis, in other words, to help make this idea spread. He explains:

"This work is purely historical; it strives, without preconceptions, to study with a critical vision and moderated language a very important series of topics [related to the prostitute] in order to offer theologians material from which they can draw conclusions."[63]

3. Presentation of the Thesis

§ 29

Von Balthasar does not follow a logical order in setting out his thesis. His work is an ensemble of interpretations on commentaries by countless authors – including various Church Fathers – on passages from the Old Testament and some from the New. He divides his study into parts without a systematic relationship, likening this or that figure of the Old Testament to this or that aspect of the Church.

Besides this free method of exposition, the work is actually more an exegetical study than the "purely historical work" that he pretends to make.

Given the lack of rigor in the fluctuating form of *Casta Meretrix*, it seems appropriate for us to present in a logical order the arguments of his thesis. In our view, von Balthasar's thesis can be summarized as follows:

---

[63] *Ibid.*, p. 193.

• In ideal terms, God's relation with Israel in the Old Testament is expressed by the husband-wife relationship.[64]

• Historically, however, Israel was unfaithful. It prevaricated by adoring the gods of other peoples. Thus, it figuratively became an adulterous wife, a prostitute who abandoned her legitimate husband (God), and chased after other men (the other peoples) to fornicate with them (adore their gods).[65]

• God, by tolerating this state of affairs and loving Israel despite its sins, assumed the position of a betrayed husband and went on to have normal relations with His prostitute wife.

• This relationship and imagery are confirmed by the testimony of various Prophets, and especially by the episode of the Prophet Osee, whom God ordered to marry a prostitute to symbolize his new type of relationship with the Chosen People.[66]

• Therefore, Von Balthasar presents the figure of the prostitute to express the situation of the Chosen People in all of the Old

---

[64] For example, von Balthasar says: "Long before Osee, the Covenant viewed as a marital union between God and His people was a common theme in Israel. By this means, the time of God's right and His love – a zealous and exclusive love, domineering but filled with faithful dedication and generosity toward His spouse, a love that expects a total response – is offered to the people" (*ibid.,* p. 194).

[65] Von Balthasar emphasizes this prostitution as the symbol of Israel's sins: "The bride, foolishly trusting in her beauty, took advantage of her 'good reputation in order to prostitute herself:' 'You bestowed your shame to the first one who presented himself,' and with the gifts of her charm she built 'high places,' those ancient places of pagan cult in Israel that were literally places of ritual prostitution to honor the goddesses of fertility" (*ibid.,* p. 197).

[66] The author writes: "A new dimension opened with the Prophets, especially Osee. By ordering him to procure a prostitute, marry her and beget children of prostitution upon whom the shame of their mother would fall, God desires to give an unheard of form to His relations with the people. It is no longer the juridical relations of an earthly spouse with her heavenly Lord, but the love relationship of a God humiliated by the betrayal of His wife. Nevertheless, in His ire He discovers His 'shame;' by marrying the prostitute, justifying her and changing the name of her children, He thus reveals the 'weakness' of His love" (*ibid.,* p. 195).

The same thinking is repeated in von Balthasar's *De l'Integration*, p. 79; the excerpt is transcribed on page – (Chap IV § 12) of this Volume.

Testament. That is, it cumulatively typifies the Jewish people and that whole historic period.[67]

§ 31

To confirm this thesis, von Balthasar interprets two other episodes of the Old Testament: the case of Rahab, a prostitute in Canaan who converted during the conquest of Jericho; and that of Tamar, the widow of two sons of Judah who disguised herself as a prostitute in order to have offspring with Judah himself.[68]

With these presuppositions, the author goes on to apply the image of the prostitute to the Church in the New Covenant. His reasoning is the following:

• The Church is essentially a society composed of men. Now then, men are sinners. Therefore, the Church is essentially sinful.[69]

---

[67] In several fragmentary passages, von Balthasar attributes the symbol of a prostitute to the whole Old Covenant:

• "In the *Book of Judges* we have the description of the beginning of this **continuous betrayal**." (ibid. pp. 194-195).

• "Jahveh is the God who, strong and tender but nonetheless **betrayed from the beginning** ... threatens inexorably; nonetheless, He gives the victory to His compassionate love" (*ibid*, p. 195).

• "From the apocalyptic perspective, the two figures [of the two prostitutes, Oholah representing Samaria and Oholibah symbolizing Jerusalem] who at the time of the Prophets intermingle in a powerful drama **(this union - with the prostitute - was the center of all ancient revelation)**, exclude one another as black excludes white" (*ibid*, pp. 199-200).

• Commenting on some lines of Rupert of Deutz, von Balthasar makes this generalization: "**Thus the action of Osee is a symbol for yesterday, today and tomorrow**" (*ibid*, p. 226).

• Many times in his work the author attributes to the entire Old Testament the expressions 'Jerusalem the prostitute,' 'the great whore Jerusalem' or 'the great prostitute Jerusalem' (cf. pp. 189, 196, 201-202, 204, 226, 252, 268). Likewise he uses the generic expression 'Israel the prostitute' on pp. 223, 226, 263.

[68] In his work, the symbolic meaning of Rahab is dealt with mainly in its Item 4: *Rahab's Motive. The Salvation and Purification of the Prostitute* (cf. pp. 207-223). The symbolic meaning of Tamar is found in its Item 8: *Tamar's Motive. The Image of the Church Prostitute* (cf. pp. 259-268).

[69] For example, Von Balthasar states:

• "If the Church did not consider all her members, she would no longer be the Church. Her destiny is marked on her members just as her members have theirs marked on her. **For, since the sins of the**

• Since the infidelity of the Chosen People in the Old Testament was symbolized by a prostitute, so also the infidelity of the Church in the New Testament can assume this figure.[70]

• Furthermore, various Church Fathers have applied the image of the prostitute to the Church. Therefore, it is legitimate to do so.[71]

---

sons and daughters revert to the mother, she must pray in her members and ask for her own salvation" (*ibid.*, p. 256).

• **"If it is true that the Church is immaculate ... this does not exclude her from continually confessing her faults, but rather requires it"** (*ibid.*)

• Von Balthasar endorses the notion of a stained Church defended by Fr. Emile Mersch (*Theologie du Corps Mystique*, Paris, 1964, vol. 1, pp. 364-368): "The bride of Christ was chosen by Him to be holy and immaculate, without wrinkle or stain of any kind, chosen by Him to make the adoption in purity and sanctity. For this reason, **it is inconceivable that she could also be a body of sin, stained with such paltriness and perversity** [the sins of her children], **that even in her most authentic manifestations her moral misery abundantly reveals itself. Nonetheless, this is what happens. The holy Mystical Body of Christ is a body in which redemption is being achieved – it is not already fulfilled. For this reason sin is always present and operating**, since each new generation in History multiplies sin again. Whence, finally, sin assumes its necessary place, the place of something that must continually be cast out, that is present in temptations and then is expelled, the place where redemption fulfills its work of suffering" (*in ibid.*, p. 281).

[70] With crude, shocking imagery, von Balthasar makes this brazen statement: "To the Church the *forma meretricis* [figure of the prostitute] fits so well ... that it defines the Church of the New Covenant in her most splendid ministry of salvation. **The exit of the synagogue from the Holy Land to go live among the pagan peoples was an infidelity of Jerusalem, the 'opening of her legs in all the roads of the world.' But this very movement that takes her to all peoples is the mission of the Church. She herself must unite and merge with all peoples and this new apostolic form of union cannot be avoided"** (*ibid.*, p. 267).

• In another text the author reaffirms the prostitution of the Church: **"In her most intimate and characteristic core, the prostitution of the new Daughter of Sion plunges into** the simple **'madness of the Cross'"** (*ibid.*, p. 205).

• He also makes this generalization: "**Israel the prostitute, a model of the Church of humanity"** (*ibid.*, p. 223).

[71] Throughout his work, von Balthasar interprets excerpts from the Church Fathers, trying to legitimize his thesis. The more significant texts will be quoted in §§ 85-91.

This is the logic upon which the author establishes his exposition in order to conclude that prostitution exists in the essence of the Church.[72]

---

[72] Someone could imagine that we exaggerate in affirming that von Balthasar defines the very essence of the Church with the metaphor of the prostitute. They could argue that he was merely trying to describe the human part of the Church, without taking into consideration her essence.

In Note 69 above, we presented excerpts in which the author proposes that the sins of the children of the Church penetrate her very constitution, her very essence.

Other excerpts that clearly attribute sin to the essence of the Church follow:

• We emphasize his mention to the essence of the Church in this already cited text: "**To the Church the *forma meretricis* [figure of the prostitute] fits so well ... that it defines the Church of the New Covenant in her splendid ministry of salvation.**" (*ibid.,* p. 267).

• Applying the symbol of Osee's prostitute to the Church, von Balthasar affirms: "**The past [that is, prostitution]** is canceled out by grace and totally superseded, however, **it confers to the present something constitutive and formal that survives the past**, without its old [historical] content" (*ibid.,* p. 260).

• Commenting on a text by Paolinus of Nola about Mary Magdalene, von Balthasar unequivocally declares: "**There is something** (and not the least apparent thing) **in the essential figure of the Church that calls to mind sin, that is conditioned by sin.**" (*ibid.,* p. 266).

• In another passage where he attributes to the Church Fathers intentions they did not have, von Balthasar makes it clear that for him there is no difference between the human and the essential aspects of the Church: "**The Fathers did not think – like Journet does – of analyzing the Church in a 'formal' life different from her 'material' life where the first element** (the indwelling of the Spirit of God through Christ in her sacramental and institutional life) **would be substantially intangible,** and the second element, the people of the Church, would belong to the Church insofar as it is structured and informed by the first" (*ibid.,* p. 276).

• Further on he repeats his interpretation: "**Thus, for the Fathers, there is no difficulty whatsoever in defining the Church as 'stained' by virtue of the sinners who belong to her**" (ibid., p. 278).

• For more confirmations see *Casta meretrix*, pp. 203, 205, 237-238, 240-241, 256, 274.

4. Observations on von Balthasar's Method of Exposition

A. Hegelian Method and Lack of Order

§ 32

As we have observed above,[73] von Balthasar adopts a Hegelian method of exposition by which he presents a thesis (the Church is chaste) and an antithesis (the Church is a prostitute), and then leaves this blatant contradiction unexplained. Doing this, he expects the dynamics of the Hegelian process to generate a new reality, a synthesis (a Church simultaneously chaste and prostitute), without any need for a logical doctrinal discussion.

We also mentioned[74] that the author lacks order in his exposition. Here we emphasize other methodological lacunae.

B. Incoherence in His Use of the Church Fathers

§ 33

To prove his thesis, von Balthasar presents a large number of texts from the Church Fathers. At times, however, he acknowledges that the Fathers used the metaphor of the prostitute in a sense opposed to his thesis of *casta meretrix*.

For example, when he speaks about Rahab, a converted prostitute in whom many Fathers saw as a prefigure of the Church of the New Covenant, that is, of the Gentiles who adored idols but later converted and entered the Church, von Balthasar admits the Fathers did not approve of Rahab the prostitute: "Rahab, the convert, the one who professed [the faith] and was incorporated into the Church, or rather the very Church of the Gentiles – and Rahab the prostitute. **The first is the only one to have found favor with the Fathers**."[75]

Further on, he writes: "**Most texts on Rahab and Magdalene stress** the change that took place over time: Before **she was a prostitute, now she is a saint.** Then, in a second analysis, they stress the Church of the Gentiles: **Before she prostituted herself with the idols, now she chastely belongs to Christ**."[76]

Speaking about Eve, he acknowledges that the Church Fathers adopted the metaphor of prostitution to refer to heresy rather than to the Church: "**Thus, it is not surprising that the Fathers ... understood heresy**, a rupture with the spirit of the Church, in an elementary way, **as a very dangerous spiritual impurity**."[77]

---

[73] § 27.
[74] § 29.
[75] *Casta meretrix*, p. 208.
[76] *Ibid.*, p. 220.
[77] *Ibid.*, p. 234.

Later, in an introduction to texts by Cassiodorus, St. Bernard, Eusebius, Origen, St. Augustine and others, he also affirms the opposite of the thesis he sustains: "All Christians are sinners, and **even though the Church does not sin as the Church,** she sins in all her members."[78]

Accordingly, the value of the author's exposition can be questioned: He sets out to demonstrate that the Church Fathers assert that the Church has the characteristic of sin and prostitution in her very essence. However, he admits that the Fathers understand the image of prostitution exclusively in the opposite sense and that they state that the Church does not sin as the Church...

This incoherence leads us to question the seriousness of the author's conclusions: First, he peremptorily and generically affirms that the Church Fathers did not distinguish the human aspect of the Church from her essential aspect and considered her a sinner.[79] Later he admits – also generically – that the Fathers did not apply the symbol of the prostitute to the Church but rather only to the pagans and heretics; they declare that the Church does not sin as the Church. How, then, should one understand the general thinking von Balthasar attributes to the Church Fathers? Can an author who indulges in such incoherent generalizations be taken seriously?

Therefore, the use of inconsistent generalizations appears as another charge against von Balthasar's credibility.

C. Superficiality

§ 34a

Throughout von Balthasar's work one also notes a singular insouciance in presenting the whole thinking of each of the Church Fathers he cites. Such a lack of concern is all the more grave given that he is dealing with the topic of the sanctity of the Church. Von Balthasar extracts short excerpts from here and there in the works of the Fathers – some of them apparently contradicting what that same Father had said before[80] – and inserts his quick commentaries, trying to give the impression that all these Church Fathers in fact corroborate his thesis.

---

[78] Ibid., p. 239.

[79] The three texts in which the author makes this statement were cited above in Note 69.

[80] For example, von Balthasar cites an excerpt from St. Ambrose affirming that the Church does not take upon herself the sin of her children: "Not in herself, my daughters, but in ourselves the Church is wounded" (*De virginitate*, 10, 48, in PL 16, 278D, *in ibid.*, p. 240). Further on, he cites another passage from the same Saint that refers

Now, if the thinking of one or two Church Fathers really supported what von Balthasar proposes, why would he not study it in depth? Would it not be more advantageous – from the apologetic standpoint – to base his thesis on a complete, systematic and detailed study of at least one or two great thinkers of the Church?

The absence of analytical depth in such a grave matter, coupled with the excessive fragmentation of the excerpts he quotes, adds another heavy charge against the already precarious credibility of von Balthasar.

D. Partiality

§ 34b

This doubt about his credibility increases when one considers the curiously biased criterion for selecting and using texts from the Fathers and Doctors that von Balthasar adopts. In fact, he affirms:

"What has been said so far teaches us to analyze critically the theological tradition from the end of the first century up to our days, without rejecting its totality. It is a matter not only of ordering its statements according to a scale of values, but also of decomposing them in order to recompose them in a new way."[81]

One cannot but be suspicious that in *Casta Meretrix* von Balthasar used this criterion of, "decomposing" the original thinking of the Fathers in order "to recompose it in a new way" – a way tailored to favor his thesis...

To these suspicions raised against the scholarly integrity of von Balthasar based on his form of exposition, we can add other critiques about the substance of the subject he addresses. They will be presented below.

We will see that in this case his generalizations – more than being suspicions – actually involve grave historical, exegetical and doctrinal errors that invalidate his thesis.

5. Analysis of the Unfounded Generalizations in the Work *Casta Meretrix*

In order to study the foundation for the work *Casta Meretrix,* we will consider as a presupposition his arguments as summarized in §§ 30, 31. Here we will demonstrate that von Balthasar's generalizations lack foundation for various reasons.

---

to the Church using the expression *casta meretrix*, which von Balthasar chose as the title of his work (*in ibid.*, p. 267-268).

[81] H. U. von Balthasar, "Mysterium Paschale," in V. A., *Mysterium salutis*, vol. III/6, p. 107.

1st Unfounded Generalization:

The Husband-wife relationship is the perfect expression of the relationship between God and His people

1st Rebuttal:

The husband-wife relationship is neither the only nor the best expression of the relationship between God and His people

§ 35

In *Casta Meretrix*, von Balthasar maintains that God's relationship with Israel in the Old Testament is ideally expressed by the husband-wife relationship. But he carefully leaves out the fact that the relations between God and His people in the Old Testament are described in other forms that occur much more often in the Sacred Scriptures than the metaphor of the husband-wife relationship. These other forms also more adequately reflect the role of God as the Creator and Sustainer of His people and their consequent subordination to Him. Thus, the relationship between God and His people in Scriptures is frequently expressed as relations between Creator and creature, King and subject, Master and slave, and Father and son, while the image of husband and wife is in fifth place (if we counted them correctly) as far as number of occurrences is concerned.

The first four images reflect mainly the transcendence of God and the unfathomable difference between Himself, the Almighty Creator, and us, simple creatures. The last image – husband and wife – is the one that allows an exegetic interpretation where the note of the inferior's dependence on the superior is much less relevant.[82]

---

[82] While Jewish scholar André Neher points out the four mentioned relationships, he emphasizes the spousal (cf. "Le symbolism conjugal: expression de l'histoire dans l'Ancien Testament," in *Revue d'Histoire et de Philosophie Religieuses,* Strasburg: Presse Universitaire de France, 1954, vol. 34, pp. 37-38).

Other progressivist authors repeat the same exaggeration of von Balthasar and treat the husband-wife relationship as the only valid one to express the relations of God with His Chosen People. Among others, are included E. Schillebeeckx, *Le Mariage*, vol. 1, *passim,* especially pp. 56-58, 67-69, 83, 86, 92-94, 95; H. de Lubac, *Catholicisme,* pp. 42-51, 154-158; Jean Daniélou, "Rahab figure de l'Église," in *Sacramentum futuri* (Paris: Beauchesne,1950), pp. 217-232; *ibid.* in *Irénikon*, Chevetogne, vol. 22, 1949, pp. 40-45; *Theologie du Judéo-Christianisme* (Tournai: Desclée et cie, 1958), pp. 326-337; Y. Congar, *Un peuple messianique*, pp. 39-43, 64.

Therefore, von Balthasar's systematic omission of the four principle forms to express the relationship between God and His people – which appear most abundantly throughout Scriptures – seems both excessive and misleading. The same can be said about his generalization of the husband-wife symbol to express the whole Old Testament.

2nd Unfounded Generalization:

The symbol of the prostitute is the archetype of the Old Testament

2nd Rebuttal:

The symbol of the prostitute is not an archetype of the history of the Chosen People; rather it is an anti-archetype

§ 36

Von Balthasar contends that "this union [of the Husband with the prostitute] constitutes the nucleus of all of ancient revelation."[83] To reach this conclusion, he makes several biased omissions.

1st Omission

The Prophets who used the figure of the prostitute were all from the same epoch and were referring to just one apostasy

To help the Reader understand von Balthasar's omission, we offer a brief summary of the historical use of the symbol of the prostitute.

A. Historical Reason for the Symbol of the Prostitute

In some places of the Old Testament, relations between God and His faithful people are compared to relations between a husband and wife.[84] Other biblical passages refer to the apostasy and idolatry of the Jews in a given phase of their history, using the rude image of

---

[83] H. U. von Balthasar, *Casta meretrix,* p. 200; in the same sense, see the excerpts transcribed above, Note 67.

[84] For example, in the *Canticle of Canticles.* According to some commentators, the marriage of Solomon with the Sulanite, described in this book is not a historical fact but rather a pre-figure of the mystical marriage of Our Lord Jesus Christ with the Holy Church (Cf. Matos Soares, *Tradução e comentários da Bíblia Sagrada,* São Paulo: Paulinas, 1964, p. 731). The same wedding image is also found in other passages of the Old Testament, as in Ezekiel 16.

In the New Testament, see: Mt 9:15; 22:2-14; 25:1-13; Jn 3:29; Eph 5:25-28; 29-31.

the prostitute. The bride with whom the Lord had made an eternal covenant betrayed the true God to adore the idols of false gods.[85] This unfaithfulness to the true Spouse and the pursuit of a religious relationship with the gods of pagan nations is a spiritual sin symbolized by the action of the unfaithful wife who, defiling the chaste bed of her legitimate spouse, gives herself over to adultery and prostitution.[86] This particular historical era is often referred to by the Prophets, and the image of the prostitute is in fact used by some of them: Isaiah, Jeremiah, Ezekiel and Osee.[87]

---

[85] The Chosen People went to the extreme of erecting an altar to the false gods in Jerusalem at the order of a pontiff (cf. 4 Kings 21:10-12).

[86] Commenting on the passage: "Go and take thee a wife of fornications" (Os 1:2), Cornelius a Lapide observes:

"Here the Prophet represents God, and the woman, the synagogue, that is, the people of Israel with their 12 tribes, as it becomes clear later. Fornication in this and other passages of the Prophets signifies sins, principally the one of idolatry. It was through idolatry that the Israelites, leaving their Spouse to lead a licentious life, attached themselves to idols and pleasures as their lovers. This is what the Prophet explains further, when he subordinates his [Osee's] marriage to the divine command. He says: "For all the land is immersed in fornication," that is, given that the Israelites completely delivered themselves to idolatry, this tendency became common among them. ... This is how St. Jerome, the Chaldean and others interpret this text" ("In Osee Prophetam" 1:2, *Commentaria in Scripturam Sacram*, Paris: Ludovicus Vives, 1874, vol. 13, p. 280).

[87] • **Isaiah**: "How is the faithful city, that was full of judgment, become a harlot? Justice dwelt in it, but now murderers" (1:21).

• **Jeremiah**: "Of old time thou hast broken my yoke, thou hast burst my bands, and thou said: I will not serve [the Lord]. For on every high hill and every green tree thou didst prostitute thyself (by adoring the false gods)" (2:20).

• "Lift up thy eyes on high: and see where thou hast not prostituted thyself: thou didst sit in the ways, waiting for them as a robber in the wilderness: and thou hast polluted the land with thy fornication, and with thy wickedness ... Thou hadst a harlot's forehead, thou would not blush" (3:2-3).

• "Hast thou seen what rebellious Israel hath done? She went of herself onto every high mountain and under every green tree, and hath played the harlot there (with idolatry) ... And her treacherous sister Juda saw, that because the rebellious Israel had played the harlot, I had put her away, and given her a bill of divorce: yet her treacherous sister Juda was not afraid, but went and played the harlot (with idolatry) also herself, and by the facility of her fornication she defiled the land" (3:6-9).

• **Ezekiel:** "But trusting in thy beauty, thou played the harlot because of thy renown, and thou hast prostituted thyself to every passenger, to be his. And taking of thy garments thou hast made the high places sewed together on each side: and hast played the harlot upon them, as hath not been done before, nor shall be thereafter. And thou took thy beautiful vessels, of my gold, and my silver, which I gave thee, and thou made thee images of men, and hast committed fornication with them. And thou took thy garments of diverse colors, and covered them: and set my oil and my sweet incense before them. And my bread which I gave thee, the fine flour, and oil, and honey, wherewith I fed thee, thou hast set before them for a sweet odor; and it was done, saith the Lord God. And thou hast taken thy sons and thy daughters, whom thou hast borne to me: and hast sacrificed the same to them to be devoured. Is thy fornication small? Thou hast sacrificed and given my children to them, consecrating them by fire. And after all thy abominations, and fornication, thou hast not remembered the days of thy youth ...

"And it came to pass after all thy wickedness (woe, woe to thee, saith the Lord God), that thou didst also build thee a common stew, and made thee a brothel house in every street. At every head of the way thou hast set up a sign of thy prostitution: and hast made thy beauty to be abominable and hast prostituted thyself to everyone that passed by, and hast multiplied the fornication. And thou hast committed fornication with the Egyptians thy neighbors, men of large bodies, and hast multiplied thy fornication to provoke me. Behold, I will stretch out my hand upon thee, and will take away thy justification: and I will deliver thee up to the will of the daughters of the Palestinians who hate thee, who are ashamed of thy wicked way. Thou hast also committed fornication with the Assyrians, because thou wast not yet satisfied: and after thou had played the harlot with them, even so thou wast not content. Thou hast also multiplied thy fornication (or idolatry) in the land of Chanaan with the Chaldeans: and neither so wast thou satisfied.

"Wherein shall I cleanse thy heart, saith the Lord God: seeing thou dost all these works of a shameless prostitute? Because thou hast built thy brothel house at the head of every way, and thou hast made thy high place in every street: and wast not as a harlot that by disdain enhances her price. But as an adulteress, that brings in strangers over her husband. Gifts are given to all harlots: but thou hast given hire to all thy lovers, and thou hast given them gifts to come to thee from every side, to commit fornication with thee. And it hath happened in thee contrary to the custom of women in thy fornication, and after thee there shall be no such fornication: for in that thou gavest rewards, and didst not take rewards, the contrary has been done in thee.

§ 37

Such a general apostasy of the people – the result of the apostasy of the priests and false prophets[88] – had to be punished in an exemplary way. Before releasing His punishment, however, God exhorted the people to penance by means of various serious rebukes. For this He used different symbols, some very rude and forceful.[89] It

---

"Therefore, O harlot, hear the word of the Lord" (16:15-35).

See also Chapter 23, which describes the infidelity of the two wicked sisters Samaria and Jerusalem.

• **Osee:** "The beginning of the Lord's speaking by Osee: and the Lord said to Osee: Go, take thee a wife of fornication, and have of her children of fornication: for the land *(of Israel)* by fornication (*or idolatry*) shall depart from the Lord. So he (Osee) went, and took Gomer the daughter of Debelaim: and she conceived and bore him a son.

"And the Lord said to him: Call his name Jezrahel: for yet a little while, and I will visit the blood of Jezrahel upon the house of Jehu, and I will cause to cease the kingdom of the house of Israel. And in that day I will break in pieces the bow (or military power) of Israel in the valley of Jezrahel.

"And she (Gomer) conceived again, and bore a daughter, and he said to him: Call her name, Without mercy: for I will not add any more to have mercy on the house of Israel, but I will utterly forget them. And I will have mercy on the house of Juda, and I will save them by the Lord their God: and I will not save them by bow, nor by sword, nor by battle, nor by horses, nor by horsemen.

"And she (Gomer) weaned her that was called *Without mercy*. And she conceived, and bore a son. And he said: Call his name, *Not my people*: for you are not my people, and I will not be yours (1:2-9).

- "If you play the harlot, O Israel, at least let not Juda offend" (4:15).

[88] * "Astonishing and wonderful things have been done in the land. The prophets prophesied falsehood, and the priests clapped their hands: and my people loved such things: what then shall be done in the end thereof? (Je. 5:30-31).

* "And I have seen the likeness of adulterers, and the way of lying in the prophets of Jerusalem: and they strengthened the hands of the wicked, that no man should return from his evil doings; they are all become unto me as Sodom, and the inhabitants thereof as Gomorrah. Therefore thus saith the Lord of hosts to the prophets: Behold I will feed them with wormwood, and will give them gall to drink: for from the prophets of Jerusalem corruption is gone forth into all the land" (Je. 23:14-15).

[89] For example, God ordered Isaiah to walk naked in public so that the people would know they would be taken prisoners by the Assyrians if they did not end their alliance with the pagans (Cf. Is 20:2-5).

was in this context – in which the wrath of God was ready to be unleashed – that He used the metaphor of the prostitute through the mouths of His Prophets.

At the end of the 8th century B.C., the Chosen People were broken into two kingdoms. Ten tribes had previously separated and formed the Kingdom of Israel in the North, whose capital was Samaria. The other two tribes – of Judah and Benjamin – formed the Kingdom of Judah, whose capital was Jerusalem.

§ 38

In this epoch the *first phase* of the great chastisement against the Jewish people struck Samaria. In 720 B.C. the Assyrians took the 10 tribes of the North in captivity to Nineveh.[90] The same armies then descended on Jerusalem and besieged the city. God, however, took pity on Jerusalem with the hope that it would convert. Thus, one night "the Angel of the Lord went out, and slew in the camp of the Assyrians a hundred and eighty-five thousand" (Is 37:36). In this way Jerusalem was saved.

§ 39

The *second phase* of this great chastisement, however, did eventually strike the Holy City, which had hardened in its sin. The Chaldeans, who in the meantime (612 B.C.) had conquered the millenary Assyrian Empire, took Jerusalem and ransacked and destroyed the Temple of the Lord (586 B.C.). The two remaining tribes were taken off in captivity to Babylon[91] where they joined the other 10,

---

He commanded Ezekiel to eat bread baked under the heat from excrements in front of all the people to symbolize the affliction they would suffer in captivity (Ez 4: 9-15).

He also commanded Ezekiel to preach to Jerusalem, comparing it to the dross to be melted by fire: "Son of man, the house of Israel is becoming dross to me: all these are brass, and tin and iron and lead in the midst of a furnace: they are become the dross of silver. Therefore, thus saith the Lord: Because you are all turned into dross, therefore, behold, I will gather you together in the midst of Jerusalem. As they gather silver, brass and tin and iron and lead in the midst of the furnace, that I may kindle a fire in it to melt it: so will I gather you together in my fury and in my wrath, and will take my rest: and will melt you down. ... As silver is melted in the midst of the furnace, so shall you be in the midst thereof: and you shall know that I am the Lord, when I have poured out my indignation upon you" (Ez 22:18-22).

[90] The deportations of the Jews to Assyria were not only to Nineveh, but also to Hala, Habor, Ara and other cities.

[91] The Jews of Judah were led to Babylon in three waves: The first group of captives included the Prophet Daniel in 609 B.C. A few years later in 599 B.C., 10,000 captives, including the Prophet Ezekiel followed. Finally, the third wave came when the city of Jerusalem fell

which had been transferred there after the destruction of Nineveh. Much of the symbology used in the Apocalypse takes as an archetype the antagonism between Babylon and Jerusalem, which finds its historic base in this chastisement, given its great parabolic expression.

§ 40   With this terrible punishment,[92] the golden age of the Hebrew people came to an end. The brilliance of David and Solomon no longer shone in the land of Canaan. The Babylon captivity lasted until the Persian King Cyrus issued an edict (536 B.C.) allowing the Jews to return to their fatherland and to rebuild the Temple in Jerusalem. This meant 184 years of servitude for the tribes of the North and 73 years for the tribes of the South.[93]

§ 41   So that they might be spared this immense chastisement, God had vigorously exhorted the Hebrew people to repent.

Given the extreme apostasy that the Jews had reached and the extreme punishment that awaited them, the dramatic character of the metaphors God used to reflect both realities is understandable.

For this reason He commanded Osee, a Prophet in Samaria before its devastation, to take a prostitute for a wife in order to symbolize how God judged Israel's apostasy (Os 1:2). For analogous reasons, Isaiah, Jeremiah and Ezekiel rebuked Israel using the same metaphor.

B. The Omission

§ 42   Von Balthasar pretends that these references to the prostitution of the Chosen People in the Old Testament are present throughout Sacred History "from beginning to end," [94] He fraudulently omits the fact that these references by Isaiah, Jeremiah, Ezekiel and Osee to the apostasy of the Jews, calling it prostitution, dealt exclusively with one epoch and all refer to the same apostasy. It does not, therefore, reflect the whole history of the Chosen People.

---

and the Temple was destroyed in 586 B.C., an event witnessed by Prophet Jeremiah (4 Kgs 24, 25; 2 Paralip 36: 5-23; Jer 52; Ez. 1:1-2; Dan 1:1-7).

[92] The cycle of Assyrian-Chaldean invasions also destroyed the great nations and civilizations of Egypt, Syria and Phoenicia. Assyria itself was ravaged by the Chaldeans, and finally the short-lived Chaldean Empire was destroyed by the Persians.

[93] For the 10 tribes of Israel, the captivity lasted from 720 B.C. to 536 B.C., a period of 184 years. As for Judah, the time from the first wave in 609 B.C. to the decree of liberation by Cyrus in 536 B.C. was 73 years.

[94] Cf. H. U. von Balthasar, *Casta meretrix,* p. 195.

We have just described the one particular apostasy of the Jews and the historical epoch to which the Prophets were referring.

It should be pointed out that of the 17 Prophets who left writings, 12 preached about that same historical era. Four of these – Osee, Amos, Isaiah, and Micheas – exercised their mission a little before the Nineveh captivity. Eight lived between the time of the Nineveh captivity and the Babylon captivity; these were Nahum, Habacuc, Sophoniah, Joel, Ezekiel, Jeremiah, and Baruch, and the Prophet Daniel was taken in captivity to Babylon as a child. The leitmotiv of their writings is almost exclusively the apostasy of the Jews during this precise historical epoch. And they include the only Prophets who used the metaphor of the prostitute – Osee, Isaiah, Ezekiel and Jeremiah.

§ 43   Thus, in the 2,000-year period of Sacred History from Abraham to Our Lord Jesus Christ, it was only for a period of around 200 years – from Isaiah and Osee to Ezekiel – that the metaphor of the prostitute was used by the Prophets to express the depth of the abyss into which the Chosen People had fallen.

One sees, therefore, that von Balthasar's generalization that the metaphor of the prostitute is a symbol of all of Sacred History not only is excessive, but actually is fraudulent since it conveys a false view of God's relationship with His people.

2nd Omission

When God refers to the Chosen People as a prostitute, He does so in great wrath and as a sign of an imminent rupture of His Covenant with them

§ 44   Omitting the preponderant role of the wrath of God, the threat of an imminent break of the Covenant and the chastisement that followed the apostasy of the Chosen People, von Balthasar pretends that God accepted as a consummate fact that His bride had become a prostitute. For even then, von Balthasar goes on to claim, God did not refrain from having a relationship with her:

"A new dimension is opened with the Prophets, especially Osee. By ordering him to look for a prostitute, marry her and beget children of prostitution on whom the shame of their mother should fall, God wants to make an unparalleled example of his own relations with the people: **It is no longer a question of the juridical relations of an earthly wife with her heavenly Lord, but the loving relations**

of a God humiliated by the betrayal of His wife, who in His ire[95] discovers His 'shame' **and, by marrying the prostitute, justifying her and changing the name of her children, reveals the 'weakness' of His love."** [96]

§ 45   An analysis of the excerpts in the Old Testament in which God calls the Chosen Nation a prostitute through the mouths of His Prophets shows precisely the opposite of what von Balthasar pretends. The texts in fact reveal the intolerance of God toward the prostitution of the people who have forsaken Him to adore false idols.

Thus, in Osee, when God warns the Jews about the chastisements He would soon unleash upon Israel, one reads:

"Judge your mother, judge her: because **she is not my wife, and I am not her husband.** Let her put away her fornication from her face, and her adulteries from between her breasts. Lest I strip her naked, and set her as in the day that she was born: and I will make her as a wilderness, and will set her as a land that none can pass through, and will kill her with drought. **And I will not have mercy on her children: for they are the children of fornication"** (Os 2:2-4).

Contrary to what von Balthasar says about God's leniency with the children of Samaria, in Osee God curses the Kingdom of Israel, symbolically referring to it as Ephraim because of its apostasy:

"I found Israel like grapes in the desert. I saw their fathers like the first fruits of the fig tree in the top thereof: but they went in to Beelphegor, and departed from Me to cover themselves with confusion, and became as abominable as those things they loved.

"As for Ephraim, their glory hath flown away like a bird from the birth, and from the womb, and from the conception. And **though they should bring up their children, I will make them without children** among men; yea, and **woe to them, when I shall depart from them.** Ephraim, as I saw, was as Tyr founded in beauty: and Ephraim shall bring out his children to the murderer.

"Give them, O Lord. What wilt Thou give them? **Give them a barren womb and dry breasts. All their wickedness is in Galgal, for there I hated them: for the wickedness of their devices I**

---

[95] When von Balthasar speaks here of the "ire of God," he is not referring to the supreme wrath of God, which was in fact unleashed in the described chastisements. He refers simply to the inconsequential ire of a betrayed husband who will soon accept his wife's prostitution as a fact of life, without breaking his normal relations with her.

[96] H. U. von Balthasar, *Casta meretrix*, p. 195.

will cast them forth out of My house: I will love them no more, all their princes are revolted. **Ephraim is struck** *(with death)*, **their root is dried up, and they shall yield no fruit. And if they should have issue, I will slay the best beloved fruit of their womb**" (Os 9:10-16).

§ 46   The wrath of God over the apostasy of Jerusalem is also manifested in Ezekiel, the Prophet who most often utilizes the metaphor of the prostitute. He foretells the chastisement that would soon fall on the unfaithful people:

"Therefore, O harlot, hear the word of the Lord. Thus says the Lord God: Because thy money hath been poured out, and thy shame discovered through thy fornication with thy lovers, and with the idols of thy abominations, by the blood of thy children whom thou gavest them: Behold, I will gather together all thy lovers with whom thou hast taken pleasure, and all whom thou hast loved, with all whom thou hast hated: and I will gather them together against thee on every side, and will discover thy shame in their sight, and they shall see all thy nakedness.

"**And I will judge thee as adulteresses, and they that shed blood are judged; and I will make of thee a bloody victim of fury and jealousy. And I will deliver thee into their hands, and they shall destroy thy brothel house, and throw down thy stews**: and they shall strip thee of thy garments and shall take away the vessels of thy beauty: and leave thee naked, and full of disgrace. And they shall bring upon thee a multitude, **and they shall stone thee with stones, and shall slay thee with their swords**" (Ez 16:35-40).

§ 47   One can see, therefore, that the use of the symbol of the prostitute in no way implies any tolerance of God with prostitution, as von Balthasar contends. He shows no tolerance toward the symbol, prostitution, nor toward what it symbolized, the apostasy of the Jews. Indeed, the Kingdom of Israel (where Osee preached) and the Kingdom of Judah (where Isaiah, Ezekiel and Jeremiah preached) were both chastised by the exemplary wrath of God, who showed no lenience or connivance with sin.

The simple consideration of the wrath of God over the prostitution of the Chosen People – that is to say, their apostasy – shows how out of place the suspect thesis of von Balthasar is. In fact, it can only make a minimum of sense if one omits the historical-theological context of the chastisement and the curse of God that surrounded the apostasy of the Jewish people.

Therefore, von Balthasar's generalization that the relationship between the betrayed Husband with a prostitute wife would symbolize the normal relationship between God and His people is misleading and groundless.

3rd Omission

In order to express the apostasy of the Jews, God used many other symbols, [97] and not exclusively the symbol of the prostitute

§ 48

By omitting the large number of other symbols used by the Prophets to express the calamitous apostasy of the Jews, von Balthasar implies that the only symbol expressing that reality is the prostitute. By insinuating this exclusive usage, he tries to impose the idea that the "prostitute Jerusalem"[98] expresses not only this epoch but the whole Old Testament.

Now, this generalization is also groundless because the Prophets who lived at that time and tried to move Israel and Judah to convert used many tragic symbols to express the apostasy of the Jews. If von Balthasar had been honest in his method, he would have mentioned the image of the prostitute along with the many others that appear in Sacred Scriptures.

We have already mentioned the rude symbols used in this period, that is, a nude Isaiah, Ezekiel eating bread cooked under excrements and Jerusalem as dross about to be melted by fire.

§ 49

Below are some other symbols used in the Old Testament to represent the apostasy of the Chosen People during this particular epoch:

• The Chosen People is a choice vineyard tended by God, but it yields only **wild grapes** (Cf. Is 5).

• The wickedness of Israel is like a **fire devouring the briers and thorns**, setting the forest thicket ablaze so that it rolls upward in a column of smoke (Cf. Is 9:18-19).

---

[97] The **1st Unfounded Generalization** showed von Balthasar's omission regarding the types of relationships between God and His people throughout the Old Testament. Here we consider his omission of other symbols referring to the specific epoch in which the apostasy took place.

[98] The expression "prostitute Jerusalem" appears on pages 196, 201-202, 204, 226, 252 and 268 of von Balthasar's book *Casta meretrix*. The term "prostitute Israel" is on pages 223, 226 and 263.

- Samaria has become **a fading flower** (Cf. Is 28:1).

- The Kingdom of Judah is like **a drunkard who covers the tables with vomit and filth** (Cf. Is 28:7-8).

- The Chosen People is like **the clay that revolts against the potter** and **the pot that does not recognize its maker** (Cf. Is.29:16).

- Israel shall be completely smashed like **a piece of pottery** that breaks into many pieces (Cf. Is 30:14).

- Jerusalem is like the **slumbering drunk who has taken the cup of Our Lord's wrath and drained it to its dregs** (Cf. Is 51:17).

- The wicked of that time are like **the raging sea, whose waters toss up mire and dirt** (Cf. Is 57:20).

- The people have abandoned God, the fountain of living water, and have dug for themselves cracked **cisterns that can hold no water** (Cf. Jer 2:13).

- The Chosen People, a choice vineyard, became **the degenerate shoots of a foreign vine** (Cf. Jer 2:21).

- The people are like **a wild and lustful donkey** (Cf. Jer 2:23-24).

- The generation of Jews living at that time is like **a ravening lion**; their own sword devours their prophets (Cf. Jer 2:30).

- Faced with the chastisement, Jerusalem cries out in anguish like **a woman in labor** (Cf. Jer 4:31).

- The inhabitants of Jerusalem have made their faces harder than **stone** and refused to repent (Cf. Jer 5:3).

- The Jews have become like **horses, lusty stallions** (Cf. Jer 5:8).

- The people of God are like **corrupted metals** that cannot be refined (Cf. Je. 6:27-30).

- The people of Israel are all running down the path of sin as swiftly as **a horse galloping into battle** (Cf. Je. 8:6).

It would take too long to list all the metaphors used by the Prophets who lived at that time. The metaphors used by Isaiah and others from the first chapters of Jeremiah cited above as examples seem sufficient to illustrate the almost inexhaustible richness of the images God used to try to convert the people.

We thus arrive at the conclusion that von Balthasar's systematic omission of this great variety of symbols and his quotation only of the symbol of the prostitute in order to represent the apostasy of the Jews constitutes another fraudulent practice.

§ 50

We conclude our analysis of the **2nd Unfounded Generalization** summarizing.

To present his argument that the prostitute is the archetype of the whole Old Covenant, von Balthasar omitted that:

• The metaphor of the prostitute was not used throughout the Old Testament, but only in one epoch of general apostasy.

• God was tolerant neither with the symbol of the prostitute, nor with what it symbolized, the apostasy of the people.

• The symbol of the prostitute was not the only one used to express the apostasy of that time.

Therefore, the symbol of the prostitute cannot be used as an archetype of the whole Old Testament. Since it expresses the general apostasy of a people who should have been faithful, it really represents an anti-archetype of the Chosen People in the Old Covenant.

3rd Unfounded Generalization:

Tamar and Rahab reinforce the prostitute as the archetype of the Old Testament

3rd Rebuttal:

The episodes of Tamar and Rahab do not support the thesis that the prostitute is the symbol of the Chosen People or of the entire Old Testament

§ 51

We have just seen that the basis of von Balthasar's argumentation to legitimize the prostitute as an exclusive symbol of the Old Covenant is weak on account of groundless generalizations and biased omissions. It is, in fact, so frail so as to become unsustainable.

Trying to reinforce his argument, however, von Balthasar uses two isolated episodes from the Old Testament: that of Rahab, a prostitute of Canaan who converted during the conquest of Jericho, and that of Tamar, the widow of the two sons of Judah, who disguised herself as a prostitute to have Judah's offspring.

How could two isolated cases – with 400 years between them – that occurred in Sacred History strengthen von Balthasar's argument that the prostitute is a model of the Old Testament? Especially since the more recent episode – that of Rahab – took place 500 years before the beginning of the apostasy being analyzed here? Far from strengthening his thesis, those incidents would only reveal the exceptional character of the symbol of the prostitute.

They do not reflect, however, even this exceptional character since Tamar was not a prostitute and Rahab is not a symbol of the Chosen People.

A. Tamar Was Not a Prostitute

§ 52

Tamar was not a prostitute. She was successively a widow of two sons of Judah who had no children. In order to raise a progeny, Tamar feigned to be a prostitute to seduce Judah, her father-in-law, and have his offspring. There is no record that anyone except for Judah had relations of this kind with her. Nor is there any evidence that she was a prostitute before or after that episode.[99] Therefore, the statement that Tamar was a prostitute is unfounded.

This does not exclude the fact that Tamar committed the sins of incest and adultery, according to Fr. Cornelius a Lapide.[100]

B. The Case of Rahab Did Not Represent the Chosen People

§ 53

Rahab was a prostitute who played a key role in the conquest of Jericho by hiding the two spies sent by Joshua to scout the area. She hid them on the roof of her house and helped them to escape on a scarlet cord through her window. When Joshua conquered Jericho he spared Rahab, who had converted. [101]

Historically, however, neither Rahab's prostitution nor her conversion is related to the vocation of the Jews. At that time the Jews, after 40 years of exodus in the desert, were in a phase of fidel-

---

[99] Cf. Gn 38:16.

[100] Cf. C. a Lapide, *Commentaria in Scripturam Sacram*, vol. 1, p. 347.

[101] Upon receiving the scouts, Rahab made a profession of faith in the true God, "for the Lord thy God he is God in heaven above, and in the earth beneath" (Jos.2:11). According to Cornelius a Lapide, "Rahab, moved in part by miracles and wonders, in part by God's illumination, understood that the idols of the Chananites were false and fictitious gods, and that only the God of the Hebrews was the true God" (*ibid.*, vol. 3, p. 14).

ity; for this reason they were beginning to conquer the Promised Land. One can even say that this phase that starts with Joshua's conquest of Jericho and goes until David's conquest of Jerusalem constitutes the heroic phase of fidelity of the Chosen People, which produced the golden age of their history under the reigns of David and Solomon. Thus, the symbolism of Rahab – either as a prostitute or a convert – has nothing to do with any known infidelity of the Jews in that period. It does reflect the infidelity of the inhabitants of Jericho, who failed to heed God's warning. Only a prostitute among them responded to the divine appeal.

§ 54

Thus, one sees that, historically speaking, it is not objective to propose that the episodes of Tamar and Rahab would corroborate the thesis that the prostitute is the symbol of the Chosen People or of the entire Old Testament, as von Balthasar insinuates in Item 4 and generalizes in Item 8 of his work.[102]

---

[102] If he were to use the Rahab episode as a symbol of the Old Testament, von Balthasar would frontally clash with almost all the texts he cites of the Church Fathers, who interpret Rahab as a symbol of the pagans rather than the Jews. He avoids this clash harmful to his thesis by resorting to insinuation. In Item 4, twice he makes comments that try to generalize the Rahab episode and transform it into a symbol of the whole Old Testament.

Commenting on an excerpt by Origen, he writes: "**The noteworthy peculiarity**, the singularity of this statement, **lies in the fact that** here also .... **Origen understands 'until today' in the sense that the episode of Rahab still applies today**. It is not so much that her transformation from a prostitute into holy Church is in progress, but primarily that **the Church of the pagans is being inserted into the Church of the Jews**" (*Casta meretrix*, p. 212). In other words, the two would come to be one same thing. Thus, the symbol of the prostitute could be applied to the whole Old Testament.

The same insinuation appears further on in his criticism of how the Church Fathers have interpreted the Rahab episode: "**Patristic theology (and nearly all the theology that followed) reflected less on the fact that 'salvation came from the Jews' or that paganism was grafted onto the 'sacred trunk [of Judaism],'** than on the fact that **the *theologumena* of the people of the Old Testament** [including the thesis of the prostitute as a symbolic expression of it] **are assumed by the people of the New Testament**" (*ibid.*, p. 222).

Von Balthasar's intent to reinforce his thesis of the prostitute as a figure of the Chosen People becomes even clearer in Item 8 of his work. In the first text he employs the expression "the prostitute Israel" to refer to the entire Old Testament; in the second he clearly

4ᵗʰ Unfounded Generalization:

The Catholic Church is the heir of the prostitute of the Old Testament

4ᵗʰ Rebuttal:

Deicide was the supreme sin of the Jews, and in this sense it was prostitution. But the Holy Church is not the heir of a prostitute synagogue, but of a holy synagogue, whose legacy was transmitted through Our Lord and a small remnant of the faithful.

On this matter, Von Balthasar makes another historical error in *Casta Meretrix.*

§ 55   While generalizing the figure of the prostitute as a symbol of the whole Old Testament, he omits, however, the supreme apostasy of the Jews during the epoch of Our Lord, which was the crime of Deicide, symbolically a prostitution. He conveniently skips over this rejection of Our Lord, and, instead, emphasizes secondary points related to that time.[103] Then, he turns his attention to the "Church of the pagans," that is, the converted Gentiles, and again applies to them the figure of Rahab, generally interpreted as a symbol of the Gentiles.

§ 56   Further, von Balthasar also neglects to point out the note of continuity between the fidelity that existed in the Synagogue and nascent Church.[104] One could say that he failed to consider the whole legacy of fidelity that comes from the Old Testament.

---

affirms that Tamar is a symbol of the whole synagogue. He attributes to St. Augustine this comment, without a corroborating text:

"Augustine presents **the prostitute Israel** who is transformed into the Church by means of a *confession.* In fact, this transformation and [Tamar's] matrimonial contract present themselves earlier in the secret of the heart..." (*ibid.*, p. 263).

He goes on to attribute to St. Jerome, also without a text, this interpretation that suits his thesis: "**Jerome's interpretation of 'the prophetic prostitute'** ... **applies to Judaism. For him, Tamar is the image** either of the Church of the pagans or, what seems more fitting, **of the synagogue**" (*ibid.*).

[103] Cf. H. U. von Balthasar, *Casta meretrix*, Item 3.

[104] The only citation that would appear to differ from what we said is an excerpt from Origen: "**Afterwards, Rahab remained among the Chosen People until today**. This cannot be understood literally. If you want to understand more clearly how Rahab remained in Israel,

It is, however, of utmost importance to point out who the sinners were and who the faithful were during that epoch in order to properly understand how and to whom the metaphor of the prostitute can be applied. Then one can answer the question: Does the symbol of the prostitute represent a model or an anti-model of the Church?

§ 57   It would seem that these omissions by von Balthasar are intended to divert attention from the sin of Deicide and the apostasy committed by most of the members of the Synagogue at the time of Our Lord, facts well-known to everyone. By making such omissions, he certainly intended to prevent the symbol of the prostitute from appearing to his readers as a clear anti-model of the Church.

---

consider how the wild olive was grafted onto the trunk of the good olive tree, and you will better understand how those who were grafted onto the faith of Abraham, Isaac and Jacob are rightfully considered a part of Israel to this day. In fact, we, the wild olives, were taken from the pagan peoples – we who once were prostituted by adoring stones and trees instead of the true God - we have been grafted onto the good trunk even to this day" (*Homiliae in librum Josue,* 3.4, in von Balthasar, *Casta meretrix*, p. 211).

Although Origen admits the continuity between the Old and New Testaments, in his comment on this excerpt, von Balthasar makes an acrobatic interpretation to conclude, opposed to Origen's context, that it would be the note of prostitution that is transmitted in the continuity between the Synagogue and the Church. The first part of this quotation was already cited in Note 102 for another purpose. Commenting on Origen, von Balthasar says:

"**The noteworthy peculiarity**, the singularity of this statement **lies in the fact that** here also ... **Origen understands 'until today' in the sense that the episode of Rahab still applies today**. It is not so much that her transformation from a prostitute into holy Church is in progress, but primarily that **the Church of the pagans is being inserted into the Church of Jews. No other Church Father sensed so strongly the insuperable character of the Old Testament and the ancient economy** [that is, the figure of the prostitute] **and the ancient people as a radical reality onto which the Church of the pagans must be continually grafted,** since she owes her salvation and sanctification to her insertion into the people of God chosen from the beginning. The conscious awareness of the fact of this incorporation is in opposition to a theology of the Church that either forgets or ignores that the Church was assembled from among the Jews (and considers and defines the Church of the New Testament simply as the Church of the Gentiles). Or it sees the synagogue, an 'unfaithful wife,' as abandoned by God, thus allowing Christians through the centuries to view it the same way" (*ibid.*, p. 212).

§ 58

Indeed, the Deicide was the result of the supreme apostasy of the Chosen People. Even though there is no record of the Jews practicing formal idolatry at the time of Our Lord as they did in the epoch of the Prophets, the rejection of the Messiah and the crime of His death constitute a kind of "prostitution." In this sense one may say that the Synagogue prostituted itself.

That applying this expression to the apostate Synagogue is correct can be seen by analyzing the parallel between the two great apostasies in Sacred History.

§ 59

The first, already examined in this Appendix I, was the abandonment of the true Faith, the profanation of the Temple and the killing of the Prophets. It was punished with the captivity of the Chosen People, the flight and dispersion of those who were not imprisoned, the destruction of the Temple and the city of Jerusalem, and the virtual disappearance of the Jewish Kingdom. In that period, fidelity was maintained by a small remnant[105] essentially composed of the Prophets. Through that remnant fidelity was reborn in captivity, attracted the mercy of God and resulted in the return of the Jews to the Holy Land, the reconstitution of the nation and the rebuilding of the city and the Temple.

§ 60

The second great apostasy took place at the time of Our Lord. It entailed the abandonment of the true Faith – the rejection of the Messiah and the profanation of the Body of Christ, the true Temple of God[106] – through the ignominy inflicted upon Christ during the Passion and slaughter of the God-Man. It was chastised by the destruction of the Temple of Jerusalem by Titus and the dispersion of the people (70 A.D.) and, later, the final annihilation of the Hebrew State by Adrian's army (135 A.D.).

§ 61

Fidelity in this period was also maintained by a small remnant who gathered around Holiness Incarnate, Our Lord Jesus Christ, who still tried to convert the Jews. To a large extent, however, they hardened their hearts against Him and became the authors of the Deicide. It was the Gentiles who were responsive to the voice of that remnant. Thus the Holy Church was born as an institution, like a vine whose stock were the faithful Jews – Mary Most Holy and the Apostles and Disciples – and whose branches grafted onto it, were the Gentiles who entered the Church.[107]

---

[105] "Except the Lord of hosts had left us survivors, we had been as Sodom, and we should have been like to Gomorrah" (Is 1:9); other references to the remnant include Is 11:11; 49:6; Jer 42:2; Joel 2:32.

[106] Cf. Jn 2:19-21.

[107] Cf. Rom 11:11-24.

The parallel between the two situations is remarkable. Hence one may fittingly say that just as the appropriated symbol of the first apostasy is prostitution, so also the second apostasy can be symbolized by prostitution.

§ 62   But the Catholic Church is not heir to this prostitution, just as the new Jerusalem rebuilt at the time of Zorobabel, Esdras and Nehemiah did not inherit the sin of the Israelites prior to the captivity. Jerusalem was heir to the fidelity of the Prophets and those few of the Chosen People who remained faithful.[108]

The Church is heir to the Holy Synagogue, which was represented by the few who remained faithful awaiting the Messiah. These would include the Prophet Simeon and the Prophetess Anna, who lived in the Temple, the priest St. Zacharias, Joseph of Arymathea, who was a member of the Sanhedrin, as well as other representatives of the Synagogue who make the official links between the Old and the New Covenants. If these can be called the representatives of the ecclesiastical institution, from among the faithful the great figure of St. John the Baptist along with his disciples stand out. This handful of people found its most noble expression of fidelity in the Holy Family. Therefore, the true Synagogue was constituted by that nucleus who gathered around the Supreme Pontiff Jesus Christ.[109]

And it was from Him that the true Church was born.

§ 63   On the contrary, the sin of the Jews – their prostitution – was not taken on by the Church but by the current Jewish Synagogue, which even to this day obdurately rejects the true Faith and refuses to recognize the Messiah, Our Lord Jesus Christ.

Summarizing one sees that:

§ 64   • The apostate and false Synagogue, which rejected Our Lord and killed Him, can be properly symbolized by the prostitute. But the prostitute was not the model of the Old Testament; on the contrary, it was clearly its anti-model.

• From the true Synagogue all the fidelity of the Old Covenant harmoniously merged into the Holy Church, despite the persecutions she suffered from the apostate Synagogue.[110] For this reason it is a great historical error to state that the Holy Catholic Church

---

[108] Some 40,000 people returned from captivity in Babylon to rebuild Jerusalem and the Temple (cf. Esd 2:64-65).

[109] Cf. Heb 5, 7, 8, 9 and 10.

[110] The *Acts of the Apostles* narrate some episodes of the relentless persecution waged against the Christians by the apostate Synagogue:

came forth from the prostitute, understood as a symbol of the unfaithful Synagogue in the Old Testament.

• If someone today were to use the symbol of the prostitute in a way consistent with the teaching of the Prophets, he should apply it to the present Jewish Synagogue or, perhaps, to some crime similar to the Deicide that is being perpetrated in the Church in these days.

Hence one can conclude:

• These omissions of von Balthasar are fraudulent because they deliberately avoid facing powerful arguments against his thesis.

• Furthermore, his very thesis is historically faulty because it purposely fails to consider the apostasy of the Jews at the time of Our Lord.

5ᵗʰ Unfounded Generalization:

A Great Number of Church Fathers defended that the Church is a prostitute in her essence

5ᵗʰ Rebuttal:

The excerpts from the Church Fathers compiled by von Balthasar do not demonstrate that the Church is a prostitute in her essence

§ 65   It is well known that Modernists and Progressivists have long been searching the works of the Latin and Greek Church Fathers for elements to justify their theses, using the "return to the sources" among other methods.[111] In this effort to legitimize their theses, they try to oppose the theology of the early Fathers to the theology that became

---

The arrest of St. Peter and St. John at the Temple by the order of the priests and magistrates (cf. Acts 4:1-23); the imprisonment of the Apostles by the order of the high priest (cf. Acts 5:17-18); the re-imprisonment of the Apostles (cf. Acts 5:26); the martyrdom of St. Stephen who was stoned to death (cf. Acts 7:54-59); the persecution and dispersion of the faithful (cf. Acts 8:1); the martyrdom of St. James (cf. Acts 12:1-2); the imprisonment of St. Peter (cf. Acts 12:3-4) and of St. Paul (cf. Acts 21:30-34).

[111] Fr. Congar recognizes this in passing when he writes: "Scheeben, but also before him Franzelin, Schrader and Passaglia, rediscovered this doctrinal meaning [that the whole is present in the parts in the theological discourse of the Fathers] ... Today we could expand and deepen its application, **thanks to the acquisitions of 40 years of**

solidly accepted after the first seven centuries of the Church. Calvin, Baius, Jansenius and other heretics used the same method, trying to justify their theories in St. Augustine.[112]

§ 66

This progressivist tendency to use obscure or strange-sounding texts of the early Fathers is a common practice of heretics. Already in the 5th century, St. Vincent of Lérins was combating "the fraud of those who, contriving to disguise a heresy under a name other than its own, usually take obscure texts of some ancient writer and adjust their doctrine to that obscurity. Doing so, they do not seem to be either the first or the only ones to have held the things that they profess.

"I deem their wickedness worthy of a double rejection: *first*, because they do not fear to offer others the poison of heresy to drink; and *second*, because with profane hands they manipulate the memory of some holy man, as if it were dead ashes. And the things [he defended] that should be buried in silence, they spread through a new thinking, following in the footsteps of their predecessor Ham, who not

---

research in these three areas: the liturgical movement, **the return to biblical sources [*ressourcement*]** and the ecumenical dialogue. These are dimensions that the theology of 1870 did not have as we do today" (Y. Congar, *L'ecclésiologie de la Révolution Française au Concile du Vatican, sous le signe de l'affirmation de l'autorité*, in V.A., *L'ecclésiologie au XIXe. siècle*, Paris: Cerf, 1960, pp. 113-114).

A more encompassing and direct confirmation is provided by historian Fr. Roger Aubert is his work *Catholic Theology in the First Half of the 20th Century*. Speaking about the Patristic studies made by Modernists during the pontificate of Pius XI, he affirms:

"It is precisely this fruitful contact [between theology and lay culture] – existing particularly in German colleges of theology, Louvain and certain French centers of higher studies as well as in circles around professors like O. Bardenhewer (1851-1935), B. Altaner (1885-1958), J. Lebon (1879-1957) and J. Lebreton (1873-1956) – which explains the flowering of valuable studies that gradually reopened new perspectives in numerous fields of Patristics and the History of Dogma. **This burgeoning was the continuation of a movement that had started at the end of the 19th century**" ("La Theologie Catholique durant la première moitié du XXe. siècle," in H. Vorgrimler and R. Van der Gucht, *Bilan de la théologie au XXe. siècle*, vol. 1, p. 431).

[112] The Church impugned such behavior, showing that the authority of her Magisterium prevails even over a Church Father and Doctor of the stature of St. Augustine. Among the 30 Jansenist propositions condemned by Alexander VIII in a *Decree of the Holy Office* of December 7, 1690, one finds the following:

only refused to cover the nakedness of his venerable father Noah, but also announced it to others as an object of mockery.

"Doing so, Ham committed such a grave crime against piety that the curse that he drew down from his sin also fell upon his descendents. Much to the contrary his blessed brothers did not want to expose the nakedness of their revered father to their own eyes or the eyes of others, but with their backs turned to him, as it is written, they covered him, neither approving nor revealing the fault of the holy man."[113]

A. Outlines of the Authority of the Fathers

§ 67

The fountain of riches that constitute the writings of the Fathers is an inexhaustible source for Catholic thinking. In their writings broad horizons unfold, revealing an original outburst of intelligence and an unrivaled mystical and poetic spirit.

In the Fathers also shines the light of the special vocations of various peoples and regions, some of which unfortunately would later fail to flourish inside the Church. Such are the cases of St. Ephrem of Edessa (ancient Persia), St. Basil of Cappadocia, St. Gregory of Nyssa and St. Gregory Nazianzus (Pontus), and Tertullian, St. Cyprian and St. Augustine (the old Numidia in North Africa).

"*Condemned:* If one finds that a doctrine is clearly stated in Augustine, it is permitted to uphold it and teach it in an absolute way, without taking into account any papal bull" (DS 2330).

Referring to documents of Popes Clement XI, Innocence XIII and Benedict XIV against the errors of Quesnel, one reads: "It cannot be denied that in many of Quesnel's propositions one can find affinities with and allusions to the works of Augustine of Hippo. For example, in *In evangelio Joanis tractatus,* III, 8, *ad propositionem* 27-28; *Enchiridion* c.117 (PL 40, 287) ad 45; *De praedestinatione Sanctorum* c.8 § 13 (PL 44, 970) ad 17; *De correptione et gratia* c.14 § 43 (PL s44, 942) ad 13.

"Nevertheless, should there be any real or apparent discrepancy between the decrees of the Church Magisterium and the doctrine of Augustine, the true Catholic will not attribute to Augustine – as did Calvin, Baius and Jansenius – an infallible and absolute authority to which the decrees of the Magisterium must be subjected. Rather, he must take the position that all of the authority of Augustine comes from concession to and the interpretation of the Magisterium of the Church, just as the light of the moon comes from the sun. The unfortunate exaggeration of the authority of Augustine has produced most deleterious fruits, above all in Baianism and Jansenism" (Introduction, DS 2400).

[113] St. Vincent of Lérins, *Commonitorium*, I.VII, in PL 50, 647.

Likewise, the vocations of so many Greek Fathers did not burgeon, especially those of the School of Alexandria, whose countries disappeared under the merciless invasion of the followers of Mohammed. For this reason, to have a full view of the potentialities of the mission of the Church, to know her in all of her nuances, it is very useful and advisable to have recourse to the Church Fathers.

§ 68

From the standpoint of doctrine, it is difficult to find a historical epoch that has offered a more fertile ground for the Holy Church, a more authentic echo of the truths revealed by Our Lord Jesus Christ. This, which can be said *in genere* of Patristics, can be stated *in specie* of the great Sts. Augustine, Jerome and Ambrose in the West and Sts. Basil, Gregory Nazianzus, Cyril of Alexandria and John Chrysostom in the East. Alongside the true marvels in their works, however, are found some errors that the Church later condemned or doctrines that she, at the least, advised against.[114]

---

[114] Someone could object that by pointing out certain errors of the Church Fathers, as we shall proceed to do, this Work would incur the same criticism made above about the heretics who lacked respect for the teaching of holy men (§ 66). This, however, is not the case. We have the greatest veneration for those who number among the first and most brilliant defenders of the Holy Church and provide a sound foundation and inexhaustible source of elucidation for the Catholic Magisterium.

If we recognize some errors in their writings, it is with the sole intent of defending the Catholic Church, to whom the progressivists unduly seek to attribute various obscure passages of the Fathers as if they were Church doctrine.

We have no desire to disparage the work of any one of these Fathers, let alone their work as a whole. By acknowledging that even the greatest Masters of the Church can reveal the fallibility of human thinking in some points, our aim is exalt the infallibility of the perennial and universal teaching of the Church – especially that of the extraordinary Papal Magisterium – which is inerrant by the special assistance of the Holy Ghost.

In so doing, we do not believe that we incur St. Vincent of Lérins' severe denunciation of those who defame the Fathers, whom he rightly calls the followers of Ham. On the contrary, we believe we are following the recommendations of that same Saint when, further on in his work, he states:

"Whatsoever a person holds that is different from or contrary to all [the teaching of the Church], even though he be holy and learned, a bishop, a confessor or a martyr, let that be regarded as a private opinion of his own, and be separated from the authority of the common, public and general sentence [of the Church]. By so doing, we

§ 69   Such is the case, for example, of certain millenarist tendencies that appeared at the very start of the Church with Papias and were later defended in mitigated versions in various writings of St. Justin, St. Irinaeus, St. Hippolytus and St. Methodius.[115] So also Tacianus, an early apologist of the Holy Church who wrote many good works, later became a heretic. His errors were fiercely combated in the writings of St. Irinaeus.[116]

§ 70   Analogously, Tertullian, who was long a brilliant defender of the good cause, broke with Pope St. Zepherinus to adhere to the Montanist heresy.[117]

§ 71   Notwithstanding his various writings against the heretics of his time, St. Hippolytus was accused of heresy by Pope St. Callistus and became schismatic. He came into conflict with Popes St. Zepherinus and St. Callistus and founded the "petite Church," placing himself at its head. It was only after he was arrested under Maximinianus and deported to Sardinia that he returned to the Catholic Church, reconciled with Pope St. Pontian, also exiled there, and died a martyr.[118]

§ 72   The heterodox thinking of Origen, the famous master of the School of Alexandria, was opposed by St. Demetrius of Alexandria, who ordered him to restrict himself to sound Catholic doctrine. Speaking of Origen, Porphyry of Tyr remarked, "In his behavior he was a Christian, but in his ideas about God and the world he was a Hellenist."[119] St. Methodius of Olympus wrote against Origen's teachings on the Resurrection and called him a "centaur," half-Christian and half-Gentile.[120] St. Epiphanius, St. Jerome and later Justinian among others

---

will not follow, with great risk of our eternal damnation, the newly devised error of a single man (according to the sacrilegious custom of heretics and schismatics) and reject the ancient truth of universal dogma," (*ibid.*, I..XXVIII, in PL 50, 675-676).

Having said this, we will proceed with all due respect for the Fathers of the Church to expose some of their opinions that the Church later disapproved or even condemned.

[115] Cf. Gustave Bardy, entry "Millénarisme," in DTC., vol. 10, cols. 1760-1763.

[116] Cf. Jules Lebreton, "L'apologétique chrétienne au IIᵉ siècle," in Fliche-Martin, *Histoire de l'Église*, vol. 1, pp. 451-454.

[117] Cf. J. Lebreton, "Les écrivains chrétiens d'Afrique," *in ibid.*, vol. 2, pp. 164-185.

[118] Cf. J. Lebreton, "Les controverses romaines à la fin du IIᵉ et au début du IIIᵉ siècle," *in ibid.*, pp. 105-106.

[119] Cf. *Enciclopédia Universal Ilustrada*, entry "Origenismo," vol. 40.

[120] Cf. Fócio, *Bibl. Cod. 235, in ibid.*

accused him of Subordinationism[121] and of being the precursor of Arius and Macedonius. St. Eustache of Antioch wrote against his allegorical method of interpretation.

A general and violent campaign was undertaken against Origen after St. Ephiphanius accused him of heresy in his famous work *Adversus Haereses* [Against Heresies].[122] The combat against his teaching continued with Theophilus, Patriarch of Alexandria, who deftly won the decisive cooperation of St. Jerome and thus managed to have Origen's writings condemned by a large part of the Church. A century and a half later, accusations against Origen had gained such momentum that Emperor Justinian asked the Pope and all the Patriarchs to condemn him. In fact, the errors of Origenism were condemned in the anathemas of an edict published by Justinian in 543.[123]

§ 73 Some Saints, however, did not completely reject the teaching of Origen. For example, St. Dyonisius of Alexandria, who followed the same school of thinking as Origen and later became Bishop of Alexandria, was also sympathetic to Hellenism, and some of his writings were condemned with strong words by Pope St. Dyonisius.[124]

§ 74 Something similar occurred with St. Lucian the martyr, founder of the School of Antioch. Like Origen, Lucian upheld a type of Subordinationism, which gave birth to Arianism. The protagonists of the Arian heresy, beginning with Arius himself, were students of Lucian. St. Alexander of Alexandria came against Lucian, singling him out as the teacher of Arius and successor of Paul of Samosata.[125]

---

[121] Subordinationism designates the errors or heresies of those theologians who lost view of the equal divinity of the Three Divine Persons, namely, of the Son regarding the Father. This theory was present in many different ancient errors, Arianism being the best known of them. They were influenced by the Hellenist idea of a *Logos* [Divine Word] who would be only an instrument of God in creation and, therefore, subordinate and not equal to the Father (cf. DTC, Tables, entry "Subordinationisme," vol. 3, p. col. 4088).

[122] Cf. St. Epiphanius, *Adversus haereses, 64, in ibid.*, p. 433.

[123] Cf. DS, 403-411.

[124] Cf. J. Lebreton, *L'Église d'Alexandrie après Origène*, in Augustin Fliche and Victor Martin, *Histoire de l'Église*.

[125] Cf. J. Lebreton, *L'Église d'Antioche à la fin du IIIe siècle, in ibid.* p. 350.

For many years, St. Jerome was an admirer and follower of Origen, going as far as to call him "the first Master after the Apostles."[126] Even though he disagreed with the thinker of Alexandria on various points, the Latin Father praised him in many of his early writings. But from 394 onward, St. Jerome took a stand against the errors of Origen.[127]

The brilliant St. John Chrysostom, Patriarch of Constantinople, was deposed and died in exile in punishment for his alleged adhesion to Hellenism and for sheltering monks who supported Origen. He was accused by Theophilus, the Patriarch of Alexandria, and by St. Epiphanius of Salamis.[128]

St. Gregory of Nyssa, brother of St. Basil, was also an admirer of Origen. Because of his sympathies for some of Origin's teachings, he is not listed as a Doctor of the Church.[129]

An illustrious cluster of Church Fathers – St. Justin, St. Irenaeus, St. Hippolytus, St. Cyprian and St. Ambrose – erroneously defended the thesis, today a heresy, of the "deferment" of the punishments of Hell until the end of the world.[130]

It would take too long to list all of the doctrinal turbulences – and even some heresies – of the first centuries of the Church that were harbored in the writings of the great Church Fathers and Saints of that time. These turbulences probably resulted from the influence of the Greek and Latin schools of thought, which still had not been sufficiently disciplined by the temperance and holiness of the Church.

---

[126] Cf. St. Jerome, *Praefacium in librum de nominibus haebraicis* and the *Prologues* to the translations of Origen in *Commentaries on Micheah, Epistle to the Ephesians,* entry "Origenismo," in *Enciclopédia Universal Ilustrada,* Vol. 40, p. 433.

Pierre M. Richard, under the entry "Enfer" in the *Dictionnaire de Theologie Catholique* (vol. 5, col. 75), asks whether "it can be said that St. Jerome had too much tolerance for the brilliant teacher Origen," a position that would explain why he "cited Origen without making the necessary corrections."

[127] Cf. Georges Fritz, entry "Origenisme," in DTC, vol. 11, cols. 1568-1569.

[128] Cf. G. Bardy, "Saint Jean de Constantinople," in Fliche-Martin, *Histoire de l'Église,* vol. 4, pp. 131-148.

[129] G. Fritz, entry "Origenisme," in DTC, Vol. 11, col. 1567.

[130] Cf. P. M. Richard, entry "Origenisme," *in ibid.,* vol. 5., cols. 89-90.

§ 75   Like Christ, His Mystical Body, the Church "grows in grace and sanctity" (Lk 2:52). So also her doctrine gained robustness and clarity as the centuries passed. With the help of the Holy Ghost, the earthly Jerusalem becomes increasingly perfect. For this reason, the magnificent contribution of the Church Fathers in her early times must always be understood in light of the later definitions of the Magisterium, rather than the opposite, as the progressivists do.

§ 76   Paradoxical as it may seem, St. Thomas Aquinas himself, the Universal Doctor of the Church, had things to learn, as is clear when one considers that he did not understand the dogma of the Immaculate Conception.[131]

§ 77   For just as the sea is greater than the rivers that flow into it, so the Church is greater than her Saints and Doctors. Her authority is the source of that of her children – however great they might be – just as the light of the sun is the source for the light of the moon.

B. After the Protestant Heresy, It Is Inopportune to Apply the Symbol of the Prostitute to the Church

§ 78   In the case of the expression *casta meretrix* used by St. Ambrose,[132] who also was an admirer of certain ideas of Origen,[133] we find something similar to what took place with the other Fathers.

---

[131] In the *Summa Theologiae*, III, q. 27, a.1-3, the Angelic Doctor defended the opinion that Our Lady was conceived in original sin. Six centuries later on November 8, 1854, Pius IX defined the doctrine of the Immaculate Conception as a dogma of the Faith. In other passages and works St. Thomas upheld the same thesis opposed to the Immaculate Conception (Cf. *Summa Theologiae*, I-II, q.8, a.3; III, q.31, a.1, ad 3; *In IV Sententiarum*, 1.II, d.31, q.1, a.2; 1.III, d.3, q.1, a.2, s.1.; 1.IV, d.4, q.1, a.4; *Summa contra gentiles*, IV, c.IV, c.LII, ad 4; *De malo*, in *Quaestiones disputatae* (Turin/Rome: Marietti, 1949), vol. 2, q.4, a.6.

[132] Cf. St. Ambrose, *Expositionis in Evangelium secundum Lucam*, III, 23, in PL 15, 1599, in H. U. von Balthasar, *Casta meretrix*, pp. 287-288. The great Saint understood the expression *casta meretrix* in an allegorical way, not to be attributed to the essence of the Church. For example, in another place, he categorically affirmed her virginity: "It is not she who wounds herself, but we who wound the Church. Therefore, let us take care to prevent our falls from becoming a wound in the Church. *Caveamus igitur, ne lapsus nostre vulnus Ecclesiae fiat*" (*De Virginitate*, 10, 48, in PL 16, 278D, *in ibid.*, p. 240).

[133] On the influence of Origen on St. Ambrose, P. M. Richard writes: "Starting in 380, the influence of Origen began to permeate the West through St. Ambrose, who 're-arranges' his comments, as St. Jerome

With the passing of time the metaphor of Rahab as a symbol of the Church inasmuch as she was a converted pagan – to which St. Ambrose refers – fell into relative disuse. Only centuries later was the image of the prostitute again applied to the Church, but this time by heretics such as Wycliffe, Hus, Savonarola and Luther. That symbol would come to be a kind of rallying slogan for those who revolted against the Church.[134]

§ 79   Therefore, applying the metaphor of the prostitute to the Holy Church based on the early Fathers became extremely inappropriate because of later definitions of the Magisterium,[135] and because it can raise the suspicion of favoring heresy. It would be as flawed as trying to resurrect excerpts from Origen, St. Dyonisius of Alexandria and St. Lucian of Antioch to justify Arius' thinking and contest the Nicaea Creed, or to oppose the dogma of the Immaculate Conception based on St. Thomas of Aquinas. When the infallibility of the Church is involved in a matter, the question is closed. What her children may have thought differently in the past *ipso facto* becomes corrected.

§ 80   The infallibility proper to the teaching of the extraordinary Papal Magisterium, that is, its official definitions, dogmas and anathemas, is also present in the teaching of the ordinary Papal Magisterium, which remains constant through the ages.[136]

§ 81   In addition to papal teaching, the teaching of the ensemble of Bishops, echoing that of the Sovereign Pontiff and made uniformly throughout the centuries, also enjoys the perogative of infallibility.[137]

---

contends in his *Epistula*, 48, 7, in PL, 22, 749" (entry "Enfer" in DTC, vol. 5, col. 74). See also *Enciclopedia Universal Ilustrada*, entry "Origenismo," vol. 40, p. 433.

[134] See in this Volume, Chap. IV §§ 1, 6, 9, for offenses of Luther and other heretics who call the Holy Catholic Church a prostitute.

[135] For quotes of various papal teachings on the divine nature of the Church presupposing her holy and immaculate character, see §§ 111-113, Note 139.

[136] Speaking on the topic of the Blessed Virgin Mary as Co-Redemptrix, Fr. José Aldama writes: "Although the ordinary Magisterium of the Roman Pontiff is not infallible *per se*, if it constantly teaches a certain doctrine for a long period of time to the whole Church, as is our case [that of the Co-Redemption], one must absolutely admit its infallibility; otherwise it would lead the Church into error" ("Mariologia," in *Sacrae Theologiae Summa*, Madrid: BAC, 1961, vol. 3, p. 418).

[137] Church thinking on infallibility in the ordinary and universal Magisterium is presented in the *Dictionary of Catholic Theology*:

§ 82

As for the word prostitute applied to the Church, even though such usage has not yet been formally condemned by the Magisterium, this appellation was one of the banners of the Protestant revolt. For this reason, it is reasonable to consider it as included in the condemnations the Church issued against Luther. Further, at least since the Middle Ages, the symbol of the prostitute was no longer used in the Church[138] except in the miserablist heretical sects mentioned above.

"As for the infallible teaching in the ordinary and universal Church Magisterium, its existence was always admitted in the Church. This is demonstrated particularly by the way that many errors have been condemned through the centuries without a formal definition, but by the simple fact that they were judged to be contrary to the ordinary thinking of the universal Church" (Edmond Dublanchy, entry "Église," in DTC, vol. 4, col. 2193).

Further on is a summary of the thinking of various authors on the ways this Magisterium is exercised in the Church:

"a. The ordinary and universal Magisterium of the Church is exercised above all by the *explicit* teaching habitually communicated ... by the Pope and the body of Bishops scattered throughout the world, in which the teaching of authors especially approved by the Church participate. ...

"b. The ordinary and universal Magisterium can also be exercised by the *implicit* teaching openly contained ... in the discipline and general practices of the Church, at least in all that is truly commanded, approved or authorized by the universal Church; in this teaching ... the Church is no less infallible than in the solemn definitions of her councils.

"c. The ordinary and universal Magisterium is exercised, finally, in a simply *tacit* way by the approval the Church gives to the teaching of the Fathers, Doctors and theologians when she allows it to spread in the Universal Church in order to effectively direct the beliefs and practical lives of the faithful. For the Church would fail to successfully fulfill her mission to fully guard the deposit of Revelation if, by her silence, she were to authorize a universal teaching that would not conform to this revelation or would weaken it" (*ibid.*, cols. 2194-2195).

[138] Von Balthasar himself acknowledges the scarcity of texts using the figure of the prostitute since the Middle Ages when he cites an excerpt from St. Bernard: "This crude image [of spiritual fornication] ought to please **the Middle Ages, when the echo of the figure [of the prostitute] used by the early Fathers was fading out.** Thus, **Bernard would never call the Church a prostitute,** but he could well say that the bad shepherds, who devastated the Church instead of 'building her,' 'prostituted her' (*Sermo in Canticum Canticorum,* 77, 1, in PL 183, 1156.A)" (*Casta meretrix,* p. 258).

§ 83   After the Protestant revolt, the term prostitute became, as it
were, proscribed among Catholics. Besides, for almost four centuries
the Magisterium has been teaching with ever-greater insistence[139] that
the Holy Church is the most pure Spouse of Our Lord Jesus Christ,

---

[139] In his work *Institutiones Theologiae Dogmaticae* (Barcelona:
Herder, 1951, vol. 1, p 257), Fr. Ludwig Lercher, S.J., affirms: "John
XXII defended the sanctity of the Church against the *Fraticelli* (D
485), affirming that an ontological sanctity exists in her by virtue of
her sacred power. Against Quesnel, Clement XI taught that the
Church is holy, that is, she is not deficient in matters of faith and
customs, nor does she persecute the holy (D 1445-1447). The same
was taught by Pius VI against the followers of the Synod of Pistoia
(D 1501)"

In these documents that Lercher indicates, we can read the following:

* John XXII, in the Constitution *Gloriosam Ecclesiam* of January 3,
1318, defends the Church against the *Fraticelli,* a heretical sect that
separated from the Franciscan Order on account of disputes concerning poverty: "For this reason, the first error that burst forth from
the dark laboratory of these men imagines two Churches: one carnal, filled with richness, swimming in pleasures, stained with crimes,
over which, they affirm, the Roman Pontiff and the other lower Prelates rule. The other is spiritual, pristine in its sobriety, beautiful by
its virtue, girded with poverty; in it only they and their cohorts are,
and they also command it by virtue of their spiritual lives, if one gives
any credibility to their lies" (DR 485).

* Clement XI, in the dogmatic Constitution *Unigenitus* of September
8, 1713, condemns the following error of Quesnel, a French Jansenist
theologian: "Truths have become, as it were, a foreign tongue to the
majority of Christians and the manner of preaching them is, one could
say, an unknown language, so far are they from the simplicity of the
Apostles and so far beyond the common grasp of the faithful. It cannot be warned enough that this defect [of the Church] is one of the
greatest visible signs of the senility of the Church and of the wrath of
God on His sons" (DR 1445).

* Pius VI in the Constitution *Auctorem Fidei* of August 28, 1794
combats the errors of the Synod of Pistoia – held in September of
1786 to favor Jansenism and similar errors in Italy, condemning as
heretical this proposition: "In these later times a general obscurity
fell over the more important truths pertaining to religion, which are
the basis of faith and of the moral teachings of Jesus Christ" (DR
1501).

Other papal documents unequivocally affirming the sanctity of the
Church can be found in §§ 111-113.

essentially the opposite of what von Balthasar asserts. Four centuries of the exercise of the ordinary Magisterium on this matter *ipso facto* engages the infallibility of the Church.

§ 84

One sees, therefore, that von Balthasar's affirmation that the metaphor of the prostitute can be openly applied to the Church[140] is inaccurate, insincere and misleading.

C. Analysis of the Texts of the Church Fathers upon which Von Balthasar Bases His Thesis

§ 85

Notwithstanding what has been said about the limits of authority in the Patristic, a simple reading of the work *Casta Meretrix* by von Balthasar shows that only a few of the texts he quotes actually admit **sins in the Church** and, even then, they fail to corroborate his thesis that they are **sins of the Church**. [141]

Indeed, of the around 250 excerpts from various authors that von Balthasar cites, almost all of them do not substantiate what the author wants to demonstrate: that there would be a sinful note typical of a prostitute in the essence of the Church. Many of the authors give a clearly mystical connotation to the metaphor of the prostitute as used in texts of the Old Testament; others apply to it allegorical meanings; still others interpret it far differently from von Balthasar's thesis. Finally, some say precisely the opposite of what he seeks to demonstrate, as in the case of St. Cyprian who states: "The Spouse of Christ cannot be tempted into adultery; she is incorruptible and chaste ... Anyone, however, who separates himself from the Church to unite with an adulteress, removes himself from the promises of the Church."[142]

§ 86

The only texts that come close to the idea that there would be sin in the Church are the ones we will cite below. By our count, they are only 11, to wit:

---

[140] Cf. H. U. von Balthasar, *Casta meretrix*, p. 193.

[141] Sins in the Church: That there are sins in the men who compose the Church is a truth that has never been denied. Sins of the Church: That there would be sins in the essential nature of the Church itself is a thesis that has never been accepted by the Church and is now defended by von Balthasar and Progressivism.

[142] St. Cyprian, *De unitate Ecclesia*, 6, in PL 4, 502-503, in H. U. von Balthasar, *Casta meretrix*, pp. 236-237; See also St. Ambrose, *De virginitate*, 10, 48, in PL 16, 278D, *in ibid.*, p. 240.

• An excerpt from St. Gregory the Great in which he states, in an allegorical sense, that the Church is black in her human side, adding 'black in myself';[143]

• An excerpt from Dionysius the Carthusian in which he says that the Church is prostituted in her wicked children;[144]

• An excerpt from Clement of Alexandria in which he states that one who lives as a pagan is impure in relation to the Church;[145]

• An excerpt from St. Jerome, completely conditional, admitting that the Church could be transformed into the Jerusalem of Ezechiel **if** she is unfaithful;[146]

• An excerpt from St. Hilary of Poitiers saying that the Church is a sinner in her children and affirming in an ambiguous way, "She herself is a sinner;"[147]

---

[143] "So says the Church: 'I am black, but beautiful;' black according to your judgment, but beautiful by the radiation of grace .... black by [my] merits, but beautiful by grace; black in myself, but beautiful by grace; black in the past, but beautiful for what I shall become in the future" (St. Gregory the Great, *Expositio super Canticum Canticorum,* c.1, v.5: ed. by Heine, p. 183, in PL 79, 486-488, *in ibid.,* p. 222).

[144] "Therefore, the Church is called disfigured, errant, exhausted and prostituted with regard to the faithful who do not show evidence of love and [good] works, but instead are loaded down with vices, and their souls, far from being spouses of Christ, are adulterers of the Devil" (Dionysius the Carthusian, *In Canticum,* art. I; *Opp.* VII, 368; art. 18, 406.B, *in ibid.,* 223, based on Helmut Riedlinger, *Hoheliedkommentar des MA,* 1858, pp. 396-397).

[145] "Anyone who continues to live as a pagan in the Church, whether by deeds, words or even only thoughts, commits impurity with the Church and with her body" (Clement of Alexandria, *Stromata VII,* 14, 87-88, 1; GCS III, 62, 64, 24-25, *in ibid.,* p. 236).

[146]"What we have always said about Jerusalem refers to the Church and to the souls of the faithful **if** they give their lovers their nuptial gifts, that is, the gold (of their thoughts) and the silver (of their words) ..., and **if** they affirm that impurity is not dangerous ... **If** this miserable Jerusalem, where peace should dominate, were to accept something such as that [which I just described], **then** its highest sentiments and noblest words would be transformed into ignominy" (St. Jerome, *Commentaria in Ezechielem Prophetam,* liber 14, in PL 25, 148.D-149.B, *in ibid.,* p. 254).

[147] "The Church is composed of publicans, sinners and pagans; only her second and celestial Adam did not sin. She herself is a sinner and saves herself by begetting children who persevere in the faith" (St. Hilary, *Liber mysteriorum, De Adam,* CSEL 65, 5-6, *in ibid.,* p. 256).

• An excerpt from St. Peter Damian recognizing that there are sinners in the Church;[148]

• An excerpt from St. Bernard rebuking the evil shepherds who "prostitute" the Church;[149]

• An excerpt from St. Ambrose in which he uses the expression *casta meretrix* in such an allegorical and loose fashion that he leaves the field of Dogmatic Theology and situates himself solely in that of the elegant paradoxical rhetoric that was fashionable in his time;[150]

• An excerpt from St. Augustine saying that the Church has stains and wrinkles;[151]

• An obscure excerpt from St. Peter Chrysologus comparing the Church with the repentant St. Mary Magdalene who was guilty

---

[148] "In the Church there are several kinds of members: some who must be besieged by the arguments of sacred preaching, others whose bulwarks of infidelity or corruption must be struck by the missiles of the doctrine of salvation, and some who are already fully a part of the house. Others are still outside of it because they have gone astray as a consequence of their evil works" (St. Peter Damian, *Sermo* 57, in PL 144, 825.C-826.D; *in ibid*, p. 257).

[149] Von Balthasar writes: "Thus, Bernard would never call the Church a prostitute, but he could well say that the bad shepherds, who devastated the Church instead of 'building her,' 'prostituted her'" (*In Canticum Canticorum,* 77, 1; in PL 183, 1156.A, *in ibid.*, p. 258).

[150] "Rahab, in the symbol of the prostitute, in the Church mystery ... did not refuse her embrace to the many who came to her, and the greater the number of those with whom she unites, the more chaste she becomes: an immaculate virgin without wrinkle, immune from the sense of shame, universally public (*plebeia*) in her love, a chaste prostitute (*casta meretrix*), a sterile widow, a fertile virgin. A prostitute, because she is visited by many lovers, with all the lures of love but without the stain of guilt, for 'he who unites with a prostitute forms only one body with her;' a sterile widow because if she lacks a husband, she cannot beget. ... A fertile virgin who begat this whole rabble with the blessed gift of love, without any concupiscence" (St. Ambrose, *Expositionis in Evangelium secundum Lucam*, 23, in PL 15, 1599, *in ibid.*, pp. 267-268).

[151] "Not even the saints are free from daily sins. The Church as a whole says: Forgive us our trespasses! Therefore she has stains and wrinkles. But through confession the wrinkles disappear; through confession the stains are washed away" (St. Augustine, *Sermo* 181, 5, 7, in PL 38, 982, *in ibid.*, p. 278).

for her previous sins, probably referring allegorically to the state of the Gentiles before they converted to the Church;[152]

    • An excerpt from St. Thomas Aquinas in which he says that the Church at present has stains and wrinkles.[153]

§ 87

    Four of these 11 quotations unequivocally refer to the sins of men, excluding the possibility of any sin of the Church (those by Dionysius the Carthusian, Clement of Alexandria, St. Peter Damian and St. Bernard). Five refer to the sins of men but fail to distinguish them from sins of the Church (those by St. Gregory the Great, St. Jerome, St. Hilary, St. Augustine and St. Thomas). Two make use of allegories so loose that they can be considered poetic literature rather than dogmatic teaching (those by St. Ambrose and St. Peter Chrysologus).

§ 88

    As for the five texts that refer indistinguishably to sins of men and sins of the Church, we see that the text of St. Gregory is allegorical and its dogmatic consequence is insufficiently clear; the text of St. Jerome is hypothetical and thereby not dogmatically conclusive, and the excerpts from St. Hilary, St. Augustine and St. Thomas are very brief and do not distinguish what is divine and what is human in the Church, what cannot sin and what can sin in her. Thus their few lines on the topic do not appear to reflect a desire to define dogmatically a question of this magnitude.

---

[152] "'Behold a woman who was a sinner in the city.' In the city of infidelity (*perfidy*) this woman, that is, the Church, was laden with the gravest guilt from many previous sins. ... And thus with impetuous love she spills forth tears at the feet of the Lord" (St. Peter Chrysologus, *Sermo 95, De Magdalena*, in PL 52, 468-469, *in ibid.*, p. 279).

We have not listed another excerpt from the same sermon by St. Peter Chrysologus as favoring Balthasar's thesis because it is not sufficiently clear. Its style, however, is clearly allegorical. It reads: "'She was a woman known in the city as a sinner.' Who is this woman? The Church, undoubtedly. In what city? In the one of which the prophet spoke, 'How did faithful Sion become a prostitute of the city?'" (Is 1, Je 11:16-17; *Sermo 95*, in PL 52, 467-468, *in ibid.*, p. 220).

[153] "That the Church is glorious, with neither stain nor wrinkle, is the final goal to which we tend by virtue of the passion of Christ. This will occur only in the eternal motherland and not on our pilgrimage; according to 1 Jn. 1:8, we would deceive ourselves if we were to affirm that there is no sin whatsoever here" (St. Thomas Aquinas, *Summa Theologiae,* III, q.8, a.3 ad 2um, *in ibid.*, pp. 279-280).

§ 89

Regarding the two allegorical texts of St. Ambrose and St. Peter Chrysologus, we stress *first,* that allegorical and poetic texts like these cannot constitute a base for any dogmatic conclusion, such as the thesis of von Balthasar. *Second,* in view of the disrespectful liberty of language they adopt in relation to Holy Mother Church and the inopportuneness of the symbol of the prostitute applied to her, these excerpts certainly can be set aside as ill-sounding, similar to the mistakes we have already mentioned in other Church Fathers, which St. Vincent of Lérins recommends us to disregard as "private opinions" and "obscurities."

Therefore, the citations von Balthasar makes that would supposedly allow him to initiate a dogmatic discussion on the peccability of the Church would number no more than the five mentioned above, and these do not distinguish between sins of men and sins of the Church. Of these excerpts, the only one that actually uses the prostitute comparison is that of St. Jerome.

Here we will not analyze further the problems involved with the short texts of these five great Saints[154] or check them in their original contexts to verify they were properly cited.[155] As we have already stated (§ 24), we will not make a comparison here with the original sources.

§ 90

Notwithstanding, we can affirm that, following the inductive method used by von Balthasar regarding the thinking of the Fathers, five *clear* texts would not be sufficient to draw a conclusion about the teaching of all of Patristics. Five *unclear* texts like the ones mentioned are insufficient for any kind of generalization whatsoever.

While more texts are presented throughout *Casta Meretrix* than the ones mentioned here, nothing significant is found in the thinking of those Church Fathers and Doctors that could be directly related to sins attributable to the essence of the Church.[156]

---

[154] This subject will be addressed in the presentation of the **6ᵗʰ Unfounded Generalization** in this Appendix.

[155] As we have already stated (Cf. § 24), we will not make a comparison here with the original sources.

[156] We are obviously not considering texts that von Balthasar cites from authors like Savonarola and others, since, as he himself admits, "the shadow of condemnation hovers over them" (*Casta meretrix*, p. 270). To consider them as expressing the thinking of the Church would be an aberration.

Also omitted are passages from the writings of Erich Przywara, Hugo, Rahner and Jean Danielou which concur with von Balthasar's thesis, because they only prove that this is the position of their progressivist

§ 91   With this, we close our analysis of the documents cited in von Balthasar's work by affirming that they are not sufficient to demonstrate that the Church in her essence is a sinner and a prostitute. Therefore, his generalization of such thesis based on the Church Fathers [157] is shown to be groundless. In other words, the quoted texts do not demonstrate his thesis.

---

current. This argument is a *petitio principi* or a tautology (an argument in which the conclusion is assumed as being the premise). It does not lead to demonstrating the thesis of the author.

Finally, among these 11 excerpts we did not include the final text by Fr. Emile Mersch, doubtless a respected author, but still too recent to determine whether in the future his ideas will have the authority of the Church Fathers and Doctors as expressing Church thinking.

[157] • Von Balthasar's tendency to generalize can be noticed from the beginning of the work in his interpretation of passages from the Gospels. In the following citation, we place in bold his generalization without foundation in the Gospel: "'Go and sin no more' (Jn 8:11): upon her also [the prostitute, as a symbol of the Church] befalls the duty of not sinning anymore. Even in the vacant house, swept and adorned, the devil can return with seven others still worse than him 'and the final condition of that man is worse than the first' (Mt 12: 45). This is true for each sinner.

"With regard to Peter and the other hesitating Apostles [Jesus Christ said]: 'Simon, Simon, Satan has asked to sift you as wheat. But I have prayed for you, Simon, that your faith may not fail. And when you have turned back, strengthen your brothers' (Lk. 22:31-34). Peter, affirming that he would accompany Jesus to prison and in death, sheds light on this statement by the Lord, just as it provokes another: 'This very night, before the rooster crows, you will deny me three times' (Mt 26:34). Peter is supported by a prayer that protects him against Satan, but it is not enough to prevent him from falling and denying Jesus, thus making him like Judas.

"The same thing is said to him after he confesses the messianic character of Christ: 'Have I not chosen you, the Twelve? Yet one of you is a devil!'" (Jn. 6:70). **It would be inconceivable that these words and actions would refer only to the acts of founding the Church and have no further significance for her state after she was consolidated.** The New Testament speaks of the confirmations given to the Church of Christ only to say that she is gravely exposed to the threat of abuse, to the possibility of apostasy. **The immaculate character of the wife is never presented as an accomplished fact that the bride should simply accept without any further concern**" (*Casta meretrix*, p. 203).

• Further on, von Balthasar draws this generic conclusion that finds no apparent foundation in the texts he presents: "In his works, Ambrose cited many of these lines by Hippolytus commenting on the *Canticle of Canticles*. The presupposition to understand them correctly is a certain dynamism in Hippolytus when he says, 'The Church never ceases to generate in her heart the word that is persecuted by the wicked,' or 'Understand, o man, what has been written: The mouth of the Father spoke a pure word. And now a second word appears, spoken by the saints. She constantly begets saints, just as she constantly is proclaimed by the saints.' **In her**, therefore, **the passage from Synagogue to Church is always ongoing**; the Synagogue is the Church of the past, the past of the Church: 'I am black but beautiful, o daughters of Jerusalem.' **I am a sinner but I am even more beautiful given that Christ has conquered me with love**" (*ibid.*, p. 241).

• He cites an excerpt from St. Paolinus of Nola on Mary Magdalene, which ends thus: "Since the Church also corresponded in her symbol to her chief, Christ, she quite opportunely took the figure of the sinner, given that Christ also took the figure of the sinner." To which von Balthasar adds this general comment: "**There is something** (and not the least apparent thing) **in the essential figure of the Church that calls to mind sin, that is conditioned by sin** – and in the context we are using, all sins are infidelity and fornication – but this is still not guilt, but rather identification with the figure of sin in her chief" (*ibid.*, p. 266).

• It is in the introduction to the above-cited text of St. Ambrose (p. 113, note 11) that von Balthasar develops his thesis even further. He transfers the free, allegorical and paradoxical language of the Bishop of Milan to the field of dogmatic definitions and then presents his general conclusion: "**The *forma meretricis*** .[figure of the prostitute] ... **is so profoundly fitting to the Church that it ... defines the Church of the New Covenant in its most splendid mystery of salvation**."

• Generalizations by von Balthasar referring to all of Patristic Theology, as if it supposedly admitted sin in the essence of the Church, can be found on the texts quoted in Note 72.

6th Unfounded Generalization:

The sins of men make up the essence of Church

6th Rebuttal:

The sins of those who constitute the Church do not affect her essence

§ 92
      The only argument that remains for von Balthasar's thesis regarding the "Prostitute Church" is the fact that the men who belong to the Church do in fact sin. This is his basis to defend that the Church also sins.

      The answer to this argument demands us to make a brief exposition on what the essence of the Church is and what role the human side plays in her. It will allow the Reader to clearly see the error of his thesis.

A. Divine Attributes of the Church that Make Up Her Essence

§ 93
      Affirming the ordinary teaching of the Church Magisterium, we say that the Church – similar to the Word Made Flesh – is divine.[158] This is proved by the following reasons:

---

[158] a. In principle and in a broad sense, the Catholic Church is the ensemble constituted by the Church Triumphant, the Church Suffering and the Church Militant. Therefore, in an overview to define the essence of the Church, we should study her in this full perspective. There are very interesting questions that could be considered in this broad view:

• Is there a human-divine institutional unity simultaneously present in these three parts?

• Is Christ, as God and Man living in a glorified state, present in the three parts of the Church? How do His human and divine life, wisdom, sanctity and beauty flow from the Head to the three parts of the Mystical Body?

• How do the three parts influence one another from the institutional standpoint?

It seems to us that these and other questions could give human History a nobler perspective than what is offered by the mere chronicle of events, which is usually considered the most essential and positive in History. This is not the moment, however, to make such a study and answer these questions.

b. In principle and in a broad sense, the Church Militant encompasses in History all of the faithful who lived under natural law from the time of Adam to Moses, who lived under the written law from the

§ 94   *First,* **the origin of the Church is divine** because she was founded by the Redeemer: "Thou art Peter, and upon this rock I will build my Church" (Mt 16:18). Pius IX mentions this divine origin and institution when he teaches: "The Catholic Church, which was founded and instituted by Our Lord Jesus Christ in order to provide for the eternal salvation of men, acquired the form of a perfect society by virtue of her divine institution."[159]

§ 95   *Second,* **her mission is divine** because Christ transmitted His own mission to the Church. In *Satis cognitum,* Leo XIII states: "What did Our Lord Jesus Christ seek? What did He wish in regard to the establishment and maintenance of His Church? This one thing: to transmit to the Church the same mission and the same mandate that He himself had received from the Father, that they should be perpetuated. This He decreed to be done; this He actually did. 'As the Father has sent Me into the world, I also send you' (Jn 20:21). 'As Thou hast sent Me into the world, I also have sent them into the world' (Jn 17:18)."[160]

This mission was formally conferred by a mandate of divine power: "All power is given to Me in heaven and in earth. Going therefore, teach ye all nations: baptizing them in the name of the Father, and of the Son, and of the Holy Spirit, teaching them to observe all things whatsoever I have commanded you" (Mt 28:18-20).

Christ gave His Church the promise of divine assistance to accomplish her mission: "And behold, I am with you all days, even to the consummation of the world" (Mt 28:20).

§ 96   *Third,* **the chief end of the Church is divine** because it is to guide men to the face-to-face vision of God himself.

§ 97   *Fourth,* **the means to attain this end is also divine** because it is grace - a created gift that allows men to participate in divine life - which is conferred not only by God through the mediation of Mary Most Holy, but also through the Sacraments of the Church, all

---

time of Moses to Our Lord, and who have lived and still live under the law of the Gospel since Our Lord Jesus Christ, and constitute the Church.

The Catholic Church to which we refer is, in the strict sense, the Church historically founded by Our Lord Jesus Christ.

[159] Pius IX, Apostolic Letter *Cum Catholica* of March 26, 1860, in V.A., *Recueil des allocutions*, p. 401.

[160] Leo XIII, Encyclical *Satis cognitum* of June 29, 1896 (Petrópolis: Vozes, 1960), n. 8; see also n. 2 of that encyclical and the Encyclical *Immortale Dei* of November 1, 1885 (Petrópolis: Vozes, 1954), n. 14.

of them divinely instituted. Among the Sacraments the Holy Eucharist, which guarantees **the divine presence** of the Savior forever in the Church, stands out. In it Christ offers himself as **divine nourishment** for the faithful, thus anticipating, in a mysterious way, the union we will have with God in Heaven.[161]

But grace is not just a means to attain eternal happiness. Divine grace constitutes the very life of the Church. It is the divine breath that animates her institution and members, stimulates her development, produces her fruits of truth, goodness and beauty, preserves them in her hierarchical and sacral atmosphere and defends them against the enemies, thus fortifying her militant character. Therefore, grace is effectively the life of the Church, and since it is divine, **the life of the Church is divine.** Pius XII teaches, "The Church possesses, deriving from her Founder himself, the capacity to enjoy divine life."[162]

§ 98   *Fifth,* **as a visible society, the Church constitutes a body. This body is also divine** since Christ is her head. Pius XII teaches: "That the Church is a body is taught by many passages of Sacred Scriptures. 'Christ,' says the Apostle, 'is the head of the body of the Church' (Col 1:18). Now then, if the Church is a body, she must necessarily be one and undivided, according to the words of St. Paul: 'So we being many, are one body in Christ' (Rom 12:5). And not only must she be one and undivided, but also she must be something concrete and visible, as Our Predecessor of happy memory, Leo XIII, says in his Encyclical *Satis cognitum*: 'By the very fact of being a body, the Church is visible.'[163*]"[164]

Leo XIII also instructs: "Furthermore, the Son of God decreed that the Church would be His mystical body, with which He would unite himself as the head, just as in the human body, which He assumed in the Incarnation, the head is linked to the members by a necessary and natural union. So, just as He took to himself only one mortal body ... so also He has only one mystical body, in which and through which He makes men partakers of sanctity and eternal salva-

---

[161] Cf. Council of Trent, sess. XIII, nos. 874-893 (Petrópolis: Vozes, 1959), p. 31; Leo XIII, Encyclical *Mirare caritatis* of May 28, 1902 (Petrópolis: Vozes, 1952), *passim.*

[162] Pius XII, Encyclical *Fulgens radiatur* of March 21, 1947 (Petrópolis: Vozes, 1953), n. 2.

[163*] Cf. AAS, XXVII, p. 710.

[164] Pius XII, Encyclical *Mystici Corporis Christi* of June 29, 1943 (Petrópolis: Vozes, 1960), n. 10.

tion. 'And God hath made Him [Christ] head over all the Church, which is His body' (Eph 1:22-23)."[165]

Thus the Catholic Church is divine in her origin, mission, end and means, assisted by the divine presence itself and fed by divine nourishment, the Holy Eucharist. The Church is also divine as a visible society that forms but one single body with the Word Incarnate.

B. Definition of the Church

§ 99

In her likeness to the God-Man, the Church is essentially a single whole composed by her visible body, her created soul and her uncreated soul.[166]

§ 100

As for her body, St. Robert Bellarmine defines the Church as "the community of men gathered together by the profession of the true Christian faith and the communion of the same Sacraments, under the government of legitimate shepherds, principally the sole Vicar of Christ on earth, the Roman Pontiff."[167]

Pius XI corroborates this definition, leaving out the role of Faith and adding the social, exterior and visible nature of the Church. In the Encyclical *Mortalium animos,* he defines the Church as "a perfect, exterior and visible society by nature, destined to continue through the centuries the work of reparation of mankind under the direction of one single chief by means of a living Magisterium and through the dispensation of the Sacraments, fountains of heavenly grace." [168]

---

[165] Leo XIII, Encyclical *Satis Cognitum*, n. 10; see also n. 25 of that encyclical; Vatican Council I, Sess. III, n. 1794, (Petrópolis: Vozes, 1953), p. 7; Pius XII, *Discurso La elevatezza* (Petrópolis: Vozes, 1950), p. 3.

For the scriptural and traditional teaching on this topic. see the list of texts and authors in E. Dublancy, entry "Église," in DTC., vol. 4, cols. 2150-2155.

[166] We adopt the distinction between the created and the uncreated soul of the Church made by Cardinal Charles Journet in his work *L'Église du Verbe Incarné* (Desclée de Brouwer, 1951, 1962, vol. 2, pp. 522, 565-579), which appeared to us more complete than those by other authors, who distinguish only body and soul in the Church. However, we do not adhere to the whole ecclesiological conception of Journet, with which we disagree on several fundamental points (cf. Vol. XI, *Ecclesia*, Chap. I, §§ 26-119).

[167] St. Robert Bellarmine, *De Ecclesia Militante*, chap. 2, in C. Journet, *L'Église du Verbe Incarné,* vol. 2, p. 1181.

[168] Pius XI, Encyclical *Mortalium animos* of January 6, 1928, *in ibid.,* p. 580.

In a simple, direct and comprehensive way St. Pius X says: "The body of the Church consists of that which she has of the visible and exterior, be it either in the association of her members, or in the worship and ministry of her teaching, or in her exterior order and government." [169]

§ 101   **As for her created soul**, St. Pius X states: "The soul of the Church is that which she has of interior and spiritual, namely faith, hope, charity, the gifts of grace and of the Holy Ghost, and all the heavenly treasures that pour into her by the merits of Christ the Redeemer and the saints.'" [170]

§ 102   **As for her uncreated soul**, in the Encyclical *Divinum illud munus* Leo XIII affirms: "If Christ is the head of the Church, the Holy Ghost is her soul." He cites this comparison of St. Augustine: "What the soul is to man's body, the Holy Ghost is to the body of Christ, which is the Church." [171]

In *Mystici Corporis Christi*, Pius XII gives greater precision to the definition of the Holy Ghost as the uncreated soul of the Church: "Moreover, by that more profound communication, interior and altogether sublime ... Christ our Lord bids the Church live from His supernatural life, makes His divine power penetrate the whole of her body, and feeds and sustains each member according to the place which it occupies in the body, in much the same way as the vine-stock nourishes and fecundates the branches adhering to it.[172*]"

"If we carefully consider this divine principle of life and power given by Christ inasmuch as it constitutes the very source of every created gift and grace, we shall easily understand that it is none other than the Paraclete, the Spirit who proceeds from the Father and the Son and who in a special manner is called 'Spirit of Christ' or 'Spirit of the Son' (Rom 8:9; 2 Cor 3:17; Gal 4:6). For it was with this Spirit

---

[169] *Compendio della dotrina cristiana prescitto da sua Santità Papa Pius X alle diocesi della provincia di Roma* (Rome, 1905), p. 119, *in ibid.*, p. 568.

[170] *Ibid.* Almost the same definition can be found in St. Robert Bellarmine, *De Ecclesia Militante*, chap. 3; René Billuart, *De regulis Fidei*, dissertatio 3, a.3, *Utrum Ecclesia sit visibilis?* vol. 3, p. 302, Louis Billot, *De Ecclesia Christi,* (Rome: Aedis Universitatis Gregorianae, 1921), in C. Journet, *L'Église du Verbe Incarneé,* vol. 2, pp. 566-568.

[171] Leo XIII, Encyclical *Divinum illud munus*, in C. Journet, *L'Église du Verbe Incarneé,* vol. 2, *ibid.*, p. 522.

[172*] Cf. Leo XIII, Encyclical *Sapientiae christianae*, in AAS, vol. 22, 392; *Satis cognitum, in ibid.*, vol. 27, 710.

of grace and truth that the Son of God adorned His soul in the Virgin's immaculate womb; He is the Spirit who delights to dwell in the Redeemer's pure soul as in His favorite temple; He is the Spirit whom Christ merited for us by shedding His own blood on the Cross, the Spirit whom He bestowed upon the Church for the remission of sins, breathing Him upon the Apostles (cf. Jn 20:22).

"And while Christ alone received this Spirit without measure (cf. Jn 3:34), it is given to the members of the mystical body from that plenitude of Christ and only according to the measure that He wants to give it (cf. Eph 1:8; 4:7).

"And since Christ has been glorified on the Cross, His Spirit is communicated to the Church in abundant outpouring, so that she and each of her members may grow daily in likeness to our Savior. [173]

§ 103   In summary, the body of the Church is her external and visible aspect; her created soul is the virtues of her members, the grace and spiritual gifts that come from the Holy Ghost, and her uncreated soul is the Holy Ghost himself.

In this definition the Church is essentially constituted by divine and human aspects.

C. To What Extent Do Men Participate in the Church?

§ 104   In view of this definition and the fact that men concretely and historically make up the society of the Catholic Church and, therefore, participate in the essence of the Church, one asks whether or not their weak and sinful aspects are also present in the essence of the Church. If these aspects are not present in the essence of the Church, then the question arises: To what degree do men belong to the Church?

To respond to this question correctly, some distinctions need to be made.

§ 105   Evidently, men cannot have an essential presence in the uncreated soul of the Church, since this is the Holy Ghost himself, the Third Person of the Holy Trinity, infinitely superior to and distinct from any creature.

§ 106   Through their virtue, men certainly play a fundamental role in determining the created soul of the Church. To the extent that they welcome divine grace and the gifts of the Holy Ghost and practice the supernatural virtues of faith, hope and charity – as well as the other virtues of fortitude, justice, temperance and prudence – they will contribute to the molding of the created soul of the Church.

---

[173] Pius XII, Encyclical *Mystici Corporis Christi*, nn. 54-56.

However, to the degree that they refuse grace and the gifts of the Holy Ghost and commit sins and foster vices, they are entirely or partially cut off from the supernatural life. To what degree are they cut off also from the soul of the Church? The answer is quite difficult and mysterious because it involves a detailed and nuanced assessment of what has been rejected and what is still accepted by the sinner; it entails a judgment that must penetrate the mysterious internal dispositions of the sinner's soul. It is, therefore, an assessment reserved to the judgment of God and not to the judgments of men.

To men fall only – through a common discernment of spirit born from experience, Catholic sense, grace or a special gift from the Holy Ghost – to assess the general state of the sinner's soul in order to encourage him to repent. It also falls to men to prevent contamination from the sinner's evil.

Therefore, in conclusion, we can say that men participate essentially in the created soul of the Church to the extent that they are in the state of grace and practice virtue; this participation ceases to the degree that they sin.

§ 107   What falls to human judgment is the essential participation of men in the body of the Church. Indeed, since men constitute the external and visible aspect of the Church, it is possible for them – using wise, just and prudent criteria – to judge who belongs to the body of the Church and who is excluded from it.

The definition of St. Robert Bellarmine, cited above, contains the fundamental elements to determine who participates essentially in the body of the Church. In short, these three elements must be present: the external profession of the true Faith, communion in the same Sacraments and submission to the government of the legitimate shepherds, principally the Vicar of Christ.

According to this definition, which expresses the thinking of the Church in a splendid and brief way, by virtue of the *first* condition, infidels (Jews, Muslims and pagans), heretics and apostates are excluded; by virtue of the *second*, catechumens and the excommunicated are outside the Church; by virtue of the *third*, the schismatics are left out. The others are visible members of the Church.

§ 108   Sinners, therefore, are included in that number – not in the condition of sinners as such – by virtue of their fulfillment of the three conditions of this definition. Since these three conditions are holy, institutionally speaking, those who visibly and exteriorly fulfill these conditions are Catholics. They belong to the Church not because she accepts a part of their sins, but insofar as these sinners are still good enough to publicly profess these three holy conditions. If a man exteriorly and visibly denies one of the three conditions, he begins his process of exclusion from the body of the Church. Therefore, the essence of the body of the Church is not affected by the sins of those who compose it.

This does not exclude the fact that those who sin publicly against other visible aspects of the Church – such as criminals, the impious, those who give public scandal, etc. – wound the body of the Church. These are wounds that the Church bears on her body, but which do not stain her essence.

§ 109   The Council of Trent teaches this about the mark of holiness of the Church in the *Roman Catechism*: "It should not be deemed a matter of surprise that the Church, although numbering among her children many sinners, is called holy. For just as those who profess any art, even when they depart from its rules, are still called artists, so in like manner the faithful, although weak in many things and failing to fulfill the engagements to which they had pledged themselves, are still called holy, because they have been made the people of God and have consecrated themselves to Christ by Faith and Baptism. Hence, St. Paul calls the Corinthians 'sanctified and holy,' although it is certain that among them there were some whom he severely rebuked as carnal, and also charged with grosser crimes."[174]

§ 110   We conclude by stating that men essentially participate in the Church – in her body and her created soul – to the extent that they fulfill the three conditions of visibly belonging to the Church and to the degree that they possess the grace of God. Men do not participate essentially in the uncreated soul of the Church.

§ 111   Above the continuous voice of the faithful, who throughout History have confessed the sanctity of the Church in the Creed, louder than the grand chorus of teachings of the Magisterium whose first documents had already proclaimed her holy, we hear the grave and solemn carillon of the decrees of the Ecumenical Council of Vienne (1305-1314).[175] Its tones traverse the centuries and reach our ears with this grave and elegant message:

"And in this assumed [human] nature, **the same Word of God**, to achieve the salvation of all, not only willed to be nailed on the Cross and die on it, but, after having exhaled His Spirit, **suffered His Side to be pierced by the lance, so that, as those waves of water and blood fell from Him, that unique immaculate virgin, the**

---

[174] The Council of Trent, *Roman Catechism*, P.I, a.9, §13 (Petrópolis: Vozes, 1962), p. 149.

[175] Cf. DR 1, 4, 5, 7, 9, etc.

Holy Mother Church, the Bride of Christ, would be formed, just as from the side of the first man, sleeping, Eve was formed to be his spouse." [176]

§ 112   This is echoed in the teaching of Pope Gregory XVI: "Therefore, **it is exceedingly absurd and extremely harmful to propose a certain 'restoration and regeneration' for the Church to make her return to an early purity or to give her new vigor, as if she could be considered subject to defects, ignorance or any other human imperfections.**"[177]

§ 113   And in the teaching of Pope Pius XI: " **Never through the course of centuries has the Mystical Spouse of Christ been stained, nor can she ever in the future be stained, as St. Cyprian bears witness: 'The Bride of Christ cannot be dishonored: she is incorrupt and pure.** She knows but one dwelling, and in her chaste modesty she guards intact the sanctity of the nuptial chamber.'[178*]" [179]

§ 114   These considerations definitively establish the limits of the institutional essence of the Church and demonstrate that she is holy and divine in everything. They do not, however, completely explain the moral damage that sin inflicts on the Church. To understand this consequence, one should compare the malice of sin to the malice of those who caused the Word Incarnate to suffer in the steps of the Passion.

§ 115   As for the created soul of the Church, there are sins that cause her moral suffering, just as in the Passion Our Lord suffered from the agony in the Garden, the sleep of the Apostles, the treason of Judas, the flight of those He loved most, His consequent abandonment, the ingratitude and rejection of the Synagogue and the Jews, their scorn for proclaiming himself to be God, His delivery into the hands of the pagans, the sentence of Deicide demanded by the Chosen People, their rejection of Him in favor of Barabbas and much more – until the final cruelty of being given vinegar when, thirsting and exhausted, He requested a little water.

As for the body of the Church, there are sins that inflict sufferings on her as an institution, similar to those which tormented the Body

---

[176] Ecumenical Council of Vienne, Constitution *De Summa Trinitate et Fide catholica*, in DR, 480; in the same sense, see the Letter of the Holy Office to the Bishops of England of September 9, 14 written under the pontificate of Pius IX, in DR, 1686.

[177] Gregory XVI, Encyclical *Mirari vos*, of August 15, 1832, in DR, n. 6.

[178*] *De Catholicae Ecclesiae unitate,* 6.

[179] Pius XI, Encyclical *Mortalium animos*, in *Actes de S.S. Pie XI, 1927-1928* (Paris: Bonne Presse), vol. 4, p. 79.

of the Savior when He was buffeted and scourged, covered with spittle and blows, crowned with thorns, and made to carry the most heavy wood of torment, when His hands and feet were pierced with nails, His body was crucified, His side torn open with a lance and His Sacred Heart pierced.

Measuring the malice of sin and how much it caused the Word Incarnate to suffer, it becomes clear once again that His Mystical Body, analogously wounded by the sins of men, is pure and divine in its essence and profoundly rejects sin.

D. Conclusion on this Unfounded Generalization

The last foundation for von Balthasar's statement that the Church is a *casta meretrix* can be summarized as follows: The Church as she is known historically and visibly is composed of men. Now then, men are sinners. Therefore, the Church is a sinner.

§ 116   This simplistic reasoning is wrong. While men do in fact sin, the Church does not assume the sin of men in her essence. Sins are sufferings inflicted upon her created soul and her body. To consider the sins of men as essential parts of the Church would be as senseless as someone who, seeing the physical and moral sufferings inflicted on Our Lord Jesus Christ during the Passion, would believe that His body was in a scourged state by nature and His soul was habitually tormented.

7. General Conclusion about the Book *Casta Meretrix*

§ 117   We have seen in this Appendix that in order to prove there is a note of prostitution in the very essence of the Holy Church, von Balthasar resorted to excessive generalizations and omitted fundamental historical, exegetical and doctrinal data, without which the very presentation of the problem is falsified. Therefore, in the general structure of his work as well as in the demonstration of its parts, von Balthasar acted in a fraudulent and misleading way.

Furthermore, his thesis is false, for it is clear that the texts he produced fail to corroborate it and that the doctrine on which he bases himself is at variance with Catholic doctrine.

*

§ 118   What von Balthasar ultimately offers is a thesis on the theology of History that fails by historic omission... What a curious paradox in the work of a harbinger of Progressivism who boasts of being able to reinterpret the immutable dogma of the Church through the historical method!

*

This concludes our critique of Cardinal Hans Urs von Balthasar's work *Casta meretrix,* which expresses progressivist thinking on this theme.

§ 119   We believe that this analysis provides sufficient elements for the Reader to confront progressivists in a polemic on the sanctity and sacrality of the Holy Catholic Church.

*   *   *

APPENDIX II

Our initial idea was to present at the end of each Chapter the series of offenses contained in its texts. After reflection, however, we thought it would be better to place all the offenses in an Appendix. There are two reasons for this decision:

First, to prevent the Volume's main text from losing the tone it must have as an objective and systematic presentation of the outrages being made against the Holy Church.

Second, because, presented as a whole and in an abbreviated manner, the offenses acquire a greater force of expression.

As we compiled the list of outrages, we noticed they took the shape of a macabre "litany" that called to mind the lamentations of the Passion. *Improperia* will thus be the term used to designate this whole section.

We believe that this ensemble translates with some objectivity the hatred of progressivists for the Catholic Church as she existed for almost 2000 years, until Vatican II.

The offenses made by theologians will be presented here in their gravest aspects and uniformly presented in the form of invocations that we have constructed and, as such, do not always appear in the texts. As the Reader has seen in this Volume, these affronts have diverse nuances that, even so, do not lessen their gravity.

The most elementary common sense dictates that technical nuances have little attenuating value when it comes to insults, as we have observed in the Introduction (§ 30) of this Volume. We believe that as an expression of the *animus injuriandi* of conciliar progressivists, we should offer this ensemble to our Readers.

For those who want to verify the objectivity of each affirmation, we will indicate alongside each offense the page where it can be found.

* * *

IMPROPERIA

CHAPTER I

Christ, revealing God to the reprobates in the horrors of Hell (p. 42)

Christ, revealing God to the reprobates in the form of sin (p. 42)

Christ, traitor to divine justice (p. 42)

Christ, who makes up one single body with God's enemies (p. 42)

Christ, the one cursed by God (p. 53)

Christ, who cries out like a madman (p. 53)

Christ, who cries out more terribly than a reprobate (p. 54)

Christ, who died without communicating with God (p. 54)

Christ, who died without interior peace (p. 53)

Christ, abyss of all bitterness and despair (p. 54)

Christ, disfigured by gothic images (p. 59)

Christ, degenerated by repugnant images of the Sacred Heart (p. 59)

Heart of Christ, seat of all treachery (p. 56)

Heart of Christ, a traitor like any unfaithful heart (p. 57)

Heart of Christ, in which all betrayal & cowardice are compressed (p. 57)

Heart of Christ, given to changes of humor and sudden impulses (p. 56)

Heart of Christ, which knows not why it beats (p. 57)

Heart of Christ, whose love overflows to the enemy (p. 57)

Heart of Christ, whose folly is understood by the commerce of the flesh (p. 57)

Heart of Christ, annihilator of all barriers between good and evil (p. 57)

Heart of Christ, into which all anguish and infamies are plunged (p. 57)

Heart of Christ, into which all defiance and pride are compressed (p. 57)

Heart of Christ, narrow battlefield where the eternal struggle between heaven and hell is decided (p. 57)

Heart of Christ, betrayed by the Eternal Father (p. 58)

Heart of Christ, victim of divine wrath (p. 58)

Heart of Christ, the convergence of two hostile wills (p. 58)

Judas, representative of the acts of every sinner – Christians, Jews and pagans (p. 50)

Judas, who kissed the lips of Jesus a thousand times (p. 52)

Church, unforgivably guilty of the Protestant Pseudo-Reformation (p. 60)

Church, who strew her patrimony on the open road (p. 61)

Church, whose love travels outside her walls and lives in heresies (p. 61)

Church, who betrayed her very essence (p. 61)

Church, who denied her origin (p. 61)

Church, who strayed from her original path (p. 61)

Church, who betrays the Gospel of Christ when she refuses ecumenism (p. 62)

Church, who betrays her catholicity by falling into the temptation of power (p. 62)

Church, who betrays herself by showing pride for herself and despising others (p. 62)

Church, who betrays herself when she abuses the term 'Catholic' (p. 62)

Church, symbolized by Judas hanging from the tree, his entrails strewn about (p. 60)

CHAPTER II

Church Militant, who, by sanctioning just war, transforms man into the most ferocious of beasts (p. 83)

Church Militant, who, by sanctioning just war, promotes a ritual of sadistic cruelty (p. 83)

Church Militant, formed by assuming the bellicose temperament of the Germanic barbarians (p. 83)

Church Militant, who transferred Wotan's attributes to the Archangel St. Michael (p. 84)

Church Militant, who erred by instituting a Mass to St. Michael to obtain victory in times of war (p. 84)

Church Militant, whose Crusades were a distorted epiphany of the sacred (p. 83-84)

Church Militant, whose Crusades were a negation of the Gospel's teaching (p. 84)

Church Militant, whose Crusades were a traumatic experience for Western civilization (p. 84)

Church Militant, whose Popes erred by giving plenary indulgences to Crusaders who died in combat (p. 84)

Church Militant, who erred by incorporating prayers proper to war and battle in her liturgical books (p. 84)

Church Militant, whose reaction in the Counter-Reformation imposed a unilateral uniformity (p. 87)

Church Militant, whose Holy Inquisition was an incomprehensible stain on the Body of Christ (p. 75)

Church Militant, whose condemnation of Luther was a papal reaction of insecurity (p. 87)

Church Militant, who condemned Luther in an overly passionate reaction (p. 87)

Church Militant, who sets aside the commandment of love by fighting heretics (p. 75)

Church Militant, who distorted fundamental Catholic values (p. 87)

Church Militant, who erred gravely in her actions against heretics (pp. 82, 87)

Church Militant, who brutally and unjustly destroyed the writings of the heretics (p. 76)

Church Militant, unjust for not presupposing heretics to be in good faith (p. 76)

Church Militant, unjust for not interpreting heretics in a benign way (p. 76)

Church Militant, whose armies inflicted horrible cruelties in the Battle of Vienna (p. 79)

Church Militant, whose participation in the Battle of Vienna was disheartening and shameful (p. 79)

Church Militant, whose language of arms is not the language of Christ or His Mother (p. 79)

Church Militant, stupid and imbecile for having condemned the harbingers of the *Nouvelle Theologie* (pp. 70-71)

CHAPTER III

Jesus, Son of God, whose absence of a human father is never mentioned in the Gospels (p. 121)

Jesus, Son of God, whose natural development is denied by denying him a human father (p. 120)

Mary, whose virginity during childbirth is not binding by the Faith (pp. 112, 120-121)

Mary, whose virginity during childbirth cannot be claimed to be contained in Scriptures (p. 112)

Mary, whose tradition of virginity during childbirth is of no value even when taught by the Church Fathers (p. 116)

Mary, whose continuous virginity has nothing to do with bodily integrity (p. 114)

Mary, whose virginity is an overestimation made by earlier theologians and Fathers (p. 112, 116)

Mary, whose grandeur has nothing to do with virginity (p. 115)

Mary, whose perpetual virginity does not hold a central place in the hierarchy of Catholic truths (p. 115)

Mary, who could have had sexual relations with St. Joseph without making him a rival to the eternal Father (pp. 115-116)

Mary, whose virginal conception cannot be proved by witnesses (p. 121)

Mary, whose alleged perpetual virginity cannot stand up to a normal historical investigation (p. 119)

Mary, whose perpetual virginity insinuates the female reproductive organs should not be used for their proper biological end (p. 119)

Mary, the notion of whose virginity is influenced by Gnosticism (p. 119)

Mary, whose perpetual virginity is not supported by any biblical proof (pp. 112, 118)

Mary, whose virginity during childbirth cannot be accepted because there is no historical description of it (pp. 113, 121)

Mary, whose virginity during childbirth cannot be accepted because there were no eyewitnesses of it (p. 121)

Mary, whose parturition was probably not virginal (p. 120)

Mary, whose virginity during childbirth is a controversial concept (p. 121)

Mary, whose virginity during childbirth is only an unfortunate and *a posteriori* invention (p. 115)

Mary, whose virginal childbirth was not a necessary condition for the sinless birth of Christ (pp. 115-116)

Mary, whose virginity during childbirth is an invention of '*beatos*' and pious persons (p. 118)

Mary, whose virginal childbirth is an obsolete belief (p. 120)

Mary, who, after childbirth, forgot the disgust she felt at expelling the placenta (p. 124)

Mary, who, after childbirth, forgot the bitter shame of having others present at it (p. 125)

Mary, who, during childbirth, is not a pristine and beautiful Madonna (p. 125)

Mary, who, during childbirth, is not the Queen of Heaven (p. 125)

Mary, who, during childbirth, is just a normal woman who becomes a mother for the first time (p. 125)

Mary, whose maternity implies the opening of the birth canal (p. 117)

Mary, whose maternity implies the breaking of the hymen (p. 117)

Mary, whose maternity implies the pains of childbirth (pp. 117, 118)

Mary, whose body was ignorantly considered as a tube or canal through which Jesus passed (p. 120)

Mary, whose conception by the Holy Spirit and virginity during childbirth are comparable to artificial insemination and delivery by a cesarean operation (p. 117)

Mary, whose painless parturition has something of Docetism (pp. 117, 120)

Mary, whose painless parturition can be biologically and theologically denied (p. 117)

Mary, whose divine maternity corresponds to gnostic ideas (p. 119)

Mary, whose Immaculate Conception was proclaimed a dogma without any biblical proof (p. 108)

Mary, whose Immaculate Conception finds no foundation whatsoever in the New Testament (p. 108)

Mary, who with the dogma of the Immaculate Conception became tainted by papalism and triumphalism (p. 107)

Mary, whose Universal Mediation is a belief without basis in the New Testament (p. 108)

Mary, whose Universal Mediation should not be proclaimed a dogma in the near future (p. 127)

Mary, whose title of Co-Redemptrix is a parity with Christ (p. 127)

Mary, whose title of Co-Redemptrix is source of misunderstandings (p. 127)

Mary, to whom Pius XII and John XXIII consciously avoided attributing the title of Co-Redemptrix (p. 127)

Mary, whom the Scriptures do not describe as an example of virtue (p. 108)

Mary, who should be considered just a common good woman (p. 108)

Mary, subject to the defects and frailties of our fallen nature (p. 108)

Mary, a rough woman with callused hands, a wrinkled face (p. 124)

Mary, as intangible as the real or historic Jesus (p. 123)

Mary, of whom we know as little as we know about the mother of Abraham Lincoln (p. 123)

Mary, a fictitious figure generated by Christian legend (p. 123)

Mary, a fictitious figure generated by Christian art (p. 123)

Mary, a fictitious figure generated by Christian poetry (p. 123)

Mary, a fictitious figure generated by Christian hymnology (p. 123)

Mary, whose image is related to that of the pagan goddess Isis (p. 123)

Mary, whose devotion is related to that of the goddess Cibeles of Phrygia (p. 122)

Mary, whose devotion is related to that of Demeter of Eleusis, goddess of fertility of the land (p. 122)

Mary, whose devotion is related to that of Artemis, pagan goddess of hunting and childbirth (p. 122)

Mary, whose devotion is related to that of goddess Isis of Egypt (p. 122)

Mary, whose devotion is related to that of Aphrodite of Greece, goddess of erotic love (p. 122)

Mary, whose devotion is related to that of Venus of Rome, goddess of erotic love (p. 122)

Mary, whose devotion is related to that of the goddess Innana of Sumeria (p. 122)

Mary, whose devotion is related to that of Ishtar of Babylonia, goddess of lust (p. 122)

Mary, whose devotion is related to that of Astarte of Canaan, goddess of lust (p. 122)

Mary, whose invocation *mater dolorosa* was applied to pagan goddesses (p. 122)

Mary, whose invocation *stella maris* comes from pagan goddesses (p. 122)

Mary, whose invocation *regina coeli* comes from pagan goddesses (p. 122)

Mary, whose sanctuaries and devotions imitate the cult to pagan goddesses (p. 123)

Mary, whose devotion is spurious (p. 125)

Mary, whose devotion detracts from the Bible and Christ (p. 125)

Mary, whose exaggerated devotion was unmasked at Vatican II (p. 125)

Mary, whose devotion generates distortions (p. 127)

Mary, whose devotions are not rooted in the Mystery of Christ (pp. 127-8)

Mary, a plastic figure in traditional devotion (p. 123)

Mary, whose devotion responds to the needs of the dominant classes in Christendom (p. 123)

Church, whose devotions coming from prophecies of Our Lady are fanatical (pp. 105, 106)

Church, whose devotions coming from prophecies of Our Lady resemble utopias (p. 105)

Church, whose devotions coming from prophecies of Our Lady are motivated by fear, hatreds and partisan action (p. 105)

Church, whose devotions coming from prophecies of Our Lady are related to Montanism (p. 105)

Church, whose devotions coming from prophecies of Our Lady are related to Joachimism (p. 105)

Church, whose devotions coming from revelations, apparitions and miracles obscure the original Christian message (p. 106)

Church, whose Marian dogmas are an excrescence (pp. 106-7)

Church, who at Vatican Council II openly criticized the excesses of a theoretical and practical Mariology (p. 107)

Church, who at Vatican Council II rejected a separate document on Mary (p. 107)

Church, who at Vatican Council II expressly warned against Marian exaggerations (p. 107)

Church, who at Vatican Council II put an exaggerated Mariology into crisis (p. 107)

Church, who after Vatican Council II discouraged books and theological articles about Mary and made them a rarity (p. 107)

Church, whose glorification is unbearable (p. 99)

Church, whose monotheism is presented as a supreme form of intolerance and fanaticism (p. 130)

Church, whose prophets played a crucial role in spreading intolerance and fanaticism (p. 130)

Church, whose prophets and missionaries were examples of an unparalleled intolerance (p. 130)

Church, whose prophets and missionaries were examples of the worst kind of absolutism (p. 130)

Church, whose prophets and missionaries caused so many persecutions (p. 130)

Church, whose prophets and missionaries were responsible for religious wars and inquisitions (p. 130)

Church, whose mysticism of her Saints is not supernatural (pp. 129-30)

Church, whose mysticism of her Saints belongs to the natural order of psychology and para-psychology (pp. 129-130)

Church, whose "mysticism" is just intense psychological experiences (p. 129)

Church, whose Roman Curia must be desacralized (p. 97)

Church, whose Bishops have lordly pretentions (p. 97)

Church, whose Bishops seek prestige in their dress (p. 97)

Church, whose Roman Court and Bishops seek prestige in their insignias and heraldic symbols (p. 97)

Church, whose Roman Court and Bishops seek prestige in their retinues (p. 97)

Church, whose Bishops seek prestige in honors (p. 97)

Church, whose sacral titles are ridiculous and shameful (p. 96-7)

Church, who must desacralize herself in order to serve modern man (p. 97)

Church, whose ritualistic apparatus is rejected by modern man (p. 98)

Church, whose hierarchs were attached to the appearance of riches, especially in dressing (pp. 93, 97)

The Church, whose hierarchs donned rich garments with garish colors (pp. 93, 97)

Church, whose hierarchs bore insignia of precious metals and jewels, contrary to the evangelical spirit (p. 93)

Church, whose hierarchs must refuse titles expressing grandeur and power (pp. 180, 93)

Church, whose hierarchs must avoid bestowing and accepting privileges, priorities or preferences (p. 93)

Church, whose hierarchs have need of a most excellent reform (p. 93)

Church, whose hierarchs must simplify their garments and way of life (p. 93)

Church, whose Bishops should be like common people, riding buses and standing in lines (p. 94)

Church, whose Bishops should choose to live in poor neighborhoods and convert their palaces into schools (p. 94)

Church, whose Bishops should rid themselves of all remaining signs of richness (p. 94)

Church, who should shed all honorary distinctions fitting to the imperial era (p. 94)

Church, who must address a message of poverty to men of proletarian austerity (p. 95)

Church, whose message is made incomprehensible by marble altars, baroque pontifical Masses and strange miters (p. 95)

Church, whose message is made incomprehensible by hierarchs robed in purple and addressed as "Your Most Reverend Excellencies" (p. 95)

Church, censured by the masses for her ostentatious riches and pompous ceremonies (p. 95)

Church, censured by the masses for her exterior display and showy appearances (p. 95)

Church, censured by the masses for her acts of worship (p. 95)

Church, who must reveal her authentic, poor and divested face (p. 85)

Church, whose liturgical mysteries and Saint legends are far removed from modern man (p. 99)

Church, whose ancient liturgy was nothing but an embalmed cadaver (p. 99)

Church, whose liturgy before the reforms of Paul VI was nothing but a decomposing cadaver (p. 99)

Church, whose traditional religion is fraught with gross errors (p. 100)

Church, whose traditional religion is a survival of paganism and sorcery (p. 100)

Church, whose traditional religion makes her the object of scandal and laughter of modern man (p. 100)

Church, whose traditional liturgy asks God for what farmers ask from fertilizers (p. 100)

Church, whose traditional liturgy has magical and superstitious expressions (p. 100)

Church, whose traditional liturgy has remnants of paganism (p. 100)

Church, whose traditional Mass is considered a rite with commercial value (p. 100)

Church, who strayed by following an egoist piety and a narrow-minded religion (p. 99, 129)

Church, whose pious instructions are likened to rubbish (p. 129)

Church, whose pious instructions are likened to discarded sardine cans and tinfoil left over from a picnic (p. 129)

Church, whose pious instructions are old and rusty (p. 129)

Church, whose pious instructions deviate the sinner from Christ (p. 129)

Church, whose pious instructions are childish and foolish (p. 129)

Church, whose revelations, apparitions and miracles relegate Christ to a secondary plane (p. 131)

Church, whose hagiographic marvels no longer attract (p. 99)

Church, whose brilliant ceremonials no longer attract (p. 99)

Church, whose devotions to the Saints places Christ on a secondary plane (p. 131)

Church, whose devotions to the Saints keep people from reading the Sacred Scripture (p. 131)

Church, whose prayers, novenas and devotions are preferable to the Eucharistic banquet (p. 132)

Church, whose devotion to the Saints cause people to believe Christ abdicated his role as mediator (p. 2132)

Church, whose devotion to the Saints is a paganization of the Christian Faith (p. 132)

Church, whose devotion to the Saints is dangerous (p. 132)

Vicar of Christ, a title that obscures faith in Jesus (pp. 96-97)

Holy Father, Holy See, Sacred Congregation, sacred power, all stupid and pretentious titles (p. 96)

St. Thomas Aquinas, who dialogued with the heretics of his time (p. 96)

St. Thomas Aquinas, who showed openness by dialoguing with Arabs, Jew and Muslims (pp. 96-97)

St. Robert Bellarmine, victim of a restrictive, non-biblical concept of Church (p. 224)

St. Robert Bellarmine, who refused to recognize schismatic churches as part of the Church (p. 97)

St. Clement Mary Hofbauer, narrow-minded and reactionary (p. 97)

John XXIII, who stimulated ecumenism by refusing to define any new dogma on Mary (p. 107)

CHAPTER IV

God, who behaves toward his spouse like a deceived and humiliated lover (p. 142)

God, who reaches extreme abjection in his "frailty of love" (p. 142)

God, who is shamed as *Dieu cocu* (pp. 140-141)

God, whose ignominy was assumed and borne on the Cross by the Church (p. 141)

Christ, who plays the feminine role in relation to the Father (p. 155)

Christ, assaulted by the temptation of the flesh (p. 155)

Christ, who had a carnal weakness for the Church (p. 155)

Christ, who succumbed to the temptation of loving the Church's flesh (p. 155)

Christ, who surrendered to the temptation of delivering himself to the mysterious chaos of a body (p. 155)

Christ, who, with throbbing heart, crossed over temptation's boundary (p. 155)

Christ, united to the Church by carnal love (pp. 155-156)

Christ, conqueror of the Church who resisted him desperately, like a woman (pp. 155-156)

Christ, who entered into an unhappy and bloody wedding with the Church (p. 156)

Christ the lover, an example to follow in married life (p. 152)

Church, who receives the semen of the Word with feminine openness and availability (p. 153)

Church, who like a woman on her bridal bed does not become ruffled (p. 154)

Church, who like a woman on her bridal bed does not close herself (p. 154)

Church, who like a woman on her bridal bed does not make herself rigid (154)

Church, who like a woman on her bridal bed gives and receives in darkness (154)

Church, who like a woman on her bridal bed knows not what she receives and gives birth to (p. 154)

Church, who conceives and begets in abandonment and darkness (p. 154)

Church, who impetuously surrendered to the temptation of the flesh (p. 155)

Church, who became weak for the sake of Christ (p. 155-156)

Church, who assaulted Christ in his nudity (pp. 155-156)

Church, whose sinful battle with Christ became a struggle of love (p. 156)

Church, characterized as a prostitute (p. 139)

Church, represented by Rahab the prostitute (p. 141)

Church, as *casta meretrix*, a chaste prostitute (pp. 143,144)

Church, a venal courtesan who is purchased with gold (pp. 139, 260)

Church, handed over by the Popes to adultery (pp. 139, 260)

Church, transformed into the whore of Babylon (p. 139)

Church, with whom the kings of the world fornicated by the work of the Popes (p. 141)

Church, who became the Great Prostitute (pp. 139-140, 260)

Church, whose union with Christ is symbolized by the union of the prostitute with Osee (pp. 140, 149, 151)

Church, symbolized by the adulterous women of the Old and the New Testaments (p. 140)

Church, who is both a prostitute and the Bride of the Lamb (p. 141, 149)

Church, who strayed far from the purity of the Gospel message (p. 147)

Church, *sancta simul et semper purificanda* (p. 150)

Church, who can never present herself as a class of pure and holy people (p. 150)

Church, in whom nothing is perfect (p. 150)

Church, in whom everything is perishable and uncertain (p. 150)

Church, who need not be a model of high morality to the world (p. 150)

Church, who at night dedicates herself to prostitution (p. 143)

Church, who originates from a sinful element (pp. 144-145)

Church, in whose essence the sinfulness of men plays a profound part (pp. 144-5)

Church, an almost mythological entity, assaulted by the sinfulness of her members (p. 145)

Church, a sinner, guilty for the sins of her members (p. 145)

CHAPTER V

Church, who in her egoism imagined herself unique (p. 163)

Church, triumphalist (p. 161)

Church, isolationist (p. 162)

Church, formalist, legalist and juridicist (p. 162)

Church, unfaithful for being immutable in her institutions and laws (p. 162)

Church, who presents her message as a totalitarian system (p. 164)

Church, clericalist (p. 161)

Church, hypocritical for demanding priestly celibacy (p. 162)

Church, anti-Christian in her way of dealing with married priests (p. 162)

Church, introverted and self-centered (p. 161)

Church, pharisaic for considering Catholics superior to non-Catholics (p. 163b)

Church, dangerously pharisaic and egocentric (pp. 162, 163)

Church, pharisaically demanding that heretics and schismatics return to the true Faith (p. 161)

Church, narcissistic (p. 164)

Church, in whom the fulfillment of Christian mystery is symbolized by Narcissus (p. 165)

Church, isolated and arrogant before the modern world (p. 161)

Church, who must leave her ghetto (p. 161)

Church, who lived fortified behind bastions that must be razed (p. 161)

CHAPTER VI

Church, tyrannical (p. 170)

Church, alienating (p. 170)

Church, authoritarian (pp. 171, 172)

Church, absolutist (pp. 172, 174)

Church, imperialist (p. 172)

Church, despotic (p. 179)

Church, a usurper (p. 172)

Church, an egoist who revels in her lordliness (p. 171)

Church, who tramples men underfoot, mercyless & pityless (p. 171)

Church, whose institutional regime is intolerant (p. 172)

Church, whose institutional regime causes uncertainty and terror (p. 172)

Church, whose institutional regime enslaves men (p. 172)

Church, whose regime is devoid of love (p. 172)

Church, responsible for abuses and crimes (pp. 175-176)

Church, who abused her power (pp. 175-176)

Church, who claims to be "owner" of God's gifts (p. 179)

Church, who is no longer credible (p. 172)

Church, whose institution is an obstacle to truth (p. 172)

Church, whose institution is antiquated and sclerotic (p. 172)

Church, whose constitutions are removed from reality (p. 172)

Church, whose system is dead (p. 172)

Church, who presents the Gospel as an authoritarian system (p. 172)

Church, who used St. Thomas as an instrument of authoritarianism in theology (p. 175)

Church, who imposed theological elaborations (pp. 175-176)

Church, inclined toward dogmatic imperialism (pp. 175-176)

Church, whose ecclesiology is completely mechanical and soulless (p. 174)

Church, whose sensory aspect is monolithic, prefabricated and artificial (p. 174)

Church, whose sentiment is sacramentalist and ritually rigid (p. 174)

Church, whose Roman system of government lacks a biblical basis (p. 172)

Church, whose Faith is an ideological cover for a fixed hierarchical order (p. 176)

Church, whose clergy are obsessed by an obsolete class consciousness (pp. 177, 178)

Church, whose hierarchical institution is horrible (p. 177)

Church, whose hierarchy exercises a blind and dominating authority (p. 171)

Church, whose Bishops and theologians became mandarins (pp. 176-177)

Church, who promotes Integralism (pp. 176-177)

Church, whose colonialist, imperialist and dominating mentality is anachronistic (p. 177)

Church, whose priests hide behind a professional mask (p. 178)

Church, who developed an oppressive feeling of guilt (p. 170)

Church, who stores her treasures in dirty vases (p. 170)

Church, who carries her treasures in filthy hands (p. 170)

Church, whose religion is a caricature (p. 176)

CHAPTER VII

Holy Spirit, whose tempestuous breath must blow away everything old in the Church (p. 189)

Holy Spirit, who must unleash hurricanes in the Church (p. 189)

Holy Spirit, who must unfurl the banners of freedom on the children of God (p. 189)

Church, an old woman doomed to sterility (p. 181)

Church, an old woman who will have the last laugh when she finally conceives (p. 181)

Church, who has an archaic mentality (p. 182)

Church, who suffers from fixism and a repetitive Faith (p. 182)

Church, nostalgic for the 'times of stagnation' (p. 182)

Church, an outdated and obsolete institution (p. 186)

Church, where everything is still, silent and dead (p. 189)

Church, who is like a cadaver (p. 189)

Church, where everything old must disappear (p.189)

Church, who considers any innovator a heretic (p. 189)

Church, where the spirit of the Gospel has lost its attraction (p. 190)

Church, whose joyful and simple language became complicated and obscure (p. 190)

Church, whose theology is a passive and subservient repeater of dogmas (p. 187)

Church, whose teaching of theology was lamentable (p. 182)

Church, whose teaching of theology was abstract and sterile (p. 182)

Church, whose teaching was stuck in a sterile paralysis (pp. 144, 187)

Church, whose teaching was rigid and sclerotic (pp. 186-187)

Church, whose teaching became abstract and intellectualized (p. 190)

Church, whose Magisterium should not be accepted in a passive and unconditional way (p. 187)

Church, whose words are sterile (p. 188)

Church, whose abstract words end by being an opium of the people (p. 191, 192-193)

Church, whose language transformed the lure of the Gospel into a heavy armor of doctrines (p. 190)

Church, whose revolutionary message is the opposite of an analgesic (p. 192)

Church, whose revolutionary message is not an opium of the people (p. 192)

Church, who must stop her civilizing work (pp. 191-192)

Church subversive, whose new message of liberation does not falsely console the people (p. 192)

Church, whose Faith is dead and authoritarian (p. 193)

Church, ritualistic and esoteric, transformed into the "opium of intellectuals" (p. 193)

Church, who appears insignificant to the men of today (p. 188)

Church, who man no longer needs (p. 188)

CHAPTER VIII

Church, in whom nothing is perfect (p. 197-198)

Church, poorest of all the religions (p. 196)

Church, the mother of heretical daughter religions (p. 48)

Church, old and sluggish (p. 197)

Church, backward and vile in spirit (p. 197)

Church, confused and dispersed (p. 197)

Church, whose gaze is blurred (p. 197)

Church, whose faith became too superstitious (p. 197)

Church, whose charity became too legalist (p. 197)

Church, whose hope became too earthly (p. 197)

Church, whose children are all potential heretics (p. 197)

Church, filled with encrypted heresies (p. 197)

Church, formed by sins, like the heresies (p. 197)

Church, filled with rubble and garbage (p. 197)

Church, in whom there are sins and vices (p. 197)

Church, less faithful to the Gospel than the heretical factions (p. 198)

Church, who has less claim to be the true Church of Christ than the heretical factions (p. 198)

Church, whose Christology became inclined to Monophysitism (p. 199)

Church, whose divine elements absorb her human elements (p. 200)

Church, whose concept of God took on something of Pelagianism (p. 202)

Church, who nurtured an unconscious Docetism (p. 202)

Church, who fostered an atemporal, abstract and a-cosmic spirituality (p. 202)

Church, whose notion of grace was Pelagian (p. 202)

Church, whose morality was Jansenist (p. 202)

Church, whose teaching on Revelation was Docetist (p. 203)

Church, sado-masochist in preaching the Cross (p. 205)

Church, whose sexual morality was Stoic (p. 206)

Church of a Christianity intoxicated by a morbid dualism (p. 207)

Church, whose dogmas are arbitrary and biased (p. 209)

CHAPTER IX

Papacy, an absurd institution (p. 217)

Papacy, an immovable, insurmountable obstacle to ecumenism (p. 217)

Papacy, with its attitude of lordly absolutism (p. 217)

Papacy, a creation of history (p. 212)

Pope, who must be divested of the myth of infallibility (p. 212)

Pope, whose infallibility was fruit of Romanticism (p. 216)

Pope, whose pyramidal structure generated papolatry (p. 215)

Pope, who proliferated the servile spirit of byzantinism (p. 215)

Pope, who should be criticized as naturally as one criticizes a schoolmaster (p. 216)

Pope, the object of a devotion that has caused the church to suffer (p. 212)

Pope, the object of a devotion that is an unconscious and 'insupportable papolatry' (p. 212)

Pope, the object of a devotion that was a veritable adulation (p. 212)

Pope, the object of a devotion with unquestionably mediocre excesses (p. 215)

Pius IX, condemnable for calling the suppression of the Pontifical States sacrilegious (p. 217)

Pius IX, condemnable for stigmatizing the Modernists as his enemies (p. 217)

Pius IX, condemnable for imposing his personal thinking on Vatican Council I through morally questionable means (p. 217)

Pius X, who reacted excessively against Modernism (p. 217)

Pius X, who caused the Church to fold in and close herself off (p. 218)

Pius X, who caused the 'white terrror' (p. 218)

John XXIII, who ended the spiritual dictatorship that existed in the Church (p. 217)

Paul VI, who brought an end to 'papolatry' (pp. 212-213)

Paul VI, who introduced a climate of freedom in the Church (p. 213)

Paul VI, who was open to positive dialogue with the Communist movements (p. 218)

CHAPTER X

Church, whose theological language is closed and esoteric (p. 222)

Church, whose theology is nothing but pre-theological figurations (p. 225)

Church, whose theology is nothing but ideological poetry (pp. 225-226)

Church, whose theology is an array of unprovable myths (pp. 225-226)

Church, whose dogmatic teaching is a confused and complicated system (p. 226)

Church, whose Scholastic theology was used as an instrument of power (p. 226)

Church, whose Scholastic theology wasted time on futile questions (p. 228-229)

Church, whose teaching of Scholasticism became abstract and remote (p. 229)

Church, whose teaching of Scholasticism became rationally burdensome (p. 230)

Church, whose teaching of Scholasticism became psychologically dishonest (p. 230)

Church, whose outdated and narrow teaching of Scholasticism had to be overcome (p. 227)

Church, who owes Voltaire for abandoning a primitive theology (p. 228)

Church, who owes Voltaire for presenting a new history of secular civilization (p. 228)

Church, whose traditional theology is an old cloth that can no longer be patched with new fabric (p. 229)

Church, whose traditional theology is an old wineskin into which new wine should no longer be poured (p. 229)

Church, whose theology was in a state of underdevelopment (p. 227)

Church, whose old doctrinal foundations are no longer valid (p. 228)

Church, whose old doctrinal foundations are no longer useful (p. 228)

Church, whose pre-conciliar doctrine on Revelation was imprisoned in rationalism (p. 227)

Church, who presented Revelation as a collection of truths like geometry theorems (p. 227)

Church, whose deductive, static and universal theology did not permit criticisms (p. 229)

Church, whose conception of Revelation was abstract, Scholastic and lifeless (p. 227)

Church, whose doctrinal formulas are useless because they claim to be immutable (p. 228)

CHAPTER XI

Church, whose excessive centralization in Rome led to a pernicious uniformity (p. 234)

Church, whose excessive centralization in Rome led to a sterile rigidity (p. 234)

Church, whose excessive centralization in Rome led to a sinful Pharisaism (p. 234)

Church, whose theologians unanimously pronounce her guilty for her past (p. 234)

Church, who becomes marginal when she rejects liberty sought by means of revolt against any form of coercion (p. 234)

Church, who becomes marginal when she does not abolish her vestiges of aristocracy or feudalism (p. 234)

Church, whose theologians unanimously pronounce her sectarian (p. 234)

Church, doomed to be a small sect if she tries to achieve a homogeneous theology (p. 238)

Church, doomed to be a sect if she affirms that God is the answer to all of man's questions and needs (p. 236)

Church, whose theology became sectarian by ignoring progressivist thinking (p. 237)

Church, whose perennial theology is a sectarian orthodoxy (p. 238)

Church, whose quest for internal perfection characterizes a sectarian mentality (p. 238)

Roman Church, who gradually assumed the appearance of a sect (p. 239)

Church, who by despising the world or seeking refuge from it, becomes a sect (p. 239)

Church, who was not in tune with the world before Vatican II (p. 235)

Church, who assumed a sectarian attitude with regard to science, philosophy and politics (p. 240)

Church, whose rejection of ecumenism is a rigid and sectarian position (p. 242-243)

Church, whose centralization in Rome reduced her to a ghetto (p. 234)

Church, who must dialogue with the world in order to leave her ghetto (p. 235)

Church, who will become a ghetto if she tries to return to the homogeneous society of the past (p. 237)

Church who will become a ghetto if she is not open to the other religions (p. 237)

Church, who will become a ghetto if she does not open herself to the signs of the time (p. 238)

Church, who takes on a ghetto mentality by intransigently attaching herself to definitive formulas (p. 241)

Church, who closes herself in a triumphalist ghetto by adhering to an excessively European Christianity (p. 242)

Church, who left the ghetto and became a community open to the world at Vatican II (pp. 235, 239)

Church, whose members want to leave the ghetto to become citizens of the world (p. 242)

Church, who must place herself at the service of the world and leave her ghetto (p. 238)

Church, sterile and egocentric because she failed to open herself to the world (pp. 234, 238, 239)

Church, marginalized in our culture (p. 239)

Church, who betrays her mission by failing to recognize the signs of the time (p. 241)

Church, who fostered schizophrenia by separating herself from the world (pp. 245-246)

Church, relieved of her schizophrenia by Vatican II (pp. 245-6)

*　*　*

BIBLIOGRAPHY

ACTA APOSTOLICAE SEDIS (AAS) - commentarium officiale. Vatican City: Libreria editrice vaticana, 1909. **ABBOTT, Walter M. & GALLAGHER, J.** - *The Documents of Vatican II,* Piscataway, NJ: New Century Publishers, Inc., 1966. **ACERBI, Antonio** - *Due ecclesiolgoie,* Bologna: Dehoniane, 1975. **ALDAMA, José** - Entry "Mariologia," in V.A., *Sacrae Theologiae Summa.* **ALEXANDER VIII** - *Decree of the Holy Office* of December 7, 1690, in DS. **ALFRINK, Bernard** - Intervention in the Conciliar Hall of November 5, 1964, in R. Laurentin, *L'enjeu du Concile.* **ALSZEGHY, Zoltán** - *See* Flick, Maurizio. **ALTING VON GEUSAU, Leo** - *See* Geusau, Leo von Alting. **AMBROSE, St.** - *Expositionis in Evangelium secundum Lucam* and *De Virginitate, apud* PL, in H. U. von Balthasar, *Casta meretrix.* **ANONYMOUS** - *Il Programma dei Modernisti,* Turin: Fratelli Bocca, 1911. **AQUINAS, St. Thomas** - *De regimine principum,* in *Opuscula philosophica,* Turin/ Rome: Marietti, 1954; *De venerabili Sacramento altaris,* Rome: Marietti, 1939; *In Aritotelis librum de anima,* Rome: Marietti, 1948; *In Symbolum Apostolorum expositio,* Rome: Marietti, 1954; *Quaestiones disputatae,* Turin/Rome: Marietti, 1949; *Super libros sententiarum,* Paris: L. Lethielleux, 1929-1933; *Summa contra gentiles.* Rome: Marietti, 1934; *Summa Theologiae,* 4 vols., Turin/Rome: Marietti, 1948; *Super Epistolam Pauli, II ad Corinthios* and *Super Epistolam Pauli ad Hebraeos,* in *Super Epistolas S. Pauli lecturae,* 2 vols, Turin/Rome, Marietti, 1953. **AUBERT, Roger** - "La theologie catholique durant la première moitié du XXe. siècle," in V.A., *Bilan de la théologie au XXe. Siècle.* **AUGÉ, Claude,** ed. - *Nouveau Larousse illustré – Dictionnaire universel encyclopédique,* 7 vols. and 1 supplement, Paris: Larousse, 1897-1904. **AUGUSTINE, St.** - *Sermo 181, apud* PL, in H. U. von Balthasar, *Casta meretrix.*

BALTHASAR, Hans Urs von - *Abbattere i bastioni.* Turin: Borla, 1966; *A face mariana da Igreja,* in Wolfgang Beinert; *Casta meretrix,* Brescia: Morcelliana, 1969; "Eschatologie," in V.A., *Questions théologiques aujourd'hui; La gloire et la croix - Les aspects esthétiques de la Révélation - II Styles: De Jean de la Croix à Péguy,* Paris: Aubier-Montaigne, 1972; "La mia opera è abbozata più che terminata," *L'Osservatore Romano,* June 25-26,1984; *Le coeur du monde,* Paris: Desclée de Brouwer, 1956; *De l'intégration - Aspects d'une théologie de l'histoire,* Bruges: Desclée de Brouwer, 1970; *Mysterium paschale,* in V.A., *Mysterium salutis; Parole et mystère chez Origine; Théologie de l'histoire,* Paris: Plon, 1960. **BARDY, Gustave** - "Les Églises de Perse et d'Arménie au VIe. Siècle," in V.A., *Histoire de l'Église;* entry "Manichéisme," in DTC; "Saint Jean de Constantinople," in V.A., *Histoire de l'Église.* **BARTZ, Wilhelm** - *Sekten heute - Lehre, Organisation, Verbreitung,* Fribourg in Breisgau: Herder, 1967. **BAUM, Gregory** - 'La presenza della Chiesa nella società di domani," in V.A., *L'avvenire della Chiesa.* **BEINERT, Wolfgang** - *O culto a Maria hoje,* São Paulo, Paulinas, 1979. **BELLARMINE, St. Robert** - *De Ecclesia Militante,* in C. Journet, *L'Église du Verbe Incarné; Opera omnia,* 8 vols., Palermo/Naples/Paris: Pedone Lauriel, 1872. **BERAN, Joseph** - Intervention in the conciliar hall of September 20, 1965, in R. Laurentin, *Bilan du Concile, cronique de la quatrième session.* **BERNARD, St.** - *Obras Completas,* Madrid: BAC, 1955; *Sermo in Canticum Canticorum,* apud PL in H. U. von Balthasar, *Casta meretrix; Sermo in Nativitate, Beatae Mariae Virginis: De acquaeductu,* in PL. **BERNARDINO OF SIENA, St.** - *Quadragesimale de Evangelio eterno,* in DS. **BESCHERELLE, M.** - *Dictionnaire National,* Paris: Garnier-Frères, 1871. **BILLOT, Louis** - *De Ecclesia Christi,* Rome: Aedis Universitatis Gregorianae, 1921, in C. Journet, *L'Église du Verbe Incarneé.* **BILLUART, René** - *Summa Sancti Thomae,* 10 vols., Ibanel et Martin, 1839. **BOFF, Leonardo** -

O rosto materno de Deus - Ensaio interdisciplinar sobre o feminino e suas formas religiosas, Petrópolis: Vozes, 1979. **BONIFACE VIII** - Bull *Unam Sanctam* of November 18, 1302, in *DTC.* **BOURGET, Paul** - *Outre-Mer,* Paris: Plon-Nourrit, 1894. **BOUYER, Louis** - *A decomposição do Catolicismo,* Lisbon: Sampedro, n.d. **BRECHT, Bertolt** - *Der Kleine Brockhaus,* Wiesbaden, 1961. **BRIÉRE, Yves de la** - *Le droit de juste guerre,* Paris: Pedone, 1938. **BROWN, Raymond E.** - *The Birth of the Messiah,* New York: Garden City, 1977. **BUTLER, Christopher Basil** - Article on devotion to Our Lady, *Il Tempo,* October 28, 1963, in R. Laurentin, *Bilan de la deuxième session.* **BUTTIGLIONE, Rocco** - *Il pensiero di Karol Wojtyla,* Milan: Jaca Books, 1982.

CAPOVILA, Loris - "Quelle humour denso di umiltà," *Avvenire,* November 20, 1992. **CAPRILE, Giovanni** - *Il Concilio Vaticano II,* 3 vols., Rome: La Civiltà Cattolica, 1964. **CARDONNEL, Jean** - Declaration, *Historia* (Paris), October 1982. **CASAROLI, Agostino** - "Lettera del Card. Casaroli al rettore dell'Istituto Cattolico di Parigi," *L'Osservatore Romano,* June 10, 1981. *CATHOLIC ENCYCLOPEDIA* - 16 vols., NY: Encyclopedia Press, Inc., 1913. **CELAM** - *A Igreja na atual transformação da América Latina à luz do Council - Conclusões de Medellin,* Petrópolis: Vozes, 1980. **CHAFAREVITCH, Igor** - *Le phénomène socialiste,* Paris: Seuil, 1977. **CHARDIN, Teilhard de** - *Le coeur de la matière,* Paris: Seuil, 1976; *Le milieu divin,* Paris: Seuil, 1957. **CHATEAUBRIAND, François-René** - *Memoires d'outre tombe,* 2 vols., Librairie Générale Française, 1973. **CHENU, Marie-Dominique** - "La Chiesa e il mondo," in V.A., *I grandi temi del Concili;* "The History of Salvation and the Historicity of Man in the Renewal of Theology," in V. A., *Theology of Renewal - Renewal of Religious Thought.* **CLAEYS-BOUUAERT, F.** - Entry 'Evêques,' in *DTC.* **CLEMENT of Alexandria** - *Stromata VII,* in H. U. von Balthasar, *Casta meretrix.* **CNBB** - *Código de Direito Canônico* of 1983. Official translation of the National Conference of Brazilian Bishops, São Paulo: Loyola,1983. *CODEX IURIS CANONICI* of 1917 - Rome: Typis Polyglottis Vaticanis, 1919. **COMBLIN, Joseph** - "La théologie catholique depuis la fin du pontificat de Pie XII," in V.A., *Bilan de la théologie au XXe siècle.* **CONCETTI, Gino** - "La teologia al servizio del magistero," *L'Osservatore Romano,* December 23, 1988. **CONGAR, Yves** - *Église Catholique et France moderne,* Paris: Hachette, 1978; *La crisi nella Chiesa e Mons. Lefèbvre,* Bresica: Queriniana, 1976; *La parole et le souffle,* Paris: Desclée, 1984; *Le Concile au jour le jour – Deuxième session,* Paris: Cerf, 1964; *L'ecclésiologie de la Révolution Française au Concile du Vatican, sous le signe de l'affirmation de l'autorité,* in V.A., *L'ecclésiologie au XIXe. Siècle;* "Le rôle de l'Église dans le monde de ce temps," in V.A., *L'Eglise dans le monde de ce temps;* "Os grupos informais na Igreja," in Afonso Gregory, *Comunidades eclesiais de base - Utopia ou realidade; Pour une Eglise servante et pauvre,* Paris: Cerf, 1963; "Salvación y liberación," in V.A., *Conversaciones de Toledo - Teología de la liberación; Un people messianique,* Paris: Cerf, 1975; *Vraie et fausse reforme dans l'Eglise,* Paris: Ed. du Cerf, 1950; "1960-1970: Dix annés décisives pour l'Église et pour le monde," *ICI,* January 1,1970; Interview granted to the Author in Paris, February 19, 1983. **CONGAR, Yves & Girardi, Giulio** - "Dialogue entre les Pères Congar et Girardi - 1960-1970: Dix années décisives pour l'Eglise et pour le monde," *ICI,* January 1, 1970. **CONGREGATION FOR THE DOCTRINE OF THE FAITH** - "In margine alle osservazioni sul documento dell'ARCIC-II," *L'Osservatore Romano,* November 20, 1988. **CORRÊA DE OLIVEIRA, Plinio** - *A Igreja ante a escalada da ameaça comunista – Apelo aos bispos silenciosos,* São Paulo: Vera Cruz, 1976; *Reforma agrária - Questão de consciencia,* in collaboration with A.C. Mayer, G.P. Sigaud and L.M. Freitas, São Paulo: Vera Cruz, 1960; "Projeto de constituição angustia o País," *Catolicismo,* October 1987; *Nobility and the Traditional Analogous Elites in the allocutions of Pius*

XII to the Patriciate and the Roman Nobility, York, PA: The American Society for the Defense of Tradition, Family and Property, 1993; *Revolution and Counter-Revolution,* York: American Society for the Defense of Tradition, Family and Property, 1993; *Sou católico: Posso ser contra a reforma agrária?* in collaboration with C.D. Campo, São Paulo, Vera Cruz, 1981. *COUNCIL OF TRENT* - Petrópolis: Vozes, 1959; *Catecismo romano,* Petrópolis: Vozes, 1962. *COUNCIL OF VIENNE* - Constitution *De Summa Trinitate et Fide Catholica,* in DR. **CYPRIAN, St.** - *De unitate Ecclesia,* apud PL 4 in H. U. von Balthasar, *Casta meretrix.*

DANIÉLOU, Jean - *Rahab, figure de l'Eglise* in H. de Manoir, *Sacramentum futuri,* Paris: Beauchesne,1950; *Theologie du judéo-christianisme,* Tournai: Desclée et cie, 1958. *Dante* Alighieri - *La divina commedia,* Turin: Giulio Einaudi, 1954. **DELHAYE, Philippe** - "Histoire des textes de la Constitution pastorale," in V.A., *L'Église dans le monde de ce temps;* Interview granted to the Author, Louvain-la-Neuve, Belgium, February 28, 1983. **(D) DENZINGER, Henricus** - *Enchiridion Symbolorum,* first published 1854. **(DR) DENZINGER, Henricus & Rahner, Carolus** - The Denzinger collection updated by K. Rahner between 1946 and 1954. **(DS) DENZINGER, Heinricus & Schönmetzer, Adolphus** - The Denzinger collection with additions by A. Schönmetzer between 1955 and 1965, Friburg/Breisgau/Barcelone: Herder, 1965. **DESROCHE, Henri** - "Sciences des religions et théologie chrétienne," in V.A., *Bilan de la théologie du XXe.siècle. DICTIONNAIRE DE LA LANGUE PHILOSOPHIQUE,* Paris: Presses Universitaires de France, 1962. **DIWALD, Hellmut** - *Luther - Eine Biographie,* Bergisch Gladach: Gustav Lübbe Verlag, 1982. **DÖPFNER, Julius** - *La Chiesa vivente oggi,* Bari: Paoline, 1972. *DICTIONNAIRE DE THEOLOGIE CATHOLIQUE* **(DTC)** - ed by A Vacant & E. Mangenot, Paris: Letouzey et Ane, 1923-1972. **DUBLANCHY, Edmond** - Entry "Église," in *DTC.* **DUHAMEL, Joseph-Thomas** - *Lettre pastorale* (Ottawa), 5th series. **DULLES, Avery** - "Ecumenismo: Problemi e possibilità per il futuro," in V.A.,*Verso la Chiesa del terzo millennio.* **DUQUOC, Christian** - "Um paraíso na terra?" *Concilium,* 1979/3. **DUQUESNE, Jacques** - *Jacques Duquesne interroge le Père Chenu – Une théologie en liberté,* Paris: Centurion, 1975. **DIONYSIUS THE CARTHUSIAN** - *In canticum,* in H. U. von Balthasar, *Casta meretrix.* **DYONISIUS THE AEREOPAGITE, St.** - *La hierárchie céleste,* Paris: Cerf, 1970.

EDELBY, Neophytos - Conference in Rome of October 24, 1963, in H. Fesquet, *Le journal du Concile;* Intervention in the conciliar hall of October 5, 1964, in B. Kloppenburg, *Concílio Vaticano II.* **EGAN, Harvey D.** - *What Are They Saying about Mysticism?* New York/Ramsey: Paulist Press, 1982. **ELCHINGER, Léon Arthur** - Intervention in the conciliar hall of October 21, 1964 and intervention in the conciliar hall of November 4, 1964, in B. Kloppenburg, *Concílio Vaticano II. ENCICLOPEDIA UNIVERSAL ILUSTRADA* - 82 vols., Bilbao/Madrid/Barcelona: Espasa Calpe, 1930-1956. **EPIPHANIUS, St.** - *Adversus haereses,* in *DTC.* **EYT, Pierre** - "Igreja e mutaçöes sócio-culturais," in V.A., *A Igreja do futuro.* **FAVALE, Agostino** - ed. *Movimenti ecclesiali contemporanei,* Rome: LAS 1982.

FEDERICI, Tommaso - "Religione e religioni oggi," in V.A., *Incontro tra le religioni.* **FEINER, Johannes & Löhrer, Magnus** - *Mysterium salutis,* Petrópolis: Vozes, 1974. **FERREIRA, Aurélio B. H.** - *Pequeno Dicionário Brasileiro da Lingua Portuguesa,* Rio de Janeiro: Civ. Bras., 1968. **FESQUET, Henri** - *Le journal du Concile.* Forcalquier: Robert Morel, 1966. **FESSIO, Joseph** - "Cardinal Ratzinger Asks for Help," in Catalog, San Francisco: Ignatius Press, 1990. **FITZMYER, Joseph A.** - *To Advance the Gospel,* New York: Crossroads, 1981. **FLICHE, Augustin & Martin, Victor** - *Histoire de l'Église depuis les origines jusqu'à nos jours,* Paris:

Bloud & Gay, 1946; **FLICHE, Augustin, Foreville, Raymond & Rousset, Jean** - *Du premier Concile du Latran à l'avènement d'Innocent III, in* V.A., *Histoire de l'Église.* **FLICK, Maurizio & Alszeghy, Zoltán** - *Il mistero della croce - Saggio di teologia sitematica,* Brescia: Queriniana, 1978. **FOGAZZARO, Antonio** - *Il santo,* Milan, 1907. **FONCK, A.** - Entry "Lamennais," in *DTC.* **FOREVILLE, Raymond** - "Les grands courants hérétiques et les premières mesures générales de répression," in V.A., *Histoire de l'Église; see also* Augustin Fliche. **FOULQUIÉ, Paul** - *Dictionnaire de la Langue Philosophique,* Paris: Presses Universitaires de France, 1962. **FRANCIS DE SALES, St.** - *Traitè de l'amour de Dieu,* in *Oeuvres completes,* Paris: Vivès, 1866. **FRANZINI, Alberto** - *Tradizione e Scrittura - Il contributo del Concilio Vaticano II* Brescia: Morcelliana, 1978. **FRINGS, Joseph** - Intervention in the conciliar hall of November 8, 1963, in B. Kloppenburg, *Concilio Vaticano II; Lettre pastorale de Carême,* in Y. Congar, *Pour une Eglise servante et pauvre.* **FRITZ, Georges** - Entry "Origenisme," in *DTC.* **FROMM, Erich** - *Psicoanálysis de la sociedad contemporánea,* Mexico: Fondo de Cultura Economica Usa, 1956. **FROSSARD, André** - "Cos'é un Papa?" *L'Osservatore Romano,* March 23, 1989. **FUCHS, Joseph** - Interview granted to the Author, Rome, February 4, 1983.

GALLI, Mario von - "La relación con las religions mundiales," in V.A. *La reforma que llega de Roma.* **GALOT, Jean** - *A mulher na obra das salvação,* Ed. Universidade Gregoriana, 1984. **GAY, Jean** - Intervention in the conciliar hall of November 26, 1963, in B. Kloppenburg, *Concílio Vaticano II.* **GEUSAU, Leo Alting von** - Alcune idée sulla mariologia attuale, in V.A., I grandi temi del Concilio; "La Chiesa, 'scandalo' del mondo," in V.A., La fine della Chiesa come società perfetta. **GIRARDIL, Giulio** - See Congar, Yves. **GORCE, Marcel Maxime** - Entry "Savonarole," in *DTC.* **GREGORY, Afonso** - *Comunidades eclesiais de base - Utopia ou realidade,* Petrópolis: Vozes, 1973. **GREGORY THE GREAT, St.** - *Expositio super canticum canticorum, apud* PL in in H. U. von Balthasar, *Casta meretrix.* **GREGORY XVI** - Encyclical *Mirari vos* of August 15, 1832, in *DR.* **GREINACHER, Norbert** - "Aspetti sociologici dell'autorealizzazione della Chiesa," in V.A., *Chiesa, uomo e società.* **GUERRY, E.** - *Lettre Pastorale,* D.C., 1963, in Y. Congar, *Pour une Eglise servante et pauvre.* **GUIMARÃES, Atila Sinke** - *Collection: Eli, Eli, Lamma Sabactani?*: Volume I, *In the Murky Waters of Vatican II,* Los Angeles: TIA, 2008; Volume. III, *Animus Injuriandi II;* Volume IV, *Animus Delendi I,* Los Angeles: TIA, 2000; Volume V, *Animus Delendi II,* Los Angeles: TIA, 2002; Volume VI, *Inveniet Fidem?,* Los Angeles: TIA, 2007; Volume VII, *Destructio Dei;* Volume VIII, *Fumus Satanae;* Volume XI, *Ecclesia,* Los Angeles: TIA, 2009; *The End of the Myth of Galileo,* Los Angeles: TIA, 2005; Interview with Yves Congar, Paris, February 19, 1983; Interview with Msgr. Philippe Delhaye, Louvain-la-Neuve (Belgium), February 28 and March 1,1983; Interview with Joseph Fuchs, Rome, February 4, 1983.

HÄRING, Bernard - *Pastorale dei divorziati. Una strada senza uscita?* Bologna: Dehoniane, 1990. **HAVARD DE LA MONTAGNE, Robert** - *Histoire de la Démocratie Chrétienne de Lamennais à George Bidault,* Paris: Amiot & Dumont, 1948. **HEDDE, Rene** - Entry "Lollards," in *DTC.* **HEILER, Friedrich** - *Die Frau in den Religionen der Menschheit,* Berlin, 1977. **HILARY, St.** - *Liber mysteriorum, de Adam, apud* PL in H. U. von Balthasar, *Casta meretrix.* **HOLZER, Anton Holzer** - *Vatikanum II - Reformkonzil oder Konstituante einer neuen Kirche,* Basel: Saka, 1967. **HOMER** - *Odyssey,* trans. by E.V. Rieu, New York: Penguin Books, 1982. **HORTELANO, Antonio** - "Rivoluzione sessuale e famiglia," *Concilium,* 1984/3. **HUGO, Victor** - *Les misérables,* 2 vols. Paris: Garnier-Flammarion, 1967. **HUIZING, Peter** - "Vaticano III: una costituzione sulla Chiesa," in V.A., *Verso la Chiesa del terzo millennio.* **HUYGHE, Gerard** - Intervention in the conciliar hall of October 27, 1964, in B. Kloppenburg, *Concílio Vaticano II.*

INFORMATIONS CATHOLIQUES INTERNATIONALES (ICI) - (Paris). IONDINI, Massimo - "L'Angelo della semplicità," *Avvenire*, June 1,1993. IRIARTE, J. J. - Interview, *Le Monde*, January 6, 1963, in Y. Congar, *Pour une Eglise servante et pauvre.*

JAMES, Edwin Oliver - *The Cult of the Mother-Goddess*, London: Thames & Hudson, 1959. JANIN, R. - Entry "Pauliciens," in *DTC*. JEANSON, Francis - *La foi d'un incroyant*, Seuil, 1963. JEROME, St. - *Commentaria in Ezechielem Prophetam, apud* PL in H. U. von Balthasar, in *Casta meretrix; Praefacium in librum de nominibus haebraicis* and *Prologues* to the translations of Origen in *Commentaries on Micheah, Epistle to the Ephesians;* entry "Origenismo," in *Enciclopédia Universal Ilustrada*. JOHN XXII - Constitution *Cum inter nonnullos* of November 13, 1323, in *DR*; Constitution *Gloriosam Ecclesiam* of January 23, 1318 in *DR*. JOHN XXIII - Encyclical *Ad Petri cathedram* of June 29, 1959, in AAS; Opening Speech of the Council, October 11, 1962, in Abbott, Walter, *The Documents of Vatican II*.

JOHN PAUL II - Allocution to the Lutheran temple of Warsaw of June 9, 1991, titled "Il dovere de rispondire alla volontà di Cristo esige che restiano saldi sulla via verso l'unità tra i cristiani," *L'Osservatore Romano*, June 10-11, 1991; Allocution to the representatives of the academic world of the University of Vilnius of September 5, 1993, titled "Tra la Chiesa e la cultura è necessaria e urgente una 'nuova alleanza,'" *L'Osservatore Romano*, September 6-7, 1993; Allocution to the representatives of the cultural world in Prague of April 21, 1990, titled "Gli eventi de cui siamo testimoni dimostrano che l'Europa unità non è un'utopia del Medio Evo ma un traguardo raggiungibile," *L'Osservatore Romano*, April 23-24, 1990; Allocution to the Vicars of Rome of January 9, 1959, in Maximus IV, Letter to Msgr. Pericle Felici; Allocution to the writers of *La Civiltà Cattolica* of January 19, 1990, *L'Osservatore Romano*, January 20, 1990; Allocution to the youth in Belo Horizonte, of July 1, 1980, in *Todos os pronunciamentos do Papa ao Brasil*, São Paulo: Loyola, 1980; General audience of July 4, 1984, titled "Il 'grande mistero' dell'amore sponsale," *L'Osservatore Romano*, July 5, 1984. *Código de Direito Canônico* of 1983, see CNBB; General audience of October 15, 1980, titled "Valori evangelici e doveri del cuore umano," *L'Osservatore Romano*, October 16, 1980; General audience of October 22, 1980, titled "Realizzazione del valore del corpo secondo il disegno del Creatore," *L'Osservatore Romano*, October 23, 1980; *Insegnamenti di Giovanni Paolo II*, 18 vols., Lib. Ed. Vaticana, 1983; *Motu Proprio Tradecim anni iam* of August 6, 1982, in *Insegnamenti di Giovanni Paolo II*; Reflection on the grand jubilee of 2000, titled "La nave di Pietro fa rotta verso il duemila – Il documento riservato inviato ai cardinali per il concistoro de giugno," *Adista*-DOC, May 28, 1994; "Riflessioni sul grand giubileo dell'anno duemila," in "La nave di Pietro fa rotta verso il duemila," *Adista-DOC*, May 28, 1994; "Un'Europa unita dalla fede in Cristo," September 10, 1983, in *Insegnamenti di Giovanni Paolo II*. JOSSUA, Jean-Pierre - *Dalla teologia al teologo, in* V.A., *L'avvenire della Chiesa*. JOURNET, Charles - *L'Église du Verbe Incarné*, Desclée de Brouwer, 1962.

KELLER, L. - *Johann von Staupitz und die Anfänge der Reformation*, Leipzig, 1888, in I. Chafarevitch, *Le phénomène socialiste*. KINDT, Gerardo - *De potestate dominativa in religione*, Bruges/Paris/Rome: Desclée de Brouwer, 1945. KLOPPENBURG, Boaventura - *A eclesiologia do Vaticano II*, Petrópolis: Vozes, 1971; *Concílio Vaticano II*, 5 vols., Petrópolis: Vozes, 1966. KLOSTERMANN, Ferdinand - "Princípi per una riforma di struttura della Chiesa," in V. A., *La fine della Chiesa come società perfetta*. KOLLER, Erwin - "Cento domande a von Balthasar," *30 Giorni*, 1984/6. KÖNIG, Franz - "Il Concilio sorpresa per il mondo," *Avvenire*,

October 16, 1992; Intervention in the conciliar hall of September 28, 1965, in H. Fesquet, *Le journal du Concile.* **KÜNG, Hans** - *A Igreja,* 2 vols., Lisbon: Morales,1970; Editorial "Maria nas Igrejas," *Concilium,* 1983/8; "Qual è il messaggio cristiano?"- in V.A., *L'avvenire della Chiesa; Veracidade, o futuro de Igreja,* São Paulo: Herder, 1969. **KUSCHEL, Karl-Josef** - "Maria e a literatura," *Concilium,* 1983/8.

LALANDE, Andre - *Vocabulaire technique et critique de la philosophie,* Paris, 1960. **LAPIDE, Cornelius a** - *Commentaria in Scripturam Sacram,* 24 vols., Paris: Ludovicus Vives, 1874-1877. **LAROUSSE, Pierre, ed.** - *Grand Dictionnaire Universel du XIXe siècle,* 27 vols., Paris: Larousse: 1866-1877. **LAURENTIN, René** - *L'enjeu du Concile, bilan des quatre sessions et bilan général,* 5 vols., Paris: Éditions du Seuil, 1963-1966. **LEBRETON, Jules** - "L'apologétique chrétienne au IIe siècle," "L'Église d'Alexandrie après Origène," "L'Église d'Antioche à la fin du IIIe. siècle," "Les controverses romaines à la fin du IIe et au début du IIIe siècle," and "Les écrivains chrétiens d'Afrique," in A. Fliche and V. Martin, *Histoire de l'Église.* **LEEUW, G. van der** - *Fenomenologia de la religion,* Mexico: Fondo de Cultura Economica, 1964. **LÉGER, Paul-Émile** - Intervention in the conciliar hall of September 16, 1964, in B. Kloppenburg, *Concilio Vaticano II.* **LEO XIII** - Encyclical *Divinum illud munus,* in C. Journet, *L'Église du Verbe Incarneé;* Encyclical *Immortale Dei* of November 1, 1885, Petrópolis: Vozes, 1954; Encyclical *Mirare caritatis* of May 28, 1902, Petrópolis: Vozes, 1952; Encyclical *Quod apostolici muneris* of December 28, 1878, in AAS; Encyclical *Rerum novarum* of May 15, 1891, in AAS; Encyclical *Sapientiae christianae,* in AAS; Encyclical *Satis cognitum* of June 29, 1896, Petrópolis: Vozes, 1960; **LERCHER, Ludwig** - *Institutiones theologiae dogmaticae,* Barcelona: Herder, 1951. **LEVILLAIN, Philip** - *La mécanique politique du Vatican II,* Paris: Beauchesne, 1975. **LICHERI, Gianni** - *Chiesa dove vai? – Gianni Licheri interroga il Cardinale Franz Koenig,* Rome: Borla, 1985. **LIÉGÉ, André** - "A Igreja diante de seu pecado," in V. A., *A Igreja do futuro.* **LLORCA, Bernardino** - *Manual de Historia Eclesiastica,* Barcelona: Edit. Labor., 1942. **LOBO, Arturo Alonso** - "Comentários al libro segundo del CDC," in V.A., *Comentarios al Codigo de Derecho Canonico.* **LOEW, Jacques** - Lecture in Rome on October 22, 1965, in H. Fesquet, *Le journal du Concile.* **LÖHRER, Magnus** - See Johannes Feiner. **LONERGAN, Bernard** - "Theology in its New Context," in V.A., *Theology of Renewal.* **LUBAC, Henri de** - *Catholicisme – Les aspects sociaux du dogme,* Paris: Cerf, 1968; *Entrétien autour de Vatican II,* Paris: Cerf, 1985; *L'éternel féminin – Étude sur un texte du Pére Teilhard de Chardin,* Paris: Aubier/Montaigne, 1968; *Paradoxe et mystère de l'Église,* Paris: Aubier-Montaigne, 1967. **LUCAS-DUBRETON, J.** - *Béranger - La chanson, la politique, la société,* Paris: Hachette, 1934. **LUTHER, Martin** - *Ausgewählte Schriften,* ed. by Karin Bornkamm and Gerhard Ebeling, Frankfort: Insel Verlag.

MALDONADO, Luis - *Genesis del Catolicismo popular – El inconsciente colectivo de un proceso histórico,* Madrid: Cristiandad, 1979; *Introducción a la religiosidad popular,* Santander: Sal Terrae, 1985; *La violencia de lo sagrado,* Salamanca: Sígueme, 1974. **MALINSKI, Mieczyslaw** - *Mon ami Karol* Wojtyla, Paris: Centurion, 1980. **MALONEY, George** - "A oração e o divino pessoal," *Concilium,* 1977/3. **MANOIR, H., ed.** *Marie - Études sur la Sainte Vierge,* 8 vols. Paris, 1949-1971. **MARCHESI, Giovanni** - "La teologia di Hans Urs von Balthasar," *La Civiltà Cattolica,* January 1, 1977; "L'influsso di de Lubac su von Balthasar," *La Civiltà Cattolica,* May 17, 1997. **MARCUS, Émile** - *O que é evangelizar?,* in V.A., *A Igreja do futuro.* **MARLÉ, René** - "Nuovo linguaggio della fede?" *La Civiltà Cattolica,* June 5, 1971. **MARRANZINI, Alfredo** - "Karl Rahner ha avvicinato la teologia alle necessità spirituali dei contemporanei," *L'Osservatore Romano,* April 6,1984. **MARTELET, Gustave** -

Press statement of October 30, 1965, *in* H. Fesquet, *Le journal du Concile*. **MAR-TIN, Victory** - see Augustin Fliche. **MARTINA, Giacomo** - "Le contexte historique dans lequel a surgi l'idée d'un nouveau Concile Oecuménique," in V.A., *Vatican II: Bilan et perspectives*. **MARX, Karl** - *Contribution to the Critique of Hegel's 'Philosophy of Right,'* Cambridge: University Press, 1970. **MAXIMUS IV** - Interventions in the conciliar hall of November 14, 1962 and December 5, 1962, in V.A., *A Igreja Greco-Melquita no Concílio;* Intervention in the conciliar hall of November 19, 1963, in H. Fesquet, *Le Journal du Concile;* Intervention in the conciliar hall of October 27, 1964, in B. Kloppenburg, *Concílio Vaticano II;* Note to the preparatory commission of Vatican II in May 1962, in V. A., *A Igreja Greco-Melquita no Concilio*. **MAY, William E.** May - "Le opinioni di P. Bernhard Häring sulla pastorale dei divorziati risposati," *L'Osservatore Romano*, March 6, 1991. **MCKENZIE, John** - "The Mother of Jesus in the New Testament," *Concilium*, 1983/8. **MERCIER, Georges** - Statement about the 'poor Church,' *Equipes Enseignantes,* 1962-1963, in Y. Congar, *Pour une Eglise servante et pauvre*. **MERSCH, Emile** - *Theologie du Corps Mystique*, Paris, 1964, in H. U. von Balthasar, *Casta meretrix*. **MESSORI, Vittorio** - *Rapporto sulla Fede – Vittorio Messori a colloquio com Joseph Ratzinger*, Milan: Paoline, 1985. **METZ, Johann Baptist** - *Introduzione alla teologia,* Milan: Massimo, 1983; "La 'teologia política' in discussione," in V.A., *Dibattito sulla 'teologia política;' Más alla de la religión burguesa - Sobre el futuro del Cristianismo,* Salamanca: Sígueme, 1982; "Per una Chiesa rinnovata prima di un nuovo concilio," in V.A., *Verso la Chiesa del terzo millennio;* "Redenzione ed emancipazione," in V.A., *Redenzione ed emancipazione;* "Sulla presenza della Chiesa nella società," in V.A., *L'avvenire della Chiesa*. **MONDIN, Battista** - *Os grandes teólogos do século vinte,* 2 vols., São Paulo: Paulinas, 1979. **MOUROUX, Jacques** - "Situation et signification du chapitre I: Sur la dignité de la personne humaine," in V.A., *L'Église dans le monde de ce temps*. **MOYNIHAN, Robert** - "Casa Balthasar," *30 Dias*, August-September 1990.

NANTES, Georges de - *Liber accusationis in Paulum Sextum,* St. Parrès les Vaudes, 1973. **NEHER, André** - "Le symbolism conjugal: Expression de l'histoire dans l'Ancien Testament," in *Revue d'Histoire et de Philosophie Religieuses,* Strausburg: Presses Universitaires de France, 1954. **NEUFELD, Karl Heinz** - "Au service du Concile, évêques et théologiens," in V.A., *Vatican II: Bilan et perspectives, vingt-cinq ans après – 1962-1987*. **NEUMANN, Erich** - *Die grosse Mutter,* Zurich: Rhein Verlag, 1956.

O'DONNELL, John - "Man and Woman as *'Imago Dei'* in the Theology of Hans Urs von Balthasar," *Clergy Review* (London) n. 78, 1983. **OLIVEIRA, Plinio Correa de** - See Correa de Oliveira. **OLIVIER, Daniel** - "Perché Luther non è stato capito?" *Concilium*, 1976/8.

PACI, Stefano - "O Papa também obedece," *30 Dias*, March 1993; "O Prefeito e o quarto poder," *30 Dias*, April 1992; **PASTOR, Ludwig von** - *Historia de los Papas,* 40 vols., Barcelona: Gustavo Gili, 1886-1933. **PATROLOGIE LATINE (PL)** - Pub. and ed. by Paul Migne, 161 vols., Paris: Migne, 1841-1864. **PATTARO, Germano** - "Regno di Dio e 'ideologie'," in V.A., *Il regno di Dio che vienne; Riflessioni sulla teologia post-conciliare*. **PAUL VI** - Apostolic exhortation *Quinque iam anni, Insegnamenti di Paolo VI*, in Various Articles, "Hans Urs von Balthasar ha meso la sua conoscenza"; Brief *Ambulate in dilectione* of December 7, 1965, in B. Kloppenburg, *Concílio Vaticano II;* Opening speech at the second conciliar session of September 29, 1963 and opening speech at the fourth conciliar session of September 14, 1965, in H. Fesquet, *Le journal du Concile;* Opening speech to the second General Assembly of the Latin America Bishops Conference, August 24, 1968 and speech to the National Federation of Schools for Obstetricians on July 6, 1969, in *Insegnamenti di Paolo V;* Speech at the closing of Vatican II of December 7, 1965, in R. Laurentin, *Bilan du Concile – Chronique de la quatrième session;* Speech at the ecumenical ceremony at St. Paul Outside-the-Walls of December 4, 1965, in R. Laurentin, *Bilan du Concile – Chronique de la quatrième session.* **PERRENCHIO, Fausto** - *Communione e Liberazione,* in Agostino Favale, ed., *Movimenti ecclesiali contemporanei;* **PETER DAMIAN, St.** - *Sermo 57,* in PL, *apud* PL in H. U. von Balthasar, *Casta meretrix.* **PETER CHRYSOLOGUS, St.** - *Sermo 95, De Magdalena apud* PL, in H. U. von Balthasar, *Casta meretrix.* **PHILIPS, Gérard** - *La Chiesa e il suo mistero nel Concilio Vaticano II - Storia, testo e commento della Costituzione Lumen gentium,* Milan: Jaca Books, 1982. **PIUS VI** - *Pontificis Maximi Acta,* Rome: Typis S. Congreg. de Propaganda Fide, 1871. **PIUS IX** - Apostolic letter *Cum Catholica* of March 26, 1860, in V.A., *Recueil des allocutions;* Letter of the Holy Office to the Bishops of England of September 9, 14, in DR. **PIUS X, St.** - Apostolic Letter *Notre charge apostolique* of August 25, 1910, in AAS; *Compendio della dotrina cristiana prescitto da sua Santità Papa Pius X alle diocesi della provincia di Roma,* Rome, 1905, in C. Journet, *L'Église du Verbe Incarneé;* Motu proprio *Fin dalla prima* of December 18, 1903, Petrópolis: Vozes, 1959. **PIUS XI** - Encyclical *Divini Redemptoris* of March 19, 1937, in AAS; Encyclical *Mortalium animos,* in *Actes de S.S. Pie XI, 1927-1928,* Paris: Bonne Presse. **PIUS XII** - Allocution to the Patriciate and Roman Nobility, Allocution to the Patriciate and Roman Nobility of January 19, 1944, Radiomessage of Christmas 1944 and Radiomessage of January 5, 1942, in *Discorsi e Radiomessaggi; Discurso La elevatezza,* Petrópolis: Vozes, 1950; Encyclical *Fulgens radiatur* of March 21, 1947, Petrópolis: Vozes, 1953; Encyclical *Mortalium animos* of January 6, 1928, in C. Journet, *L'Église du Verbe Incarné;* Encyclical *Mystici Corporis Christi* of June 29, 1943, Petrópolis: Vozes, 1960. **PL** – see Patrologie Latine. **POLITI, Marco** - "Irrequieto ma ubbidiente," *Il Messagero,* February 2, 1983. **POPKES, Wiard** - *Christus traditus: eine Untersuchung zum Begriff der Dahingabe im Neuen Testamen,* Zurich: Zwingli Verlag, 1967. **POSIO, Lucia** - "L'attenzione su...," *Notizie Ecumeniche* (Bollettino di Collegamento e d'Informazione dei Giovani SAE, Resoconto del I Convegno Nazionale Giovani SAE), November 1983. **POUPARD, Paul** - "Le radici cristiane dell'Europa," *L'Osservatore Romano,* December 19, 1984. **PUYO, Jean** - *Jean Puyo interroge le Père Congar – Une vie pour la verité,* Paris: Centurion, 1975.

RAHNER, Karl - *Chiesa, uomo e società,* Rome/Brescia: Herder/Morcelliana, 1970; *Escritos de teología,* 23 vols., Madrid: Taurus, 1964; "Il significato teologico della posizione del cristiano nel mondo moderno," in V.A., *Missione e grazia; La Chiesa peccatrice nei decreti del Vaticano II,* Rome: Paoline, 1968; *Magistero e teologia dopo il Concilio,* Brescia: Queriniana, 1967; *Teologia e Bíblia,* São Paulo: Paulinas, 1972; "Theological Reflections on the Problem of Secularization," in V.A., *Theology of Renewal;* "Théologie et anthropologie," in V.A., *Théologie d'aujourd'hui et de demain.* **RAHNER, K. & Vorgrimler, H.** - *Petit Dictionnaire de Théologie Catholique,* Paris: Seuil, 1970. **RATZINGER, Joseph** - Alocución a los Obispos en Colombia – Reflexiones sobre el caso de Monseñor Marcel Lefebvre," *El Catolicismo,* Bogotá, August 28, 1988; "Contradições no livro *Infalível*' de Hans Küng," in V.A., *O problema da infalibilidade;* "Ecco perché la fede é in crisi," interview by Vittorio Messori, *Jesus* (Milan), November 1984; *Fé e futuro,* Petrópolis: Vozes, 1971; *Il nuovo popolo di Dio,* Brescia: Queriniana, 1971; Interview granted to B. Kraatz and M. Müller, "Die Kirche ist eine keusche Hure," *Der Spiegel,* September 17, 1964; "La eclesiología del Vaticano," *Iglesia-Mundo* (Madrid), October 1986; "Papa mariano, esecutore fedele del Concilio Vaticano II," *L'Osservatore Romano,* October 16, 1992; *Problemi e risultati del Concilio Vaticano II,* Brescia: Queriniana, 1967. **REGOUT, Roberto** - *La* *doctrine de la guerre juste de Saint Augustin à nos jours, d'après les théologiens et les canonistes catholiques*, Paris: Pedone, 1935. **RICHARD, Pierre M.** - Entry "Enfer" and entry "Origenisme" in DTC. **RITTER, Joseph Elmer** - Intervention in the conciliar Hall of November 19, 1963, in H. Fesquet, *Le journal du Concile*. **ROBERTS, Thomas** - Press statement of October 25, 1963, in H. Fesquet, *Le journal du Concile*. **ROUSSET, Jean** - See Augustin Fliche. **RUIZ, José Gonzalez** - "Lettera aperta al Cardinal Ratzinger," *Adista*, January 19-21, 1987.

SARTORI, Luigi - "Il linguaggio del Vaticano II," in V. A., *Il linguaggio teologico oggi;* "Regno di Dio e Chiesa," in V.A., *Il Regno di Dio che viene;* "Spirito Santo e storia - Testimonianza cattolica," in V.A., *Lo Spirito Santo pegno e primizia del Regno.* **SCHEEBEN, Matthias Joseph** - *Handbuch der Katholischen Pragmatik,* Frieburg: Herder, 1954. **SCHILLEBEECKX, Edward** - *Cristo sacramento dell'incontro con Dio,* Rome: Paoline, 1970; *Evolução e mudanças nas concepções cristãs do matrimônio,* in V.A., *Direitos do sexo e do matrimônio; Le Mariage - Realité terrestre et mystère de salut,* Paris: Cerf, 1966; "Les sacraments, organes de la recontre de Dieu," in V.A., *Catholiques et protestants; Maria, Mãe da Redenção,* Petrópolis, 1968. **SCOLA, Angelo** - "Viaggio nel Concilio e intorni," *30 Giorni,* 1985/7. **SEITZ, Paul** - Intervention in the conciliar hall of November 13, 1962, in B. Koppenburg, *Concilio Vaticano II.* **SESBOÜÉ, Bernard** - *O evangelho na Igreja - A tradiçäo viva da fé,* São Paulo: Paulinas, 1977. **SHEHAN, Lawrence Joseph** - Intervention in the conciliar hall of October 11, 1963, in H. Fesquet, *Le journal du Concile.* **SIEBER, Wigand** - *Katholisch oder Konziliar,* München/Vienna: Langen Müller, 1978. **SMEDT, Emile de** - Intervention in the conciliar hall of December 1, 1962, in B. Kloppenburg, *A eclesiologia do Vatican II.* **SOARES, Matos** - *Traduçäo e comentários da Bíblia Sagrada,* São Paulo: Paulinas, 1964. **SOCCI, Antonio** - "E chegou para Maria o dia do parto," *30 Dias,* November 1991. **STRACCA, Silvano** - "Il Concilio sorpresa per il mondo," *Avvenire,* October 16, 1992. **SUAREZ, Francisco** - *De mysterio vitae Christi,* Paris, 1866, in DTC. **SUENENS, Leo Josef** - *Cristianismo sem Deus,* in V.A., *Cristianismo sem Cristo;* Intervention in the Conciliar Hall of October 1965, in R. Laurentin, *L'enjeu du Concile; Souvenirs et espérances,* Paris: Fayard, 1991.

TILLARD, Jean-Marie - "Pluralismo teologico e mistero della Chiesa," *Concilium,* 1984/1. **TRINITE, Philippe de la** - *Dialogue avec le marxisme? – Ecclesiam suam et Vatican II,* Paris: Cèdre, 1966.

VANDERPOL, Alfred - *La doctrine scholastique du droit de guerre,* Paris: Pedone, 1919. **VARIOUS ARTICLES - *30 Dias:*** "Catecismos no espelho," February 1992; Interview with de Lubac, *30 Giorni,* July 1985. *La Civiltá Cattolica* - "Il ministero del Papa dopo i due Concilii Vaticani," November 2,1985. *L'Osservatore Romano* - "Conferito a padre Yves Congar il premio per l'unità dei cristiani," November 28, 1984; Editorial "Dal 'trionfalismo' al 'complesso d'inferiorità," October 3, 1970; "Hans Urs von Balthasar ha meso la sua conoscenza al servizio del vero che promana da Cristo," June 24, 1984; "Il cordoglio del Santo Padre per la morte di von Balthasar," June 28,1988; "Il teologo gesuita Karl Rahner morto in una clinica di Innsbruck," May 1, 1984; "La motivazione del premio," June 24, 1984; "L'incontro di Giovanni Paolo II con la Commissione Teologica Internazionale," October 6, 1988; "Nella prospettiva ecclesiologica del Concilio," June 29,1988; *Jesus* - "Perché affannarsi tanto? E cosí semplice obblidire al Papa," June 1985; *SEDOC* - "Declaração da comissão mista católico-luterana sobre o V centenário de Martinho Lutero," n. 16, Petrópolis, 1984/3.

358   ANIMUS INJURIANDI I

VARIOUS AUTHORS (V.A.) – *A Igreja do Futuro,* Petrópolis: Vozes, 1973; *A Igreja greco-melquita no Concílio,* São Paulo: Loyola, 1992; *Bilan de la théologie au XXe siècle,* 2 vols., Tournai/Paris: Casterman, 1970; *Brainwashing': A Myth Exploited by the New 'Therapeutic Inquisition,'* New York: The American Society for the Defense of Tradition, Family and Property, 1985; *Catholiques et protestants,* Paris: Seuil, 1963; *Chiesa, uomo e società,* Rome/Brescia: Herder-Morcelliana, 1970; *Comentarios al Codigo de Derecho Canonico,* Madrid: BAC, 1963; *Conversaciones de Toledo - Teología de la liberación,* Burgos: Aldecoa, 1973; "Declaration" published in a supplement of *Concilium,* Portuguese ed., January 1969; *Dibattito sulla 'teologia politica,'* Brescia: Queriniana, 1972; *Direitos do sexo e do matrimônio,* Petrópolis: Vozes, 1972; *I grandi temi del Concilio,* Rome: Paoline, 1965; *Il dialogo alla prova,* Firenze: Vallechi, 1964; *Il linguaggio teologico oggi,* Milan: Ancora, 1970; *Il regno di Dio che viene - Atti della XIV sessione di formazione ecumenica organizzata dal Segretariato Attività Ecumeniche (SAE),* Turin: Elle Di Ci, 1977; *Incontro tra le religioni,* Verona: Mondadori, 1969; *L'avvenire della Chiesa – Il libro del congresso,* Brescia: Queriniana, 1970; *La fine della Chiesa come società perfetta,* Verona: Mondadori, 1968; *La nouvelle image de l'Église – Bilan du Concile Vatican II,* Paris: Mame, 1967; *La reforma que llega de Roma,* Barcelona: Plaza & Jares, 1970; *La visita di Paolo VI alle Nazioni Unite,* Libreria Editrice Vaticana, 1966; *L'ecclésiologie au XIXe. siècle,* Paris: Cerf, 1960; *L'Église dans le monde de ce temps – Constitution pastorale 'Gaudium et spes,'* Paris: Cerf, 1967; *Lo Spirito Santo pegno e primizia del Regno,* Turin: Elle Di Ci, 1982; *Missione e grazia,* Rome, 1967; *Mysterium salutis,* Petrópolis: Vozes,1974; *O problema da infalibilidade,* coord. by K. Rahner, São Paulo: Loyola, 1976; *Questions théologiques aujourd'hui,* Paris: Desclée de Brouwer, 1965; *Recueil des allocutions consistoriales, encycliques et autres letters apostoliques des Souverains Pontifes Clément XII, Benoît XVI, Pie VI, Pie VII, Léon XII, Grégoire XVI et Pie IX,* Paris: Adrien le Clere, 1865; *Redenzione ed emancipazione,* Brescia: Queriniana, 1975; *Sacrae Theologiae Summa,* Madrid: BAC, 1961; *Théologie d'aujourd'hui et de demain,* Paris: Cerf, 1967; *Theology of Renewal - Renewal of Religious Thought,* 2 vols., Montreal: Palm Publishers, 1968; *Vatican Council I,* Petrópolis: Vozes, 1953; *Vatican II: Bilan et perspectives, vingt-cinq ans après – 1962-1987,* ed. R. Latourelle, 2 vols., Montreal/Paris: Bellarmin/Cerf, 1988; *Verso la Chiesa del terzo millennio,* Brescia: Queriniana, 1973. **VERNET, F.** - Entry "Communistes," in DTC. **VERGOTE, Antoine** - "La presenza della Chiesa nella società di domani – Riflessioni bibliche," in V.A. *L'avvenire della Chiesa.* **VINCENT OF LÉRINS, St.** - *Commonitorium,* in PL. **Virion, Pierre** - *Le mystère de Jeanne d'Arc et la politique des nations,* Paris: Tequi, 1972. **VORGRIMLER, H.** - See Karl Rahner.

WAGNER, Joannes - "La nueva litugia," in V.A., *La reforma que llega de Roma.* **WEISS,** Juan Bautista. *Historia Universal,* Barcelona: La Educación, 1927. **WENGER, Antoine** - *L'Église de son temps – Vatican II – Chronique,* 4 vols., Paris: Centurion, 1963-66. **WILTGEN, Ralph** - *The Rhine Flows into the Tiber,* Devon/England: Augustine, 1978. **WOODROW, Alain** - "A Rome: Trente théologiens du monde entier pour accomplir le Concile," *I.C.I.,* May 15, 1969. **WYSZYNSKI, Stefan** - Intervention in the Conciliar Hall of October 15, 1963, in H. Fesquet, *Le journal du Concile.*

ZIADE, Ignace - "Un nouveau style de papauté" in V.A., *La nouvelle image de l'Église – Bilan du Concile Vatican II.*

* * *

SUBJECT INDEX

ADAPTATION TO THE WORLD OR *AGGIORNAMENTO* – **Accepts** the world's errors: Introduction § 9. **Called** the Church a sect: Chap. XI § 2. **Council** showed unlimited sympathy toward the world: Chap. II § 8. **Encouraged** by *Gaudium et spes*: Introduction Note 14 e, f. **Ended** the ghetto in the Church: Chap. XI § 9. **Initiated** by John XXIII: Introduction Note 14e; Chap. XI § 8. **Synonymous** with secularization: Introduction § 11. **Unleashed** a cyclone of offenses against Church relations with the world: Chap. XI § 1. See *CHURCH-WORLD RELATIONS*

ANATHEMA – see *CONDEMNATIONS*

ANGELS – St. Michael was a replacement for Wotan: Chap. II § 30.

ANIMUS INJURIANDI, DESIRE TO OFFEND – see *OFFENSES*

APOLOGIA FOR BETRAYAL – **Christ** united with the reprobates in Hell: Chap. I §§ 5-10. Christ as a traitor of the Father: Chap. I § 5. **Conceived** by theologians: Chap. I § 2; especially by von Balthasar: Chap. I § 5. **Diverges** from Catholic doctrine: Chap. I § 10. **Father** betrayed the Son: Chap. I §§ 12, 20. Father cursed the Son: Chap. I § 17. Father was represented by Judas: Chap. I § 11. **Heart of Christ** betrayed God: Chap. I § 19. Heart of Christ betrayed himself: Chap. I § 20. **Jews** were not guilty for the death of Christ: Chap. I §§ 12, 13. **Judas** was not guilty: Chap. I §§ 13, 11-14; Judas was a victim: Chap. I § 16. The cause of Christ's death is **irrelevant**: Chap. I §§ 13, 14. Judas' **suicide** represents treasures of Protestantism: Chap. I § 23.

ARIUS, ARIANISM – Based on Subordinationism: Appendix I § 74, Note 121; see *PATRISTICS*

ASCETICISM, CATHOLIC – Was **sado-masochist**: Chap. VIII § 21. Was **Stoic**: Chap. VIII § 23.

AUTO-DEMOLITION OF THE CHURCH – **Analyzed** in Volumes IV and V of this Collection: Introduction § 28. **Confirmed** by Card. Ratzinger: Introduction § 17. **Initiated** by John XXIII and Paul VI: Introduction § 16, Note 14g. **Unleashed** a chain reaction of latent forces: Introduction § 17.

BETRAYAL – see *APOLOGIA FOR BETRAYAL*

CAPITALISM – Communist Lucio Lombardi praised John XXIII's anti-Capitalism: Introduction Note 14h.

CASTA MERETRIX (CM) – **Accusation**: Church is simultaneously CM: Appendix I § 26; in her essence: Chap. IV §§ 3, 5, Appendix I § 27. **Arguments** to present CM: Appendix I §§ 1, 30. **Background** explanation for the accusation of CM: Appendix I §§ 5-15. **Expression** CM used by St. Ambrose: Appendix I § 78; in an allegorical sense: Appendix I § 89 Notes 80, 132. **Defended** by progressivists: Appendix I Note 156, and defended by the Miserablist current throughout History: Appendix I §§ 5-7, 23. **Forbidden** after the Counter-Reformation: Appendix I §§ 78-83. **Mitigated** version of CM: Chap. IV § 21-25. **Patristic** basis for CM: Appendix I §§ 2, 3, 31. **Prostitute** as symbol of Old Testament:

Chap. IV §§ 26, 30; used by the Prophets: Appendix I § 30; tolerated by God: Appendix I § 30; confirmed by the episodes of Tamar and Rahab; Appendix I § 31; symbol of the Church in the New Testament: Appendix I § 31. CM indirectly **supported** by Benedict XVI: Chap. IV §§ 14, 17, 18, Note 21; by John Paul II: Chap. IV § 23.

CASTA MERETRIX, **Refutation of von Balthasar's book**: **I. Prolegomena**: *Limits*: Appendix I §§ 4, 24. *Method*: *Hegelian*: Appendix I §§ 27, 32; *Exegetic* rather than historic: Appendix I § 29; *Contradictory*: Appendix I § 29; *Incoherent* use of Patristic texts: Appendix I § 33; *Superficial*: Appendix I § 34a; *Partial*: Appendix I § 34b. *Objectives*: Appendix I §§ 25-28. *Presentation* of the thesis: Appendix I §§ 29-31. **II. Body of the refutation**: *1ˢᵗ unfounded generalization*: Husband-wife is not the only or the best expression of God's relations with the Chosen People: Appendix I § 35. *2ⁿᵈ unfounded generalization*: Symbol of prostitute is not an archetype of the Chosen People, but an anti-archetype: Appendix I §§ 36-54. *Omissions in this 2ⁿᵈ generalization*: A. Prophets use the symbol of prostitute for just one apostasy: Appendix I §§ 36- 42. Actual historical reason for the symbol of prostitute: Appendix I § 36. B. God refers to prostitute with great wrath: Appendix I §§ 44-47. C. God used many other symbols: Appendix I §§ 48, 49. *3ʳᵈ unfounded generalization*: Episodes of Tamar and Rahab do not support the prostitute as a symbol of the Chosen People: Appendix I §§ 51-54. *4ᵗʰ unfounded generalization*: Catholic Church is not the heir of a prostitute synagogue: Appendix I §§ 55-64. *5ᵗʰ unfounded generalization*: Patristic does not defend Church as prostitute in her essence: Appendix I, generically §§ 65-91, specifically §§ 85-9. Patristic texts are insufficient for any dogmatic conclusion: Appendix I §§ 88-90. Expression CM must be considered 'obscure thinking' of the few Fathers who used it: Appendix I § 89. *6ᵗʰ unfounded generalization*: Sins of men do not affect the essence of the Church: Appendix I generically: §§ 92-115 specifically: §§ 104-115; *Conclusion*: § 117.

CATHOLIC CHURCH (CC) – CATHOLIC PERSPECTIVE: **Constitution** of: Appendix I § 99; her *body*: § 100; her *created soul* § 101; her *uncreated soul*: § 102. **Continuity** between Holy Synagogue and CC: Appendix I §§ 56, 61-62, 64. **Definition** of CC including Church Triumphant and Church Suffering: Appendix I Note 158a; including Old and New Testament: Appendix I Note 158b. **Divine characteristics**: Appendix I §§ 93-98; Divine in her origin: Appendix I § 94; mission: § 95; end: § 96; means § 97; body: § 98. **Holiness** of CC: Appendix I § 83, Note 139. **Infallibility** of CC: Appendix I §§ 80-83, Note 137. **Men's participation** in the Church: Appendix I § 104-110; confirmed by the Pontifical Magisterium: Appendix I § 109, 111-113. **Militancy** of CC: Chap. II § 1. **Persecuted** by the Jews: Appendix I § 64, Note 110. **Powers** of CC: Appendix I § 10. Whether **sin** enters CC: Appendix I §§ 104-110, 114, 115. Sins in the Church, sins of the Church: Appendix I § 85, Note 141. Church as *societas perfecta*: Appendix I §§ 12, 13. Should influence the **temporal sphere**: Chap. II § 1; should have primacy over the State: Appendix I § 13 Notes 11, 12. PROGRESSIVIST PERSPECTIVE: CC **alienated** from the Gospel: Chap. VII § 10. Her **apostolate** was sterile: Chap. VII § 2. Her **asceticism** was sado-masochist: Chap. VIII § 21. She **betrayed** her mission: Chap. I § 24. Her **defensive** position must be abandoned: Chap. II § 33. She **denied** her catholicity: Chap. I § 25. Her **ecclesiology** was Monophysitist: Chap. VIII §§ 13, 9-14; heretical: Chap. VIII § 4. Her notion of **grace** was Pelagian: Chap. VIII § 15. She should be **indulgent** with heresies: Chap. I § 23. Her **institutions** were two-thirds *cadaver*: Chap. VII § 16; filled with *garbage*: Chap. VIII § 7; *lethargic*: Chap. VII § 17; *insignificant*: Chap. VII § 14; *paralyzed*: Chap. VII § 7; nothing is *perfect* in her: Chap. VIII § 7; she is the *poorest* of all religions: Chap. VIII § 3; *sclerotic* Chap. VII §§ 6, 7; *stagnant*, putrid: Chap. VII § 13. Her **love** was Monophysitist: Chap. VIII §§ 11, 12. Her **mentality** was Nominalist: Chap. VIII § 19. Her **militancy** must disappear: Chap. II § 2; she is not an army: Chap. II § 3; should not combat Communism: Chap. II § 4. Her **morality** was Jansenist: Chap. VIII § 16; was Dualist: Chap. VIII §§ 24, 25. Her **preaching** should avoid formulas to reach heaven that deny human freedom: Chap. VII § 22; should not propose a dead faith, an opium of the people: Chap. VII § 22. Her notion of **Revelation** was Docetist: Chap. VIII § 18. She is **represented** by Judas with his bowels strewn about: Chap. I § 23. Her **spirituality** was Docetist: Chap. VIII § 17; was Deist: Chap. VIII 20. Her **teaching** was narrow: Chap. II § 32. Her **traditions** made a prison: Chap. VII § 18. She should abandon her **triumphalism**: Chap. II § 3. Should not be **visible**: Appendix I §§ 5-9, 15. See *CHURCH-WORLD, MORALS, ASCETICISM, MYSTICISM*

CHOSEN PEOPLE (CP) – **Apostasy** in one particular period of Old Testament: Appendix I §§ 37, 41, 42, 43. **Captivities** of Nineveh and Babylon: Appendix I §§ 37-40, Notes 90, 91, 93. **Chastised** by God in two phases: Appendix I §§ 38, 39, Notes 90, 91; **Rigor** of God with CP: Appendix I §§ 37, 44-47, Notes 89, 92. Many **symbols** to reflect God's relation with CP: Appendix I §§ 35, 48, 49.

CHRIST – **Condemned**, defeated and miserable: Chap. I § 21. **Identified** with sin: Chap. I §§ 5-10. See *APOLOGIA OF BETRAYAL, DESPAIR*

CHRISTENDOM (C) – Nostalgia for C destroyed at Vatican II: Chap. II § 40. See *CHURCH-WORLD*

CHURCH OF THE POOR – Initiated by John XXIII: Introduction Note 14g. See *SACRALITY, SINNING CHURCH*

CHURCH-WORLD RELATIONS (CW) – CATHOLIC PERSPECTIVE: **Doctrine** on CW: Appendix I §§ 9, 11, 13, 14, Notes 11, 12. **Concept** of ghetto: Chap. XI § 5. **Concepts** of sect: Chap. XI §§ 3, 4, Note 6. PROGRESSIVIST PERSPECTIVE: **Barriers** between CW must be razed: Chap. XI § 12. **Distinction** between CW is schizophrenic: Chap. XI §§ 31, 32. **Ghetto** – The Church is a ghetto when she constructs a separate world as in *Christendom*: Chap. XI § 24; assumes *definitive formulas*: Chap. XI § 24; is wrapped in *fears* and mediocrities: Chap. XI § 12; is not a member of the *global village*: Chap. XI § 26; is not a citizen of the universe: Chap. XI § 26; is not universal: Chap. XI § 13; does not preach her message of salvation to all men: Chap. XI § 13; is only European: Chap. XI § 25; does not listen to the *signs of the times*: Chap. XI § 24. **Sect** – The

Church is a sect when she does not attack *aristocracy* and feudalism: Chap. XI § 6; is *centralized* in Rome: Chap. XI § 7; *closed* in herself: Chap. XI § 18; closed in one sector of theology: Chap. XI § 16; is not *ecumenical*: Chap. XI §§ 19, 27; defends the *established order*: Chap. XI § 28; is not interested in *history*: Chap. XI § 19; does not support *liberty*: Chap. XI § 6; is marginalized from *modern science*, philosophy and politics: Chap. XI § 21; is alienated from modern thought, history and concerns: Chap. XI § 30; defends herself against *society* and disdains it: Chap. XI § 21; tries to make a homogenous society: Chap. XI § 14; forms groups outside of society: Chap. XI § 21; tries to make a *uniform theology*: Chap. XI § 15; establishes a system of eternal certainties: Chap. XI § 23; does not *wake up*: Chap. XI § 29; is not integrated with the *world*: Chap. XI § 12; is not open to the world: Chap. XI § 22; does not speak the language of the world: Chap. XI § 15; does not serve the world: Chap. XI § 17. Criticism of **traditional teaching**: Chap. XI §§ 1, 2.

CLERGY – Should **abandon** its anachronistic lifestyle: Chap. VI § 20; **become** a part of the world: Chap. VI § 20. Will only be **respected** when it competes with other professions: Chap. VI § 20.

COMUNIONE E LIBERAZIONE – Movement that received the support of conciliar Popes: Chap. IV § 14, Note 21.

COMMUNISM (C) – **Church** should stop attacking C: Chap. II § 7; change her notion of God before attacking Atheism: Chap. II § 6. **Dialogue** between Conciliar Church and C: Chap. VII Note 29. C is not the **enemy** of the Church: Chap. II § 7. **Favored** by John XXIII and Paul VI: Chap. IX § 17; by dialogue with Progressivism: Chap. IX § 17. **John XXIII** helped Italian Communist Party in elections: Introduction Note 14a; received USSR *Izvestia* editor Alexei Adzhubei: Introduction Note 14a; affirmed C should not be condemned by the Church: Chap. II §§ 4-7; was praised by Communist Lucio Lombardi: Introduction 14h. Charles **Peguy** was a socialist: Chap. I § 15. Angelo **Roncalli**'s solidarity with Ranica strikers: Introduction Note 14a; Roncalli's support for Italian Socialist Party: Introduction Note 14a.

CONDEMNATIONS BY THE CHURCH (C) – **Pre-conciliar condemnations**: against Michael *Cesana*: Appendix I Note 35, the *Fraticelli*: Appendix I Notes 34, 139; those who deny the *holiness* of the Church: Appendix I Note 139; *Jansenism*: Appendix I Note 139; *Lamennais*: Appendix I Note 48; *Luther*: Appendix I Note 43; William of *Occam* and: Appendix I Note 35; *Quesnel*: Appendix I Note 139: *Synod of Pistoia*: Appendix I Note 139. **Post-conciliar condemnations:** mere *admonishments*: Introduction 19, Note 10; should *end*: Chap. II § 8; *examples* of: Introduction § 19; Note 11; *renounced* by Paul VI: Chap. II § 8; *rigor* of Congregation of the Doctrine of the Faith is a myth: Introduction Note 10. **Value** of C: Introduction § 19. See *HERESY, HERETICS, NOUVELLE THEOLOGIE*

CONSERVATISM – Attacked by **John XXIII** in the Opening Speech of the Council: Introduction Note 14d. Attacked by **Paul VI** during the Council: Introduction Note 14n.

Divine comedy – Favored **miserablist** current: Appendix I § 15 Note 13; von Balthasar **misquoted** Dante to favor his thesis: Appendix I Note 14. See *Casta meretrix, Miserablism, Poor Church*

Docetism – **Definition**: Chap. VIII Note 23. Church **spirituality** was Docetist: Chap. VIII § 17. Notion of **Revelation** was Docetist: Chap. VIII § 18.

Doctrinal condemnations – See *Condemnations by the Church*

Dogmas – **Assumption**: Chap. III § 25. **Immaculate Conception**: Chap. III §§ 25, 26. **Virginity**: *perpetual virginity*: Chap. III § 26b, Note 39; *virginitas in partu*: Chap. III § 26b Note 39. See *Mariology*

Dualism – **Church-World** relations was dualist: Chap. VIII § 25. **Definition**: Chap. VIII Note 36. Church **morality** on sex was dualist: Chap. VIII § 24.

Ecumenism (E) – **Caused** by Rome renouncing her monopoly on truth: Chap. V § 11. **Explained** by the spirit of tolerance: Introduction § 11. Previously **forbidden** by the religious authorities: Chap. VI § 5. Existence of **papacy** harms E: Chap. IX § 13. **Sign of the times**: Chap. II § 25. **Sophism** of E: Chap. V Note 14f. See *Tolerance*

Eternal feminine – See *Cosmic Mary*

Existentialism – Concept of **ontological** and ontic: Chap. X Note 15. **Relation** between Martin Heidegger and Karl Rahner: Chap. X § 8. See *Transcendental Anthropology, Nouvelle Theologie, Progressivism*

Excommunications (E) – Not a consequence of new condemnations: Introduction §§ 19, 20. See *Condemnations*

Fatima, Apparitions of – See *Mariology, Revelations*

Feminism – Angelo Roncalli's correspondence with Adelaide Cori: Introduction Note 14a.

Forgiveness, Asking – For the **Battle of Vienna**: Chap. II § 23. Of **schismatics** and heretics: Chap. II § 8; Chap. IV Note 6a, Appendix I § 22, Note 55.

Free Speech - **Denied** by the Church previously: Chap. VI § 5. **Established** in the Church by Paul VI: Introduction §§ 14, 16. **Prepared** by John XXIII: Introduction § 16. **Requested** by theologians of *Concilium*: Introduction Note 5d. **Theological pluralism**: Introduction Note 5a. See *Tolerance*

Gaudium et spes – **Initiative** of John XXIII: Introduction Note 14 e, f. **Represented** the opposite of the *Syllabus* and *Pascendi*: Introduction Note 14f.

Ghetto – Concept of Ghetto: Chap. XI § 5. See *Church-World Relations*

God – Church should **change** her notion of God: Chap. II § 6. **Traditional** notion of Providence was a *caricature*: Chap. II § 6; *garbage*: Chap. II § 6; *opium of the people*: Chap. II § 6.

Heart of Christ – Has **bizarre** anatomical contours: Chap. I Note 36. **Similar** to: the heart of the world: Chap. I § 19, 20, Note 35a; a center of energies of the

MAGISTERIUM, CHURCH (CM) – CATHOLIC PERSPECTIVE: **Definition** of the Church by St. Robert Bellarmine: Chap. V Note 14a. **Catholic sinner** compared to just men outside the Church: Chap. V § 12, Note 14. **Outside** the Church there is no salvation: Chap. V Note 14e. PROGRESSIVIST PERSPECTIVE: CM preached only **abstract** truths: Chap. X § 13; must abandon abstract, static, universal truths; Chap. X § 18. **Abused** its power: Chap. VI § 14. **Authoritarian**: Chap. VI § 14; used St. Thomas to impose authoritarianism: Chap. VI § 14. A **caricature**: Chap. VI § 16. Produced **dead speculations**: Chap. VII § 4. Its **dogmas** became taboos: Chap. VII § 18; it is a repeater of dogmas: Chap. VII § 11; its dogmas are useless immutable formulations: Chap. X 15. **Entangled** in a false anti-Protestant polemic: Chap. VII § 6. MC fostered **fixism** and repetition: Chap. VII §§ 3, 11; mummified: Chap. VII § 4; stagnated: Chap. VII § 3. **Imperialist**: Chap. VI 15; had despotic ownership of God's gifts: Chap. VI § 21. Its **language** was *dead*: Chap. X § 4; *esoteric*: Chap. X, §§ 1, 2, 5, 6; made up of primitive *figurations*: Chap. X § 9; *inaccessible*: Chap. X § 3; *magical*: Chap. X § 4; should adapt to *modern man*: Chap. X § 9; *rationalist*: Chap. X § 5; *separated* theologians from the faithful: Chap. X § 5; a *strange* idiom: Chap. X § 3; *wordy*: Chap. X § 7. CM was **Manichaean** in its combat against Communism: Chap. IX § 17. Should not be an ensemble of **metaphysical truths**: Chap. VI § 16. Had a **Monophysitist** Christology: Chap. VIII §§ 9, 10. **Needs** new foundations: Chap. X § 18. Was **obsolete** in its teaching: Chap. VII § 10. **Opium of the people**: Chap. VII § 19; a guarantee of order: Chap. VI § 16. **Pelagian** in its concept of grace: Chap. VIII § 16. **Positivist**: Chap. VIII §§ 27, 28. **Rationalist**: Chap. X § 13. **Sclerotic**: Chap. V §§ 5, 10. **Sterile**: Chap. VII §§ 4, 5, 9-11, 14. **Underdeveloped**: Chap. X § 14. See *SCHOLASTICISM*

MANICHAEISM (M) – John Paul II **accused** the Church of M: Chap. VIII Note 39. Pius XI's **combat** against Communism was M: Chap. IX § 17. **Definition**: Chap. VIII Note 36. **Theology of the body** freed us from M: Chap. VIII § 26.

MASOCHISM – **Definition**: Chap. VIII Note 31; see *SADO-MASOCHISM*

MASS, TRIDENTINE – Acquired a commercial value: Chap. III § 12;

MARRIAGE (M) – As symbol of the whole history of salvation: Chap. IV § 27. See *CASTA MERETRIX*

MARIOLOGY (M) – CATHOLIC PERSPECTIVE: **Co-Redemptrix** coldly received by John XXIII: Chap. III § 17, and by Pius XII: Chap. III § 54. **Fatima consecration** coldly received: Chap. III § 17. **Mediatrix of all graces**: Chap. III Note 75. **Overview** of M: Chap. III § 16. **Theologians** would be punished for lacking respect for M: Chap. III § 46. **Virginity** of Our Lady, papal documents: Chap. III Note 39. PROGRESSIVIST PERSPECTIVE: **Christmas** was a legend: Chap. III § 50; had many prosaic aspect*s*: Chap. III §§ 50, 51. **Devotion** to Our Lady is *deformed*: Chap. III § 55; *deviates* from Christ: Chap. III §§ 19, 51, and the interior life: Chap. III § 17; harms *ecumenism*: Chap. III § 18; is *excessive*: Chap. III § 24; *filled with abuses*: Chap. III § 19; imitates *pagan cult* to goddesses: Chap. III § 47, Note 65; is *spurious*: Chap. III § 51; filled with *sterile affection*: Chap. III § 19; and *vain credulity*: Chap. III § 19. **Dogmas** of M are *excrescence*: Chap. III § 23; *triumphalism*: Chap. III § 24. *Co-Redemptrix* suggests parity with Christ: Chap. III § 54. *Immaculate Conception* has no base in the New Testament: Chap. III §§ 25, 26; or in Tradition: Chap. III §§ 28, 29; denied by Vatican II theologians: Chap. III § 28. *Mediatrix of all graces* lacks basis in the New Testament: Chap. III § 25; suggests parity with Christ: Chap. III § 54. There was no *painless parturition*: Chap. III §§ 32, 36, 40. *Perpetual virginity* is not important: Chap. III § 34; does not resist historical investigation: Chap. III § 42; is cosmic, not biological: Chap. III § 35; is not physical virginity: Chap. III §§ 32, 40 36; to believe in biological virginity is naïveté: Chap. III §§ 35, 38; is influenced by Gnosticism: Chap. III § 42, by Docetism: Chap. III § 43; should be dismissed: Chap. III § 41. *Virginal conception of Jesus* is open to discussion: Chap. III § 45; is not in the New Testament: Chap. III § 45; is just a narrative: Chap. III § 45; lacks witnesses: Chap. III § 45. *Virginitas in partu* contested by *Lumen gentium*: Chap. III §§ 26a, 26b; comparable to artificial insemination and caesarean births: Chap. III § 36; exaggerates original sin: Chap. III § 34; is not a historical fact: Chap. III § 31; lacks basis in Tradition: Chap. III § 27; must be understood in a spiritual way: Chap. III § 32; is just a representation: Chap. III § 30; a pious story: Chap. III § 31; doesn't require the belief of the faithful: Chap. III § 28. **Marian revelations** were expressions of fanaticism: Chap. III § 20; the fruit of pious imaginations: Chap. III § 20. *Revelations of Fatima* were utopic: Chap. III § 20; comparable to Montanism: Chap. III § 21; to Joachinism: Chap. III § 21. **Mary** was a *common*, vulgar woman: Chap. III §§ 48,49; was a *cosmic* element: Chap. III §§ 32, 33, 34; *feminist*: Chap. III § 53; her *legend* is false: Chap. III § 48; she was model for *social liberation*: Chap. III § 53; *subversive*: Chap. III § 52. **Vatican II** rejected a separate document on M: Chap. III § 24; inaugurated a crisis in M: Chap. III § 24.

Mentality – Synonymous of state of spirit: Introduction §§ 6, 7.

Method of exposition – of this Volume II: Introduction §§ 18, 24, Note 16; Chap. I § 22; of Volumes II to V: Introduction §§ 25, 28; of Volumes VI to XI: Introduction Note 17; of the five first Volumes of this Collection: Introduction § 31; position of the Author regarding theologians: Chap. I Note 19. Why more texts of Saints are not quoted: Chap. III Note 78.

Militancy (M) – Catholic perspective: **Best synthesizes** the Church: Chap. II § 1. **Foundations** for M in the Gospel: Introduction § 8. **Praised** by St. Bernard: Chap. II § 22, Note 42. Knights **Templar** as its archetype: Chap. II § 22. Progressivist perspective: **Abandoned** by Vatican II: Chap. II § 33. **Aggressive** statements should be avoided: Chap. II § 5. Called an **assimilation** of paganism: Chap. II § 30. **Attacked** by the conciliar Popes: Introduction §§ 11, 12; papal basis to attack M: Chap. II §§ 7-10. **Combat** against heretics in theology should cease: Chap. II § 19, combat against Protestantism was a manifestation of insecurity: Chap. II § 36, *Civiltà Cattolica* no longer combative: Chap. II § 10. **Criticized** by John Paul II: Chap. II § 10. Should **disappear**: Chap. II § 2. **Intolerance** is an ignominy: Chap. II § 41. Sets aside **love**: Chap. II § 19. Is **negative**: Chap. II § 2. Is **opposed** by the Council: Chap. II § 2, by texts of

Vatican II: Chap. II Note 19b. Pope renounces **polemics**: Chap. II § 8, Faith should not generate polemics: Chap. II § 8. War is a ritual of **sadistic cruelty**: Chap. II § 29. Is **sinful**: Chap. IV § 3. Leads to **sterile** polemics: Chap. II § 2. Church should not have persecuted **witches**: Chap. II § 28. See *Counter-Reformation, Holy Office, War*

Miserablism (M) – **Divine Comedy** favors M: Appendix I Note 13. **Movements** defending the Church should not have property: Appendix I §§ 16-25; from the beginning of the Church to Protestantism: Appendix I §§ 16, 17; pre and post Protestantism: Appendix I § 18; in the French Revolution: Appendix I § 19; in Romanticism: Appendix I § 20, Note 48; in Modernism: Appendix I § 20 Note 49; in Progressivism: Appendix I § 21; in Vatican II: Appendix I § 22. The Church should not have **power,** property or goods: Appendix I §§ 5, 8, 15.

Modernism (M) – Anti-M **combat** was outdated: Chap. II § 34. M **continued** in Progressivism: Introduction 14b. Congar's **definition** of M: Introduction Note 14b. John XXIII **opened** the doors to M: Introduction Note 14b. Angelo Roncalli **suspected** of M: Introduction Note 14a. See *Progressivism, Nouvelle Theologie*

Monophysitism – Attributed to the Church: Chap. VIII §§ 9-14. Definition: Chap. VIII Note 11.

Morals, Catholic – **Harsh** regarding conjugal relations: Chap. VI § 5. **Laxity** of Catholic teaching after the Council: Introduction § 11. **Immature** and legalist: Chap. VI § 13. **Jansenist** in its teaching on sexuality: Chap. VIII § 16. **Stoic:** Chap. VIII § 22. **Painful** in marriage processes: Chap. VI § 5. Must be **revised**: Chap. VI § 13. **Theology of the body** freed us from Manichaeism: Chap. VIII § 26. **Turned** toward exterior things: Chap. VI § 8.

Mutual support of moderates and radicals (M) – In the **Council** and post-Council: Introduction §§ 22-24, Note 14. In the **French Revolution**, Introduction: §§ 20, 21 Notes 12 b, c, 13. See *Strategy*

Mystical body of Christ – **Prayer** of Our Lord for the Apostles: Chap. I § 10. Cannot enter a **symbiosis** with the Devil: Chap. I § 9.

Mystical body of the Devil – **Constituted** by the society of the evil: Chap. I Note 18. **Defined** by St. Thomas: Chap. I § 9, Note 17.

Mysticism, Traditional – Was **Deist** in spirituality: Chap. VIII § 20; **Docetist**: Chap. VIII § 17. Nothing more than **para-psychological** phenomena: Chap. III § 58.

Narcissist, Narcissism (N) – **Definition** of N: Chap. V Note 19. Church is N when she presents her message in a **superior**, totalitarian system: Chap. V § 17. Church **turned** toward herself is N: Chap. V § 18.

Nominalism – **Definition**: Chap. VIII Note 26. Church had N **mentality**: Chap. VIII § 19.

Nouvelle Théologie or New Theologie (NT) – *In genere*: **Attacked** by Holy Office, NT counter-attacks with Frings-Ratzinger intervention: Chap. II § 13, Notes 24, 25. **Condemned** by *Humani generis*: Chap. II § 20. **Encouraged** return to Patristics: Chap. VII § 4. **Punishments** suffered by NT leaders: Chap. II Note 39. Leaders under **suspicion of heresy**: Introduction § 23, Note 15, Chap II § 20 Notes 39, 40. Regarding its leaders: *Civiltà Cattolica* praised von Balthasar: Chap. I § 4. **Confused** thinking of Karl Rahner: Chap. X § 9, Note 17. **John XXIII** rehabilitated NT leaders: Introduction Note 14c. **John Paul II** admired NT: Introduction Note 14o, 14q; praised de Lubac: Introduction Note 14p; made de Lubac and Congar cardinals: Introduction Note 14r; praised Teilhard de Chardin: Introduction Note 14s; praised Rahner: Introduction Note 14t; gave von Balthasar international prestige: Chap. I § 3, Note 1; considered him a prophet: Chap. I § 3, Note 4; made him a cardinal: Chap. I § 3; praised him at his funeral: Chap. I § 3, Note 6. **Joseph Ratzinger** founded Casa Balthasar: Chap. I § 3, Note 7; praised Hans Küng: Chap. VIII Note 3. **Lubac** praised von Balthasar: Chap. I § 4. **Paul VI** was an admirer of NT: Introduction Note 14i, 14j; invited de Lubac to concelebrate at the Vatican: Introduction Note 14j; received and encouraged Rahner: Introduction Note 14k; gave him prestige: Chap. III Note 42; received Congar: Introduction 14l; summarized a work by Chenu in *Populorum progressio*: Introduction Note 14m; made Danielou a cardinal: Introduction Note 14m; appointed Rahner, Congar, de Lubac, Ratzinger and von Balthasar to the International Theological Commission: Introduction: Note 14m. *Osservatore Romano* praised von Balthasar: Chap. I Note 4; Congar: Chap. IX § 1; and Rahner: Chap III § 27 Note 42.

Obedience – **Different ways** the Church pays O to the Pope: *potestas vicaria, potestas ex pacto, potestas dominativa* or *domestica*: Appendix I § 10. **Emperor** must obey the Pope: Appendix I § 13 Notes 11, 12. **Promise** of O secular and regular clergy make to the Pope: Appendix I Note 9. **Vow** of O Bishops make to the Pope: Appendix I Note 9.

Offense, Offenses (O) – **Difference** between O to the honor of doctrine and O to doctrine: Introduction § 27. **Ingratitude** O represent: Conclusion § 4. **Meaning** of O in this Volume: Introduction § 26. **Role** of nuances in O: Introduction § 30. **Rejecting** O to follows the Passion of the Church: Chap. VII § 1, Conclusion §§ 4,5. Calling the Church **sect and ghetto** are O encouraged by Conciliar Popes: Chap. XI § 3. **Tolerance or approval** of O by the highest religious authorities: Conclusion §§ 1-3.

Ontology – Progressivist **concept** of O different from Aristotelian-Thomistic: Chap. X Note 15. **Definition**: Chap. X Note 15. **Distinction** from Ontic: Chap. X Note 15. See *Transcendental anthropology, Existentialism; Nouvelle Theologie, Progressivism*

Opium of the people (OP) – **Defense** of order by theologians is OP: Chap. VII § 19. **Original** text of Marx: Chap. VII Note 28. **Social doctrine** of the Church cannot become OP: Chap. VII § 20, 21, 22. **Traditional teaching** on God is OP: Chap. II § 6.

Origen, Origenism – Heterodoxy of: Appendix I §§ 72-74; see *Patristics, Subordinationism*

Pact of the Catacombs – **Heading** to miserablism in the Church: Chap. III Note 8. **Influenced** by Congar's book *Toward a Servant and Poor Church*: Chap. III Note 8. **Made** at the end of the Council: Chap. III § 2, Note 2a. See *Miserablism*

Papacy (P) – **Devotion** to the Pope is insupportable papolatry: Chap. IX §§ 2, 6, 8; is adulation: Chap. IX § 3; a manifestation of a servile spirit, an exaggeration: Chap. IX § 10; mediocre: Chap. IX § 11; is romanticism: Chap. IX § 12. **Infallibility,** different from infallibilism: Chap. IX § 10; blind obedience to the P ended: Chap. IX § 12; created an absurd situation for ecumenism: Chap. IX § 13; became a dictatorship: Chap. IX § 14, absolutism: Chap. IX § 14. **Petrine primacy** is a creation of History: Chap. IX § 2; cannot exist without the consent of the Church: Chap. IX § 7; must be identified with the Church: Chap. IX § 15; is a kind of imperialism: Chap. IX §§ 6, 9; is sickening: Chap. IX § 5; a morbid obsession: Chap. IX § 9; imposed personal thinking on Vatican I: Chap. IX § 15; became a white terror under Pius X: Chap. IX § 16. **Symbols** of the Papal power: Appendix I § 14. **Title** Sovereign Pontiff is pagan: Chap. IX § 4. Faithful should criticize P: Chap. IX § 12.

Patristics (P) – **Basis** for von Balthasar's work *Casta meretrix*: Appendix I § 2. **Contribution** of P to the Church: Appendix I §§ 67, 68. Must be **controlled** by the Church: Appendix I §§ 75, 77, 79. **Encouraged** by Progressivism: Chap. VII § 4, Appendix I §§ 65, 66, Note 111. **Errors** or heresies in Church Fathers: Appendix I §§ 68-74. **Heretics** often used P to spread their errors: Appendix I § 66, Note 112. **Legitimacy** of pointing out errors in P: Appendix I Note 114. **Obscurities** in Church Fathers must be avoided: Appendix I § 66, Note 114. See *Casta meretrix*

Pelagianism (P) – **Church** is P: Chap. VIII § 15. **Definition**: Chap. VIII Note 19.

Pharisaism, Pharisaic (Ph) – **Definition**: it is to accept a visible Church: Chap. V § 4; to have a concrete and immutable Church: Chap. V § 10; to construct her own world: Chap. V § 9; to consider herself better than other religions: Chap. V § 11; to follow Catholic Morals: Chap. V § 16; to demand celibacy of the clergy: Chap. V § 15 to claim the monopoly of truth: Chap. V § 11; to fulfill the law: Chap. V § 14; to identify the Catholic Church with the Church of Christ: Chap. V § 13. Ph as **hypocritical**: Chap. V § 4. **Meanings** of Ph: Chap. V: §§ 1-4, Note 1. See *Sinning Church*

Piety, Traditional – Became **magical** and superstitious: Chap. III § 12; **similar** to rubbish: Chap. III § 57.

Pilgrim Church – Contains the Kingdom inchoately: Chap. III § 9.

Pluralism – See *Theological pluralism*

Poor Church (PC) – Church should **divest** herself of riches : Chap. III Note 3d, as condition of fidelity to the Gospel: Chap. III Note 3e. **Divine Comedy** favors PC: Appendix I Note 13. **Encouraged** by abandonment of tiara: Chap. III Note 1b. **Example** of poverty for Bishops given by Paul VI: Chap. III Note 2b. **Goals** of PC: Bishops should reform lifestyle: Chap. III Notes 2b. 3a; renounce palaces: Chap. III Notes 2a, b, 3c; properties: Chap. III Note 2a; episcopal temporal power: Chap. III Note 3a; fine food, luxurious means of transportation: Chap. III Notes 2a, 3c; noble clothes and insignias: Chap. III Notes 2a, 3a, § 7; honorific treatment: Chap. III Notes 2a, 3a, 3b, 3c; receiving and giving privileges: Chap. III Note 2a, 3d; having worldly prestige: Chap. III § 7; using ostentatious religious buildings: Chap. III Note 3a; employing pomp and ceremony: Chap. III Note 3d; saying baroque Pontifical Masses: Chap. III Note 3c. **River of heresies** demands PC: Appendix I §§ 5-9. **Symbolically** established by the Pact of the Catacombs: Chap. III § 2, Note 2a. See *SACRALITY, PACT OF CATACOMBS, MISERABLISM, CASTA MERETRIX*

POPE – see *PAPACY*

POSITIVISM (P) – **Definition**: Chap. VIII Note 40. **Theology** was based on evangelical P: Chap. VIII §§ 27, 28.

PROGRESSIVISM (P) – **Attack** against the Church surpasses that of heretics: Chap. IV § 7; Appendix I § 23. **Conciliar Popes** favored P: See *NOUVELLE THEOLOGIE*. **Differences** from heretics who accuse the Church of prostitution: Chap. IV §§ 3-7. **Encouraged** return to Patristics: Chap. VII § 4. **Favored** by John XXIII in the opening speech of the Council: Introduction Note 14d. **Modernism** continued by P: Introduction Note 14b. **Spirit of the Council** and P: Introduction §§ 22-24. **Vatican II**'s sympathy with P: Introduction § 22. **Reasoning** that defends *Casta meretrix*: Appendix I § 1. See also *CASTA MERETRIX, NOUVELLE THEOLOGIE*

PROTESTANTISM – **Concept** of *Ecclesia reformanda* entered Vatican II: Chap. V § 7, Note 7. **Lutheran ideas** adopted by the Council: Appendix I § 22, Note 54.

PROSTITUTE – Received brand on shoulder: Chap. IV Note 51, see *CASTA MERETRIX, SINNING CHURCH*

RAHAB – As **prostitute**: Appendix I § 53; as converted: Appendix I § 53, Note 101. **Role** in the taking of Jericho: Appendix I § 53. As **symbol**: Appendix I § 54.

RELATIVISM (R) – **Dogmatic** R: Introduction § 11. **Established** in the International Theological Commission: Introduction Note 5g, h.

REVELATIONS (R) – **Appeal** to rigorous morality: Chap. III § 21. **Characterized** by fanaticism: Chap. III § 22. **Comparable** to Joachinism: Chap. III § 21, to Montanism: Chap. III § 21. **Condemn** the world: Chap. III § 21. **Considered** more important than the Scripture: Chap. III § 21. **Obscure** the Scripture: Chap. III § 22. **Raise** a spurious interest in the faithful: Chap. III § 22. See *MARIOLOGY*

REVOLUTION (R) – **Metamorphoses** of R: Introduction §§ 20, 21, Notes 12, 13; in the French Revolution: Introduction Note 13.

ROMANTIC SCHOOL (GERMAN) – Role of Döllinger and Möhler: Chap. III Note 25.

SACRALITY OF THE CHURCH (S) – **Abolition** of Bishops lifestyle by Pact of the Catacombs: Chap. III Notes 2, 3. **Attacked** by conciliar Popes: Introduction § 11; by Bishops at Vatican II: Chap. III § 3, Note 3; by the Pact of the Catacomb:

Chap. III § 2, Note 2. **Created** by devotions to the Saints: Chap. III § 56. **Destruction** of S by conciliar Popes: *John XXIII* initiated destruction: Introduction Note 14g; disliked use of *sedia gestatoria*: Chap. III § 1, Note 1a. *Paul VI* abandoned *sedia gestatoria*: Chap. III § 1, Note 1b; fisherman's ring: Chap. III § 1, Note 1e; the tiara: Chap. III § 1, Note 1b, Appendix I Note 52. *John Paul I* abandoned papal coronation: Chap. III Note 1c. *John Paul II* abandoned majestic plural: Chap. III Note 1d; *Benedict XVI* abandoned the throne in papal 'inauguration': Chap. III Note 1f. **Disfigured** after Vatican II: Chap. III § 4. **Episcopal** garments ridiculed: Chap. III § 6. **Liturgy** proclaimed dead: Chap. III § 12. **Opposed** to modern man: Chap. III §§ 8, 11. **Overview** on attacks against S: Appendix I §§ 5-15. **Ritualist** Church apparatus cannot be taken seriously: Chap. III § 8. **Roman Curia** must be desacralized: Chap. III § 5. **Titles** using 'holy' and 'sacred' are stupid: Chap. III § 5; title Sovereign Pontiff is pagan: Chap. IX § 4; title Vicar of Christ should be abolished: Chap. III 5. See *Liturgy, Pact of Catacomb, Poor Church*

Sadism – Definition: Chap. VIII Note 31. See *Sado-Masochism*

Sado-Masochism (SM) – **Definition**: Chap. VIII Note 31. Catholic **suffering** was SM: Chap. VIII § 21.

Saints (S) – **Cult** to statues must end: Chap. III § 15. **Role** of devotion to S in the Church: Chap. III § 56. **Offenses** *in genere*: S do not attract modern man: Chap. III § 12; devotions favor paganism: Chap. III § 64; deviate faithful from Christ: Chap. III § 64; from the Eucharist: Chap. III § 64; S were intolerant and fanatical people: Chap. III § 59. *In specie*: *St. Clement Marie Hofbauer* was vile: Chap. III § 63. *St. Peter* was the greatest sinner: Chap. III § 60. *St. Robert Bellarmine* had a non-biblical conception of the Church: Chap. III § 62. *St. Thomas Aquinas* was ecumenical: Chap. III § 61.

Schismatics (S) – **Lifting** excommunications of S: Chap. IV Note 6b. **Nullity** of this action: Chap. IV Note 6b.

Schizophrenia – Definition: Chap. XI § 31, Note 39. See *Church-World*

Scholasticism (S) – **Burdensome** and dishonest: Chap. X § 19. **Confused** and complicated: Chap. X § 9. **Contradictory**: Chap. X § 9. **Lacked** historical fidelity: Chap. X § 19. **Produced** sterile debates: Chap. VII § 6; specious and futile questions on the death of Christ: Chap. X § 17. **Outdated**: Chap. VII § 15; narrow and archaic horizons: Chap. X § 11. **Taught** fictions: Chap. II § 32; lifeless conceptions: Chap. X § 12. St. **Thomas** erred on Immaculate Conception of Our Lady: Appendix I § 76, Note 131. **Transformed** Revelation into geometric theorems: Chap. X § 12. **Used** as instrument of power: Chap. X § 10. See *Magisterium*

Sect – **Current concept** used by progressivists: Chap. XI § 4, Note 6. **Etymological concept**: Chap. XI § 4 Note 6. **Meanings** of: Chap. XI §§ 4, 5. See *Church-World Relations*

Secularization – See *Adaptation to the Modern World*

SENSUS FIDELIUM – **Common sense**: Introduction § 30. **Shocked** by text of von Balthasar on Christ in Hell: Chap. I § 5, by affirmation that Christ united with the reprobates: Chap. I § 8, by comparison of the Church to a prostitute: Appendix I §§ 82, 83.

SEX, SEXUALITY – **Basis** of von Balthasar's theology: Chap. IV § 28, Note 47. **Christ** and the Eternal Father relations based on sexual act: Chap. IV § 28. **Christian** and Christ relations based on sexual act: Chap. IV § 28. **Church** and Christ relations based on sexual act: Chap. IV §§ 29, 30; Church teaching on S was Jansenist: Chap. VIII § 16.

SIN (S) – **Attributed** to institution of the Church: Chap. IV §§ 4, 11, 15, 17. **Distinction** between peccability and peccantness or sinfulness: Appendix I Note 3. **Our Lord** could not sin: Chap. I § 7, identified with S: Chap. I §§ 5-10. See *CASTA MERETRIX, SINNING CHURCH*

SINNER, CATHOLIC – Compared to the just man outside the Church: Chap. V § 12, Note 14.

SINNING CHURCH (SC) – **Church** sins through men: Chap. IV §§ 4, 11, 15, 17; has sin in her essence: Chap. IV §§ 15-20, Appendix I § 27; is simultaneously sinner and holy: Chap. IV § 5. Church is guilty of perpetual divisions: Chap. V § 13. **Concept** of SC adopted by Vatican II: Chap. IV Note 4, Appendix I §§ 22, 23, Note 56. **Definition** of sin: to have fixed doctrinal formulas: Chap. IV § 3; juridical and institutional power: Chap. IV § 3; a militant character: Chap. IV § 3; properties and pomp: Chap. IV § 1. **Holy and sinning** Church is mitigated version of *Casta meretrix*: Chap. IV §§ 21-25. **List of sins** of the Church: Chap. IV §§ 19, 20. **Progressivist** reasoning on SC: Appendix I § 1. **Prostitution** is having a visible Church: Chap. IV §§ 1, 2. Prostitution defines the Old Testament: Chap. IV § 10, Note 13; the New Testament: Chap. IV § 10; all of History: Chap. IV § 26; the Church: Chap. IV §§ 8, 11. **Recourse** to Scripture to favor the thesis *Casta meretrix*: Chap. IV § 6; to Patristics: Chap. IV § 7. **Separation** is a sin against the Spirit: Chap. VIII § 8. The **sin** of being inspired by Greek philosophy: Chap. IV § 20; by Roman Law: Chap. IV § 20; sin of Church considering herself complete: Chap. V § 10; of Pharisaism: Chap. V §§ 1-4, Note 1; of presenting her message as a totalitarian system: Chap. V § 17; of professing ecclesiocentrism: Chap. V § 20. See *CASTA MERETRIX*

SOCIAL DOCTRINE, CATHOLIC – **Cannot** become opium of the people: Chap. VII §§ 20, 21. **Should** fight to end oppression and not become opium of the people: Chap. VII § 22.

SOTERIOLOGY – Definition and applications: Chap. III Note 33.

SOULS OF THE DEAD – Go to the center of earth: Chap. I Note 35a.

SPIRIT OF THE COUNCIL (S) – **Definition** *in theory*: Introduction § 3; *in practice*: Introduction §§ 6-12; other definitions: Introduction §§ 6, 8-10, 12, Note 4. **Difference** between S and state of spirit: Introduction §§ 6, 7. **Hostility** toward militancy: Introduction §§ 9, 24, 25; toward sacrality: Introduction §§ 9, 10, 12; toward hierarchy: Introduction §§ 9, 10, 12. **Meaning** adopted in this

Introduction: § 16. T of **authorities** toward error and evil: Introduction § 8. **Classical** notion of T killed by Vatican II: Chap. II § 39. **Establishment** of International Theological Commission: Introduction §§ 13, 15. **God** in the Old Testament was tolerant with the sin of the People: Chap. IV §§ 10, 12; Appendix I, *passim*. **Intolerance** is ignominious: Chap. II § 41. **Mercy** as synonymous with T: Introduction, § 8. **Milestones** in establishing T: Introduction: § 15. **Symbolized** by a current of fresh air to renew the Church: Introduction § 16.

TRANSCENDENTAL ANTHROPOLOGY – **Based** on Existentialism of Martin Heidegger: Chap. X § 8; on German Idealism: Chap. X § 8; on Pantheism: Chap. X § 8. **Necessary** to reform theology: Chap. X § 9. **Synthesis** of Modern Philosophy: Chap. X § 8, Note 14. See *ONTOLOGY, NOUVELLE THEOLOGIE, PROGRESSIVISM*

TREASON – Etymology: Chap. I § 11. See *APOLOGIA FOR BETRAYAL*

VATICAN – No longer combats Communism: Chap. II § 4.

VATICAN II – **Assumed** the notion of a Sinning Church: Chap. IV Note 41; Lutheran positions: Appendix I Note 54. **Avoided** condemning any enemy of the Church: Chap. II § 8; using the word militant: Chap. II § 9, Note 19a. **Differences** between the New Church to the Catholic Church: Chap. V § 8, Chap. IX § 15. **Ended** the Constantinian era: Chap. II § 39. **Freed** teaching from rationalism: Chap. X § 13. **Finished** with the paralysis of Vatican I: Chap. VII § 12. **Gave in** the privileges of Bishops: Chap. VI § 12. **Opposed** the militancy of the Church: Chap. II Note 19b. **Overcame** the spirit of caste: Chap. VI § 12. **Overrode** definitive positions of Trent: Chap. VII § 11. **Reached** a point of no return with *Gaudium et spes*: Chap. VII § 3. **Rejected** a document on Our Lady: Chap. III §§ 24, 51. **Renounced** to attack Atheism: Chap. II §§ 4, 5. **Revolution** initiated by John XXIII: Chap. II §§ 33, 39. **Rupture** with the past: Chap. VII § 5. **Shook** carapaces and archaisms: Chap. VII § 17. **Stopped** Mariology from progressing: Chap. III § 24. **Transcended** the *Syllabus*: Chap. II § 40. **Undid** the work of the Counter-Reformation: Chap. V § 8.

WARS, CATHOLIC (W) – **Against** the language of Christ: Chap. II § 23. **Battle** of Vienna was shameful: Chap. II § 23. **Correct** Catholic doctrine on right of just war: Chap. II Note 44. **Cruelties** committed in W: Chap. II § 23.. **Forgiveness** should be asked for W: Chap. II § 23. **Religious wars** were a dark night of the faith: Chap. II § 25; against human rights: Chap. II § 26. **Originated** from paganism, Wotan god of war: Chap. II § 30. See also *INQUISITION, CRUSADES, MILITANCY*

WORKER-PRIESTS – **Became** *periti* at the Council: Chap. VII § 9. **Made** speeches that influenced *Presbyterorum ordinis*: Chap. VII § 9.

WORLD – See *CHURCH-WORLD, ADAPTATION OF THE CHURCH TO MODERN WORLD*

* * *

WORD INDEX

Abelard, 203 (n. 26).
Abraham, 53, 226, 286, 295 (n. 104).
Absolutist Church, 72, 130, 169, 174-177, 217,
Ad Gentes (AG), 69 (n. 19), 241.
Adam, 53, 56 (n. 35), 116, 228, 310 (n. 147), 316 (n. 158).
Adrian's army, 296
Aggiornamento, 16-17, 28 (n. 14c), 41, 85, 86, 186, 231, 234-235, 244, *see also* Subject Index: *APOLOGIA FOR BETRAYAL*
Aeolian bag, 22.
Agobard, Bishop of Lyons, 262.
Albigensians, 262.
Aldama, José, 306 (n. 136).
Alexander, St., 303.
Alexander III, 117 (n. 53).
Alexander VIII, 299 (n. 111).
Alfrink, Bernard, 65-66.
Alszeghy, Zoltán, 206.
Altaner, B., 299 (n. 111).
Ambiguity, 15, 17, 18 (n. 4d), 36, 98, 221.
Ambrose, St., 43 (n. 14), 277 (n. 80), 301, 304, 305-306, 305 (n. 133), 311, 312, 313, 315 (n. 157).
Amos, 286.
Anabaptists, 263.
Animus Delendi-I (Vol. IV), 15 (n. 1), 24 (n. 11), 24-25 (n. 11), 25, 29 (n. 14g), 34, 96 (n. 4), 142 (n. 18), 164 (n. 14).
Animus Delendi-II (Vol. V), 24-25 (n. 11), 35-36, 59 (n. 39), 142 (n. 18), 231 (nn. 2,3,5), 233 (n. 7), 237 (n 7), 244 (n. 37).
Animus Injuriandi I (Vol. II), 33, 36, 247.
Animus Injuriandi II (Vol. III), 24-25 (n. 11), 33, 36, 48 (n. 19), 54 (n. 34), 59 (n. 39), 70 (n. 2), 76 (n. 37), 160 (n. 8).
Anna (prophetess), 297.
Annas, 50.
Anselm, St., 203, (n. 26).
Antoniutti, Ilbebrando, 71.
Aphrodite, 122.

Apocalypse, 135, 138, 139, 285.
Apostasy, of Church 240, 314 (n. 157); of Jews 138, 280-288, 292, 294-296; symbols of 289-291; two great, 296-298.
Apostolic Brethren, 262.
Apostolic Letter *Cum Catholica*, 317.
Apparitions, *see* Prophecies
Aquinas, St. Thomas, 43-44 (nn. 14, 15), 45-46, 45 (n. 17), 46 (n. 18), 130, 169, 175, 226, 305, 306, 312.
Arditi, 18 (n. 4d), 26, 29 (n. 14f).
Arius, Arianism, 303, 303 (n. 121), 306
Arnold of Brescia, 262.
Artemis, 122.
Assumption of Mary, 107 (n. 34), 108.
Astarte, 122
Atheism, 41, 65-66.
Athenagoras, 137 (n. 6), 190.
Aubert, Roger, 299 (n. 111).
Augustine, St., 164 (n. 14), 202 (n. 20), 207, 277, 294 (n. 102), 299, 299 (n. 112), 300, 300 (n. 112), 301, 311, 311 (n. 151), 312, 320.
Auto-demolition (of the Church), *see* Subject Index.
Avignon captivity, 259, 261 (n. 14).

Babeuf, 264.
Babylon captivity, 284-286, 296, 297, 297 (n. 108).
Baius, 299, 301 (n. 112).
Barabbas, 324.
Bardenhewer, O., 299 (n. 111).
Barrault, J. L., 188.
Baruch, 286.
Basil, St., 304.
Basil of Cappadocia, 300.
Battle of Vienna (1683), 79-80.
Bea, Augustin, 137 (n. 6).
Beatrice (*Divine Comedy*), 258-259.
Beghards, 263, 264 (n. 37).
Beguines, 262.

*   *   *